THE
DAISY
CHAIN

THE
DAISY
CHAIN

How Borrowed Billions
Sank a Texas S&L

JAMES O'SHEA

POCKET BOOKS

New York   London   Toronto   Sydney   Tokyo   Singapore

POCKET BOOKS, a division of Simon & Schuster
1230 Avenue of the Americas, New York, NY 10020

ISBN: 0-671-73303-6

First Pocket Books hardcover printing March 1991

10 9 8 7 6 5 4 3 2 1

POCKET and colophon are registered trademarks of
Simon & Schuster

Printed in the U.S.A.

DESIGN: Stanley S. Drate/Folio Graphics Co., Inc.

To Nancy, Brian, and Bridget

ACKNOWLEDGMENTS AND SOURCES

Writing and reporting *The Daisy Chain* was a struggle and challenge that I could never have done without the support of so many friends, sources, colleagues, and a few scoundrels I met along the way. It would be impossible to thank everyone; some sources explicitly requested their names not be used. A thank-you in a plain brown envelope will have to do. There are a number of people who deserve more, though.

Doug Frantz of the *Los Angeles Times* gave invaluable advice and support. Allen Pusey, a *Dallas Morning News* reporter who truly broke the S&L story, helped, too. Nikki Murray, the world's nicest and best court reporter, took much time from her busy schedule to work on transcripts. Many thanks also to Commanche Campisi, my friend who taught me of Dallas and its wacky ways. Michael Kilian of the *Chicago Tribune* gave good advice and referred me to Dominick Abel, a literary agent in every sense of the word.

Not many journalists are fortunate enough to work with colleagues like mine at the *Chicago Tribune*. When I started this book, Jim Squires was the editor of the *Tribune*. By the time I finished, Jack Fuller had taken over. Both provided me with invaluable time and support, but Jack Fuller added understanding at a time when it was truly needed. I'd also like to thank F. Richard Ciccone, a managing editor who is a real class act, and Washington editor Nick Horrock. To many of my colleagues in the *Tribune* Washington bureau, I extend my heartfelt apologies for boring you with so many S&L stories.

I can't adequately express the gratitude I owe to Marja Mills, my good friend and colleague at the *Chicago Tribune* who did the original research for a series that I wrote on the S&L crisis. She read the manuscript and served as a soft voice of encouragement. This book would not have been completed without the help and enthusiastic support of Jane Rosenman, my editor at Pocket Books, who taught me how to write it. Special thanks, too, to Iowa Congressman Jim Leach, a man of integrity and intelligence who encouraged me to write about the mess in the S&L industry.

Most of the incidents and events in *The Daisy Chain* are based upon sworn court testimony or on-the-record interviews with participants. When there were discrepancies in elements of the story, I chose the version that seemed consistent with available records and sources. A few anonymous quotes have been used when they would not change the meaning or thrust of a passage. The quotes from the board meetings are based upon tape recordings of the actual sessions. I owe a great deal of thanks to many court clerks and government employees in seven states and numerous cities for helping me dig out the records. In some cases, individuals refused to be interviewed or I was unable to track them down. Don Dixon would not sit down for a long interview about the events in this book. That was too bad. I tried to reflect his perspective based upon depositions and testimony. Nevertheless, I still owe him: he gave me what every newspaperman lives for—a good story.

Lastly I'd like to thank my mother, Dorothy Hanley, for believing in me when few others did. And my deepest and most sincere thanks must go to my beautiful wife, Nancy, and Brian and Bridget O'Shea, two world-class kids. No amount of success will ever repay the lonely hours I spent without them while writing this book.

CONTENTS

THE
DAISY
CHAIN

1 Roots

The phone rang at R. B. Tanner's vacation home on Lake LBJ not far from Austin, Texas. It was early 1981. There was a bounce in the step of the man who took the call. At sixty-five, Tanner hardly looked his age. A youthful glow robbed years and wrinkles from his face. His wavy, silver hair shined like a 1964 quarter; his frame was sturdy as an oil rig. Yet the aura of youth couldn't hide the years of hardship in his brown eyes. Tanner's knowing stare dated him as surely as his old felt hat or the ribbed-cotton underwear that showed through his white dress shirt. He spoke with a slow, deliberate twang.

Tanner had picked cotton, shined shoes, pumped gas, and shod horses during a long journey from the son of a destitute sharecropper to the major shareholder and guiding force behind Vernon Savings and Loan, a thrift institution located about three hundred miles to the north of Austin in Vernon, Texas. Over the past two decades, he had built Vernon Savings into the cleanest little S&L in Texas—loan by loan, deposit by deposit, customer by customer. A deeply religious man with a keen eye for business, Tanner was as trusty as the local church bell. Folks around Vernon who placed their life savings in R. B. Tanner's vaults could rest assured that he wouldn't lend the money foolishly and that R.B. would always get repaid. "He carried a Bible in one hand and a butcher knife in the other," said Vernon resident Jack

Eure. At one time or another, it seemed as if every one of the town's 12,500 farmers, laborers, oil field roughnecks, truck drivers, and businessmen had passed through the doors of Vernon's only savings and loan seeking a place to stash or borrow some money. But Tanner had never met Donald Ray Dixon, the Vernon native whose voice he heard once he picked up the telephone.

At first, Tanner didn't know what to make of the call. He listened patiently as Dixon explained his roots in Vernon, how he had grown up there, left the little town for college, and had founded a highly successful building business in Dallas. Tanner had never set eyes on Dixon. Yet he was favorably disposed to the younger man. He remembered Dixon's mother, Frances, a kind, warm, handsome woman who had run a beauty parlor in Vernon. She had lived in Castlebury Park, one of Vernon's best neighborhoods. Like everyone else in Vernon, Tanner had heard of Dixon's father, too. An enterprising newspaperman and radio announcer, the elder Dixon had become a local legend with a noontime radio show that was literally the talk of the town. But W. D. Dixon had died at a relatively young age—years before Tanner had even moved to Wilbarger County.

Tanner soon learned that W.D.'s son hadn't called to reminisce about home. A few minutes into the conversation, Dixon said he was in the market for a savings and loan and had heard that Tanner might be interested in selling out. The subject caught R.B. off guard. It wasn't as if selling Vernon Savings was out of the question. Tanner had given it some serious thought lately. Over the past two decades, the savings and loan business had been good to him. Years of hard work had produced the rewards that a man of his era had come to expect in America—a nice home in Vernon, the vacation place near Austin, an Oldsmobile in good repair, and enough Vernon stock to make him a wealthy man. He had a devoted wife and a lovely family. But making good money in the S&L business was getting rough, particularly with the government's erratic economic policies. Interest rates were 12 percent one month, 18 percent another. Inflation raged like a summer storm. Things were no longer predictable. People had stopped putting their money in a savings and loan forever; they'd pull it out six months later to get a better deal in these money market funds, which were really unregulated savings and loans with no deposit guarantees. To Tanner's way of thinking, all of this was no good. It seemed excessive, greedy—the work of Satan. In just three months' time, Vernon Savings would post the first loss in the thrift's twenty-one-year history. Selling Vernon Savings definitely was not out of the question.

Yet Tanner didn't know what to say to Dixon. He had talked with his wife about retiring. He had confided in a friend who sold mortgage insurance that he might consider an offer—if the price was right. But the discussions had been vague. Nothing definite had come along to command his attention until this Don Dixon had surfaced with a proposal. It was funny. Dixon said all of the right things; it was as if he could read the older man's mind. After listening to Dixon for about a half hour, Tanner decided to take up the subject with his family first. His son, Ray, didn't display much interest in taking control one day. Maybe a possible sale would jar his thinking. Meanwhile, he'd hear Dixon out. "I didn't tell him I would sell it," Tanner recalled, "but I told him I would listen to his proposal."

Back in Dallas, Dixon hung up the phone. The conversation had gone well. The information passed along by the mortgage-insurance man was right; Tanner was interested in selling out. He hadn't said yes. But more important, he hadn't said no. Don Dixon had a lot of experience with people who didn't say no. He'd have a proposal at Tanner's front door within days.

At forty-three, Dixon looked every bit his age. A faint hint of the Indian blood on his father's side of the family colored his plump, tanned face. In appearance and style, Dixon was a Cuisinart cowboy, one of those Texans who mixed the old—western vests and cowboy boots—with the new—tailored western shirts and gold medallions that hung from the neck. He had curly, long hair and a thick mustache. Dixon stood just under six feet. He was not an imposing man by any means. His barrel chest and firm build made him look like an athlete. But he had never fared well in sports; he couldn't shake off a loss. His smile could be pleasant and friendly, but he had a cunning look in his eyes. He had a flair for art, home design, and music and affected a professorial air with the pipe he cupped in his hand. Yet Dixon was fiercely competitive in business and cut deals as fast as a snake strikes.

Like a lot of smart people, Dixon was a good listener. Friends marveled at his deftness and brains. "He had a mind and a memory that were unreal," said Gary Roth, who worked in a California loan office set up by Dixon. "We had an office up at Solana Beach in a building where there were four small offices in a row. We'd have borrowers in each office, and Don would walk from one to another like he was a doctor calling on patients. The amazing thing was, he never referred to a piece of paper. He had all the deals in his head. He would walk into one of the rooms and say approve this one, move next door and say make the profit participation bigger in that one. These were three-million-dollar deals and up. I'd be fumbling around trying to find a piece of paper in a file, but he didn't need anything."

Dixon had spent years around people like Tanner—slow, stodgy, conservative bankers whose idea of a big risk was a game of checkers. A decade ago their kind of thinking had nearly pushed him under. It had happened when he was in his thirties, on his second wife, driving a Mercury, and making it. A building business he'd started in his office at home had become a major player on Dallas's fast-paced real estate market. A bad recession hit in 1974, though, and bankers like Tanner had refused to ride out the hard times with him. Had they given him just a few extra months, things would have been fine; everyone would have made a lot of money. But no; they wouldn't take a risk. It was easy for people who played it safe to say he hadn't paid enough attention to piddling details. But where would America be without risk takers—entrepreneurs. It would be where Dixon ended up just months before the 1974 recession ended. Those crusty old bankers had forced him out of the construction company that he had led from nowhere to the No. 2 builder in Dallas. It was a bitter experience. But it wasn't a total loss. He had learned a valuable lesson: It was better a lender than a borrower be.

A few days after he had hung up his phone, a plane on the morning run from Dallas pulled up to the airport terminal in Austin. R. B. Tanner and his wife quickly spotted Dixon and Richard Little, one of Dixon's key aides. "He didn't come wearing a devil's hat," said Tanner. "He was low-key, very nice." The four Texans climbed into Tanner's car and soon were in the front room of Tanner's lake home, where Dixon delivered a sales pitch to buy Vernon Savings with characteristic charm and beguiling sincerity. "He knew all of the right things to say," recalled Mrs. Tanner. "He said he knew how hard R.B. had worked and that he had never forgotten his roots in Vernon. He told us he could do wonders with Vernon Savings and do something for the people of Vernon at the same time. He was the smoothest-talking, coolest man. He said he wanted to run it the same way that R.B. had."

Tanner said there was no hint of chicanery in Dixon's presentation. He came off as level as a church pew. "You would just think that this is the guy who wears the white hat. He said he was looking for a savings and loan so he could be the lender instead of the borrower." Dixon told Tanner he wanted to keep all of the local Vernon folks on the board of directors, including R.B. himself.

Once Dixon left town, R.B. and his wife agonized over what to do. Don Dixon's proposal to buy Vernon Savings made a lot of sense. Thanks to Tanner's reputation and years of hard work, Vernon Savings took in far more in deposits than Tanner could ever prudently invest in a small town like Vernon. He needed other outlets for new loan business. He had two offices out of state and already had tentative approval from the state commissioner to open an office in Dallas. But Tanner's constitution wasn't what it used to be; he was getting old; he feared that he couldn't handle the strain of expanding the operation at Vernon. Maybe it was time to sell out to a younger man—one who knew the booming Dallas real estate market well enough to benefit Vernon Savings. Then again, Vernon Savings was his whole life. He had labored long and hard to make it what it was. It was more than a business—he had infused his reputation and very identity into the thrift. Tanner finally reached for the right answer by doing what he had always done in times of hardship and uncertainty. He bowed his head, took his wife's hand, and prayed. God would tell him what to do.

A few days after the meeting in Austin, Woody Lemons picked up the phone at the Vernon Savings home office. A local boy from nearby Crowell, Lemons had left a job at Shell Oil in Houston a decade earlier to return home and learn the S&L business at Tanner's knee. A practical man with an eye and ear for detail, Lemons knew from the echo in the line that Tanner's call was long distance. He also figured out that R.B. was seriously thinking about selling out; Tanner told Lemons to bring some important books and records from Vernon to an office on the LBJ

Freeway in Dallas. Tanner's prayers had been answered. The address was the headquarters of the Dondi Group, Dixon's real estate operation.

As he piled the ledgers and balance sheets in his car, Lemons could see what was coming, and he wasn't too surprised. Owning a savings and loan had been a dream deal for decades, particularly in Texas. From its very inception, Texas had been a capital-importing state with a voracious appetite for borrowed money. Part of the reason was the state's oil and cattle industries, both of which require a lot of upfront cash. Texans had a penchant for thinking big, too. Give a Texan a real estate license, and he'll soon be wearing a Rolex, chatting on his car phone, and thinking about changing his name to Trammell Crow, the legendary Texas real estate developer.

The state legislature was well aware of Texas traits when it passed the laws authorizing state-chartered savings and loans. To encourage a vibrant local industry, the lawmakers in Austin also passed liberal regulations that gave Texas S&Ls latitude to invest depositors' money in loans for a wide range of money-making ventures. By the mid-1970s, S&Ls like Vernon resembled money machines. The federal government, which guaranteed the safety of S&L deposits, didn't want financial institutions engaging in the kind of destructive competition for deposits that had characterized the Great Depression. So it adopted laws that limited the interest rates any federally insured S&L could pay depositors. Thanks to the liberal rules implemented in Austin, though, Texas S&Ls had a leg up on their counterparts in many other states.

It was an ideal situation. The government's guarantee of safety gave S&Ls a steady flow of incoming deposits from Americans seeking a secure haven for their savings. Meanwhile, federal interest-rate lids limited the major cost faced by most savings and loans—the interest rate paid to lure deposits into their vaults. But S&Ls chartered in Austin had it even better: They got deposit insurance by paying a minuscule premium to a government-backed insurance fund, but they could invest more of their federally insured deposits in ventures such as oil and gas loans, which carried a far higher potential for profit.

The legal anomaly created a Texas savings and loan industry that was more entrepreneurial but also more parochial in nature and spirit. Every once in a while, some faceless federal bureaucrat in Washington would frown upon the more liberal powers in Texas and try to crack down. But Texas S&L men would simply turn to their supporters in the state legislature. Pretty soon a bill would sail through the Texas statehouse preempting the Dudley Do-Rights in Washington.

One guy in Washington had even tried to threaten Texas financial institutions by restricting their right to deposit insurance in 1971. But Texas financiers showed him they knew how to handle someone who messes with their money. A sitting governor, the chairman of the state Democratic committee, and a slew of aides, all of whom had suddenly struck it rich on a lucrative stock investment, pushed a bill through the legislature providing a way around the federal efforts. An anonymous Texas lawmaker explained to the *Dallas Morning News* one reason why the bill had such strong support. It was hard to maintain a family, a big mortgage, three cars, a pleasure boat, and a small lake cabin on a legislator's salary: "It's hard to be pious because in all honesty I could use the money," he said in an article headlined "Honesty Isn't Easy."

By the time Lemons pulled into Dixon's parking lot in Dallas, though, even Tanner was having trouble making money in the S&L business. Federal efforts to contain inflation and deregulate the S&L industry had reversed the fortunes of the healthiest S&Ls in Texas. The government had removed controls from the interest rates S&Ls could pay to depositors so the savings industry could compete with the emerging money market funds. That meant people like Tanner had to pay savers interest rates of 12, 15, or even 18 percent to keep their money in his vaults. But even with the more liberal Texas investment regulations, they were earning only 6, 8, or 10 percent on the deposits; most had been invested in old fixed-rate home loans that wouldn't be fully repaid for decades. Tanner wasn't the only S&L owner thinking about selling out. Making money in an S&L was going to be a far different proposition in the future.

Lemons parked his car and took Vernon's books and records upstairs to Dondi's corporate offices in north Dallas. Dixon and some trusted aides such as Rick Ramsey started poring over the books while Lemons and Tanner answered questions. A CPA by training and inclination, Ramsey already knew about the interest-rate problems of S&Ls. But he didn't make too much of the ones on Vernon's books. Dixon had a game plan for Vernon

Savings, and Ramsey knew it. A bunch of low-yielding home loans buried in Vernon's portfolio wasn't the problem. The important thing was getting R. B. Tanner's signature on a piece of paper.

About a month after he had first called Tanner, Dixon pulled up in front of Tanner's four-bedroom, two-story home in Vernon with the big white columns. Even in February, R.B.'s beloved pecan trees spanned the large, spacious yard with grace and dignity. Dixon crossed Tanner's threshold and headed for the dining room, where he spread the papers across the table. As he and Tanner went over the deal, the phone rang. "It was a gentleman from Houston," said Tanner. "He called and asked me not to sign the contract. He was interested. He said please don't go through with this. But when I make a commitment, I honor it. Don Dixon was at our dining room table." Tanner signed the deal. Dixon had acquired his hometown savings and loan for $5.8 million in cash. The price was fair—about 1.4 times the association's book value. All that was needed to conclude the deal formally was approval from state regulators in Austin and their federal counterparts in Little Rock, Arkansas. But that wouldn't be a problem; Tanner had already received verbal approval from the authorities.

The contract that Dixon carried out of R. B. Tanner's dining room gave him a lot more than a savings and loan. In its current condition, Vernon Savings was no prize catch. But Dixon was looking toward the future. For a real estate developer, owning a savings and loan was about to become a mixture of bare necessity and golden opportunity. The big developers in the Dallas real estate markets had already hopped into the savings and loan business. Dixon and Ramsey had grown frustrated seeing competitors offer attractive financing terms from a captive S&L to get potential buyers into their homes and condos. But the competitive advantages of an S&L were nothing compared to the potential they held. Federal lawmakers were about to approve a sweeping financial deregulation bill that would make an S&L in the hands of a real estate developer resemble a federal mint.

Ever since he'd started building homes in Dallas, Dixon had scrounged around for capital. He'd tried outside investors, government loan-guarantee programs—the works. If he wasn't borrowing funds from his mother or some independent investor, he was over at the Republic Bank wheedling money from some loan officer at two over prime. It was a real chore. The loan officers at the banks belonged in the Kremlin; all they cared about was paperwork and reports. Being able to tap your very own S&L would change all that.

Under the rules being contemplated by Congress, a developer who picked up an S&L could continue to operate a development business. It was unbelievable. Why borrow money from a commercial bank at 2 or 3 percent over prime, which was then 15 percent? A developer who wanted to build a twelve-story hotel in Coconut Grove could simply have the S&L set up a development subsidiary and use FSLIC-insured deposits to fund the venture. It would cost him far less.

Old conflict-of-interest rules prohibiting savings associations from financing projects owned by their stockholders or officers didn't apply; the institution itself, not an individual or company owned by an insider, was actually the developer. In effect, the new rules would allow Dixon and several hundred others like him to treat federally insured savings and loans as if they were personal piggy banks, borrowing billions of dollars at bargain interest rates for all sorts of ill-conceived projects. Building hotels would prove the start of something big. Why not hunting lodges, too, or ski resorts, or golf courses? One could buy a boat. Why not acquire a whole town that was dry and make it wet for people who wanted to spend Sundays with Jack Daniel's instead of Oral Roberts? If religion struck your fancy, go build a church on spec.

Best of all, thanks to the Reagan administration and Congress, Dixon and his ilk would never have to worry about a shortage of funds. Even though it deregulated the industry, the federal government would continue to guarantee that all depositors in federally insured S&Ls would get up to $100,000 of their money back, no matter how the S&L had invested the funds. In other words, the government deposit-insurance fund bore all of the risk. And if depositors started pulling their money out, all the owner had to do was raise interest rates a little, and the funds would rush back in. Those fellows in the Reagan administration sure understood the free markets. They were Dixon's kind of guys.

A few months after the initial deal was signed, Tanner's phone rang once again. Only this time it was a disturbing call from Dixon. "He said he'd lost one of his financial backers and would be unable to pay cash." Tanner didn't like the sound of it, but Dixon assured him everything was okay. He had a new deal set up that he would explain in person.

Just weeks before, Dixon had contacted Dale Anderson, the top aide to a Louisiana entrepreneur and financier named Herman K. Beebe, a shrewd and crafty businessman whom Dixon had befriended in a series of business deals. Beebe owned a string of banks, insurance companies, and nursing homes and understood exactly what could be done with a savings and loan in the new era of deregulation. "Dixon came to us with Vernon Savings," recalled Anderson. "He said he wanted to buy it and showed me the numbers and said it would be a good deal. He and I decided how to structure the deal, and I went to Herman and said I thought we should do it." Within days, Anderson and Dixon showed up at the Mercantile Bank in Dallas and applied for a loan of about $1 million. Initially, the bank balked at the request. "They said they didn't like it because Dixon had gone broke before," said Anderson. "We had a Holiday Inn in Gretna, Louisiana, and I told them we would pledge a half interest in it as collateral for Dixon's loan. That was more security than they would need, and they agreed to do the deal." For his role in the transaction, Beebe demanded a 25-percent interest in Vernon Savings.

A few days later, Tanner showed up at Dixon's offices and heard the details of a new deal firsthand. Instead of $5.8 million in cash, Dixon would give Tanner and a handful of minority shareholders $1.1 million in cash and a note for $4.7 million. The note would be paid off in quarterly installments over the next seven years at 8 percent interest. It would personally be guaranteed by Dixon and Beebe's AMI, a company that reportedly had a net worth of $19 million.

Tanner didn't know what to think. He'd been sizing up people for more than forty years and had never really gotten stung. Dixon seemed like a fine young man. He dressed in expensive clothes, drove nice cars, and always seemed to have plenty of money. He hired the best—a good sign to Tanner. Dixon's lawyers were from Jenkins and Gilchrist, one of Dallas's leading and most reputable law firms.

Even as Tanner sat in Dixon's offices, the winds of change were howling across Dallas. Deregulation, inflation, and the oil boom had infected many Texans with an ethos of greed that was as foreign to Tanner as a Ferrari. Larry Vineyard, a prominent Dallas lawyer, would later characterize the era in a courtroom speech right before being sentenced to jail for fraud:

> It is a terrifying thing to realize at the age of thirty-eight that you have been operating with a major character flaw—the reckless pursuit of gain, of personal success above all else. I grew up in Abilene, Texas, the son of simple but intelligent, God-fearing, law-abiding, hardworking, middle-class parents. My parents set high moral values and instilled those values in me. That simply straightforward kid from Abilene began to worship the wrong god—the god of money, power, and success. I allowed my greed and pursuit of material wealth to overshadow my good judgment and my understanding of the real values of truth and honesty. Now I understand this lesson.

But the clock within Tanner ticked to a different time. To Tanner's way of thinking, proper law firms and banks like the ones with which Dixon associated didn't take on unsavory clients. They simply had too much to lose. Dixon's high-powered financial references impressed him. He placed a call to the chairman of the Mercantile Bank, where Dixon said AMI had long-standing relationships, to check out Herman Beebe. "I called the chairman of the board, who I knew, and he said AMI was okay. He said he had been doing business with AMI for years. He told me, 'You won't ever have any trouble with those people,' " recalled Tanner.

On July 10, 1981, R. B. Tanner signed another contract accepting Dixon's new terms. The interest payments were to start in October. He sold his summer home near Austin and prepared to retire and enjoy the fruits of a lifetime of work. It took about six months before the federal regulators in Little Rock finally approved Dixon's acquisition of Vernon Savings. No one raised any doubts about the deal. In early January 1982, everyone assembled at Jenkins and Gilchrist's law offices at the Mercantile Bank building in Dallas so the final papers could be signed. Dixon was late for the meeting, but that didn't matter. Dixon's lawyer took care of everything. After it was over, everyone shook hands. Vernon Savings had been sold to Don Dixon. Everyone was happy, everyone was smiling. The only person who raised any doubts in the minds of Tanner and his wife was Dixon's lawyer. There was something about him that made Tanner and his wife uneasy. His name was Larry Vineyard.

2 The Boy in a Covered Wagon

I t was August of 1922. The covered wagon pulled out of a farm about thirteen miles southeast of Weatherford for the long trek across the flat, hot plains of west Texas. The summer sun beat down relentlessly on the wagon and its passengers—an itinerant farmer, his wife, and a young boy. R. B. Tanner would never forget the odyssey. It would become as much a part of his life as the quiver in his jaw or the gentle drawl in his voice. "We were farmers, but the crops were bad. We'd stop where things looked good to get some work pickin' cotton. But there was no place for us to stay. So we'd sleep in the wagon or in the barn with the animals." He was six years old.

The Texas landscape that stretched before young Tanner's eyes wasn't one of glitzy cities, concrete interstates, or oil rigs bobbing up and down like rocking horses on the horizon. Parched land, blacktop roads, withered crops, and dry throats awaited them. The family stopped periodically and tried to plant some roots. "My dad would sharecrop during the day and help at a blacksmith shop at night. In 1926, in Anson, he helped build the local high school." But the odd jobs would always end and the Tanners would have to move on. In January 1927, they moved one stop too many. "My family became totally destitute," said Tanner, tears welling in his eyes. "We didn't have any food; we survived on corn bread and sorghum molasses."

13

Tanner got his first inkling that he wanted to be a banker while scrounging around the pockets of poverty in west Texas. To help support the family, he got a job shining shoes at the local barbershop in McCaulley. "I got ten cents a shine and made about a dollar fifty a week. The president of the local bank used to come in. His name was Sam Hardy, and he was real nice to me. One day he came in for a shine and looked down while I was shining his shoes. I'll never forget how he said, 'Why don't you get into the banking business?' " To Tanner, working in a bank seemed as remote as owning an oil well. You needed an education to be a banker; he had started school in fourth grade but had been forced to drop out in sixth, just three months after the start of the year. Nonetheless, Sam Hardy had planted a seed in the lad's mind. If hard work was all one needed to be a banker, then R. B. Tanner would become one, because from that day forward a banker is what he wanted to be.

A few months later, opportunity struck. Tanner was in the fields picking cotton. It was about a hundred degrees when he saw two strangers walking down the road. Suddenly they veered into the field and approached R.B. He didn't know the men, but Tanner recalled that they knew all about him: "They were from the local Baptist church. One of them, a man named Cloyce Jones, wanted me to come to work for him in a gas station, and I would be able to go to school. I worked there, too. I swept out the school and carried coal to the boiler." It was an epiphany for Tanner in more ways than one. The experience not only fired his passion for an education; it instilled within him a religious fervor that would serve Tanner for the rest of his days. "From then on I worked every day, but I only missed one day of school. I finished high school, and the only thing that kept me from being valedictorian was my average. It was only ninety-six."

Tanner's journey to college proved no easier than finding a school that would accept him. He walked and hitchiked about about fifty miles to Abilene only to find that schools didn't cotton to kids who started in fourth grade and had no money. He was rejected at a local college. But the head of an Abilene business school agreed to give him a chance and helped him get a job washing dishes at Poffs Cafeteria to pay tuition. "I also got a job working in a gas station for one dollar a night, nine hours a day, seven days a week. I had no social life. But I took more courses than they wanted me to take. I graduated in twenty-four months."

Tanner's chance to get into the banking business came just after he got his first job as an auditor at a west-Texas utility company in Dalhart. "They had strung a line from Dalhart to Sunray, but no one had kept count of how much equipment they'd used. So they supplied me with a pickup truck, and I set out to count each pole. It took me two and one-half months, but I got a count of everything." Shortly after he returned, he got a call from a man in the State Banking Department, where he'd applied for a job months before. "The government had taken over a bank near Dumas and needed someone to go up there. He asked me if I was still interested in the banking business. I told him I sure was, and he asked how long it would take me to get loose."

Two weeks later, R. B. Tanner drove into Dumas, a little town of about 12,000 people forty-eight miles north of Amarillo. "I'll never forget that. I got into town early in the morning. It was still dark. All I had was an old map. I looked around and couldn't find the bank. Finally I pulled my car over under a streetlight in front of a building so I could read the map." When Tanner looked more closely at the building he'd parked in front of, though, he saw a small sign that barely caught the glow of the streetlamp. It said THE FIRST STATE BANK OF DUMAS.

The bank was a one-room institution full of hard luck and bad loans. The next morning, Tanner set out to visit with each borrower. He went from farm to farm and porch to porch, but the stories were the same. Borrowers wanted to repay their notes, but they had no crops to sell. You can't grow crops with tears; you need rain, and it hadn't rained in those parts for seven years. Tanner didn't have much experience in banking, but he knew a lot about people and hard times. His guts told him these Texas farmers were good for the loans. They had plenty of collateral and a lot to lose. Foreclosure wouldn't do any good; the bank needed paying customers, not land. Finally Tanner filed a report that said the government would have to wait for rain, just like everyone else. When the storm clouds finally drifted over Dumas and moisture fell from the sky, the crops rose from the parched soil and the money flowed back into the bank. R. B. Tanner had been right; the farmers paid off their loans. Tanner had passed the ony test that counts with a banker—the one where you have to get the money back.

Tanner didn't suspect that he'd end up running a savings and loan in Wilbarger County when state officials called him in 1954 and asked for help with the First State Bank in Vernon. Even though he was employed as a private banker by then, Tanner had earned a good reputation as a troubleshooter for the state. Soon after getting the call from the state commissioner, Tanner showed up at the bank in Vernon and spotted the problem almost immediately—a portfolio of sour loans and a bank plagued by weak management. This time, though, Tanner also spotted a good opportunity. With the right management, he knew that the bank could be restored to financial health. He made a proposal, and the next thing he knew he owned the place.

For the next six years, Tanner plunged into the job of making the bank a first-class financial institution. By 1959 the job was complete and R.B. was settling down to run a prosperous institution when the phone rang. On the other end of the line was Judge Alter L. Vandergriff, the state official in charge of Texas savings and loans. A group of businessmen from around Vernon were thinking about seeking a charter for a local savings and loan, but Vandergriff thought Tanner was a better candidate. Why didn't he apply for a charter? "There was no financing for home loans in Vernon, Texas," said Tanner. "The only way you could get a home loan financed there was to go to an insurance company." R.B. thought over the idea and decided he liked it. It seemed like a natural way for a kid who grew up in a covered wagon to make money—lending people the funds they needed to buy the home he never had. Once he had analyzed the numbers, he also realized he could make a small fortune. He applied in 1960 and won almost immediate approval.

Vernon Savings and Loan originally was chartered at a small office on Fanin Street just down the block from the Sears catalog store. From the outset it was an institution that focused solely on developing a market for home loans, which the town's three banks ignored. Tanner had hardly opened Vernon's doors when he started a search for a new home for the S&L and settled on a down-and-out block on the south side of the square, across the street from the Wilbarger County Courthouse. Tanner tore down some flophouses and shuttered stores and replaced them with a modern, one-story brick building and parking lot. In 1962, he sold his interest in the Bank of Vernon and went into the S&L business full-time.

From its inception, Vernon Savings was a classic example of the savings and loans that had sprung up around the country. The nation's first savings and loan had opened in Frankford, Pennsylvania, in 1831, or about 130 years before Vernon appeared on the scene. The fledgling institution had a folksy character that savings and loans would emulate for decades.

Actually the institutions originally operated like neighborhood credit unions, often serving Americans ignored by the banks. None of the thirty-seven individuals in the group that started the Oxford Provident Building and Loan Society in Frankford had saved enough to buy a home on his own. At the time, anyone wanting a house had to save his own money or borrow the funds from a rich person. As a result, not many Americans owned their own place. The folks who formed Oxford had a different idea; if they pooled their savings, they figured they could assemble enough cash for one of the members to buy a house. On January 3, 1831, the thirty-seven organizers of Oxford Provident each contributed an initial deposit of five dollars to the institution and pledged to continue depositing three dollars a month thereafter until all members had obtained the funds they needed to buy their homes. On April 11, the neighbors drew straws to determine who the lucky first borrower would be. Comly Rich, the village lamplighter, won. He borrowed $500 and used $375 to acquire a house at 4276 Orchard Street in what is now Philadelphia. He used the remaining $125 to remodel it. The house survives today. Comly wasn't so lucky. He was supposed to repay his loan so another neighbor could draw a lucky straw. In an ominous sign for the future of the nation's thrift industry, Comly had a little trouble repaying the loan, and his relatives had to bail him out.

Over the next century, savings and loans changed a lot. In Comly's time, they didn't pay or charge interest. That wasn't the case by the time Tanner appeared on the scene. But the basic idea behind savings and loans remained pretty much the same. They gathered deposits from people in the neighborhood by paying interest on savings. They then lent the funds in their vaults to other neighbors who wanted to borrow the money to buy homes. The institutions charged the borrowers a higher interest rate than they paid the savers and pocketed the difference as profit, once they covered their costs. In most cases, the owners set aside enough money in a rainy-day fund they referred to as capital to cover any unexpected losses. In some cases, the S&Ls were called mutuals because, like Oxford Provident, they were technically owned by depositors. In other cases, such as Tanner's, they were owned by stockholders. In all cases, though, the control was strictly local.

Tanner entered the savings and loan business at the dawn of its golden years. The Great Depression had been just as vicious on people who had their money in savings and loans as it had been on those who chose banks. Between 1930 and 1934, nearly six hundred savings and loans had failed, largely because depositors lost faith in the institutions and rushed to take their money out. Frank Karsten, a former Missouri congressman who went to Washington in the early years of the first Roosevelt administration, recalled the gut-wrenching scenes of those who lost more than faith in the early 1930s: "Depositors stood in lines in futile efforts to withdraw their savings. Farmers stood in lines with shotguns to try to stop tax sales and foreclosures. The homeless and unemployed stood in lines for bread and local relief. It was not uncommon to see newspaper advertisements which read: 'Need money? Bring your savings passbook and leave it with us. We pay ten cents on the dollar.' "

In response to the financial crisis that engulfed the nation, Congress passed numerous laws that would later benefit S&L owners like Tanner handsomely. The most important was the National Housing Act of 1934, which created the Federal Savings and Loan Insurance Corp. (FSLIC), the federally backed deposit-insurance corporation. For the first time in the nation's history, it guaranteed the safety of all deposits of up to five thousand dollars to keep depositors from staging the run on deposits that had toppled the strongest financial institutions.

By the time Tanner opened the doors of his new office on the Vernon town square, the savings and loan industry boasted of being "Your Partner in the American Dream—Homeownership." The economy was expanding steadily, inflation was low, housing starts were as strong as real estate sales, interest rates were stable, competition for savings was limited, and loan demand was strong. The only thing missing was a mint and a printing press for greenbacks. The key ratio for the savings and loan business had become three-six-three—pay depositers 3 percent, charge borrowers 6, and be on the golf course by three.

Tanner's board of directors read like the roster at the local Rotary. Charles Sullivan, who owned the funeral home, joined the board. So did William Brown, a chiropractor, and Clyde Ham, a builder. Although Tanner controlled most of the stock, other minority shareholders included a local doctor, the owner of the dairy and creamery; Cleddie Palmer, an abstractor and attorney, and Gerald Carter of Tom Toasted Peanuts. Tanner recruited Leon Speer, a rancher from Crowell, to join the board and drum up some business from his hometown, which was about thirty miles down Highway 70. Roy Norsworthy became a director, too. He ran the music store across the street and could keep an eye on the place.

Vernon Savings and Loan reflected the prosperity of the times. Tanner had started more than a decade earlier with a few thousand dollars that he and his minority shareholders had put up. By mid-1977, Tanner had lured about $45 million worth of deposits into Vernon's vaults. He didn't do anything really special; the government regulated the rates he could offer depositors. They were slightly above those allowed for banks. Federal law also allowed him to offer customers special premiums to put their money in Vernon Savings such as free toasters or waffle irons. It was the government's way to stimulate money for home loans, which was how Tanner invested the deposits. He recycled more than 90 percent of the $45 million into home-mortgage loans taken out by cotton farmers, packing-plant employees, workers at the uniform factory just outside of town, or oil field roughnecks. By and large they were God-fearing people, conservative Texans who placed a premium on honest living and repaying their debts. Each month they'd collectively send Tanner about $275,000 in interest payments on their loans, and he'd pay depositors $245,000 in interest for keeping their money in Vernon's vaults. Most of the remaining $30,000 would be stuffed back into Vernon's capital account to bolster its net worth, the financial backbone of the institution and the source to be tapped if an unexpected loss surfaced. Salaries, taxes, and other expenses would usually be covered by income from other sources, such as the loan fees Tanner charged, and the only real extravagance was the dividends he declared, which totaled about $5,000 a month.

"Our lending was strictly home ownership," Tanner said. "Homeownership was very, very important to me because I never had a home when I was growing up. And I made money making home loans." By the late 1970s, Vernon Savings was the strongest financial institution in Wilbarger County.

It would take a trained eye like Tanner's to see the problems start cropping up on Vernon's books. A novice reading Tanner's June 1978 financial report filed with federal officials in Washington wouldn't have suspected anything was wrong. Vernon's total income for the first six months of the year was $2.5 million, up sharply from the $1.9 million during the same period in 1977. By almost every measure, Vernon appeared as healthy as Tanner. The board declared its usual modest dividend, and Tanner plowed most of the thrift's $311,000 net profit back into the institution, just as he always had. But the numbers obscured a disturbing trend that would soon weaken Vernon and virtually every other savings and loan in the nation. Although Tanner's deposits were up by 18 percent, his cost of deposits soared by 26 percent. In other words, he had to pay savers higher interest to keep their money in Vernon's vaults.

There were lots of reasons for the troubling development, and few of them had anything to do with the way R. B. Tanner ran his savings and loan.

The main reason for the problems was inflation. Ever since the Vietnam War, the government had been fighting rising prices. But it hadn't fared much better than the troops dropped in the Southeast Asian rice paddies by the Pentagon. Economics texts are littered with culprits in the losing battle. Some historians pin the blame for the problems on President Lyndon Baines Johnson's guns-and-butter economic policies. An equally convincing case is made that the Federal Reserve Board during the Nixon and Ford administrations made America safe for inflation. Regardless of who is right, though, one thing is clear: The politics of the times provided few incentives to control inflation; Republicans and Democrats alike engaged in an extraordinary round of economic mismanagement that would literally destroy many savings and loan operators like Tanner.

Tanner had some sympathy for the people who started demanding he pay them higher interest rates. A cotton farmer who wandered into Vernon Savings and deposited $1,000 during the mid-1960s probably got a fair shake. After a year, he'd lost about $25 thanks to inflation; the $1,000 he put in Tanner's S&L in January typically bought 2.5 percent less by the time December rolled around. Under the federally imposed interest-rate ceilings in effect at the time, though, Tanner would pay him anywhere from 4.75 to 5.25 percent interest on his money, depending on how long he tied it up. In other words, he would earn up to $52.50 in interest on the $1,000 deposit, more than making up for the purchasing power he lost to inflation. It wasn't the greatest bargain in the world, but it was a better deal than he'd get at the bank, and it served Tanner and his customers well. The deposits generated earnings for the savers and gave Tanner a stable source of funds to make fixed-rate mortgage loans that wouldn't be fully repaid for thirty years.

The roaring inflation that plagued the economy in the 1970s changed the equation, though. By 1974, the cotton farmer at Tanner's S&L was getting clobbered. If he put his $1,000 in Vernon Savings during January, it would be worth $110 less, or only $890, by December. Prices rose 11 percent during the year. Thanks to the federal interest-rate controls, though, the most he could get from Tanner in interest was 7.5 percent, or $75. He didn't even earn enough to make up for the $110 he lost to inflation. It wasn't a very good deal, even if Tanner offered him a Texas-sized toaster.

It didn't take the people on Wall Street long to figure out how to make a buck off the situation. People with big money had a way to fight inflation. An investor with $10,000 in the bank could buy a corporate or government bond, which usually came in $10,000 denominations and paid higher interest rates. Real rich people had an even better deal. Under the laws governing S&Ls, interest-rate controls didn't apply to deposits of $100,000 or more. Well-heeled investors could earn whatever the market would bear. They could do a lot better than some cotton farmer with $1,000, who was stuck with the rates offered by R. B. Tanner.

In 1972, though, a New Yorker named Bruce Bent came along and started something called the Reserve Fund. The idea was to get 100,000 cotton farmers with $1,000 each to invest. Bent would pool their money and buy a $100,000 certificate of deposit. Ideally he'd get 8 percent interest on the $100,000, keep about 1 percent for himself and pass the remaining 7 percent along to the cotton farmers, who got a higher rate than the one offered by Tanner and who didn't have to tie up their money until their kids were out of college. Of course, the money wasn't insured against loss. And it took Bent years to get his idea going. But when it caught on, savers began abandoning neighborhood thrifts like Tanner's for money market funds touted by Bent and huge investment companies like Merrill Lynch.

The government could have attacked the root problem—inflation. But that would have required some political courage by Democrats and Republicans alike. By the late 1970s, inflation had developed quite a political constituency. It served the middle class in America well, driving up the value of homes, triggering cost-of-living increases, and creating the illusion of prosperity. Few lawmakers wanted to tamper with a system that made voters think they were striking it rich. Instead Congress and the White House started slowly dismantling the controls the government had placed on interest rates Tanner and others could pay depositors. The process would take years and would progress at a pace that allowed money funds to enjoy explosive growth, primarily at the expense of savings and loans like Vernon.

Unfortunately, the wise Washington heads who eased the controls on interest rates paid to depositers didn't apply the same logic to the mortgage end of Tanner's business. Congress refused to liberalize the regulations on mortgage lending, and Tanner was stuck making fixed-rate mortgage loans as the cost of his deposits soared. "We had a lot of loans that were earning about six percent, but we were paying twelve, fourteen percent for our money. That's where the pressure came," said Tanner.

By 1979, Tanner was still making money on his mortgage portfolio. But his profits were slimmer than before. By 1980, the equation would reverse. Tanner would lose some money on his mortgage-loan portfolio. And things wouldn't get any better in the future.

On October 6, 1980, a tall, lanky, cigar-chomping government bureaucrat walked into the marble halls of the Federal Reserve Board and told a group of reporters that the nation's central bank was about to adopt a revolutionary change in the way it conducted its monetary policy. With the change, Paul Volcker removed any restraints that held interest rates down.

Volcker vowed to break the back of inflation. As it turned out, he'd break a lot of other things, too. Interest rates soared far beyond anything Volcker would imagine. R. B. Tanner had never seen anything like it. In June 1981, Vernon Savings posted the first loss in its history. The government had also decided it was time to further deregulate the savings and loan industry—let S&Ls invest those high-cost deposits in something besides money-losing mortgages. Just before he turned over his S&L to Don Dixon, Tanner confided in the young man that the last several years had taught him a lesson. "Don, I know I've been too conservative with the place," Tanner recalled telling Dixon. "I know I've tried to be too safe."

Dixon knew exactly what he meant.

3 Faulkner Points

There would be none of this *Little House on the Prairie* stuff for Vernon Savings and Loan under Don Dixon. Before signing the papers in Larry Vineyard's office, Dixon might have told Tanner that he'd run Vernon Savings the same way R.B. had. But Dixon knew better. Following Tanner's lead in Dallas's fast-paced real estate market would be like riding a bike in the Indianapolis 500.

It was January 1982. In just eight months, President Reagan would sign the Garn–St. Germain Depository Institutions Act, which would dramatically expand the kinds of ventures in which most savings and loans could invest federally insured deposits. S&Ls chartered in Texas didn't have to wait that long, though. The regulations that Texas legislators had already approved allowed many of the reforms sought by federal officials. "Hell, man, we were the model for the feds," said Durward Curlee, a former Texas Savings and Loan League executive and a consultant for Dixon. By the time Dixon acquired Vernon, S&Ls in Texas were already taking advantage of their competitive edge.

Oil drives Texas like government drives Washington, Wall Street drives New York, and cars drive Detroit. The Texas economy was booming. A decade of oil embargoes, price decontrol, Middle East political instability, and inept U.S. government policies had pushed the price tag on a barrel of crude to $34.30

by 1981, a staggering 1,000-percent increase in less than ten years.

The rising prices sent the freewheeling Texas real estate market into orbit, too. In contrast to the gas lines and recession that formed around other parts of the nation, Texas saw new office buildings, condominiums, homes, and apartment buildings sprout from the ground. The state became a global symbol of prosperity. Texas economist M. Ray Perryman recalls the euphoria:

> The art world craved Southwestern paintings, sculpture, and architecture. The Austin sound swept the music scene. The Dallas Cowboys became America's Team, and their cheerleaders attained international celebrity. Fashion turned to boots, hats, and jeans, and *Urban Cowboy* became a rousing success at the box office. *Dallas* was the most-watched television show in the universe, and people across the globe waited anxiously to find out just 'Who Shot J.R.?' People from throughout the country who had never even found Houston on a map were seriously considering moving to Luckenbach!

Dixon fit right in the Dallas scene. From his offices on the LBJ Freeway, he presided over the Dondi Group, an umbrella organization of seven companies that acquired, developed, managed, and marketed real estate properties on their own or in partnership with others. Dixon wasn't in a league with major developers like Trammell Crow or Lincoln Properties. He was a medium-sized apartment builder who dabbled in a few smaller commercial deals.

But he was on a fast track. Between 1978 and 1982, Dixon had developed nearly four thousand condominiums at fourteen projects in Texas, Florida, and Louisiana, plus three residential developments involving nearly five hundred lots. Outside of his earlier brush with bankruptcy, he had a reputation for building quality units at a good price. Once a year he'd travel west and return with award-winning ideas and southern-California-inspired condominium designs. He was determined to become more than just another developer in a city where the mayor once told the industry to "keep the dirt flyin.'"

Even before he acquired an S&L, Dixon's headquarters was an exciting place to work for Rick Ramsey and other Dondi employees. Dixon was a flashy boss—an impulsive, irreverent guy who came to work in Western vests, medallions, and cowboy boots; wore his hair fashionably long and thought big time. "Don was a natural-leader kind of person," Ramsey recalled. "He'd come in a room and just take over, give everyone a sense of mission. One time he came into the office, sat down, drew up a set of floor plans, tossed them on my desk, and said, 'Here, this is what I want.' Then he got up and left."

Dixon was also generous with employees, and he made work fun. As a marketing and sales-promotion gimmick, the staff once had some three-dollar bills printed with Dixon's picture in the oval, complete with the long hair, mustache, a pipe, and the inscription "In Don We Trust" printed on one side. Dixon signed the fake currency as "Chairman of the Bored," and the ovals on the flip side bore renditions of two trademarks on the hundreds of condos he built around Dallas—weeping-mortar brickwork and red-tile roofs, which the staff dubbed Red Tillibus Roofum. The currency bore the stamp of the Department of Corrections.

Like many people with Texas-sized egos, Dixon had an aloof, almost shy, side, particularly in crowds. He had few close friends, fewer heroes, and always kept employees at a distance in social settings. "He didn't socialize at all with the people he worked with," said Ramsey. "He wasn't the type to open himself up. You never got a good picture of him. He would come to the company parties and stand off in a corner waiting for people to come to him—come to the king."

Dixon wasn't the kind of man who focused on what he had. He was always more interested in what the other fellow had that he didn't. Buying R. B. Tanner's savings and loan came naturally. Like Tanner, other mom-and-pop S&L operators across the state had started fearing their life investments would be ravaged by inflation and were selling out to scores of developers who competed with Dixon. By the late 1970s, a savings and loan had become something a Texas developer just had to have to keep up with the other guy.

"What gave us the idea for a savings and loan was the competition," said Ramsey. "We found that other developers had gotten into the savings and loan business. When you wanted a loan, they'd give it to you, but then they'd demand an interest in the development. We figured if you wanted to be in the real estate business in the South, you needed a savings and loan.''

Crucial to an understanding of what happened after Dixon got his hands on the cleanest little thrift in Texas is some knowledge of the places, professions, and personalities that were important to Dixon and vital to the atmosphere in which he thrived.

First on the list is Dixon's second home—Dallas. Long a mecca for drifters, dreamers, and defrocked Yankees, Dallas routinely lured to its neon skyline legions of hustlers eager to grab the brass ring. Local folks call it the Big D because of its glitzy nightlife, cultural attractions, and major league financial institutions. Many Texans consider Dallas too cosmopolitan for the rest of the state. But real estate developers like Dixon love the place, mainly because of its less restrictive zoning laws and prodevelopment attitudes typified by the infamous comment of one of its past mayors, Robert Thompson, who said: "You've got to build a city, the damn things don't grow like mushrooms."

An insight into real estate developers and their passion for the liberal use of other people's money helps in understanding Dixon's ascension, too. Real estate pros in Dallas and elsewhere have been creating deals with other people's money—and little of their own—ever since Dad Joiner brought in the Daisy Bradford No. 3 oil well in east Texas and gave Dallas a reason to exist as a service and financial center for the oil industry. A developer with a $100-million project often borrows extra money—$110 million or far more to finance his deal and pay the interest, fees, and expenses he incurs while the project is under construction. A legitimate developer figures he will add value to the project and generate the earnings he needs to repay the loan by creating an income-producing development or by selling the thing. Debt is like mother's milk to developers; things just don't happen without it. Equity is something they create with imagination and brains. Sitting in his office building in downtown Dallas, Preston Carter, the "Crocodile Dundee" of Texas real estate developers, explains how it works:

> See this building here we're in; it was built in 1952. The Republic Bank owned it and had a bunch of minorities in here making MasterCards. It was a pretty shitty deal. I bought the building for $40 a square foot. The

reason I bought it was that I knew I could finance the whole thing with Travelers Insurance for $6.7 million. And I also knew that I could get Atlantic Richfield to lease a ton of space at $11 a square foot each year for a long time, which worked out to $110 a square foot. Less my operating expenses at the time, it was worth about $60 a square foot, and I was paying $40. That created a big equity right there. And then I knew a developer building next door needed a parking garage, and I could sell him mine. So all of a sudden I had beaucoups of equity. You see, I inherited $900. I had to learn to create equity right away.

Prior to the 1980s, developers had never been able to own federally insured savings and loans. Under the prevailing wisdom, allowing a developer to own a savings and loan was considered crazy; he'd be able to tap federally insured deposits to finance his own ventures. But common sense took a beating when Congress passed the 1982 laws deregulating financial institutions. The new laws not only allowed developers to own S&Ls, they also contained few prohibitions on how they could invest the deposits under their control. Even before the laws were passed, entrepreneurs such as Dixon had started snapping up S&Ls like they were used cars, licking their chops at the prospects of what was to come. The institutions were headquartered in places like Mesquite, Lubbock, Tyler, or Paris, but the real action swirled around the offices they had set up in Dallas. The combination of soaring oil prices and easy money fueled a real estate boom of unprecedented proportions. Building permits in Dallas would soar from $4.3 billion in 1976 to $17 billion by 1983.

But Dixon didn't prosper merely because he was in the right place and in the right profession. Crucial to an understanding of the forces that allowed him to thrive were other personalities— colorful Texans such as Danny Faulkner and Ernie Hughes. They helped create the "anything goes" atmosphere in which no deal could go wrong and the money flowed like champagne. The story of Vernon's prodigal son simply could not have happened without them.

An itinerant housepainter and sixth-grade dropout from Kosciusko, Mississippi, Faulkner was a flamboyant and charismatic character. Once he hit Dallas, he became what every Texas hustler yearned to be—an American success story with a rags-to-riches résumé. He'd started off in Dallas painting seats in Texas Stadium. By the time his son got married a few years later, he could hire the Tulsa Philharmonic to play the theme from *Rocky* at the wedding and station a uniformed guard at the entry to the Dallas North Tollway, tossing quarters from a large sack into the automatic gate so his guests could drive up the road for the reception.

He had abandoned his paint bucket in the 1970s to take up a career as a Dallas builder with a Rolls as a family car and a helicopter as a taxi. Throughout the late 1970s, he developed hundreds of condominiums and apartments along a nineteen-mile stretch of Interstate 30 running from Dallas east to Lake Ray Hubbard.

Faulkner had started out just like Dixon—building condos and selling them to consumers who got their loans from places like Empire Savings. But he soon figured out that he—and the savings and loan—could make a lot more money by acquiring the land and then selling it at inflated prices to private investors, who could borrow all they needed from the friendly S&L, which also made a ton off the loans. There was none of this mumbo jumbo about adding value or creating a profitable concern. Inflation in land values and a little deal called a "land flip" would take care of everything. To one degree or another, it was a path that Dixon and many others would follow.

To keep his deals cooking, Faulkner needed converts to the cause, people like Ernie Hughes. Just a few years before he met Faulkner, Hughes had hitchhiked twenty miles to his first closing as a real estate agent because his car had been repossessed by a finance company: "I stayed in the house after the deal was settled, because I didn't want the buyers to know that I didn't have a car."

Fate compensated for his hard luck when his phone rang in the early 1980s, though. A friend on the other end of the line offered to repay Hughes a favor by putting Ernie into a condo deal with a developer who had an in at Empire Savings, a fast-track Mesquite S&L that operated even faster and looser than Vernon.

Hughes jumped at the opportunity. "Most of the condos in Dallas at the time were conversions [in which existing apartments were converted into condominiums]. But this involved building new condominiums. I thought it was a good idea, a new market, you know—the cutting edge, supplying housing to the masses who couldn't afford it." Another factor appealed to Hughes, too. He didn't have to come up with any of his own money; Empire would lend him all he needed. All he had to do was supply a financial statement and an income tax return to paper the deal and make it appear legit. He found the proposition irresistible.

The deals struck by Texans like Faulkner and Hughes were crude models for dozens of other S&Ls like Vernon. They became so outrageous that Dixon's more sophisticated twists wouldn't look so bad to regulators stunned by the excesses at Empire Savings.

Within weeks of Hughes's initial phone conversation, a group of investors at Faulkner Point West "flipped" four acres of land they had acquired weeks earlier, marking up the price sharply and selling it to Hughes and three others for $4.50 per square foot. Empire Savings lent Hughes and his partners all the money they needed to close the deal. "The way it broke down was, on the first tract of land, which was just over one acre, we built thirty-two condos." Empire also provided the construction loan for the condos, and its alter ego, a subsidiary named Statewide Services Co., became a fifty-fifty partner with the Hughes group on the project. "It would take the sale of sixteen of those condos to pay off the construction loan and the land loan on all four acres," said Hughes. "That left us with the remaining three acres and sixteen condos free and clear. Statewide got eight of the condos and we [the four investors] got two each. They were selling for anywhere from thirty thousand to forty-five thousand dollars each, depending on the square footage. You wound up with sixty to ninety thousand dollars' worth of property you could sell or rent."

That was just the first wrinkle to the deal. The developer had originally set aside fifty cents per square foot from the land loan for development costs—things like utilities and streets. But he needed only twenty-five cents per square foot. So, according to Hughes, the Faulkner development kicked back twenty-five cents per square foot to the investors. That meant Hughes and his partners got a check for about $12,000 for going along with a no-money-down deal in which they made a bundle.

After the first one closed, Hughes said he couldn't wait for the next deal to come along. Everybody involved in the scheme had made money. The original Faulkner Point investors made money on the land flip. Hughes got a kickback, some condos, and some land. Empire not only got condos; it had charged Hughes and his cohorts 18 to 20 percent interest on the loans plus 12 points (or a 12-percent fee) for financing the deals. Hughes said Faulkner and Co. would reenter the scene once construction was under way. "They had their builder in there. He's doing all of the construction. You wanted to do business there, you used their builder. They sold hte contractor all of the lumber. They had landscaping, carpeting, everything. I discovered the concrete contractor is supposed to pour streets that are four inches thick, but he's only pouring an inch and a half. At some point in time, I discover I'm paying Faulkner and his son nineteen dollars a yard for eight-dollar-a-yard carpet."

Hughes overlooked the profiteering, though. He could make up for it when selling or renting the condos. The costs were buried in the sales prices or rents. Potential buyers wouldn't have any trouble getting a mortgage loan, either. Empire was his partner in the deal. It would later come along and make a mortgage loan to the poor sap who bought the final product at an inflated price. Best of all, the whole scheme was probably legal as long as no one falsified any documents.

Ernie Hughes became a believer. "I got into sixteen deals," he said. In the constant quest for fresh blood to keep the schemes rolling, Empire officials also promised Hughes and others $10,000 for each new investor they brought in. Hughes pitched the deals with enthusiasm. "I got real involved," Hughes said. "At one point, I got a gum disease and my regular dentist sent me to an oral surgeon. I'm under anesthesia and as I'm coming out of it, the surgeon and his anesthesiologist tell me that I'm pitching a condo deal. So when they get through with me, they say, 'Okay, now tell us some more about this.' So they got involved."

From then on, things really started rolling. Kickbacks of fifty cents a square foot became routine for investors getting into no-money-down deals. Hughes brought his real estate partner in, and pretty soon his partner had many of the fifty-eight real estate agents in the office involved. One day Hughes got a check for $160,000, simply for bringing in new investors. Real estate agents used to making $15,000 a year hustling single-family homes could suddenly make that much money on a single deal. "It was like a drug. All of a sudden they had fifty percent more income. A lot of these people got in on six or seven or eight deals, and they've been making eighty thousand to one hundred thousand dollars or better," Hughes said.

They bought Ferraris and Rolls-Royces; new homes, boats, jewelry, and dreams. At times, it seemed as if anything were possible. One real estate agent who had joined Hughes's staff was a cute woman with a chest as flat as west Texas. "Catherine wasn't doing that well in real estate," Hughes said. "But she was married, and together she and her husband had some assets and a good financial statement." Catherine and her husband became investors in a deal on Faulkner Point, two parcels of land that jutted into Lake Ray Hubbard near Mesquite. "She made about eight thousand to ten thousand dollars on her first deal, and then she kind of disappeared for a while," recalled Hughes. "People started wondering what happened. One day we were sitting in the office bullin' and Catherine walked in, and she's just grinnin' from ear to ear." As Catherine approached Ernie and the others at the bull session, Hughes noticed she was wearing more than a fresh smile: "She came up to us and pulled open her blouse. She didn't have a bra on. Then she said:

" 'I just wanted to show you boys what I did with my first check. I got me a couple of Faulkner points.'

"They were just great," Hughes recalled years later with a smile.

Faulkner and another associate, James Toler, the former mayor of Garland, Texas, soon started hosting Saturday breakfasts at Wise's Circle Grill on Interstate 30 near Bobtown Road. "When I first got involved, most of the people were tradespeople that Faulkner would buy breakfast," said Hughes. "It was a rah-rah type thing. But it quickly changed in a month or two when the investors started participating, and you got the politicians coming out here in droves."

Hughes recalled an atmosphere that was zanier than the deals. As politicians like Texas attorney general Jim Mattox shook hands and wolfed down steak and eggs, Sparkles, a jeweler who had attracted Faulkner's fancy, worked the room with his wares crammed in a couple of big valises. "Sparkles was selling Rolexes out the ass and all sorts of jewelry," Hughes said. "Every

Saturday there was all this money and jewelry floating around."
Once breakfast was done, a big ten-gallon cowboy would be
passed among the throng to be stuffed full of cash for the visiting
politico in case things got out of hand and everyone needed a
friend to cool things off. "If two politicians showed up, they'd
pass the hat twice," said Hughes. "The message was pretty clear.
You've got to contribute if you want to get into any more deals."
More than one hundred investors had flocked to the Empire
deals, and more were waiting in the wings. A $1,000 contribu-
tion from each would net a quick $100,000 for a cash-starved
political campaign.

The profits from the land deals were astonishing. On one
day, an Empire subsidiary bought eighty-two acres of land on
I-30 for $1.86 million, or fifty-two cents per square foot, and sold
it a few hours later to Faulkner and Toler for $3 million, or
eighty-five cents a square foot. That was a lot quicker way for an
S&L to make money than by sinking it in thirty-year fixed-rate
home mortgages. Faulkner and Toler would then turn around
and sell the land again to some of their cronies.

Faced with the prospect of huge profits, investors figured
the political contributions at the breakfasts were a small price to
pay. Meanwhile, S&Ls that had seen their capital depleted by
years of inflation also suddenly saw a chance to earn it all back
through acquisition and development loans similar to those
pushed by Empire. The deals generated extraordinary fees and
paper profits for the S&Ls, which then dipped into their feder-
ally-insured deposits to pay fat dividends to their owners. The
deals would eventually generate an unprecedented glut of unsold condos, but no one seemed to care. The new era of liberal
rules and financial deregulation made it all seem so dynamic.
S&L regulators in Washington thought it was a miracle.

A few of the federal regulators who showed up to view the
Dallas spectacle felt some nagging doubt tugging at their guts.
But they ignored their instincts. "I went down there," one federal
official explained, "and this Texan showed me this piece of land
and told me how this guy had sold it to that guy, and that guy
had sold it again, until it had been sold about six times, and I
said, 'My God. That's terrible,' and he said, 'Only if you're
sixth.' "

The deals made Ernie Hughes as rich as Danny Faulkner—
for a while. Faulkner turned over the sales operation to Hughes.

"Faulkner and Toler had a breakfast meeting at the Circle Grill," Hughes recalled. "Faulkner got up and said it was time to change the guard and that my friend here Ernie Hughes is going to take over sales and marketing and all of the land sales. He then stuck a Faulkner Point pin on my lapel. What a favor he did for me, I'll tell you. The son of a bitch came back and asked me for the pin a couple of months later; it had a little diamond in it."

Hughes could overlook such slights, though. He was rich and powerful. Faulkner confided in him. At one point, Faulkner summoned Hughes to a local bank for a meeting and told him that a loan broker both men knew had fallen on hard times:

> He wanted me to help him out. He wants me to buy a couple of his Rolls-Royces. These are Rolls-Royce convertibles—$156,000 automobiles. Faulkner tells me that the guy's willing to let me have them for $110,000. In fact, he's talked him down to $110,000 just because it's me. In addition, the guy's got this priceless necklace which Faulkner's got there with him. It's made of technically matched Burmese rubies and diamonds all set in platinum, and the thing is gorgeous. He said the thing was priceless; that you couldn't even get it appraised and that it had to be worth $1 million. He wanted $260,000 for the necklace. So I'm rolling in it and I go and write out a check right then and there for $480,000 because Danny wanted me to. I learned that you got to have two Rolls-Royces because you've always got one or two in the shop. The necklace I brought home and showed it to my wife. My wife isn't big on jewelry anyway. She was sitting there; she had on a pair of shorts and a Mickey Mouse T-shirt. She put on this priceless necklace and was just prancin' around.

The euphoria was everywhere. Other investors clamored to get in on deals. At one point Hughes walked into the hall of an office building to attend a closing involving a flip with multiple sales:

> The tables were lined all of the way down the hall, and the investors were lined up in front of the tables. The loan officers would close one sale and pass the

papers to the next guy, who would close another sale at a higher price. It was unbelievable. It looked like kids registering for college. If an investor raised a question, someone would come over and tell them to get out of the line, they were out of the deal.

With Faulkner, Hughes, and others building hundreds of condos on the plains east of Dallas, it was not unusual to see thrifts such as Empire quadruple their outstanding loans in a year or two. As a result, it didn't seem at all unusual when Dixon opened a Vernon Savings office in Dallas's northern suburbs. He was just one more developer who had hopped into the fray. Dixon took to the competition like a real pro. He already had plenty of experience building condos with his Dondi Group of companies. And he didn't need the likes of Danny Faulkner to learn about the wonders of the savings and loan business. When raising the money he needed to buy Vernon Savings, Dixon had taken on his hidden partner—Herman Beebe, a man who knew a lot about the fast track.

Trim and dapper at about five foot eleven, Beebe was a Louisiana entrepreneur and financier with a shady background and a taste for the good life. He would sweep into Dallas with an entourage in a limousine, dine at the Old Warsaw, and stay at the finest hotels. He had met Dixon a few years back when the young builder needed funds for his expanding condo operation. "We had an interest in Continental Savings, and Dixon had borrowed a lot of money from us," recalled Dale Anderson, Beebe's top aide. "It was about twenty or thirty million dollars. One day Herman came in and asked me what I knew about Dixon. I told him that I had met him briefly at the Dallas airport and that Dixon had asked me for a favor. He wanted a stall for a horse at the Shreveport racetrack. Herman told me to set up another meeting with him at Continental's offices in Houston. He said, 'I want to know anyone who has borrowed that much money from us.' "

One meeting led to another and a business and social rela-tionship that would extend beyond a few loans. To get enough money to buy Vernon Savings, Dixon needed the financial cre-dentials that he could get with backing from someone like Beebe, who presided over a multimillion-dollar network of banks, in-surance companies, and nursing homes from a Shreveport building that looked as if it had been designed by Darth Vader. Beebe needed young hotshots like Dixon to assume high-profile positions and obscure Beebe's ties to the financial institutions in which he had an investment. His brushes with federal authorities extended back to the Texas Rent-a-Bank scheme, a bank-busting plot that made headlines in the 1970s when leveraged buyouts were still considered a scandal.

Dixon wasted no time plunging into the booming Dallas market. Soon after Dixon won approval of his acquisition of Vernon Savings from federal regulators at the regional Federal Home Loan Bank in Little Rock, Dale Anderson showed up at Dixon's offices to help design a corporate reorganization of Dixon's empire that would foster rapid growth at Vernon Savings. Ramsey said that soon, "the whole attitude changed" toward the real estate operations he ran. "Up until then, developers' attitude had always thought what makes the deal is the deal itself. After we got involved with the S&L, it became what makes the deal is the borrower. Once you had him, they seemed to think the deal would take care of itself. I remember how the S&Ls had coffee cups that said, 'You Do the Work; I Bring the Money and We Split 50–50.' "

By the fall of 1982, Dixon had discovered what Danny Faulkner had seen months earlier. One day as Ramsey sat at his desk, Dixon walked in. Ramsey recalled the conversation:

> He said to me, "You know, Ricky, it takes a lot fewer people to lend money than to build these things. This is bullshit. We go out as the builder and develop a deal and we get half the profit. Why should we be the developer and get half the profit? Why not finance it and get half the profit without any unhappy homeowners? If the borrowers can't finish it, we can take it over and finish it ourselves.

By then, President Reagan was about to award Dixon and his colleagues for their belief in the free enterprise system in a big way. On October 18, 1982, Reagan walked into the Rose Garden to sign the Garn–St. Germain Depository Institutions Act. It was a bright day, and as Reagan signed the bill, dozens of S&L executives, lobbyists, and politicians looked on. "All in all," said the President as he set down his pen after signing the bill into law, "I think we've hit the jackpot."

4 Edwin J. Gray

Ed Gray wore his best smile as he walked into the U.S. League of Savings Institutions convention in New Orleans. It was November 1982. Just months before, Gray had left his job with the Reagan administration in Washington to return to San Diego. His old boss, Gordon Luce, the chairman of San Diego Federal Savings and Loan and a member of Reagan's kitchen cabinet, was about to reorganize the thrift. "The lease for our house came due. My wife wanted to get back; I wanted to go home and Gordon wanted me to come back." So Gray, a born PR man and aide to Ronald Reagan in Sacramento and Washington, returned to San Diego and the S&L business.

Overall he had worked in the industry for only seven years. Nevertheless, Ed Gray could hold his head high as he mingled with other members of the industry's most powerful trade group in New Orleans. His mentor, Ronald Reagan, would address the convention within hours. From the day he'd hit Washington, Reagan had made the S&L industry a test case for deregulation. The industry loved it. Gray's credentials as a Reagan insider undoubtedly enhanced his stature.

Gray's and Reagan's paths had first crossed in 1966 just after Gray had gotten a job as a publicist for a California utility company. The company had decided to send him to San Francisco when Reagan won the California governor's race and called

37

the utility for some help. Gray's employer volunteered his services for the inaugural, and when Reagan needed a Bible for the swearing in, Gray was dispatched to Carmel for a two-hundred-year-old book used by missionary Junípero Serra. After Reagan took his oath of office, Gray got a job as an assistant press secretary for the governor, his first tour as a foot soldier in the Reagan Revolution.

"Four years later the president of San Diego Savings invited me to go to work there, but Ed Meese, who was then the governor's chief of staff, said I couldn't leave. And so I said that I'd stay if Gordon Luce would keep that job open. He did and I finally called him in the summer of 1973. He said to come down. I went and I stayed. But in 1980 the Reagan people called, and I went back to the campaign."

From the outset, Gray believed in Reagan and his policies. He wasn't one of the rugged Westerners in the administration. His favorite sport was fly-fishing in the California high country, not riding horses. And he wasn't like the conservative Ayn Rand ideologues who populated the Reagan movement; he liked reading real history, particularly accounts of the Dark Ages in Europe.

Yet Gray viewed Reagan as the embodiment of the American dream, not so much a spokesman for big corporations but an average fellow just like himself—someone who would always do the right thing. When Gray joined the White House staff after the successful campaign against Jimmy Carter, he worked as a deputy assistant to the President on the domestic-policy staff. "My particular job was to make sure that the issue papers that went to the President and the cabinet council were unskewered so that people could make their decisions. We always took the position that if Ronald Reagan had all the facts and all the arguments, he could make a good decision. So I was fairly conversant with the issues and the arguments having to do with deregulation."

Once he left the White House staff to return to San Diego, though, Gray figured his political career was over. "I'd never worked for any other politician except Ronald Reagan, and I never had any desire to."

Soon after he entered the convention hall in the fall of 1982, Gray learned otherwise. His White House connections carried more weight with the deregulated S&L industry than he'd imagined. As Gray chatted with acquaintances, Leonard Shane, a beefy California S&L executive who also headed the U.S. League at the time, pulled him aside and gave him some startling news: The powerful California delegation wanted Gray to become the chairman of the Federal Home Loan Bank Board, the federal agency that regulated the thrift industry. Pretty soon other S&L executives approached him, emphasizing the importance of his White House contacts for an industry emerging from decades of government regulation. Richard Pratt, a free-market purist, had decided to step down from the chairman's job, and the industry wanted the torch passed to a true believer. Even Gray acknowledges the industry viewed him as a nice guy—a toady who would do as he was told. "They all wanted me in this job for one reason. I was their boy. I think some of them thought basically I'd be there to do whatever they wanted. I'd be their cheerleader; their guy in the White House. A lot of people came up and begged me to take the job."

From a government perspective, being tapped as chairman of the bank board wasn't exactly like being named secretary of state. In all, four government agencies engaged in federal financial regulation—a job that Federal Reserve Board Chairman Arthur Burns once called a competition in laxity. The comptroller of the currency in the Treasury Department regulated national banks; the Federal Deposit Insurance Corp. watched over state banks; the Federal Reserve monitored bank holding companies; and the bank board rode herd on savings and loans.

By almost every measure, the bank board was the worst of the lot. Created after the bank runs of the 1930s, the board's duties included prevention of financial failures at savings and loans, enforcement of the law, and the prevention of conflicts of interest. The President appointed the three board members, who had to be confirmed by the Senate, and he named the chairman. At least one of the members had to be from the opposite party, and they presided over a network of twelve regional Federal Home Loan Banks, whose stock was owned by the local savings and loans in their regions.

On paper the board was a powerful organization that could pull a thrift's charter, examine its books, pass sweeping regulations, and set broad policies for the industry, such as the standards for minimum capital. Actually, though, the whole system functioned as an industry booster under the thumb of the trade associations, particularly the U.S. League. It was virtually impossible to be named bank board chairman without the support of the U.S. League, and the industry financed the entire system through annual fees and assessments paid by federally insured savings and loans. No government money was involved. In other words, the thrift industry actually owned its own regulatory system. It could tell the watchdog when to bark and knew how to pull its chain.

The government's only exposure to loss in the system was through the U.S. Treasury's backing of the S&L deposit-insurance fund—a guarantee of solvency that would turn out to be fatal for American taxpayers. Being named chairman of the system was kind of like running the Metropolitan Sanitary District in Chicago. You were pretty important to people with sewer problems, but most citizens had never heard of you.

In all, nineteen Americans had held the bank board job before Gray was asked to consider it. Overall they were a pretty lackluster group. Pratt, the man the industry wanted Gray to replace, was from Utah. It was easy to see why thrift executives hated to see him go. A finance professor and staunch advocate of deregulation, Pratt belonged to a pack of free-market economists, political operatives, and assorted right-wing loonies that Reagan had unleashed upon Washington to make "regulation" a dirty word.

Pratt became chairman of the bank board in the midst of the industry's problems with interest rates in 1981. He intoned the virtues of a deregulated industry in a deep, rolling voice that was music to the ears of Don Dixon and Danny Faulkner. In his perfect world, the savings and loan industry would be totally free of government involvement. But eliminating the entire regulatory system was clearly too radical. Instead Pratt suggested the industry resolve its interest-rate-mismatch problem by easing restrictions on how thrifts could be run, who could run them, and how deposits could be invested. The Garn–St. Germain act was a crucial component of his strategy; it encouraged savings and loans to engage in riskier but more profitable acquisition, construction, and development loans to offset their losses. Equally important, though, were a set of rule changes that Pratt rammed through the bank board. Accounting procedures for routine exams were eased; a requirement that thrifts have at least four hundred stockholders was scrapped, eliminating the concept of community control. Worst of all, the Pratt board also dramatically altered the capital requirements, permitting S&L owners to put up less of their own cash in reserve and allowing them to substitute assets such as raw land for capital—the crucial measure of an S&L's financial health.

To the layman or the average depositor in an S&L, the rules changes sounded like gibberish. But knowledgeable pros like Herman Beebe and Don Dixon knew better. Back in Dallas, Pratt's new math made a lot of sense. The law that originally set up the industry's deposit-insurance fund required federally insured savings and loans to set aside at least 5 percent of their deposits in a reserve that could be tapped in case of an emergency, such as an unexpected loss. In 1972, rapidly growing S&Ls in Florida had successfully pressured the board to liberalize the regulation and require thrifts to set aside reserves equal to 5 percent of their average deposits over the past five years. In effect, by averaging deposit growth the board had lowered the reserve requirement, especially for fast-growing S&Ls. Faced with the continued losses in 1980, the board had reduced the requirement even further to 4 percent and finally to 3 percent when Pratt took over.

An entrepreneur with a keen eye for finance could see the advantages immediately. Under Tanner's conservative hand, Vernon grew slowly. Just before the sale closed in 1981, Vernon's deposits totaled about $72 million, up from $62 million in 1979. Under the old rules, Vernon needed capital of about $3.4 million. But Tanner had $4.6 million in capital, or far more than was required.

Thanks to the Pratt board, things were different for Dixon. Once he took over, Vernon grew rapidly. Three years later, Vernon's deposits stood at an astonishing $820 million, up by more than 1,000 percent. Yet under the liberalized rules that permitted him to average his deposits, Vernon had to set aside only $7.4 million in reserve. In other words, Dixon could lure an additional $750 million in federally insured deposits into Vernon Savings to be invested in his deals. But he had to invest only an additional $2.8 million of his own money in capital. Best of all, Dixon didn't even have to put up cash as his contribution. The definition of capital had been expanded to include land, stock, or other assets.

By the time Pratt was thinking about stepping down, consultants from coast to coast were staging seminars on how real estate developers and other entrepreneurs could take advantage of the new rules to tap federally insured deposits for their ventures.

The bank board wasn't the only problem. As Dixon and his cohorts revved up their S&Ls in Texas, Reagan populated the federal bureaucracy with other free-market zealots who equated more government with castor oil. Concern over conflicts of interest were brushed aside along with the wimps from the Carter administration. True Reagan men wanted to get the government off everyone's back so entrepreneurs could earn real profits and make America No. 1. They seemed determined to create the savings and loan crisis that would eventually evolve.

Nowhere was the sentiment for financial deregulation stronger than in the Treasury Department, headed by Donald Regan, the Wall Street executive that Reagan had tapped to run the huge agency. A former head of the Merrill Lynch & Co. brokerage firm, Regan also headed the Depository Institutions Deregulation Committee, called DIDIC, and he used his position to accelerate deregulation of the financial industry.

Regan had quickly made it clear to Washington insiders that he was no friend of the S&L industry. One reason for his animosity stemmed from his background at Merrill Lynch. Stockbrokers traditionally viewed the thrift industry with a mixture of envy and disdain. Brokers figured the money that poured into thrifts would have been theirs to invest were it not for the safety provided by federal deposit insurance. They chaffed at the prospect of competing with institutions that enjoyed federal help. Thrifts were viewed as a coddled, inefficient industry that needed a dose of free enterprise.

The relationship between Regan and Ed Gray didn't help, either. The two men met at the dawn of the Reagan administration and disliked each other immediately. In Washington, Regan made no secret of his feelings toward Gray, and Gray sensed Regan's disdain. Recalled Gray:

> I was not from Wall Street. I was a pol that Ronald Reagan brought from California. What could I know about anything? I was in the cabinet council meetings with him. I despised him. He was so arrogant. He had his opinion and made up his mind before anything was

said. One time I had to go and talk with him, and he said he was worried I wouldn't be a team player. I told him no one had to tell me anything about being a team player; I had been with Ronald Reagan since 1966. It wasn't until later I realized he wasn't talking about Ronald Reagan's team; he was talking about his.

Regan's old employer on Wall Street had a vested interest in seeing the government remove the regulatory wraps on the thrift industry. Merrill Lynch made a lot of money scanning the financial markets looking for the best interest rate available for clients who had megabucks—deposits of $100,000 or more, sometimes called brokered funds.

Prior to 1982, the megabuck market had been limited by a federal regulation that said brokered funds could not exceed 5 percent of a savings and loan's deposits. Once enough S&Ls hit the 5-percent threshold, brokers such as Merrill Lynch had nowhere to place the deposits. But in March 1982, the DIDIC committee, led by Regan, removed the 5-percent limitation. Suddenly Merrill Lynch had plenty of places it could invest its customers' megadeposits; Dixon and other S&Ls in Texas drew huge deposits into their vaults from outside their area simply by taking out ads in the *Wall Street Journal* and offering investors high interest rates.

The rule change would dramatically increase the exposure of the American taxpayer to losses. Merrill Lynch was one of the biggest players in the money fund markets. For their fees, the brokers would split the megabuck deposits into smaller denominations to take advantage of federal deposit insurance. A broker with a client who wanted to deposit $900,000 in Vernon Savings to capitalize on a one-quarter-percent interest-rate advantage would split the money into ten $90,000 accounts, thereby qualifying for federal insurance on accounts of $100,000 or less. The high-cost deposits fueled a surge in demand for riskier loans that carried the higher returns needed to pay the interest to the big depositors.

Thrifts started investing in the futures markets, financial options, and other more exotic investments permitted under deregulation. Dixon looked toward acquisition and development loans to fund the dramatic increase in brokered or jumbo deposits at Vernon.

"You have to understand," Gray recalled, "that the DIDIC with Don Regan as chairman was moving full speed ahead. It was created in 1980 and had six years to take the controls off. But my God, it was nearly 1983 and they were almost finished." S&L owners could take on huge increases in deposits without being forced to add much of their own capital, particularly with the averaging rules and lower capital requirements enacted earlier. The Regan forces seemed mesmerized by deregulation. It was as if they wanted to deregulate the industry as fast as they could, before anyone realized the possible damage that could result.

"I kept arguing they were going too fast, that they were going to harm the thrift industry," said Gray. "But I was on the losing end of most of the votes. Paul Volcker had some reservations. He said, 'Well, yeah, we have to go to this deregulation, but you can't just ignore the consequences of this.' "

The forces for a slower pace were hopelessly outnumbered, though. At the Office of Management and Budget, David Stockman threw the weight of his powerful staff squarely behind the efforts to deregulate by cutting the bank board's manpower. Even in their heyday, thrift industry examiners were a powerless lot. The U.S. League felt they had too much clout during the Depression and that they had closed institutions that should have remained open. When the federal system was set up in the 1930s, examiners were relegated to a mere fact-finding role. They could spot a problem within an institution, but they couldn't do anything about solving it. That was a job for a separate staff controlled by the regional banks.

"This was a sleepy little agency when Ed Gray came, totally ill-equipped to deal with a deregulated industry," Robert Sahadi, a onetime bank board official, told the *American Banker*. "Many of the examiners had cobwebs."

But the White House budget office made a bad situation worse. Because the Treasury guaranteed the solvency of the deposit-insurance fund, the OMB had to pass on the bank board's budget. Entry-level examiners at the bank board earned a mere $14,390 a year, far less than at the other bank regulatory agencies. OMB and the White House Personnel Office not only resisted pay and staff increases, they pressed for reductions in the size of the examination force. It was all in the name of

deregulation. The examiner staff actually fell during the years
when the industry experienced its most rapid expansion. Examiners had faced a struggle when they were merely scrutinizing
institutions full of home loans. Suddenly they were expected to
analyze far more demanding and complex land transactions.
They didn't have a chance.

Since the whole system was financed by the industry, the
OMB and White House cutbacks saved the taxpayer nothing. But
the push for deregulation was ideologically driven. Everything
was viewed through a free-market prism. Deregulation had become the administration's buzzword and predominant philosophy. By the time Pratt was ready to leave, industry analysts and
White House insiders felt he had worked wonders with the
agency. He was credited with leading the industry out of the
heavily regulated nineteenth century and into the twenty-first.
He had prepared the industry well for his successor. The White
House and the industry were looking for another good soldier to
take over. Ed Meese knew Gray from their days in the Reagan
state house in California. He was just what the administration
needed—a not-too-bright fellow who would do as he was told.
In short, an industry toady.

Gray got a call from the White House Personnel Office a few
weeks after the U.S. League convention had ended. The President had made a decision on his senior staff. He wanted Gray to
take over for Dick Pratt. Recalls Gray:

> I had to go and discuss it with my family. We had
> just left Washington, and my wife didn't want to go back
> because she couldn't stand it. But I told her I would get
> an apartment and come back home when I could. I
> didn't have any doubt that I wanted to do it. Of course,
> I didn't know then that my whole philosophy would
> change. I couldn't have known that at the time. I didn't
> know that I would find that the administration's policy
> was wrong, either. I thought it was a good policy then,
> but that's because I didn't know enough.

Within days, word leaked in Washington's gossip mill that
Gray would be the new bank board chairman. On March 24,
1983, he became a member of the bank board. His nomination

sailed through the Senate, and two months later Edwin John Gray was sworn in as the twentieth chairman of the Federal Home Loan Bank Board.

A month later, he accepted an invitation to speak to the Texas S&L industry's annual convention. He arrived a hero, a man who had framed the preamble to the Garn–St. Germain bill and hung it near his desk. His speech, entitled "A Sure Cure for What Ails You," was on the administration's favorite philosophy—deregulation. Even as Gray spoke, Pratt packed up. He was leaving the agency in good hands. He would take a job in private industry—with Merrill Lynch.

5 Homecoming

The picture on the front page of the December 1982 *Vernon Daily Record* signaled a major change of command at the savings and loan on the town square. Roy Dickey, Jr., and Woody Lemons stared into the camera as they went over some expansion plans. In a story below the photo, Vernon residents learned that Dickey would soon leave his local CPA firm to assume the presidency of Vernon Savings, replacing Lemons, who would continue as the chairman of the board and an officer in the thrift's holding company, Dondi Financial Corp. in Dallas.

"Vernon Savings is going to become a major financial institution in the state of Texas under its new owners," Lemons told readers. "In order to get this done, we are going to have to have more expert help, and this is one reason we turned to Roy," who, as the town's mayor, had the kind of credentials Dixon liked. Lemons said he himself would continue to maintain an office in Vernon plus one in the thrift's newest expansion in Dallas. But Dickey would be responsible for most of the thrift's Vernon operations. "I think Roy's getting a promotion, and I'm definitely getting a promotion."

For the town's 12,500 residents, the shuffling of jobs at the local savings and loan was big stuff. Vernon is a hardscrabble town on the flat, red, dusty plains of north central Texas. The nearest town of any consequence is Wichita Falls, where the

47

tallest building is a grain elevator, and when people want to have fun, they go to Oklahoma, which is fifteen miles to the north. It's an obscure place with paved streets for white folks and clay for the blacks and Hispanics. No one really knows why Vernon is even called Vernon. One story printed on the town map says Vernon was originally named Eagle Flat because so many eagles nested in the area. But the Post Office Department objected. Towns with Eagle in their names littered the Texas landscape. So some faceless federal bureaucrat in Washington changed the name to Vernon in honor of George Washington's home, Mount Vernon. He dropped the "Mount" because there were no mountains around.

In many towns, a new face at the local savings and loan would not be a big deal. But it was front-page news in Vernon. That Dixon, a local boy made good, had engineered the changes made the news more compelling. Dixon hadn't lived in Vernon since he'd graduated from high school. But his family had a rich history there. His dad once wrote for the newspaper that announced Don would be acquiring the savings and loan. And Don credited his upbringing in Vernon for the values that had made him such a success down in Dallas.

The Dixons first showed up in Wilbarger County around 1925. Welcome D. Dixon, Don's father, moved to the town to start a career as a newspaperman and radio announcer. Welcome was born in Oklahoma and reared in New Mexico and Paducah, Texas. He moved to Vernon when he was around twenty to take a job as a cub reporter on the *Vernon Daily Record*. Welcome had some formidable problems to overcome, not the least of which was his name. Friends said the elder Dixon's full name was Welcome Darling Dixon, which is not good form in a state where every third male is named Bubba. As the story goes, Welcome's mother, a full-blooded American Indian, didn't know what to name him when he was born but gazed lovingly at the newborn and said, "I don't know what we'll call him, but he's a welcome darling." The name stuck. Welcome got around it with another time-honored Texas tradition—he used his initials as a name. For years people around town called him W.D. or Dick Dixon. People just assumed the *D* in W.D. stood for Dick.

Dixon's father unquestionably was the source of his entrepreneurial instincts and zest for a deal. W.D. was a hustler and workaholic who started his day at five A.M. and didn't stop until eleven at night. He squeezed in some time to marry a beautiful young woman from Waco named Frances Amiott. But he spent most of his time on business ventures, including an unsuccessful effort to launch a newspaper in Wichita called the *Post*.

Donald Ray Dixon was born at five-fifteen P.M. on November 20, 1938, about nine years after his folks had married. By this time his father's career had mushroomed. He was business manager for the newspaper and radio station and the author of "Party Line," a popular local newspaper column that he also read over the airwaves. Like a lot of towns with a Calvinist streak, Vernon is dry. People get their kicks listening to Eddie West sing "Touch of the Master's Hand" at the First Baptist Church rather than sitting in a saloon sipping whiskey and watching the Cowboys massacre the Redskins. W.D. figured out how to tap the reservoir of self-righteousness with a column that poked fun at his strait-laced neighbors and provoked rage. He once went on a satirical campaign to ban red fingernail polish. Readers rewarded his ingenuity with letters, comments, and complaints, making him an immensely popular and controversial figure. He was literally the talk of the town.

Young Don idolized his father. An Eagle Scout and an A student, Don grew up a quiet, well-behaved boy, known for his brains and ability. One teacher recalled, "He was kind of chubby and wore glasses early on. He sat close to the front of his class. He was always there and had his lessons done. He wasn't one of those boys full of vinegar." A manipulative nature and lifelong passion for cars, planes, yachts, blondes, and high living seemed to evolve from a doting mother and materialistic dad. Dixon wasn't an only child; he had a sister. But he might as well have been. His mother was a kind, gracious woman who spoiled her son rotten. "His Daddy would set goals for him and always reward him with a goody—a bike or something like that—if he achieved it," said a former wife. "Don's dad was his only real hero. But I think that's where he also got this thing about having a lot of toys."

Tragedy struck just before Don turned fourteen. The family had gone on a rare vacation to New Mexico. "I remember we went hunting the morning before they left, and W.D. was saying he was worried that he hadn't spent enough time with Don," a family friend recalled. "He told me to look around for a car for the boy. He was going to give him one for his fourteenth birthday.

You could drive at fourteen in Vernon those days." But W.D. suffered a massive heart attack in New Mexico and died.

The family returned to Vernon, where Dixon's mother maintained W.D.'s minority interest in the newspaper and ran a beauty parlor. But the death of his father also marked the start of something new for Dixon. To escape the insufferable heat of Texas summers, Dixon's mother traveled west to southern California to visit family and friends. The trips expanded Dixon's horizons beyond Wilbarger County. He would return from the vacations with news of the latest music and fads, like the black leather motorcycle jacket he wore to the local Dairy Queen. Other kids started looking to him for a more worldly view, and he liked the attention. He graduated from Vernon High near the top of his class, and his mother gave him a pea-green, two-seater Thunderbird as a graduation gift. He, too, was soon the talk of the town; he was the only kid with a sports car. He used it to drive right out of Vernon, Texas.

Dixon's triumphant homecoming more than twenty years later didn't occur without controversy. Once federal regulators in Little Rock approved his acquisition of Vernon Savings, he made it clear that he would keep Tanner and all of the local residents on the Vernon board. In a show of confidence, he elevated Lemons, R.B.'s handpicked successor. But it also became immediately clear that Dixon wasn't going to run Vernon Savings the old-fashioned way, despite what he had told Tanner. Strains on the board developed almost instantly.

Memories differ on exactly why R. B. Tanner stepped down. "The first thing he did was at the first directors' meeting after he took possession," said Tanner. "He'd already bought an Indian statue and paid $125,000 for it, or so he purported to the board, and he asked the board to approve it." The board was stunned by the request for an after-the-fact approval for the *Watcher of the Plains*, a limited-edition bronze casting by Charles Marion Russell, a Western artist who had once exhibited at the World's Fair in St. Louis. But Dixon and his new team pressed for a quick decision. They couldn't believe the board members. What a bunch of bumpkins! Didn't they know that investment art was a hedge against inflation? Dixon could see he had a lot of work to do dragging these guys out of the dark ages. "I wasn't going to be a rubber stamp," fumed Tanner. "I spoke out against it, but when no one would go along, I quit." Other board members said

Tanner's outrage over the statue actually came later, after he had quit over a dispute with minority shareholders who had accused him of trying to evade his fair share of the fees associated with the ownership transfer.

Regardless of the reason, though, Tanner had stepped down by the time a work crew set the life-sized Indian sculpture in the lobby of Vernon's home office, where it would sit in a cross-legged trance. Any restraints on Dixon walked out the door with Tanner, who was on the outside looking in as paintings, pottery, and other gilded inflation hedges streamed through the front door. Dixon soon approached Woody Lemons and told him the future would be different, too. As Lemons recalled the conversation, Dixon thought the staff needed some fun therapy: "He told me, 'We're going to have to teach these people how to let their hair down.' "

To most of the townsfolk, the young man who had left more than twenty years before had become a legendary success, a native who'd struck it rich and returned home to share his good fortune with neighbors. Dixon immediately ordered a $250,000 renovation project at the company headquarters and created jobs in the community at a time when other savings and loans were closing their doors. Vernon paid a premium for new employees it lured away from local banks and other competitors and pumped wealth into the community. Lemons vowed that Dixon would make Vernon the anchor for his expanding empire. "He had the reputation of an alchemist," said Raylan Loggins, a Vernon employee. "He was the guy who could turn dirt into gold."

Actually, Dixon had experienced a checkered financial history before his return as a conquering hero. He originally left Vernon because he had plans to design buildings, and enrolled in Rice University to study architecture. But a summer job in an architectual firm taught him that the real action centered around the guy who built a project, not the one who designed it. After two years at Rice, he left for the less oppressive air of southern California, where he graduated from UCLA with a business degree in 1960.

Dixon got into the real estate development business in a roundabout way. For college graduation his mother sent him on a cruise to Europe. He was in the tourist section of the ship when he met a Wisconsin girl named Sherry who was first class in

more ways than one. He courted her with his usual zeal and
charm and made her his wife a year later, taking a job with a
Milwaukee outdoor-advertising firm where his new father-in-law
also worked. Dixon soon discovered that selling billboard space
in a snowy place full of people who ate sauerkraut and drank
schnapps was no life for a Texas boy. He took Sherry back to
Dallas, where real men ate jalapeños and drank whiskey. He got
into the real estate business while designing and building their
first home.

From the outset, Dixon cultivated an image of a young
entrepreneur willing to risk his money on an uncertain future.
Actually, Dixon funded his early ventures with some stock he
acquired at a bargain price through his father-in-law and through
loans from his mother. He knocked around Dallas building small
clusters of homes. By the mid-1960s, he had dumped Sherry and
married her best friend, Diana Kincannon, a Corsicana, Texas,
native who had discovered her football-star husband wasn't
much to cheer about when he wasn't carrying a pigskin. As the
1970s dawned, Dixon and an ex–SMU football player named
Raleigh Blakely formed Raldon, a home and apartment building
firm that rapidly became a major force in the Dallas and Houston
markets.

Dixon's experience at Raldon would be a catalyst for the
lending philosophy he would adopt at Vernon years later.
Thanks to a relatively healthy economy, Raldon rocketed from a
thinly capitalized building firm to the No. 2 company in the
Dallas market. Dixon displayed a remarkable ability to finance
his rapid growth by borrowing huge amounts of money from
banks and private investors. "He took incredible risks," said a
former Raldon executive. "And why not? All he had was about
five hundred dollars of his own money tied up in the company.
The rest was borrowed. He didn't have anything to lose. He
didn't see it as an enormous risk: he wasn't out to screw anybody. He just didn't know when to stop. I think it's part of the
culture down there. There must be something in the Dallas water
supply that makes them think growth will never end."

The growth ended with the recession. Dixon wasn't the only
builder in Texas that hit hard times when the economy slumped
in 1974. But not many were so overextended. Raldon had about
$30 million in debt, including $20 million in land loans and $10
million for construction of homes that couldn't be sold. Dixon

tried all sorts of tricks to keep the operation afloat. He believed that real estate was the best investment in the nation. Dixon told his bankers the market would turn around and that Raldon would be profitable again, once the economy bounced back. They agreed with his philosophy, but the bankers wanted to rejuvenate Raldon without Dixon and Blakely, who were forced out of the company in 1975. Dixon, the borrower, never forgot it.

Once he acquired Vernon Savings, Dixon, the lender, vowed he wouldn't undercut any struggling developers. In effect, Vernon Savings would become a partner in the projects it financed by taking a profit participation in the venture. All that baloney about running a traditional S&L was Tanner talk. Dixon felt that a developer's lender should share in the profits or losses with its borrower and not be so quick to yank his financing in times of trouble. Vernon, he told Lemons, would be a developer's bank, run by developers, and for developers.

"He went over to the Federal Home Loan Bank of Little Rock and told them exactly what he was going to do," said Lemons. "After the meeting, they said we need more men like you. Things couldn't have gone on like they were, because we were paying fifteen percent for money and our loan portfolio was yielding only about ten percent. He told them we were going to make construction loans, land loans, and take profit participations in projects. Dixon was like most real estate developers I've ever met; he had a mind-set that didn't focus on problems but on how to solve problems. This worked for a while and everything we touched turned to gold. The regulators held us up as a model."

The regulators weren't the only ones who heard of the Dixon philosophy. As Dixon geared up to become a developer's bank, Harvey McLean walked into a cocktail party in Shreveport, Louisiana. After a few minutes' mingling with guests, the Harvard-trained developer ran into his first ex-wife. After a few minutes more, McLean's second ex walked through the door. After a few minutes more, he decided that Shreveport was too small a town. He left the party and moved to Dallas shortly thereafter.

Shreveport's all-star wheeler-dealer, Herman Beebe, put McLean into contact with Dixon after Harvey decided to develop a project along the I-30 corridor and needed financing. Dixon spelled out his theories of high finance, telling McLean that experience as a developer gave him an insight and appreciation into the problems that real estate men had with lenders, such as their irritating insistence on being repaid. McLean recalls:

> In acquiring Vernon, Don said he intended to oper-
> ate it differently. In order to enhance Vernon's position,
> he said it would take a profit participation in the deal—
> a fifty-percent profit participation—but if there were
> any losses, that Vernon would also split those. He also
> philosophized about the real estate cycles in the market,
> arguing that if you can hang on until the real estate
> cycle comes back, you can sell the property at a profit,
> especially in a dynamic growth community like Dallas.
> Vernon would not require us to repay any loans that we
> had until they could be disposed of profitably, and they
> also would carry any losses until the project could be
> sold at a profit.

McLean wasn't the only developer who couldn't believe what he had heard. Real estate men of all stripes would flock to Dixon's doors. "I met Ron Finley when I worked at Western Savings," said Raylan Loggins. "He was an ex–Casual Corner salesman from California who had come in to get a loan for a liquor store in a small shopping center he'd developed. We turned him down. By the time I went to work at Vernon a few years later, this guy had borrowed nearly one hundred million dollars. It was unbelievable."

Jack Atkinson ran a building supply store until 1982, when he decided to set aside his light fixtures and plumbing supplies to devote all of his time to developing real estate financed by his friend Don Dixon at Vernon Savings. "There is an old axiom in lending called the Golden Rule," Atkinson's lawyer later said. "To paraphrase, it says he who has the gold makes the rule. While Jack Atkinson successfully developed and sold real estate in the Dallas area for many years, he was not known as a big-time developer or heavy hitter when he began his relationship with Vernon in 1982. His relationship obviously was dictated by the Golden Rule."

Dixon's terms were mouth-watering. All real estate developers borrow as much money as they can to maximize their leverage and make profits off other people's money. But a bank usually demands a track record and some assurance that the funds will be invested in a sound deal before giving a developer a highly leveraged loan. Vernon gave developers like Finley and Atkinson, favored customers with ill-conceived deals, 100 percent financing and then some, a technique permitted under Texas law and under the terms of the Garn–St. Germain bill. A developer with a big project could not only borrow the $10 million he needed for a deal, but also enough money to pay Vernon's fees and the first two or three years' interest. At closing, the three years' worth of interest would be set aside in a separate interest-reserve account. As each monthly or quarterly interest payment became due, Vernon's employees would simply transfer money from one account to another to pay the interest and keep the loan current. Even better, usually included in the loan proceeds, was an up-front developer's fee of 2 to 4 percent. In other words, a developer could borrow $10 million with no cash down and take anywhere from $200,000 to $400,000 immediately as compensation for his management of the project. It was a more sophisticated form of the kickback that Ernie Hughes got in his deals.

The loans benefited Vernon Savings handsomely. The thrift's earnings soared because it charged loan renewal fees twice as high as the rest of the industry, routinely rolling over loans every six months instead of the standard one year. Vernon's interest rates were always higher than others in the industry, and it charged fees or points that were twice as high as most S&Ls. Vernon typically demanded 20 to 50 percent of the profits from the projects it financed, a split that generated a lot of income in an inflationary economy.

But Vernon also attracted borrowers who couldn't get loans elsewhere. "I recognized a lot of the names when I got there. They had all been turned down for loans at Western," said Loggins. A lot of the deals were racy, too. Jack Atkinson walked in during 1982 and borrowed $7.2 million to buy 345 acres of land known as Spring Park. Because of the way the loan was structured, Vernon initially had to advance only $2 million of the money. But Atkinson had to pay the full $400,000 in loan fees. Before he was scheduled to get the other $5.2 million, Atkinson got the land rezoned and sold it for a fat profit at the height of land inflation in Texas. Vernon's share of the profits generated another $2 million in earnings. Overall, the thrift earned $2.4 million on the deal even though it had advanced only $2 million on the loan. Initially the volume of the deals was astonishing. During a twenty-month period starting in April 1982, Vernon officials approved $706 million in construction loans, including seventeen that totaled more than $10 million. Developers flipped entire building projects. By mid-1983, Vernon was in danger of violating federally imposed limits on loan volume despite the more lenient rules under deregulation. Dale Anderson, Beebe's right-hand man, soon showed up at Vernon and went to work with Dixon on a way around the problem.

Back in Vernon, the board members were baffled. They had spent more than twenty years approving relatively simple home loans. Suddenly people such as Yvonne Robinson, R. B. Tanner's original secretary, who had remained on the board, were faced with complex development loans that involved interest reserves, profit participations, and exotic ventures in far-off places. "They ran the business; we were just figureheads," said Robinson. "We were totally in the dark. They let us know what they wanted us to know." Yet the directors and the employees at the thrift didn't object. Vernon had taken on a new philosophy. Everything was geared to profit. "Anything that was done that was not profitable was just kind of a no-no around here," one employee would later tell federal regulators. Vernon Savings couldn't miss. As long as inflation drove land prices upward, Vernon and its customers could always unload the most ill-conceived deal at a profit.

Dixon himself seemed to fade into a behind-the scenes role up in Vernon, leaving everything to the home-grown boy, Woody Lemons. Dixon wasn't even an officer of the S&L; he controlled the operation through his position in the Dallas-based holding company and avoided most contact with the people in Vernon. Said one employee, "The only one that we never sent anything to and never had anything to do with was Don Dixon."

But Dixon was involved. He and Anderson launched a complex reorganization in mid-1983 to cope with the problems of loan limits and other bank board rules. The federal regulators in Little Rock ignored the potential trouble posed by the new plan and Beebe's involvement in Vernon. As far back as 1976, bank board officials had tracked Beebe to a savings and loan that incurred troubles during the Texas Rent-a-Bank scandals spawned by the downfall of a little bank in Carrizo Springs, Texas. Yet the regulators didn't object when Beebe's AMI assumed an ownership stake in Vernon. They actually praised

Dixon after Beebe's right-hand man started shuffling Vernon subsidiaries around as if they were a deck of cards.

Dixon sold the plan to the regulators as a capital contribution to Vernon Savings. The S&L industry's prime problem was a lack of capital. Dixon proposed to bolster Vernon's net worth by contributing his Dondi Group of companies to the thrift, making them subsidiaries of the savings and loan. "The whole idea was to increase Dondi's cash flow and Vernon's net worth so it could grow fast to a billion dollars and Dixon could be a big player," said Ramsey. On paper, the contribution would increase Vernon Savings' net worth by $9.2 million and expand its ability to make more and bigger construction loans. The regulators praised Dixon's proposal. That's what deregulation was all about—luring new capital to an undercapitalized industry. He was a hero—one of those free-market entrepreneurs Reagan always talked about, a guy who shunned government handouts. He was injecting more than cash to the S&L, he was contributing sweat equity—the companies he had worked so hard to build.

Anderson was amused. Actually, the Dondi Group was starting to encounter troubles. Texas S&Ls like Empire had funded millions of dollars' worth of condo loans. Who cared if the units weren't occupied; who cared if they were poorly built. S&Ls making loans on the deals were generating huge fees, bolstering their incomes and justifying fat dividend checks to their owners. So what if Dallas faced a glut of unsold condos. That was a problem for tomorrow. Besides, inflation would eventually drive up the land value and bail everyone out. This was Texas, land of opportunity and oil.

Within months, the Dondi Group would learn that there were more condos than buyers. But that didn't really make any difference in the short run. By making the companies a subisdiary of Vernon Savings, Dixon could use the thrift's deposits to cover Dondi's growing debts. The value of the companies Dixon contributed to the S&L was nowhere near $9.2 million. But the regulators were so tickled that he would contribute them to the S&L that they quickly approved the reorganization. The board members did, too.

Dixon was on a roll. The reorganization also made Vernon Savings a subsidiary of Dondi Financial Corp. He had it both ways. The S&L could be used to cover the debts of the Dondi Group, its corporate children on the new organization chart. But it would also declare dividends to its parent, Dondi Financial, the corporate head of the family. By 1983, the board authorized dividends in excess of $1 million, or five times as high as the total authorized over the past five years by that old skinflint Tanner. And 1983 was just the start of something big. This deregulation was wonderful. So was Reagan. He was Dixon's kind of guy, one who didn't pay attention to all of those silly details. Things had gone well for Dixon. Vernon Savings was doing great.

6 "Gastronomique Fantastique"

G ary Roth pulled up to the stunning glass-and-wood house where Dixon said to meet him. It was perched high above the Pacific on the bluffs just north of Solana Beach. What a view; what a place. Dixon knew how to live; no question about that. Maybe he'd get lucky and get the job.

It had only been a few months since Roth had met Dixon while working as a California mortgage broker trying to line up a $12-million, no-money-down loan for a client:

Interest rates were twenty percent, and I had been to five hundred lenders over the past two years. I went everywhere. I went offshore. I met the brother-in-law of the sheik fifteen times but never the sheik. Then a broker friend here told me a Texas group he knew wanted to talk with me. I put on my three-piece suit and went up to the LaCosta Country Club, expecting to meet some silver-haired bankers in one of the high rises. Instead I went into an apartment, and there were three guys sitting there in golf outfits. It was Herman Beebe, Don Dixon, and Woody Lemons, in that order—number one, number two, and number three. I made my presentation and they said let's go see the project. So I took them out there. Herman Beebe looked around and said,

59

"Let's do it," and it was done. After two years I finally got this guy his loan. And what did he do? He fired me.

Roth ran into Dixon a few weeks later at the Carlsbad city hall and told him of his sorry fate. Dixon said to stop by the Solana Beach house the following Monday to talk about a job. Roth had never seen anybody quite like Dixon. From his earlier encounter, he knew Dixon owned a savings and loan headquartered in some two-bit little town in Texas. Yet he had a West Coast lending office in a posh beach house on the bluffs high above the Pacific. He financed multimillion-dollar deals on the spot. What was with this guy?

Actually, Vernon Savings didn't own the house. A California real estate developer named Walter Van Boxtel had acquired the beachfront land in 1979 for $150,000 and built a six-bedroom, 5,000-square-foot home on the site. By the time he was ready to rent it out, he had sunk about $520,000 into the place, but it was worth about $1 million. In 1981, Van Boxtel got a call from a local real estate agent who said she had some clients who wanted to buy the house. The next thing Van Boxtel knew he was deeply involved in a tax-free real estate swap engineered by Dixon and Beebe. "Don was a remarkably friendly front man. He had a little bit of that Southern drawl," said Van Boxtel. "You know how he did it? He had this little chuckle. He knew how to laugh at just the right time. He made everything seem like it was so much fun."

Beebe and Dixon could have paid Van Boxtel $1 million for the house and that would have been the end of it. They had the money. But that would have been too simple—no imagination involved there. They were deal makers who measured every angle to a transaction. Had they simply given Van Boxtel his $1 million, he'd have had to pay taxes on his profit of $480,000. Under the deal that they cut, Van Boxtel wouldn't have to give any of his hard-earned cash to Uncle Sam.

The swap involved four steps. Van Boxtel would get everything started by transferring ownership of the beach house to a Texas real estate venture controlled by Dixon. The Texas venture would then trigger step two by giving Van Boxtel thirteen new condos to be built in Dallas's sizzling real estate market as partial payment for the house. Step three involved refinancing the beach house and using it as collateral for a $750,000 loan from a bank controlled by Beebe. About $480,000 of the loan proceeds would go to Van Boxtel. Since borrowed funds are not taxed as income, Van Boxtel would get all of his equity out of the house tax-free. Another $120,000 of the loan money would be used to remodel the place, and the remaining $150,000 would be set aside in a reserve to insure that the original first mortgage of $148,000 would be paid off. Finally the Dixon venture would repay the $750,000 loan by leasing the beach house as an office or by renting it out to friends of Vernon Savings—other developers and wheeler-dealers who got fat loans from the Texas thrift. Once the deal closed, Vernon Savings became the only thrift in Texas with a pricey West Coast lending office.

Roth walked through the front door at the appointed hour after his chance encounter with Dixon at city hall. The inside of the two-story house had a masculine decor amplified by a stunning view. From the second-story deck, Roth could see the Pacific surf pounding the beach a hundred feet below as surfers paddled their boards out to catch the next wave. It was a breathtaking view. Roth was equally astonished when he found Dixon sitting naked in a Jacuzzi ready to conduct the job interview. Dixon didn't seem to be bothered, though. He asked Roth a few questions and hired him on the spot for $36,000 a year: "He said he would be out here every weekend, and he would tell me just what to do."

Roth soon learned that Dixon traveled in some fascinating circles. Potential clients such as the infamous Hunt brothers and former Texas governor John Connally showed up for weekend parties at the beach house. Roth learned that Vernon Savings also had another place closer to home—a $1.9-million, eight-bedroom, seven-bath, two-story ski lodge in Beaver Creek, Colorado, an exclusive resort where former president Gerald Ford had a home. Vernon was like no savings and loan Roth had ever seen. Dixon soon had Roth taking care of his classic-car collection: "At one time I had eleven antique cars to take care of. Eventually he had fifteen to eighteen of them stored in a warehouse up by the Palomar Airport Road."

Back in Vernon, many of the thrift's employees and the townsfolk didn't know what to think, either. As it turned out, Tanner's prudent, conservative business ways had a downside.

When Roy Dickey took over as president of the office in Vernon, the institution had no personal computers, and some of the books were still done by hand. The volume of loans generated in Dallas quickly taxed the resources of the home office. Employment in Vernon grew to reach 140 to 150 people, but the complexity and volume of the loans proved to be too much. Tensions erupted between the old guard and the new, pitting the Tanner types in Vernon against employees in Dallas. "The reason we started having so many problems with loan documentation was the people in the home office; they were ignorant," said one Dallas-based vice-president. But Dickey and his employees in Vernon blamed the problems on the slipshod operators in Dallas.

Soon other people in Vernon also started wondering just what was going on. Curtis Johnson, president of the Herring National Bank, recalled playing golf at the local country club as airplanes emblazoned with Dixon's initials roared overhead, ferrying employees to Dallas and back. "People started coming into my bank asking why we weren't paying as high an interest rate as they were. But I wasn't going to compete. The only way I could have done it was to go after high-priced money. And then you have to make marginal loans to make up for that, and I wasn't going to do it." Customers didn't have to worry about that, though. They were getting record interest rates on their savings, which were insured by the federal government.

Dixon knew why everyone was having trouble. Under Tanner, Vernon Savings had limited horizons. People had to start thinking Big. The savings and loan business had gotten into trouble because government regulators made all of the decisions, not the owners themselves. Dixon would show them how it was done. Lending money on home loans wasn't thinking Big. It was one of the worst ways to make any money. S&L owners had to start pondering new and different approaches—like investing in French restaurants. That was thinking Big.

The sunrise on Friday, October 6, 1983, was brilliant as the Westwind jet pulled out of the hangar at the Addison airport to pick up three couples. Just days before, Gary Roth had learned that the boss wouldn't be coming to California for a couple of weeks; he was going to France to conduct a market study for a French restaurant to be built and opened in Dallas. As the plane taxied out of the hangar, Dixon climbed aboard. He had dumped his second wife, Diana, months before and had married a third time, to Dana, an interior decorator from Fort Worth, a town, in the words of one Texan, "where the only mistake a man could make was to overdress." Dana climbed aboard the plane, too. She was followed by Woody and Paula Lemons, and Dixon's right-hand man at Dondi Financial Corp., Richard Little, and his wife, Carol. The plane would stop first at an antique-car show in Hershey, Pennsylvania, and then go on to New York, where the Dixons and the Littles would board the Concorde for Paris.

From its inception, the trip was designed to be a whirlwind experience. There were none of those tacky Cook's tours of the Eiffel Tower for Don Dixon; he'd show these bumpkins in Vernon a thing or two. He had a Parisian playboy and ex-husband of a beautiful princess on his staff for just such an occasion. Dixon had him organize a memorable culinary romp across the French countryside. Now that was thinking Big.

Dixon had hired Philippe Junot, the former husband of Princess Caroline of Monaco, who called himself a *conseiller financier*, soon after he'd acquired Vernon. Officially Junot functioned as a restaurant and public relations consultant and important source of financial contacts among European royalty for what every Texas S&L needed—a Geneva-based Swiss subsidiary named Vernonvest. In reality, though, Junot didn't do much for his sizable salary except impress Texans. "That Philippe, I'll tell you, was a real party animal," said one former Vernon executive.

The restaurant trip actually grew out of Dixon's hiring of Junot in Dallas during 1983. Junot recalled the experience with a haughty French flair:

> During my stay in Dallas, Don Dixon mentioned the possibility of building a restaurant across from his office. Vernon Savings and Loan was lending money to a developer, and they had a piece of land available to build a restaurant and he stated that he wanted to have here a restaurant of haute cuisine. And I said, "What do you call that cuisine?" And he said, "Well, let's go have some dinner in a restaurant in Dallas." My opinion about the cuisine was quite different than haute. So I said to Mr. Dixon, I'll be delighted to show you what

exactly is the culinary art of haute cuisine in our country at the occasion of your next trip. So we went on a
trip.

Philippe didn't work for free. He drew money from several
Vernon subsidiaries, $100,000 a year and more. But one former
Vernon executive said Philippe's paycheck was nothing com-
pared to his expense accounts.

"I saw some of Philippe's expense accounts that ran as high
as five thousand to ten thousand dollars a month," said Raylan
Loggins. But Philippe commanded such prices because of his
trained palate and vast experience and schooling in the restaurant business. During a legal fight over some restaurants Dixon
wanted to build in Dallas and New York, Philippe told an
inquisitive lawyer that he had built over twenty-five restaurants
in France. "I never built a restaurant in the United States," which
is what Dixon wanted to do, he said. "But I trained in the United
States prior to this operation for a period of four months with a
company in California."

"What company was that?" asked the lawyer.

"It was Food Maker, Inc.," said Junot.

The company owns Jack in the Box, which Junot agreed was
not exactly "haute cuisine."

Philippe wasn't the only Francophile on Vernon's staff. "We
had another one," recalled Loggins.

We called it our Rent-a-Frenchman program. Besides Philippe, Dixon hired another guy named Raymond Pousaz to run Vernonvest. He was a real ass, too.
We used to call him Inspector Clouseau after the detective that Peter Sellers played. He talked like that. Once
he brought this girlfriend named Yanou to Dallas. We
gave him the keys to the company's condo near the
office and had a limo drop them off. Some guy had just
wallpapered the place and had done a sloppy job. Pretty
soon we got a call from Raymond. He's talking real
snooty and says, "Yanou and I cannot stay in des apartment; there is sperm all over the carpet." Ray Jeter told
him, "That's wallpaper paste, you dumb shit."

Dixon's hiring of the Frenchmen paid off when the Concorde landed in Paris for the start of his market study, though. Junot and Pousaz might not have been much as capitalists, but they were terrific as tour guides, bon vivants, and freeloaders. "We knew we were truly into the adventure, that it was really happening to us, when we were greeted by Philippe's smiling face and his immediate quick witticisms," according to a written account of the trip by Carol Little. For the next two weeks, the Dixons would live like real royalty—on someone else's money. The trip would cost Vernon Savings $22,000. But that's how people who thought Big did things.

The Old World suites at the Bristol Hotel were superb. Philippe and some old friends from Paris stocked the place with fresh fruits and flowers. But the rooms were nothing compared to the Tour de France of the tongue that the Dixons and Littles would experience. First there was dinner at Castel's—a chic private club in Paris. Philippe's close friends Yolande and Jean Castel helped Junot organize the culinary tour and decided to tag along. If you're going to check out French chefs, why not have one along?

Over the next fourteen days, private planes dropped them off for lunch overlooking the River Ille in the west of France and waited so they could be ferried to dinner that night in Roanne. Chauffeured cars whisked them across the countryside for the roebuck in Alsace. Philippe picked up the group the first day in a 1954 Silver Dawn Rolls-Royce for lunch near Versailles. Unknown and unimportant people waited in lines, but the Dixons and their growing entourage didn't. Raymond Pousaz joined them. So did Philippe's mother as they relished the divine meals at La Tour d'Argent and the Sunday brunch on the Boulevard St.-Germain.

One day Sophie Hapsburg, an Austrian archduchess and lovely blonde with striking turquoise eyes, joined the tour and showed them how to shop along Avenue Montaigne. Another day would bring another fresh face. They visited the wine cellars of Château Mouton-Rothschild, took a side trip to Marbella, Spain, where Philippe had a place, and hit classic-car shows in Nice, and Bern, Switzerland. The most impressive performance came near the end of the trip, though, in Lyon at the kitchens of the famous French chef Paul Bocuse.

Carol's account caught the spirit of the show:

> We flew to Lyon and motored to the restaurant of
> Paul Bocuse. He is the most fun-loving, flamboyant,
> ebullient of the chefs. We went first to the large restau-
> rant where banquets are served, and as we entered, we
> were suddenly and enthusiastically greeted by patriotic
> French music being played on a huge antique calliope
> that occupied the entire end of the room and had
> amusing mechanical figures. There followed "The Star-
> Spangled Banner" and more, including discotheque
> music. In between, Monsieur Bocuse, with a chuckle,
> would dash back to initiate the next selection. In that
> party atmosphere he had created for us, we were served
> delicious champagne and special hors d'oeuvres.
>
> Finishing there, we drove up the road to the regular
> restaurant for lunch. At our places when we were seated
> were personalized cover plates Monsieur Bocuse had
> made especially for our party. In the center, they said
> (in French), "At the helm is Jean Castel, the captain,
> and his cabin boy, Philippe Junot." Circling this was
> our menu and the wines we were to be served. The
> plates were then packed and ready for us to take when
> we left.

The highlight of the lunch was the truffle soup Monsieur
Bocuse had invented in 1975:

> It is served in a bowl with a high pastry toque. One
> eats down through the pastry taking a bit with each
> spoonful of soup. Also unforgettable was the fish in
> pastry—the pastry resembling a fish, including the
> sculptured scales. Everything, as usual, was very dra-
> matically presented, and Monsieur Bocuse joined us to
> kibitz between courses.

After lunch, as the Dixons were saying good-bye, Bocuse
organized the grand finale. He had his chefs—twelve that day—
line up in the courtyard and insisted that the men in the party
"pass and review" the troops. It was spontaneous and fun until
the end. And it was Big.

As they headed home, they had visions of twenty-seven Michelin stars forever in their heads, a good idea of what kind of restaurant was needed in Dallas, and some extra baggage.

Gary Roth's phone rang early in the morning soon after Dixon's plane touched down. "It was six A.M. California time. Dixon was in Texas so it was later for him. He told me he had just returned and had a car shipped from Europe to Los Angeles. I said, 'Okay,' and he said, 'No, you don't understand. I had it shipped air freight. It will be there today. It's a gray Mercedes. I had it air-freighted from Europe. You'll have to go up to L.A. and meet it.' He hung up."

Roth couldn't believe his ears. Dixon might as well have Fed Exed the car. Air freight from Europe? The shipping must have cost a fortune. He got out of bed, got dressed, and headed for L.A. International Airport. "When it came in, it was a real pain. They had drained all of the oil out, and I had to run around and get oil and gas. It had those air shocks. One was broken and I couldn't get it fixed. So I drove it home with one side higher than the other."

Dixon didn't bill the savings and loan for his cars; he paid for them himself. By this time he was earning more than $200,000 in salary and pulling down twice that in the dividends that Vernon Savings paid to its parent firm, Dondi Financial. Nevertheless, Dixon and Beebe had figured out a way to take care of various expenses, such as maintenance of the cars and the Solana Beach house. By 1983, Vernon was doing a lot of business in California, financing time-share units, office parks, and apartments. Included in Vernon's fees for many of the multimillion-dollar loans was 1 to 1.5 points that would be funneled into a special account maintained by Roth. "I used that money for the house and other expenses," said Roth. Sometimes Vernon and its partners would deduct $60,000 to $100,000 before splitting the profits on one of their land deals to meet lease payments on the Solana Beach house, which became Vernon's West Coast party palace.

One day Dixon told Roth that Vernon's board of directors would be coming to California in the near future for a special board meeting. "He said he wanted to arrange something special for them like a cruise and that he would probably need my help." Roth didn't think much more about the request until

Dixon approached him a few weeks later. "He said he had arranged for a cruise in the San Diego harbor after the meeting and that he wanted me to get some liquor and find eight female escorts." Roth was stunned by the request. "I wasn't shocked; I just didn't know how to go about lining up female escorts. So I called a friend and he gave me Karen's name."

Although Roth didn't suspect it at the time, his call to Karen Wilkening would one day echo far beyond San Diego's discreet call-girl circuit. Within a few years, her name would consume gallons of ink in California newspapers as a key figure in the Rolodex Madam scandal, involving an exclusive call-girl ring patronized by the city's powers. Scandal writers would have a field day describing the FBI's frantic efforts to get their hands on Wilkening's Rolodex, which reputedly contained the names of leading local politicians and judges. At the time of the phone call, though, Roth didn't even know what to ask her. "I called Karen and told her I wanted eight girls. She asked me what I needed them for. I didn't know what to say." Roth went back to Dixon with Karen's question. Dixon looked at him in the way he looked at people who didn't think Big. "He said, 'What do you think you hire girls for?' So I called Karen back and said, 'I need them to entertain men.' She said it would be a hundred and fifty dollars a girl."

Roth couldn't believe what Dixon was about to do. He had seen the board members on a trip to Vernon. They were Bible toters—guys whose idea of a cruise was two hours in a bass boat on Lake Lugert near Vernon. The town music-store owner, funeral director, and other captains of industry, and a chiropractor had remained on the Vernon board. Dixon had made it clear that things were going to be different from when R. B. Tanner ran the place. But the idea of getting the directors involved with Karen and her Rolodex was a Big difference.

When the directors back in Vernon heard about the meeting in California, they were excited. Don Dixon was one good owner. Even since he'd taken over, dividends were higher and Vernon was more fun. Once a year Vernon Savings would bring favored borrowers and celebrities like Philippe Junot to Vernon for a bird hunt. The directors could rub shoulders with major Dallas developers and blow little birds out of the sky. It was fun. When the idea of a trip to California arose, there was one problem—the board's token female, Yvonne Robinson, R. B. Tanner's original secretary, who looked like a vicar's wife. Woody Lemons took care of her; he pulled Yvonne aside and explained it would be a boys-only trip and that she wasn't invited. "I wouldn't have gone if I was," she said. "My impression was the trip was social—for the men to go and play golf and look over some of our property."

When the plane carrying Dixon and the boys on the board touched down at the Palomar airport, Roth was there to pick them up in a stretch limo. "They were half bombed from drinking on the plane," said Roth, "and I took them to the Solana Beach house for the board meeting." Once the meeting ended, the fun started. The boys soon found themselves zipping down the freeway from Solana Beach to the Sheraton Inn in downtown San Diego. Moored in the harbor near the hotel was a fifty-foot sailboat that would take them to dinner at a fancy restaurant on Coronado Island. Also on the scene were eight of Karen's finest beauties to help pass the time.

Once everyone was aboard, the yacht slipped gracefully into the harbor for the forty-five-minute twilight cruise. Roth soon learned that these Texas boys were landlubbers: "Woody Lemons got seasick, the poor guy." The yacht took a tour of local sights before docking at Coronado. It was a beautiful evening in more ways than one. The boys and the girls had a sumptuous dinner at the Chart House, a restaurant known for its tasty seafood, fine wine, and spectacular views. "If these guys would have died on the spot, they all would have died with a smile on their face," said Roth.

Karen had done a first-class job in selecting the girls. They were beautiful young women who knew how to make old men think they were in their prime. The shenanigans would be exposed years later and would shake the folks back in Vernon. "When it came out about the kept women," said Donna Karcher, who works at the Vernon Chamber of Commerce, "that was terrible. They preached about it in church. These were men who sat in the front pew! People just wouldn't believe it. People talked about it in the coffee shop. It was appalling. You can steal money here. Texans are used to graft. But sex? Oh, no."

After dinner, the yacht carried eight happy sailors back to the pier in San Diego. "Once we got back to shore, we had a slight problem with the girls," said Roth. "I had to do some renegotiating. The one hundred fifty dollars only covered four hours, and it had taken us that long to eat dinner." Roth soon rectified the situation by giving the girls another $150 each. The eight girls and eight guys climbed into cars for the trip back to the house high above Solana Beach. "I took them directly to the house. I left the girls in the house and the eight directors in there, too. I opened eight bottles of wine, and I left for the night."

Weeks later, Roth had to figure out how he would cover the $3,000 he had spent that night. "I called Dallas and asked how I should report this. The guy there said, 'That's a good question.' " It was nearing Christmastime, 1983, and Roth asked if he would be getting a Christmas bonus. "That's it," said the voice on the other end of the line. "We'll call it a Christmas bonus."

7 The Tattoo Tuna

R
ick Ramsey picked up the morning newspaper and headed back into his suburban Dallas home. He didn't have to turn any pages in the November 27, 1983, edition of the *Dallas Morning News* to decide which story he wanted to read. The headline on the page-one story wasn't exactly a grabber for anyone not in the real estate business: "Condo Land Deals, Price Spiral Probed."

But Ramsey anxiously read every word of the story by Allen Pusey and Christi Harlan:

> From LBJ Freeway eastward to Faulkner Point, Lake Ray Hubbard and beyond, an area that once was undeveloped grassland has become the site of thousands of condominium units.
>
> A two-month investigation by the *Dallas Morning News* reveals that many of those condo developments have been built on hundreds of unusual land sales, inflated land appraisals and more than $500 million in questionable real estate loans.

Ramsey sat down in a chair to pore over the details of the *News* investigation. As the head of Dixon's condo building operation and an officer of Vernon Savings, Ramsey obviously

71

was relieved that neither venture was even mentioned in the story. But that didn't mean the Dondi Group and Vernon Savings wouldn't be affected by the scandal.

Pusey and Harlan had broken the story of how a closely knit group of real estate investors and developers, including Danny Faulkner and Ernie Hughes, had engaged in land flips and bogus sales designed to inflate the price of condos sold to unsuspecting consumers along the I-30 corridor. Thanks to the land scam, Dallas had an artificial condominium building boom. A glut of unprecedented proportions threatened condo markets in some sections of suburban Dallas with an astonishing 12.5-year supply of condominiums. One federal housing official told Pusey and Harlan that the glut was the "worst we have seen in years." Thousands of potential condo customers already burdened by soaring interest rates had spent their Sunday morning doing the same thing as Ramsey—reading the gory details of the scandal in the newspaper. Ramsey didn't know what impact the publicity would have on the consumer traffic through the condominium projects developed by the Dondi Group, the Vernon Savings subsidiary he ran. He hoped the story would be like most newspaper scandals; something that would stir up a lot of dust but not much heat. He should have known better. It gets hot in Dallas—even in November.

On paper it would have been hard to detect that the headlines represented much of a threat to Vernon Savings. It had been nearly two years since Dixon had acquired control of the thrift, and everyone thought he had the Midas touch. Huge profits generated by Vernon's less conventional investments more than covered the past losses in Vernon's residential-home-loan portfolio. In his report to Vernon's employees, customers, and shareholders for 1983, Woody Lemons reported "record growth in assets, deposits, capital, and most importantly, earnings." Dividends had soared and local citizens marveled at the Vernon Savings' generosity. At a fund-raiser for the Red River Valley Museum in Vernon, the thrift had donated an entire room to house exhibits in the museum, which was Vernon's idea of the Smithsonian, and had contributed a week's use of the Beaver Creek lodge to the auction.

Contrary to his promises to R. B. Tanner, Dixon categorically rejected the *Little House on the Prairie* approach. By mid-1983,

Vernon had become part of a baffling pile of interrelated corporations designed to pump money into Dixon's and Beebe's
corporate pockets.

At the top of the heap was Dondi Financial Corp., the
holding company in which Dixon and Beebe were majority
stockholders. On the organization chart, Dondi Financial had
four subsidiaries that fed it revenue. In reality, almost all of
Dondi Financial's cash came from dividends declared by one of
the four—Vernon Savings.

On its own, Vernon Savings also had subsidiaries—six of
them that helped invest federally insured deposits in land, real
estate, commercial ventures, and most important, paper shuffled
between Vernon and a handful of savvy investors.

By far, the largest Vernon subsidiary was the Dondi Group,
the umbrella organization run by Ramsey that acquired, developed, managed, and marketed condo projects and other real
estate developments. Seven more subsidiaries fit under the
Dondi Group umbrella, and each fed business and profits to one
another. One subsidiary, Dondi Residential Properties, Inc.,
would acquire land and build condos. It would then hire another
subsidiary, Dondi Designs, an interior design firm run by Dana
Dixon, to decorate the units, and still another, Dondi Marketing,
to help sell them.

Each of the subsidiaries operated as a semiautonomous unit
with its own president and unique set of goals. As a dollar of
profit rolled in, the subsidiary kept twenty cents and passed
eighty cents on to its parent, Dondi Group, which passed its
profits on to Vernon Savings. In some cases, the Dondi Group of
companies developed projects on their own. In some cases, the
group became a partner in projects with other developers. In all
cases, though, the goal was to create a money machine that
would enable Vernon to declare hefty dividends to its parent
firm, Dondi Financial. Vernon's other subsidiaries worked in
much the same way.

Dixon imbued the organization with a psychology of reckless growth that didn't stop with the projects Vernon owned.
Powerful incentives existed to boost the subsidiaries' contribution to Vernon Savings. The bank board's 1982 resolution approving Dixon's acquisition limited dividends that Vernon Savings could pay to its owners to 50 percent of the thrift's income.

If Vernon earned $1 million, it could pay only $500,000 to Dondi Financial. If it earned $10 million, it could pay its parent $5 million. The more money that Dixon could flush into the subsidiaries, the higher his dividends.

Vernon soon became intricately involved as a partner in projects that it financed, often demanding that loan applicants hire its subsidiaries for certain services. When Dallas developer Harvey McLean applied for his loan to build condos along the I-30 corridor, Dixon demanded the right to approve the plans and specifications before the loan would be made. "We submitted our [plans] to Vernon for their approval. But Mr. Dixon didn't like them. He felt while they might be okay for a strict apartment, that we were dealing in condominiums that were to be rented as apartments for a brief period of time and that we should build higher-quality and larger units that he felt would be more suitable for conversion. [Eventually] the overall quality of the apartment project went up, and the size of the individual units went up by about twenty percent," said McLean. The amount of money McLean needed to borrow went up, too. The construction budget jumped 35 percent, and McLean got not-so-subtle hints that he should hire Dana Dixon's interior decorating firm, Dondi Designs, to decorate the apartments.

"Woody Lemons suggested to me that if I wanted to have a continuing relationship with Vernon and Mr. Dixon, that I'd better hire Don's wife to do the decorating," McLean said. He had already contracted for an interior decorator on the project, so he hired Dondi Designs on another apartment complex he was building. "They insisted, of course, that we write the insurance through their agency. And they insisted that we use a certain computer company for production of monthly financial reports," said McLean.

Such heavy-handed tactics might sound sleazy to the average American. But few real estate developers would flinch at Vernon's approach. More than one lender has forced big borrowers to hire a certain firm for appraisals or inspections. In fact, it's done all the time. It usually isn't done on the scale that existed at Vernon Savings, where the approach was also a tad crude. But it worked. By late 1983, Vernon's assets had soared under Dixon's leadership, reaching $800 million, up more than tenfold from the $72 million reported when he took over. Earnings surged, too. Nationwide, Vernon ranked second in profitability in a survey by Kaplan, Smith and Associates, a prominent Los Angeles financial consulting firm. *Dunn's Business Month* would soon cite it for its professional real estate investment acumen.

"It had a reputation of a highly profitable, rapidly growing company in a dynamic real estate market," said McLean. "I was specifically told by people at Vernon that the federal and state regulators were very happy to have the management team in Vernon and that they approved and actively encouraged the method of operation. It was represented, for example, by Jenkins and Gilchrist, one of the leading law firms in Dallas." It was represented by Caplin and Drysdale in regulatory matters, a Washington law firm whose chief senior partner is Mortimor Caplin, the former commissioner of Internal Revenue.

Dixon himself took great pride in the organization he had built. In early 1984 he described it as "one of the most dynamic forces in real estate." Thanks to its new ownership, Dixon said, Vernon could talk the developer's language and position itself as a "real estate developers' bank run by developers for developers."

But Ramsey knew better. An accountant by training and an ex-Marine by temperament, the soft-spoken and deliberate CPA understood that the rosy financial reports and elaborate corporate reorganization chart obscured some potentially severe problems in the condominium operation. Ever since his days at Raldon, Ramsey had watched Dixon grab the brass ring. Of the two men, Dixon was the visionary—the man with the grand ideas who traveled west and returned to Dallas with California-inspired condo designs. He was always one step ahead of everyone. Ramsey, by contrast, was the deliberate one—the sticks and bricks man, a construction executive who stayed behind and actually got things built. When the two joined forces in the Dondi Group during the early 1980s, Dixon established a blistering pace for the condo-building operation and Ramsey blazed the trail. He launched a construction blitz, starting nearly five thousand condominium units in sixteen separate projects in Texas, Florida, and Louisiana.

By 1983, Dixon had all but abandoned management of the condo operation to play with his new toy—Vernon Savings. But Ramsey more or less stayed behind to keep the condo operation afloat. It was no easy job. The economy had slowed, and interest rates had remained stubbornly high. Ramsey admits that he started feeling like a corporate stepchild.

"We [in the condo and building operation] were used to seeing all of the growth, and then suddenly it seemed like all anyone cared about was the savings and loan." Ramsey could understand why. To a real estate developer and deal junkie like Dixon, the savings and loan business was like a dream come true. Developers could tap into millions of dollars in other people's money as easily as they could write a check. Why borrow money from a commercial bank, pay 2 percent over the prime, and worry about nosy loan officers? Under financial deregulation, a developer could buy a savings and loan and lend federally insured deposits to one of his development subsidiaries. In effect, he was lending the depositors' money to himself. The interest rate on the deposits usually was about two-thirds the rate charged by banks, and there were no loan officers to worry about. The only potential problem was a group of under-staffed regulators who overlooked everything except the most serious abuses.

Dixon had plunged into the S&L side of the business with gusto, particularly after he discovered that a developer with a savings and loan didn't even have to build anything to make money.

Ramsey watched in awe as people like Jack Atkinson, the appliance dealer that Dixon turned into a deep-pocket real estate developer, flocked to Vernon Savings.

The pace of the deals was mind-boggling. Atkinson and Dixon flipped land deals around as if they were pancakes. In mid-1983, Atkinson got a loan from Vernon to buy a 48-acre tract of land in Dallas with no money down. The dirt cost $2.8 million, or $1.35 per square foot, but Vernon lent Atkinson over $3 million, or about $200,000 more than he needed. Atkinson used part of the extra $200,000 to pay Vernon Savings the $122,000 in loan fees the thrift charged for making the loan. The rest was his. Vernon also demanded—and got—a share of any profits that would be generated by the venture. Atkinson never developed the land, though. Just six weeks after he bought it, he sold a portion of the land at a profit, peddling 14.8 acres of the tract for $2 a square foot. The profit worked out to be $154,000, which he split with his partner, Vernon Savings. And who paid $2 a square foot for the land valued at $1.35 just six weeks earlier? Dondi Properties, Inc., a subsidiary of Vernon. A month later, Dondi had some second thoughts and decided it didn't want the land after all. So it sold the 14.8 acres back to an Atkinson partnership for $2.85 per square foot, or yet another markup. Vernon Savings got a piece of the action on both sides of that transaction. The price the Atkinson partnership paid to reacquire the tract generated a $548,000 profit for Vernon's Dondi Properties subsidiary. But Vernon also lent the Atkinson partnership the money it needed to reacquire the 14.8 acres. For the loan, it earned another $42,000 fee. Overall, Vernon and its subsidiaries made nearly $800,000 in fees and profits between June 30 and September 19 flipping around a piece of land on which nothing was built except inflation. With profits like that, who needed to worry about building condos? Eventually, Vernon could lend some developer enough money to buy the land for $3 per square foot. He could build a shopping center and charge rents high enough to cover all of the illicit profits. Store owners would then mark up the price of their goods, and the public would pick up the final tab in higher prices. It was a financial wheel of fortune with inflation as the hub.

From his position at the helm of Dixon's condo operation, Ramsey could see how the whole scam could fall apart, though. The land flips worked as long as everyone was willing to pay higher prices. But what would happen if the developers couldn't find tenants for the shopping centers and were unable to repay their loans? Such a slump was already occurring in the condo markets, and he seemed to be the only one in the organization who was worried about it.

Things had changed dramatically since he and Dixon had started building condos in the early 1980s. The Texas economy was no longer booming. Oil prices stood at $26 per barrel. But they were $5 per barrel off their 1981 peak. Interest rates remained high, too, as Paul Volcker continued his relentless war against inflation. A prudent businessman might have cut back once he saw signs of an economic slowdown. But real estate developers don't think that way, particularly real estate developers who work for someone like Don Dixon. Ramsey—like practically every other developer in Texas—had continued to expand. Ramsey didn't really have much choice. Condos are far different from residential housing projects. A homebuilder can start a sixteen-house development and quit midway if the economics turn against him. Once a condo project is started, though, it has to be finished. "If you say you are going to build 146 units, you have to build 146. That's the law," said Ramsey. By late 1983, though, there were too many condos and not enough buyers.

The glut was already evident to builders and real estate pros. When Pusey and Harlan's story hit, though, the glut also became evident to consumers. Ramsey hoped the initial exposé would be the end of the newspaper stories. But the headlines kept coming. Two days later, Pusey and Harlan had two more stories. One told how a state senator named Ted Lyon had made thousands of dollars dealing with Mesquite developers, and another detailed how investors were offered bonuses to pledge their financial statements in the smelly deals. Each story reminded the *News* readers that the Dallas-area developers had created a 12.5-year oversupply of condominiums.

As November faded into December, the stories kept coming. Savings and loans were in trouble because of the I-30 deals; politicians were involved; appraisers were under investigation for phony real estate appraisals and kickbacks. The headlines gave the public a well-justified skepticism about investing in any condominium project, and the Dondi Group soon found itself in deep trouble, with hundreds of unsold units on its hands. "The serious deterioration began in the later part of 1983. Condominium sales continued to decrease every month. The traffic was not coming to the sales offices, the marketplace had just all but abandoned us," Ramsey said. The Vernon subsidiaries that had passed their profits up the line to the parent company now faced the prospect of passing their losses on to Vernon Savings.

Dixon didn't like losses of any kind. But the declining markets threatening the condo operation represented a particularly thorny problem. Just six months before, he had given the Dondi Group of companies to Vernon Savings as a noncash capital contribution to the thrift. Because Dixon placed a high paper value on the Dondi Group assets, the gift had doubled the thrift's net worth, enabling Vernon to make far larger loans and pleasing federal regulators immensely. If Vernon's earnings dropped precipitously less than a year later because of losses from the condo operation, though, the transaction would surely raise questions at the Federal Home Loan Bank Board, which had already sent examiners into Vernon for a routine exam.

Once everyone realized the stakes that were involved, Dixon decided the projects had to go before they became a drag on Vernon's earnings and inhibited the thrift's ability to pay dividends to you-know-who. Vernon soon embarked on a strategy to sell the condo projects to a third party, so it could shield Vernon's income statement from any losses, and cut overhead.

But Ramsey and Dixon had a falling-out when Vernon officials started scratching around for buyers. Dixon wanted to carry the unsold condos on Vernon's books at an artificially high value—one that would avoid any embarrassing write-downs and losses. The last thing he needed was some federal examiner poking his nose into deals like the ones he had cut with Jack Atkinson. But Ramsey wouldn't go along with the treatment. Part of the reason was his background as a CPA who understood the legal implications of Dixon's position. Ramsey was in charge of—and responsible for—the condo operation, and he didn't want any legal liability coming back on him. But Ramsey's standards were also a cut above his old partner's. Internally he was considered weird by other staffers, who joked about his tendency to field-strip his cigarette butts as required in the Marine Corps. "You'd go into his office and you'd see these little cigarette butts he had stacked in a pile," said one former officer. But Gary Roth recalled Ramsey for other reasons. He was a straight arrow, a square who didn't participate with the women out in California at all.

Ramsey insisted that accounting rules required Vernon to write down the unrealistic value of the units on its books until they were sold. "Sometime in December 1983," Ramsey recalled, "Dixon came by my office and invited me to lunch. I thought it was sort of odd. We hadn't had lunch together in years. Woody Lemons and Dick Little were there, too. We got into Dixon's car and drove over to his house. He had his maid make up some tuna sandwiches, and we went into the study and sat down to have lunch." Dixon joined his hands together in front of him as if he were about to say a prayer. Then he lifted his hands and began spreading them apart. "He said, 'Ricky, you are going one way, and the company is going another. Be a team player or you are out.' I called it the tattoo tuna lunch.'' By branding him as a loner, Dixon gave Ramsey his tattoo. Then he got his tuna sandwich.

Within weeks, it was apparent to almost everyone that Ramsey had fallen from grace. Dixon had a highly visible system of perks that left little doubt about who was in and who was out in Dondi's offices on the second floor of Vernon's building. Dixon had the corner office—the biggest one, with the wet bar, the shower, the stained glass, and the best view of the pond outside. His desk was elevated on a platform so he would sit above anyone who sat in the chairs before him. The second-in-command had a smaller, less luxurious office next door. The pecking order continued down the hall. The farther an employee sat from Dixon's office, the lower the rank. Within days of the tattoo tuna lunch, Ramsey voluntarily abandoned his office next door to Dixon for one farther away. He continued to resist Dixon's treatment of the condos on the books, too. A few months later, Ramsey unilaterally booked a loss on the condos in a routine internal financial report that landed on Dixon's desk with a thud. Dixon was livid. "I remember the day very well. It was June nineteenth, my birthday, and Mr. Dixon came in and demanded that we reverse the loss, that I had lost sight of our objectives, and that [the loss] was not acceptable to him.'' Ramsey, who was also chief operating officer at Vernon Savings, resigned on the spot and left the organization a few months later. To Don Dixon, the problems with the condo operation went out the door with Ramsey. It would take him a while to learn that Rick Ramsey left a few things behind.

8 No More Mr. Nice Guy

Joe Settle didn't know what hit him. A genial North Carolinian who had spent seventeen years in the commercial banking business, Settle had been president and the principal federal thrift regulator at the Federal Home Loan Bank of Dallas since 1979 when Ed Gray summoned him to Monterey, California, in April 1984. It had been months since the Empire Savings scandal broke, and the bank board was in California for a meeting concerning the mortgage market. Settle had no idea what to expect when he walked into the room at the Hyatt hotel and saw Gray and his two fellow board members, Mary Grigsby, a Texan, and Donald Hovde.

After Empire, Gray had reviewed supervision of S&Ls in the Dallas district and got the strong impression it was like a country club with Joe Settle as the golf pro. The other board members had expressed reservations about the action Gray wanted to take. They saw Settle as a weak but well-meaning federal regulator who couldn't be blamed for the failure of a state-chartered savings and loan. Nevertheless, Grigsby and Hovde finally agreed to go along with their new chairman.

"We've reviewed the situation, and we're not happy with the supervision in your district," Gray bluntly told Settle once the meeting began. "We've decided to replace you. You can stay on as the president of the bank, but you'll have to give up as the PSA [the principal supervisory agent]."

Settle was stunned. He was the first supervisory agent to be fired in the fifty-year history of the Federal Home Loan Bank system, and he asked the board members if the reason was the Empire scandal. "No, no, no, no," said Gray. "I specifically looked at other cases, too." But the decision was final. Gray knew it would only be a matter of time before Settle would leave the bank. Being the bank president but not the PSA was like being captain of a ship with no sailors. He was right. Settle resigned soon afterward.

The sacking of Joe Settle shocked the Texas S&L industry. Dixon and his cohorts didn't know what to think. Just ten months earlier, Ed Gray had shown up at the Texas industry's annual convention in Dallas and seemed like the ideal federal regulator—the kind of guy who wouldn't make waves. Texas S&L executives ushered him around Dallas in a regal blue Rolls-Royce. Settle and Texas savings and loan commissioner L. Linton Bowman III gave Gray a brief warning that trouble might surface at Empire Savings. But most of the visit was social. *Washington Post* reporters David Maraniss and Rick Atkinson would later report how the regulators and regulated partied in the penthouse atop Dallas's Registry Hotel. Bowman and Durward Curlee—a chubby, ribald lobbyist for the local industry—plucked their guitars and serenaded Gray, crooning "I'm Walking the Floor over You" and "Lovesick Blues." Gray seemed to like the show—the one in the penthouse and the one on the local industry's balance sheet. Yet here he was less than a year later firing the compliant head of the Dallas bank, chastising the local bank board directors for their lack of vigilance, and insisting that Settle be replaced with an outsider—Roy Green, an Arkansas-born thrift executive who worked for the California-dominated U.S. League of Savings Institutions.

Although Dixon and the rest of the Texans didn't know it, the sacking of Joe Settle represented the first shot in a war that would erupt between the bank board and the Texas industry. Eventually the battle would consume much of Dixon's time and lead to a running confrontation that would seal the fate of Gray, Dixon, Vernon Savings, and many other powerful people. Dixon, Curlee, Bowman, and other Texans were about to learn that Ed

Gray was not the malleable regulator they had come to expect from the system.

But in April 1984, no one suspected that anything so dire loomed on the horizon. Gray's behavior merely puzzled Texans such as Dixon; they didn't understand what had happened to the guy. What was he trying to do? Was he going crazy?

If there was a catalyst for Ed Gray's epiphany, it was the same thing that triggered Dixon's troubles with Rick Ramsey— the I-30 condo scandal. The headlines started just six months after Gray became chairman of the Federal Home Loan Bank Board. The stories humiliated him. Because Empire's deposits were federally insured, the bank board's field examiners had alerted Washington to the imprudent loans, conflicts of interest, sloppy records, and no-money-down deals at Empire. But deregulation so dominated the administration's thinking that signs of trouble were ignored. Gray's predecessors didn't dare interfere with the doings of a state-chartered S&L. The idea of deregulation was to get the government off everyone's back. Examination reports on the blatant abuses at Empire Savings had languished in government in-boxes along with exams of other troubled S&Ls. When Gray assumed the chairmanship, he knew little about the problems and did less to find out more. Linn Bowman had issued a vague warning to Gray about Empire, and Settle had twice raised the subject. But Empire Savings' troubles seemed postponable. Gray had heard lots of stories about S&Ls having trouble adjusting to deregulation. A troubled S&L in Texas just wasn't the main thing on his mind.

Gray was a creature of the huge and powerful California savings and loan industry, which had gotten him his job. The California S&Ls didn't care about some troubled thrift in Texas. They feared the developing markets for brokered funds—huge deposits that could be steered into savings and loans by Wall Street brokers because of some 1980 rules passed by Gray's predecessors. Charlie Knapp—a flamboyant operator who had gained control of a large S&L in California—was offering savers high interest rates and luring billions of dollars of deposits into his S&L from Wall Street brokers, who earned a fee for placing the money in a federally insured thrift. Within no time, Knapp's thrift had become the fastest growing in the state, raking in deposits from pensioners and Arab potentates looking for a safe place to park their petrodollars. Traditional California S&Ls saw the cost of their deposits soar as they upped interest rates to keep their customers from defecting to Knapp. The California industry let Gray know it wanted to go back to the pre-1980 rules, when federally insured S&Ls could have only 5 percent of their deposits in brokered funds. Slapping restrictions on brokered deposits would not only correct a legitimate problem; it would give Charles Knapp his comeuppance and please the California S&Ls. Soon after he took office, Gray focused almost all of his attention on brokered funds: "I got my first briefing in August about this phenomenon, and I really got concerned very quickly. Remember, I'm new in the job. And I'm trying to get to know where the bathroom is. I'm trying to pull together my team, trying to get to know the people there. And then I get this briefing, and it scares the hell out of me."

Gray and the California S&Ls weren't the only ones concerned. Banks didn't like paying savers higher interest rates, either, and bankers had complained to William Isaac, the chairman of the Federal Deposit Insurance Corp., which insured deposits in commercial banks. After discussing the problem, Gray and Isaac decided to issue joint regulations restricting brokered deposits. But they ran into stiff opposition from Wall Street, the Texas S&L industry, which relied heavily on brokered deposits, and Donald Regan in the Treasury Department.

Determined to contain the festering problem, Gray and Isaac prepared to issue their new regulations in early January 1984. But three days before they unveiled their plan, Bowman, the Texas S&L commissioner and advocate of brokered funds, decided to move against Empire. No one has ever explained why the state of Texas waited seventeen months after its examiners had first urged immediate action against Empire to close the thrift. But by moving against Empire in January 1984, Bowman forced Gray's office to divert some of its attention to Empire Savings, a thrift that quickly became the bank board's most pressing issue. Gray's office dispatched a consultant named Frank Augustine to Dallas to evaluate Empire's holdings while other federal officials moved swiftly to limit the exposure of the federal fund that guaranteed the safety of Empire's deposits.

A wintry chill lingered in Washington when Ed Gray assembled his staff in a sixth-floor conference room to decide if Empire should be declared "hopelessly insolvent." A decision to shut down the place would create the largest insolvency in the fifty-year history of the deposit-insurance fund, which stood to lose a staggering $165 million. No Texas thrift had ever been declared insolvent by federal regulators.

Augustine, a former World War II bomber pilot, had flown over the I-30 corridor with a video camera strapped to a plane he had chartered, and Gray was about to see a videotape of the trip. A staff assistant slid the cartridge into a videocassette recorder, and for the next twenty minutes Gray and the others sat in stunned silence. "I felt physically sick," Gray said. Augustine's camera took them on a tour of the I-30 corridor ventures financed by Empire Savings. The projects that flashed onto the screen would become the property of the FSLIC if the board voted to take over Empire.

An unseen narrator gave the board members the bad news in a wooden monotone:

> Looking west toward downtown Dallas, we can begin to see the hundreds and hundreds of units that are under construction, none occupied. . . . Building after building, probably twenty-four to thirty complexes, all unoccupied. . . . Other mature projects, probably complete for a year . . . no occupancy. . . . The problems of security, vandalism, fire, control, completion—all are readily apparent from pictures like these. A project called Snug Harbor—vacant. On Faulkner Point North, numerous projects, numerous buildings, virtually totally vacant. No sales effort, no leasing effort, and across the street, more slabs and active construction. Notice the incredible waste, the total lack of contractor control. . . . Evidence of arson is already available. . . . In the distance, numerous projects, virtually one hundred percent complete, no occupancy, and the land between the camera and the building is being prepared for more development. . . . This particular series of buildings made up one project, apparently totally vacant, with severe freeze damage inside each unit.

Once the video ended, Gray remained silent. He later described the film as "fiduciary pornography." He couldn't believe his eyes. The warnings about Empire had not prepared him for anything like what he'd seen. The news stories and headlines couldn't begin to describe it. This was no isolated scandal. Something had gone seriously wrong in the deregulated savings and loan industry he had been appointed to oversee. Now it had been dumped into his lap, and he was seething with anger. The board quickly voted to close Empire Savings and forever ban its majority stockholder, Spencer Blain, from working in the savings and loan industry. The board's staff also started work on a massive lawsuit and initiated criminal referrals to the Justice Department against more than one hundred companies, and individuals such as Ernie Hughes, Blain, and Danny Faulkner.

But the legal actions didn't quench Ed Gray's thirst for revenge. He took the tape over to Capitol Hill and showed it to House Banking Committee chairman Fernand St. Germain. He showed it to Federal Reserve Board chairman Paul Volcker. He fired Settle, and the tape invigorated his campaign against brokered deposits. Gray correctly equated the reckless growth in deposits steered into Empire by money brokers with the thrift's bad-asset problems: "All you had to do was walk up to a money broker and say you need so much in deposits. What's he going to do? He's going to tell you, 'Okay, this is what it's going to cost you.' So you say, 'Okay, I'll take it,' and you pay a high interest rate. And you turn around and lend it. So that puts a premium on lending it out in riskier deals because you've got to make a higher rate on the loan to pay the rate demanded by the money broker." At one point, 83 percent of Empire's deposits came from brokers.

On January 15, just three days after Bowman moved against the Mesquite thrift, Gray and Isaac had released for public comment a proposed rule that said deposits in excess of $100,000 from any one deposit broker would not be covered by federal insurance. Opponents had until late March to comment on proposed rules before Gray decided whether to implement the new regulations. There was little doubt what he would do.

Texans reacted bitterly to Gray and his criticism, particularly his treatment of the Dallas bank board. Gray knew that the government had moved the district bank from Little Rock to Dallas less than a year ago. Gray himself had voted to approve the shift only three weeks after taking office. The move ended a longtime political feud over the location of the district bank, which provided jobs and prestige to the city in which it was located. But most of the employees stayed behind in Little Rock. Indeed only two of the eleven employees who moved with the bank were supervisory agents. As Gray well knew, they had responsibility for overseeing 480 S&Ls in Arkansas, Louisiana, Mississippi, New Mexico, and Texas. The district bank had to recruit and train an entirely new staff at the very time thrifts such as Empire and Vernon Savings were growing at astonishing rates. It was no wonder that the board had problems. Criticism from someone who had made the move possible stung.

Robert D. Mettlen, then chairman of the Dallas district bank, was furious, particularly at Gray's demand that the board hire Roy Green as president of the bank. Mettlen and Gray swapped insults over the telephone and in an equally spirited cussing match in a hotel banquet room. But Gray got his way. The president of a district bank is also the principal supervisory agent, a job ultimately controlled by the bank board chairman in Washington. The Texas district board begrudgingly approved Green, but local savings and loan officials never forgot why. They resented Ed Gray and would remember how he had treated them.

The anger at Gray's handling of the Settle paled in comparison to the outrage generated by his drive to curtail brokered funds, though. This step would hit thrifts like Vernon right in the wallet. "I wanted to stop the dam, turn off the spigot, you know? Because every several weeks when I'd have this briefing, things were getting worse," said Gray. Vernon Savings and the Texas industry attacked Gray's proposal as discrimination against the little guys. "In the current competitive environment, the major national banks have a decided advantage because of their ability to mount nationwide ad campaigns to attract deposits," Roy F. Dickey, then president of Vernon Savings, wrote to the bank board. "The use of deposit brokers by small banks and savings and loans becomes a valuable option in their efforts to compete for deposit dollars." The proposals drew fire from the Treasury, too. Regan himself couldn't jump into the fray. As a prime advocate of brokered funds at Merrill Lynch, the Treasury chief had to recuse himself in the fight. But his minions didn't. One Regan aide, R. T. McNamar, a deputy Treasury secretary, spent seven hours on the phone trying to talk Gray out of imposing his brokered-funds regulation.

Even the U.S. League had some reservations. Although the

trade group publicly backed Gray in his campaign, industry officials privately expressed concern about the intensity of Gray's campaign. He was publicly calling attention to the industry's problems and risked scaring off customers. Said Gray:

> The people over in my own administration were going crazy because their own guy is the one who is leading the fight on this. You can't believe the calls I got. Don Regan couldn't do anything about it. So they didn't know what to do. I had to use incredible arguments. The strategy I used was not about the growth. I would have never made it on that. I said that if you turn over the collection of deposits to the money brokers, you would give away the store and you'll never get it back again. Hey, that was a pretty good strategy. A lot of them got my point. They didn't like it. But it was enough.

On March 26, 1984, Isaac and Gray announced they would adopt their brokered-fund regulation effective October 1. Opponents remained determined to stop them. News stories about Gray soon surfaced in the press, obviously leaked by his opponents at the Treasury and the bank board. Questions were raised about his intelligence. He was derisively nicknamed Mr. Ed after the talking horse on television.

The Texans weighed in with their Capitol Hill clout. The state has long enjoyed a big and powerful congressional delegation, composed of legendary lawmakers such as Lyndon Johnson and Sam Rayburn. In Gray's tenure, House Speaker Jim Wright was like a household word. Rep. Jack Brooks, another Texas Democrat, chaired the Government Operations Committee, responsible for oversight of government agencies such as the bank board. Suddenly Mr. Ed was hauled before a House Government Operations subcommittee to defend his proposals.

"This was right after we had closed Empire and cited it as a great example of a disaster of brokered funds. And of course, Doug Barnard, the subcommittee chairman, was all for brokered funds. So I was walking right into the jaws of a lion. And he got real angry with me because he says I didn't tell him in advance that we were going to close Empire. He said I did him dirty."

Gray started feeling increasingly isolated:

> I was considered a real strange duck. . . . I wasn't
> playing ball. Something had happened to me. I mean,
> first of all, I was supposed to be the buddy of the thrift
> industry. Secondly, I'd gotten carried away. They'd say,
> Where'd you get this guy? He started out in the Dark
> Ages. He's a Neanderthal. He doesn't understand that
> this is the day of free markets. I rapidly became known
> as the great reregulator. You never hear the word 'rereg-
> ulation' today. But then it was the worst perjorative. I
> remember I went over to see Jim Baker. I had worked
> with him in the campaign in 1980. He said, 'How does
> it feel to be the great reregulator?' I said, 'It doesn't feel
> very good. I don't like it.' "

A few months later, Ed Gray's campaign ended. A trade
association for the big Wall Street investment firms like Merrill
Lynch had launched a court challenge of Gray's authority to
issue a brokered-fund regulation. On June 20, 1984, a federal
judge gave the money brokers a resounding victory. The bank
board, he said, lacked the authority to ban brokered funds; only
Congress could do so.

Gray had been manhandled by Wall Street and Donald
Regan. He was angry at the outcome and depressed by his loss.
But Ed Gray's problems were just beginning. By year-end 1984,
fifteen more federally insured thrifts had failed. They were not
the neighborhood savings and loans that regulators once quietly
folded into another institution. One of them, San Marino Savings
in California, would cost the FSLIC $200 million, or $35 million
more than Empire. Texas was not the only place with problems.
California, where savings and loans accounted for nearly one
third of the industry's assets, obviously had big troubles, too.
Empire Savings, Gray and his staff were coming to realize, was
no aberration.

Traditional savings and loan operators struggling to overcome their interest-rate problems of the early 1980s had watched
the Don Dixons of the world use brokered deposits and risky
lending practices to grow out of the troubles. Federal regulators
had not stopped or even criticized the practices; they praised

them. Free enterprise and free markets were at work. The traditional thrifts emulating high-fliers like Dixon were ticking time
bombs waiting to explode in Ed Gray's face. Gray could still feel
the welts from the political lashings he'd received during the
brokered-funds fight. But he had learned a lesson. The next time
some flashy Texas savings and loan operator surrounded by fancy
cars and fly-by-night loans got into trouble, Ed Gray wouldn't
ignore the problem.

9 The Divorce

ixon looked Dale Anderson in the eye. So Herman Beebe wanted to split up their empire. Dixon had no doubt that the short, husky Anderson spoke for the Louisiana entrepreneur. Anderson was Beebe's right-hand man. But Dixon had a hard time disguising his delight at the prospect of ditching Beebe. Anderson could see Dixon wanted out of the corporate marriage as badly as Beebe.

It was about time that Dixon got some good news. Ever since the condo markets had turned sour, things had not been going so well. The unyielding publicity about the I-30 scandal killed the condo market. In March 1984, one of Vernon's subsidiaries was forced to take a $337,000 loss when federal regulators forced it to sell a huge chunk of stock it had acquired in a Florida savings and loan. Ramsey quit a couple of months later, but Vernon's outside auditors kept harping about the value Dixon had placed on the unsold condos he couldn't unload. Meanwhile, the regulators had become a nuisance. At the conclusion of a routine exam, they had pounded Vernon with complaints about unsafe lending practices, inadequate books and records, weak appraisals, excessive deposit growth, loan documentation deficiencies, violations of conflict-of-interest regulations, and complaints about a $700,000 loan to another savings and loan holding company partially owned by Woody Lemons. Not in the

91

report were the verbal concerns the regulators expressed about Dixon's relationship with Beebe. Federal officials had asked for a meeting with the thrift's top management and board in June to discuss a supervisory agreement that would cramp Dixon's style. Getting rid of Beebe would no doubt make them quite happy and ease their concerns about Vernon.

Dixon and Beebe's friendship had been drifting downhill for some time anyway. When they first met, the two men discovered they had a lot in common. Dixon liked cars, women, airplanes, California beach houses, and the fast life. So did Beebe. Both were consummate deal makers and quick studies. Dixon admired Beebe's wealth, his toys, and the pizzazz he displayed when he swept into Dallas with his entourage.

Both men also had something the other needed. At the outset, Dixon needed Beebe's financial credentials. Despite his success with Dondi, Dixon's past troubles at Raldon had continued to haunt him in the early 1980s. Even Texas bankers balked at big loan requests from someone with a checkered history. Like a college kid who needed his parents to cosign a loan, Dixon needed someone with hard assets to back up his requests for money at the banks. That someone became Herman Beebe.

Beebe needed someone like Dixon, too. Herman was no choirboy. Past brushes with regulators and the U.S. Securities and Exchange Commission and rumors of unsavory business ties had tarnished his reputation among federal authorities. He needed gutsy executives like Dixon to serve as front men in his complex financial deals.

Before long, the two men became close friends and even closer partners. In 1981, Beebe invited Dixon into his family of fast-paced financial deals by asking him to buy $600,000 worth of stock that Beebe wanted to unload in return for access to Beebe loans in the future. Dixon jumped at the chance. When Dixon later married Dana in Las Vegas, Herman Beebe was the best man.

Dixon quickly learned that Beebe ran with some fast and strange traffic. At one time or another, Beebe's business relationships included deals with Dallas Cowboys founder Clint Murchison; Fort Worth millionaire T. Cullen Davis; and former Texas lieutenant governor Ben Barnes. Some of his associates had questionable backgrounds. Beebe lent about $10 million to Rex Cauble of Denton, who was convicted in 1982 on charges of leading a marijuana smuggling ring known as the Cowboy Mafia. Beebe also had ties to people like Herman Ricky Wolfenbarger, otherwise known as Hair Wolfe. Convicted of securities fraud during 1967 in Kentucky, Wolfenbarger moved to Texas, shortened his last name, and started borrowing money from banks, secured by his financial interests in race horses alive and dead. Some of his customers went to the opposite extreme. Beebe helped finance the television ministry of the Reverend Robert Tilton, who ran the Word of Faith Outreach Center Church in Farmers Branch, Texas.

By mid-1983, Dixon and Beebe were intricately tied into a partnership that would prove hard to end. They would simply have difficulty in extracting themselves from the illicit deals they'd concocted. Dixon learned that the paperwork seldom reflected the "real world" of a Beebe deal. "We'd just back into a deal," said Anderson.

> Let's say you wanted to build a development. First we would say let's see how much can he build it for, maybe five million. Okay, we'll need five million to start off. Now I want one million for me. Then you'd say, we'll want to reserve two years' interest and we'll have to pay five points. Okay, so that's about eight million to eight-point-five million to borrow. So you go get an appraisal that the thing will be worth that much once it is done. Then you'd borrow the money. Nobody worried that the deal wasn't worth it. With inflation, it would be worth that much two years down the road. We'd lived with inflation all of our adult lives. Who would have thought that it wouldn't keep going?

Often the feasibility of a deal was a minor consideration. Nobody cared if the project made no sense as long as it generated fees, commissions, and side deals. In the spring of 1983, for instance, Beebe put together a group to acquire an 18,000-acre ranch near Vernon and develop it into a hunting club. On paper, the transaction looked simple enough. Beebe and his cohorts took out a $4.4-million loan from State Savings, a Lubbock institution run by Terry Barker, a friend of Dixon and Beebe. Around $3.4 million of the loan proceeds were to be used to acquire the land and create the Sugarloaf Hunt Club, a private game preserve with a hunting lodge near Lemon's hometown of Crowell. Around $1 million would be used for working capital on the project. An appraisal accompanying the loan application said the land, once developed, would be worth $5.5 million, more than enough to justify a $4.4-million loan. The loan would be repaid from membership fees paid by wealthy Texans who could hunt and enjoy the 10,000-square-foot lodge.

Actually the loan made no sense for several reasons. One was the price of a Sugarloaf Hunt Club membership. Originally the organizers were going to sell thirty-five memberships for $185,000 each. Because of the way the deal was structured, the membership fees would be tax deductible and would generate more than enough money to repay the $4.4-million loan. For their money, members would not only get the use of a posh club, they would also get all sorts of other amenities. At one point, two potential investors envisioned ferrying members to the ranch on helicopters purchased by the club.

The trouble was even Texans didn't want to pay $185,000 to hunt little birds. There were plenty of farms nearby where a hunter could pay a fraction of the Sugarloaf fee and shoot all of the birds he wanted.

The site was a problem, too. "To hunt birds, you've got to have a bird dog," said Vaughn Mitchell, a Dallas mortgage broker and avid bird hunter hired by the government to investigate the Sugarloaf loan. "Now bird dogs can't smell anything when they get around cedar trees, and that thing was located smack dab in the middle of eighteen thousand acres of cedar trees. I'll tell you, true blue, I hunt birds, and if anyone would pay $185,000 to hunt birds there, he needs a saliva test."

The birds, or more precisely, the lack of them, were another problem. "Don took me up to the hunting lodge," said Tom Gaubert, a fellow Dallas savings and loan owner who also got into hot water with the regulators. "I always thought of a hunting club as a sort of rustic place. But this place had oriental rugs, down pillows, king-sized beds, designer sheets. It didn't look like it was for hunting to me. It looked like it was for something else. Besides, it didn't have any birds. Don told me he'd hired a couple of guys from Texas A and M to increase the bird population and I told him, 'Hell, Don, you don't need any Aggies, you need some birds.' "

It didn't make any difference if the club or the financing

behind it made any sense, though. Beebe, Dixon, and their pals borrowed $4.4 million from State Savings of Lubbock to build Sugarloaf. Within weeks, they drew down $2.8 million of the loan proceeds to buy the land and to cover State Savings' fees. Another $500,000 to $600,000 was set aside to build the lodge and have Dana Dixon decorate it. That brought the total amount of loan proceeds used up to $3.4 million. The loan rose to $4.4 million because the Beebe group figured that it deserved $1 million for being smart enough to think up the deal. One month after the initial draw from State Savings, the loan officer received a $1 million request for "working capital" for Sugarloaf to be wired to an account in the Mercantile Bank in Dallas. Instead of being sent to Sugarloaf, though, the $1 million was transferred to Beebe's Bossier City Bank & Trust Co. "Beebe got a fourth," said Anderson, while a front for Dixon and two other partners got the rest.

Even though they now had the $1 million, the original group was still responsible for repaying a $4.4-million loan. But membership sales weren't going well. So Vernon officials approached Jack Atkinson and asked him to take over the hunt club. To sweeten the deal, Atkinson was offered a developer's fee of 2 to 4 percent if a partnership he formed to develop Sugarloaf took over the project and the responsibility for repaying the State Savings loan. Given the volume of loans that Atkinson had received from Vernon, he was in no position to refuse. By December 1983, Atkinson bought Sugarloaf Hunt Club and assumed responsibility for repaying the loan to State Savings. That meant Beebe and the others had their $1 million free and clear.

Things didn't work out so well for Atkinson, though. By early 1984 he ran short of cash and Vernon started lending him more money to pay construction cost overruns, operating expenses, and even interest payments to State Savings. Eventually Vernon Savings dumped an additional $1.2 million of federally insured deposits into Sugarloaf. They pitched in to help Atkinson sell memberships, too, by leaning on major borrowers to buy the $185,000 Sugarloaf memberships so the club could pay off its debts to State Savings and Vernon. Prospective members could borrow all or a portion of their membership fees from Vernon. All they had to worry about were monthly payments. "I never was in any negotiations where someone put a gun to someone's head and said join the club or else," said Ramsey.

"What they would say is, you've gotten millions of dollars in loans from Vernon and made a lot of money. We shared the profits with you. Now we want to start a club and we need you to join."

The Sugarloaf lodge was built; Dana Dixon decorated it with Indian rugs and chairs made of deer horns. A couple of Vernon subsidiaries acquired memberships; Dixon and other Vernon executives would occasionally use the place. But it never really got off the ground. Even the birds found the place wanting. Sugarloaf officials once had to import some so important guests would have feathered friends to blow out of the sky. Eventually the club ran out of money, defaulted on its loans, and suffered the same fate as Dixon and Beebe's partnership.

The strains between the two men didn't start with business problems. "Dixon's wife and Beebe's girlfriend, Shirley, had a falling-out," said Anderson. Shirley blamed Dixon for leading Beebe astray, and Dana had it the other way around. The animosity soon spread to the business dealings, though.

Although Dixon and Beebe had much in common, their vastly different styles and competitive drives created friction. "Dixon was sharp. He had good business instincts and was a good thinker. But he delegated everything," said Anderson. "Beebe was different. Beebe wouldn't delegate anything. I used to say AMI had an organization chart with one big square and thirty-five hundred little ones running off it. The one big square was Herman; the other thirty-five hundred were the rest of us. The two of them would drive up to a parcel of land and Dixon would say, 'Herman, I think we could build two hundred condos here and make money,' and he would never go back again. Herman would be back there the next day."

Beebe was more authoritarian. An impeccable dresser with close-cropped gray hair, Beebe ran AMI as a benevolent dictator. When Beebe quit smoking, he banned smoking in his Shreveport headquarters. When Beebe embarked upon the Spartan diets of Nathan Pritikin, the chefs in AMI's executive dining room cooked Pritikin. He could be charming and generous but also turn selfish and cruel. When things went wrong, Beebe "was one of those guys who always blames someone else," said Anderson.

Dixon was less disciplined. If things went wrong, he wouldn't blame anyone; he'd deny that anything *was* really wrong. He had a flamboyant and flashy style. "I'll tell you one thing he used to do," said Gaubert. "You'd go up there to meet with him, and he'd have his barber come into the office and cut his hair while the meeting was under way. I'd say, 'Who's making the decisions, Don, you or your barber?' But I thought that was really neat. When I got back to my office, I called my barber and said, 'Sal, would you come over to my office and give me a haircut?' He said, 'Sure, but while I'm gone I'll lose six customers so I'm gonna charge you one hundred and fifty dollars.' I said the hell with you."

In contrast to Beebe, Dixon dressed casually, usually with an open shirt and Western vest. His hair was long, his voice soft. But he hated to be told that something couldn't be done or that there was an answer other than his.

The longer the two men were together, the more they grated on each other's nerves. Both had towering egos and hated to lose. If Beebe got a car, Dixon got a bigger one. When Beebe bought a Learjet, Dixon bought a Falcon 50. The competition wasn't limited to toys. It began affecting their deals, too. At one point, Beebe was accused of converting to his personal use more than $130,000 in loan proceeds deposited in his Bossier City bank for Van Boxtel's Solana Beach house. Vernon officials witnessed nasty public exchanges between the two men. Beebe would treat Dixon with contempt in meetings. He once referred to his one-time protégé as a "curly-haired Texas Jew," which was not exactly a compliment from a man who grew up in Lena, Louisiana. But the insults and slights simply made Dixon more determined to beat Beebe.

The friction caused plenty of gossip around Vernon Savings offices. By mid-1984, the two men hardly spoke to each other. "By the end, Dixon wouldn't give Herman the time of day. I don't think he liked Herman very much. In fact, he probably hated him," said Anderson.

Then the federal law enforcement and regulatory officials entered the picture. In Louisiana, Joe Cage, the U.S. Attorney in Shreveport, got on Beebe's case. Cage had indicted a man named Albert Prevot in the early 1980s on charges of using a U.S. Small Business Investment Corp. to divert funds to himself and a business partner. While the investigation was under way, Prevot agreed to help Cage unravel the finances of Beebe, whose activities had also come under suspicion. Cage then launched an intensive investigation of Beebe's far-flung business empire. By mid-1984, the youthful prosecutor was preparing to indict Beebe on charges of defrauding the government through Savings Venture Capital Corp., a small-business investment company in which Beebe had been involved. Aware of Cage's case and Beebe's background, federal and state regulators started looking harder at Vernon and Don Dixon.

One day Anderson said he was sitting in his office in AMI's new tower just outside of Shreveport when Beebe walked in and started a conversation. Vernon Savings, Beebe said, was growing too fast. Dixon was heading for a fall, and Beebe told his right-hand man he didn't want to be around when it occurred. "Herman said he thought we should end our relationship with Dixon and that I should take care of it."

A few days later, Anderson was on a plane to Dallas for a meeting with Dixon at the Vernon Savings office near Addison. Anderson set the tone for the meeting by somberly informing Dixon about Beebe's fate, and Cage. "I said that I was sure he knew how this U.S. Attorney Joe Cage was now bearing down on us. I told him some of this might spill over on your organization. As a practical matter, it might be in the best interests of all concerned if we split up. I told him Herman was prepared to get out of this by dividing any projects now being developed and for five million in cash."

Dixon got the message. Here was Beebe's right-hand man telling him that Herman was under investigation by a U.S. Attorney. Over the years, Dixon and Beebe had done many deals together. Beebe was in trouble because a former business associate had fingered him to save his own skin. It would cost Dixon $5 million to avoid the threat of a similar situation. "He wanted to get away from us as bad as we wanted to get away from him," Anderson said.

Dixon agreed to the deal with Anderson, and Dale hopped on a plane for the short trip back to Shreveport. When he returned, he found Beebe and told him the good news. But Anderson was surprised at Beebe's response. "He seemed kind of shocked." In one day, Dixon had agreed to split up for $5 million. Maybe he hadn't asked for enough. Beebe remained silent, listening as Anderson recounted the meeting. When his aide was done, Beebe had only one response: "Go back and get five million more."

Within days, Anderson was back in Dallas in Dixon's office:

> I went back and said, Don, we've put a lot of deals on your books that ought to make a lot of profit down the road. We feel that it is only fair that we get something for that, too. Dixon said that's probably true and suggested we make a list of them. So we got this yellow legal pad out and we made up a list. And we went over the projects one by one. I'd say that one ought to pay out pretty good one day, and we'd agree on a figure for it and move on to the next one. Finally I said that Herman would settle the whole thing for another five million. By this time, the whole exercise was just numbers to Dixon. Money had lost all of its meaning. It was just a way of keeping score. He wanted to be the next Donald Trump. He agreed to the deal.

Anderson said part of the money paid to Beebe came from the larger-than-normal Vernon Savings dividend that federal regulators approved in 1984. The regulators fully expected Beebe to be indicted and didn't want to call any attention to the government's approval of him as a major investor in Vernon. The sooner he was out, the better. In August, Vernon Savings signed a supervisory agreement—one of those "the devil made me do it" documents used by government bureaucrats to give the illusion of action. By signing it, Vernon more or less admitted it had done a few things wrong and promised to correct them as long as no one got real tough. The agreement required adoption of a business plan to control deposit growth, required diversification of Vernon's loan portfolio, and "addressed" conflicts of interest and loan rule violations. Vernon officials signed the government deal, and Dixon went on to ignore it.

Beebe didn't get off so easily. In early 1985, he was indicted on charges of conspiring to defraud the U.S. Small Business Administration. The agency charged that a government-aided company under Beebe's control lent $100,000 to a company owned by Dallas businessman George Owen for a nursing home investment. Owen told a federal court jury that he never received the money. Others testified that it went to a company controlled by Beebe's children. A judge sentenced him to five years' probation.

But the 1985 conviction marked the beginning of the end for Beebe's empire. A determined Cage would continue his investigations of Beebe's deals. The notoriety of his conviction would focus the attention of bank regulatory agencies on any institution in which he was involved. With the IRS and federal prosecutors on his trail, Beebe's lawyer finally called the Justice Department and said his client would plead guilty to one charge in Louisiana and one in Texas to get everyone off his back. "It was incredible," said one former top federal prosecutor active in the case. "We started going through all of our files to find an illegal transaction we could use in a plea agreement. There were a lot of questionable transactions, but we couldn't find anything that was outright illegal. Finally we had to call his lawyer and ask him for one."

The transaction selected got Beebe one year in jail. It was the diversion of $1 million from the loan proceeds that financed the Sugarloaf Hunt Club.

10 Joy Love

As the blue-and-tan Falcon 50 bearing Dixon's initials pulled onto the tarmac at Austin's airport, L. Linton Bowman picked up his bag and walked toward Vernon Savings' sleek corporate jet. A tall, lanky, and easygoing man who wore a thin gold bracelet on his wrist, the Texas savings and loan commissioner was a veteran of the local industry. A former thrift executive from the northeast Texas town of Greenville, Bowman had gone to work for the state savings and loan department in 1980 hoping to find a quiet job without a lot of controversy. Two years later he had been tapped to head the department.

It was March 1985, and Bowman knew the savings and loan that owned the plane he was about to board was not run by a bunch of choirboys. In many respects, Vernon Savings was a lot like Empire. It had lured a huge amount of brokered deposits into its vaults and had invested them in risky commercial real estate deals and condo projects. The thrift and its officers flaunted their rising fortunes with airplanes, steep salaries, and expensive perks. Bowman knew that the wages of greed were good. During 1983, Dixon had hired Pat King, Bowman's deputy and partner in a local real estate investment, to run a Vernon subsidiary headquartered in Austin. About a year later, Dixon promoted King to president and moved him to Dallas to oversee Vernon's far-flung operations. Bowman discussed the thrift's

101

affairs often with his old friend in Dallas. He knew the inner workings of Vernon better than most of the S&Ls under his gaze.

A cautious man with many friends in the S&L industry, Bowman was uneasy with the fast-paced deals that thrifts like Vernon churned out to generate their soaring earnings. To a traditional S&L man, the investments seemed a scary and foolish way to handle deposits insured by the federal government. But the commissioner was also racked with doubt about how the state should handle the Don Dixons of the world. Even as he had moved against Empire and its owner, Spencer Blain, Bowman wondered where genius stopped and mistakes began. "What if I'm wrong and he's right?" Bowman asked himself. His self-doubt was reinforced each time he left his Austin office and looked up and down the streets of the Texas capital, which had replaced Dallas and Houston as the real estate mecca of the Southwest. The symbols of the go-go development promoted by thrifts such as Vernon were everywhere. As he strolled toward the blue-and-tan jet for the trip out west, Bowman didn't know what he should do—stop the growth or encourage it.

Unfortunately, few answers came from his colleagues in government. On the federal level, things were deteriorating rapidly. The thrift industry had long enjoyed cordial relations with federal regulators. After Ed Gray took over and Empire failed, though, things changed. It seemed like every day brought another new or revised rule. Gray seemed to despise Texas thrifts, which were seething at his barrage of new regulations. If Gray actually started enforcing some of the rules he was proposing, Texas S&L operators warned Bowman, the bank board chief would wreak havoc on the system and the state. Just what was wrong with this guy? they asked. Highfliers such as Dixon had even formed a special lobbying group that met once a month to develop strategies to deal with these kooks in Washington.

If things were bad on the federal level, they were worse at the state. The Texas S&L department had long been a tool of the local industry. There were a few voices urging old-fashioned prudence. But most S&L operators seemed to envy the growth that Dixon and his ilk enjoyed. Even if the state regulators had had the gumption to crack down on the industry's highfliers, the government would have been hard-pressed to do much. The state laws had been drafted to boost the fortunes of the S&Ls, and the department's pay and budget didn't exactly attract Rhodes scholars. Just after Bowman had been appointed commissioner, a state examiner went to Lubbock to scrutinize the books of a local S&L. The next thing everyone knew, Darwin Adrian Fowler's picture was in the paper, and it wasn't because he'd been chosen Man of the Year at the Chamber of Commerce. Fowler showed up in a story on Texas's most-wanted list after he shot two men in a dispute at a Lubbock car wash. Dixon and his executive team shook their heads in disbelief. Just a few months earlier Fowler had been in Vernon examining the thrift. "We saw this story and said, 'Hey, there's our examiner.' We laughed our asses off. That's the kind of people they had in there examining our books," recalled one former Vernon executive. Bowman said his staff worked long and hard riding herd on the state thrift industry, but he acknowledged they were poorly trained and ill equipped for the job.

The state examiners had just entered Vernon for their first exam in two years when Bowman stepped into the cabin of the Falcon 50. The feds had given Dixon a pretty rough time in their last inspection. On a scale of 1 to 5, they rated Vernon 4-D, near the bottom and a sharp contrast to the 1's that Vernon had always received when Tanner was running things. Because of the poor grade, the feds had required Vernon to sign the supervisory agreement to straighten things out. But Dixon had ignored the document. Vernon was a state-chartered thrift; any regulatory problems it would encounter would come from the state, not the feds, Dixon had told his aides. He was determined that Vernon would maintain good relations with the Texas commissioner.

Bowman was surprised to see Dixon sitting in the cabin of the plane. When he'd told his old friend Pat King he had to go to California on business a few weeks back, no one had said anything about Dixon's coming along. King and Pat Malone, another friend and Vernon officer, had led Bowman to believe they had business in California, too. "They said why don't you just ride along on the company plane," Bowman recalled.

Bowman should have known better. Those boys from Vernon Savings were always full of surprises. Just weeks before, King had invited his old boss to dinner in Dallas. When Bowman arrived at the restaurant that night, King was not alone; two voluptuous women had joined him. Bowman could tell from appearances that they weren't Camp Fire Girls, particularly his date. At five foot six with sandy-brown hair, the only thing more unbelievable than her

body was her name. Only in Dallas would a woman call herself Joy
Love. Dinner was wonderful. Dessert promised to be even better.
"Joy was good-lookin' and well built," said a former Vernon executive who knew more of Joy than her name. "Her eyes? What color
were her eyes? Hell, I don't remember what color her eyes were.
That's not where I was lookin'. I can tell you this, though, that girl
could suck start a Harley."

Dixon reached out to shake Bowman's hand as the commissioner entered the cabin of the sleek ten-seater jet. Malone, a
onetime Texas Savings and Loan League executive, was on the
plane, as was King. Unbeknownst to Bowman, Dixon had ordered King to line up the West Coast trip with the commissioner
a few weeks back so Dixon could show Bowman a good time.
Dixon gripped the commissioner's hand, according to Bowman's
account, and said, "When I heard you were going to California, I
decided to go along and show you a few things I'm doing out
there." Bowman wasn't offended. This wasn't the first time he'd
been put in an awkward position by the people from Vernon,
and it wouldn't be the last.

Actually Bowman took a gallant attitude about the situation.
If savings and loan executives were going to jet off to sunny
California for a weekend of fun and games, then the Texas state
savings and loan commissioner had an obligation to go along
and find out what they were up to—firsthand. Sure, it took up
more of his time. Sure, it didn't look too cricket. But there would
be none of this "Send the Marines" stuff for L. L. Bowman. He'd
go to the front lines himself. He'd risk the nasty headlines. Why
pass it off on some underling? The Falcon 50 turned and taxied
out to the runway. As the thrust of the jet engines pressed
Bowman back into his seat, the commissioner relaxed. He'd like
San Francisco.

Back on the ground, Bowman's examiners had started a
review of the books at Vernon as of January 31. Several weeks
had passed and the state crew was troubled. Vernon Savings,
some of the examiners felt, had some potentially severe problems. Although Dixon had been able to shove Herman Beebe out
the door, he had never solved the troubles in Rick Ramsey's old
condo operation. Even Vernon's outside auditors worried about
the unsold units still on the books at inflated values. No buyers
were in sight, either. But the condos were only one of the items
that bothered examiners. Vernon also had a potential problem

with the "quality" of its earnings—a fault that would prove to be
an Achilles' heel for Dixon and hundreds of other savings and
loan owners.

Like dozens of other thrifts run by entrepreneurs and real
estate developers, Dixon operated far differently from the normal
thrift. If a customer wanted a loan to buy a $100,000 house, an
S&L specializing in home loans typically demanded a $10,000
to $20,000 down payment before the thrift would make a mort-
gage loan on the remaining $80,000 to $90,000 that was needed.
If the loan got into trouble, the S&L could foreclose on the
property and sell it for $80,000 to $90,000 to recoup the federally
insured deposits it had loaned to the borrower. In other words,
it had a $10,000 to $20,000 cushion.

If a developer, by contrast, walked into Vernon seeking a
loan to build a $10-million office tower, he'd usually ask for a
$12-million loan, just as they did at Empire Savings. It was Dale
Anderson's real world at work. First the developer needed $10
million to acquire the land and the sticks and bricks to actually
build the tower, hopefully within a year. An office tower pro-
duces no income while it is under construction, though. So he'd
ask for an additional $1.3 million to cover a year's worth of
interest at 13 percent. That meant he'd need $11.3 million. Next
Vernon allowed the developer to borrow his 2.5 to 4 percent
development fee up front. On a $10-million deal, that's at least
$250,000. That takes the total needed to $11.55 million. Then
add the 4.5 points, or fees, that Vernon Savings gets for making
the loan. That takes the total to $12 million. Dixon didn't
demand a cash down payment at all. Instead Vernon officials
demanded that the developer split the profits on the completed
project before they would approve the loan. In other words,
Vernon's cushion was an agreement entitling it to a share of
future profits. Dixon was betting that the developer could finish
the project and make money.

On the day that the loan closed, everyone was understandably happy. Vernon would take $12 million in federally insured
deposits and credit $10,250,000 to the developer—the $10 million to be invested in the construction project and $250,000 for
his up-front fee. An additional $1.3 million prepaid interest
would be set aside in a special interest-reserve account at
Vernon. When the monthly interest payment on the loan was
due, Vernon would simply transfer money from the interest-

reserve account to a loan-repayment account, always keeping the loan current. Lastly Vernon would book the $450,000 in points or fees as income, or the source of cash used to pay expenses such as salaries and dividends. In effect, Dixon's thrift was borrowing its earnings.

If history was any guide, a Texas office tower that cost $10 million to complete in the early 1980s might have fetched $14 million by the time the last carpenter left the job. The developer would have the resources to repay the $12 million he had borrowed from Vernon Savings, and Vernon would have the $12 million it needed to repay depositors. Meanwhile, the developer would would split the $2 million profit fifty-fifty with Vernon. Thus Vernon got its fees, more than covered its interest payments, and earned an extra $1 million in profit. And who was paying for all of this? Inflation-hardened tenants who paid the high rents for space in the office tower.

In the early part of the 1980s, the profit participations, high fees, and high interest rates had propelled Vernon to the top of the S&L heap. By 1985, though, troubling signs were afoot. Oil prices had dropped for the third consecutive year, a disastrous freeze had hurt crops in the Rio Grande Valley, agricultural markets were off, and the Texas economy faced big troubles. Suddenly the developers who had borrowed $12 million from Vernon to build $10-million office buildings were in trouble, too. They couldn't find anyone to buy the buildings for $10 million, much less $14 million. The interest reserves set up to service their loans had kept the accounts current. But examiners started questioning what would happen when the reserves ran dry. Where were the developers going to get the money to pay the $12 million back? And where was Vernon going to get the $12 million to repay its depositors?

Dixon could see why these guys worked for the government and he was a millionaire; they had no imagination. When the $12-million loan came due in a year, Vernon or another friendly savings and loan could simply lend the developer an additional $2.1 million—$1.6 million for another year's interest reserve, $100,000 for another developer's fee, and $400,000 in points of renewal fees that, once again, would be counted in Vernon's earnings. If Vernon didn't have the $2.1 million in the till, it could just bump up the interest rates it offered to pay savers on federally insured deposits and the money would flow in. The thrift would then have more than $14 million in federally insured deposits invested in the deal. Once the real estate markets recovered and inflation resumed, though, the developers could sell their holdings, make a killing, and share the profits with Vernon Savings. Everyone would come out okay. Time and inflation would take care of everything.

Vernon officials didn't think much about what would happen if the developer didn't make a profit because a poor economy had depressed real estate values. That was a problem, and Dixon didn't believe in dwelling on problems; they were something to be overcome.

But Bowman's examiners thought a lot about the impact of a poor economy. The huge fees and points that Vernon had included in its income when the $12-million loan was booked were based entirely on the presumption that the borrower would repay his loan. If the loan was not repaid, Vernon would have to take a hit on its earnings to set the record straight. Moreover, if the developer who had borrowed $12 million spent his money on a project that was now worth only $8 million, the thrift faced a potential $4-million hole in its balance sheet. Who would fill the hole with cash so the S&L would have enough money to repay its depositors? Where would an undercapitalized thrift get the $12 million, particularly if it had squandered most of the profits it had reported on perks and high living?

It would have been one thing if Vernon Savings had one $12-million loan secured by one project worth $8 million. But by 1985, Vernon had about $700 million worth of construction loans on its books, including many to developers who had used the proceeds to cover interest reserves, points, fees, and closing costs. The loans were secured by construction projects, all right, but no one knew how much the building ventures were worth in the Texas economy of 1985.

The situation may have bothered regulators, but it didn't seem to trouble Don Dixon. He was a real estate developer. Everyone knew that when he first acquired Vernon. The state and federal government approved the deal. What did they expect him to invest in—birdbaths? If a thrift didn't have enough money to repay its depositors, then the government had a problem. Uncle Sam was the one who guaranteed depositors would get their $12 million back—not Don Dixon.

As the plane banked and headed toward California's Gold

Coast, Dixon briefed Bowman extensively on Vernon's good fortune in California. "Dixon was always talking about his cars and his houses and all of that," Bowman said. He was careful to avoid any discussion of regulatory matters, though, particularly the questions that examiners were raising back at Vernon. Dixon may have been worried that the state bureaucrats might cramp his style, but he had a plan to deal with regulators. He'd get to Bowman, their boss.

In January 1985, the same month the state had shown up, Dixon had moved John Vaughan Hill from Florida to Dallas. A short, thin, and balding engineer, Hill had been president of a Vernon investment subsidiary in southern Florida. But he was better known as Vernon's ambassador to the lowlife. In any given situation, he could bring out the worst in anyone. A few weeks after he was on the job, Dixon summoned Hill to his office for a chat. "Don Dixon told me that he was going to go out to the West Coast with Linn Bowman and said that he would like to get Shelley [a woman Hill and Dixon knew from Florida] to go along as Bowman's date. And he asked me to arrange it."

Actually Dixon had tried to set up a similar trip weeks earlier. He had Bowman's friend, Pat King, invite the commissioner on a pheasant-hunting trip to Kansas. When Bowman accepted, Dixon raised the idea of taking some women along. King and Woody Lemons objected. They argued it was simply too risky. Bowman was a married man. Discreetly lining up a night with Joy Love in Dallas was one thing. Vernon did that sort of thing all the time. At first, King didn't even tell Bowman that Joy was a prostitute and that Vernon had paid for her time. The scuttlebutt was that Bowman thought it was love. They all got a good laugh out of that, even Bowman when he later learned the truth. But inviting the commissioner on trips where numerous Vernon executives would see him with a strange woman was another question. Dixon agreed and dropped his plans for the hunting trip.

When Bowman accepted the ride on the plane to California a few weeks later, though, Dixon brought up the idea of taking some girls along again. Don Dixon was a quick study. His ability to size up a situation instantly extended far beyond financial statements; he could read people, too. Linn Bowman was a Texas boy, and every Texas boy Dixon ever knew had a little lust in his heart. He'd give King and Lemons a lesson in self-regulation.

Bowman would like the ladies; Dixon was sure of that. And if the commissioner faced a hard call on Vernon's troubled deals down the road, Dixon wouldn't have to do a thing. The memories of Shelley and Joy Love would dance in Bowman's head and regulate the regulator.

Bowman could feel the plane losing altitude as the jet approached the San Diego area. Dixon had briefed him on Vernon and Dixon's investments in California, which had gradually been rising since 1982. At first the thrift had financed office buildings, condominiums, and mixed-use development projects, including some with Beebe. Californians familiar with construction-site signs that said "Financing for this project was provided by the Bank of America" suddenly saw projects underwritten by Vernon Savings and Loan. "I remember one deal in my district. I couldn't figure out why anyone would want to build there. I asked where they'd gotten the money and someone told me Vernon Savings and Loan. I said, 'Who is that?' and they said, 'It's some guy from Texas,' " recalled one California congressman.

From the outset, Dixon's experience in California was terrific. Bowman's counterpart in California, Larry Taggart, was a firm advocate of deregulation. Rapidly growing California thrifts had more than a friend in the statehouse; they had a partner. Vernon couldn't miss in the California real estate market, either. Prices zoomed upward, giving Vernon plenty of profits to cover any troubled loans. Dixon told Bowman he had big plans in California that would offset any temporary problems he might be experiencing in Texas.

Dixon was prospering personally in California, too, sometimes maximizing profits in his own business deals by capitalizing on his ties to Vernon Savings. At one point, Dixon cut another deal with Van Boxtel to acquire some beachfront land just north of Moonlight Beach in Encinitas and convert a run-down house and sixplex into some condominiums.

The deal started off simple enough. Dixon, Van Boxtel, and Woody Lemons formed the Moonlight Beach Joint Venture and borrowed some money from Anchor Savings and Loan of Kansas City to develop the site. Van Boxtel did the construction work, and Dixon was responsible for marketing the units. Once construction was done, Dixon gave Van Boxtel a lesson in banking Texas style. "I told those guys they should write a book," said Van Boxtel.

The two Vernon natives formed the Moonlight Beach Club, which promptly borrowed $5.5 million from Sandia Savings and Loan, a New Mexico thrift controlled by some of Dixon's friends in Texas. The beach club then used the proceeds of the $5.5-million loan to acquire the condo project from the Dixon–Lemons–Van Boxtel joint venture. And just how would the club repay the $5.5-million loan from Sandia? It would sell memberships to wealthy Texans.

Pretty soon, big customers seeking loans at Vernon Savings started hearing about this great beach club near San Diego. The sales pitch was similar to the one for the hunt club. No one said a $10-million loan request for a shopping center would be denied if the developer didn't join the beach club. But everyone got the message. "I don't think you had to join," said Ross Ikemeir, a Dallas architect, Vernon client, and member of the club. "You would just go to get a loan and they would say, 'Okay, you can have the loan.' Then they would say, 'By the way, we have a beach club over here and we need to sell some memberships.' No one thought they were doing anything wrong. They were just taking advantage of the loopholes. It was kind of a sport." Vernon eased the pain by offering to finance the $77,500 to $155,000 the prospective member needed to join the club. For their money, the members got the use of one of the club's six condos and a car for two months each year. Van Boxtel was amazed. Lemons and Dixon even awarded themselves a bonus for setting up the deal. After all of the papers were signed, it turned out that the remodeled house and part of the land were not involved in the sale to the club. Interests representing Dixon and Lemons kept them for themselves. "I guess they got it for the development skills," said Van Boxtel.

Vernon's jet glided to a halt in the San Diego airport. Ernie Osuna was waiting nearby in Dixon's $600,000 antique Duesenberg. A gentleman's gentleman and member of one of the area's founding families, Osuna was a personal valet of sorts hired by Dixon to make restaurant reservations, service antique cars, and keep house accounts in California. As Dixon, Bowman, King, and Malone approached, he opened the car doors for the ride north to Solana Beach.

Dixon normally arrived in California at an airport up the coast a little farther, near Carlsbad, where Don and Dana were well known. But Dixon had given Osuna specific instructions to meet them in San Diego. The ride up the coast was always a pleasant one. The white stucco homes with red-tiled roofs dotted the hills of southern California. As the road twisted toward the Pacific, the visible signs of prosperity paled in comparison to the natural beauty of the surf. The ride gave Bowman a feel for the wealth, climate, and pace of southern California.

"Suddenly, Don said we were going to stop for lunch at a place between San Diego and Solana Beach and that two women would be meeting us," according to Malone. At first, Shelley had not wanted to make the trip from Florida to California when Hill approached her. But he was an expert at these things. "She had a friend, Regina, that she wanted to accompany her," Hill later recalled, and he worked things out. Shelley and Regina would be flown from Florida to California, courtesy of Vernon's investment subsidiary. They would then meet the four men at a restaurant just north of San Diego for lunch and a lovely weekend. To say that Shelley was "statuesque" was like saying the *Mona Lisa* was a snapshot. She had been handpicked for Bowman by Don Dixon, and Dixon had exquisite taste. True to his policy of following corruption to the source, Bowman stayed for lunch. If thrift executives were tempting government employees with the likes of Shelley, then L. L. Bowman had a duty to be the man on the scene. Temptation didn't scare him.

After lunch, Dixon and his guests agreed to meet the girls later at the Solana Beach house. The boys had business to attend to. The tour of the area was complete. Dixon showed Bowman the fantastic business opportunities available for a man who was willing to take a risk. The last thing Bowman wanted back in Texas was another troubled thrift like Empire on his hands, and Dixon showed him how Vernon would avoid such a fate. The rules and regulations being pushed by Ed Gray were creating a need for a new and even more profitable investment climate, such as the one in California. In tony La Jolla in the north of San Diego, Dixon showed Bowman the car dealership he wanted to acquire through a Vernon subsidiary. It would require Bowman's approval, but it would make money for Vernon—lots of it.

If Bowman had any doubts about Dixon's personal wealth, they faded during the tour of the Vernon native's personal residence under construction in Rancho Santa Fe, an exclusive community near La Jolla.

When the four men pulled up to the Solana Beach house

later in the day, Gary Roth was there with two other women courtesy of the Rolodex Madam. Shelley and Regina soon reappeared, too. From all appearances, Dixon's instincts had once again proved correct. Bowman didn't shy away. Four men and four pretty women had drinks and a lovely dinner on a house perched high above the Pacific. They had an even lovelier evening. "Everyone," Malone recalled, "sort of went off—two to a room. Mr. Dixon wanted to take off early in the morning."

Bowman, Dixon, Malone, and King—their dates in tow—saw the sun rising from the windows of the Falcon 50 as it headed toward the Glendale-Burbank airport the next morning. Bowman wanted to review a computer-software system being set up for the state of Texas by a Glendale savings and loan consultant. The system would be used by regulators to monitor the finances of Texas savings and loans. Malone, who ran Vernon's government-relations division, went into the consultant's offices to inspect the program with Bowman. Dixon and the others waited out in the hall. Once business was out of the way, it was off to San Francisco.

Dixon had thought of everything. Lunch in the city and a stroll through Fisherman's Wharf before checking in at the Fairmont, the stately AAA hotel atop Nob Hill, where a two-bedroom suite goes for $700 a night. There was a room for Malone, one for King, and a two-bedroom suite with a spectacular view of the Bay and San Francisco for Dixon, Bowman, and their dates. They had cocktails in the suite; dinner in Chinatown. They'd even drop Bowman off in San Antonio the next day at a Texas Savings and Loan League convention before returning to Dallas. You had to hand it to Don Dixon. His instincts were incredible. There was only one tiny oversight, and he wouldn't find out about it for years. At the time, Bowman says he was impotent.

11 The Board

P at King looked around the meeting room at the Vernon Municipal Airport. The Vernon Savings board of directors, minus Yvonne Robinson, had assembled for the June 1985 session. Back in Dallas, Dixon was preparing to board the Falcon 50, which would soon stop in Vernon to pick up board members for the annual directors' trip to California. Vernon's officers' staff were jockeying to see who would get to ride on Vernon's Falcon or the Learjet. The thrift's Citation was the plane to avoid. "You didn't want to get stuck on it because you had to stop in Albuquerque to refuel, and you didn't want that," said one former officer. Some of the directors wore their Hawaiian shirts, others dressed as if they were going on a picnic. All were smiling. They didn't know it yet, but King was about to drop a big one on them.

A former deputy to Linn Bowman and son of the Wilbarger County sheriff, King was Vernon's Mr. Law and Order. Everyone called him Commander. He looked like a cop—short hair, husky, and square jawed. "Pat's favorite magazine was the *Law Enforcement Observer*," said Raylan Loggins. "All the rest of us had the *Architectural Digest* or something like that on our desks. But he had this thing with little blurbs about a big drug bust like in the tabloids or a story about the latest in handcuffs." A former criminal investigator for the Texas attorney general's office, King's onetime duties as the Texas deputy savings and loan commissioner and his continuing friendship with L. L. Bowman gave him the mantle of propriety at Vernon Savings. If Pat King was for something, it usually suggested that it would pass muster with Bowman and the state officials. "Pat was a former state regulator," said board member Leon Speer. "I figured he knew the laws. He'd keep us from doing anything wrong."

The first order of business on King's agenda was board approval for a new subsidiary that Dixon had already set up in southern California. "Don got real interested in this," King said as the board members sat up and listened. Dixon wanted to acquire a California car dealership—an unusual investment for a savings and loan in the heart of rural Texas. But the directors were aware that Vernon Savings was not your typical S&L.

Normally the man near King's side—Woody Lemons—ran the meetings. Aggressive and crafty with a closely cropped mustache, Lemons looked like a chubby version of Adolf Hitler with dark, plastic-rimmed glasses. Due to his local roots and history with Tanner, Lemons had also earned the respect and trust of the board members. He had learned the S&L business at R.B.'s knee: "We all had a lot of respect for Woody," said Speer, a native of Lemons's hometown of Crowell. "He was a guy who had worked his way up, sat in every desk. His dad and I were friends before he was born. I knew him when he was in stocking feet."

Usually there was no doubt that Lemons—not King—was in charge. Dixon purposely never held a seat on the board, although he sat on the committee that approved loan requests before they were sent to the board. Lemons was viewed as Dixon's personal emissary. The directors deferred almost totally to his judgment.

"I remember going before the board with a deal," said Gary Roth. "I got all dressed up in my best suit and tie. I usually prepared for these things and brought maps, appraisals, and paperwork, the kind of detail that board members usually want to see before they approve a big loan. I had this elaborate, detailed presentation, but when I got there, it seemed like all they wanted to know was 'When are we going to go huntin'.' I started to brief them on the loan, but Woody Lemons cut me off and said, 'Give them the Reader's Digest version.' "

On paper, the board members were the guardian angels of Vernon stockholders and the public citizens who placed their savings in the institution. They had obligations—legal and moral—to protect the public's interest against harm and ensure that the people running the place didn't violate state and federal regulations.

In practice, though, the board was a joke. The directors were clearly dazzled by Dixon, who was the dominant shareholder in more ways than one. Just a few years before, the board's idea of a weighty decision was whether to open a new branch in Wichita Falls or Paducah. Once Dixon took over, they made decisions involving the fate of glitzy Dallas real estate developers. High-priced lawyers and accountants approached the board as if they were altar boys seeking the directors' blessing for multimillion-dollar deals in faraway places. It was pretty heady stuff.

The board members considered Dixon and Lemons the gold dust twins. "They viewed Don as the Great Don Ray Dixon," said Loggins. "They said they didn't know how he did it. He could take dirt and turn it into gold. Woody wasn't as smart as Dixon. But he'd been at Vernon for twenty years. He could talk about loan swaps and participations. He would move loan one over here, another over there; it was like he was at a pinball machine lighting up all of the lights."

In dealing with the board, Lemons had history on his side. The board had grown accustomed to a strong man in the chairman's seat. The same people had been meeting at the same time of the month for the past twenty years to approve loans and oversee the affairs of Vernon Savings. Other financial institutions may have had strong-willed, independent boards of directors who challenged management decisions on loans and investments. But Vernon didn't. Even in R. B. Tanner's day, Vernon board members looked for a strong individual who would provide the board with leadership and direction. Lemons told them what to do, and they usually did it.

For the most part, the directors were small-town, naive folks who had known each other for most of their lives. The board included three men who owed their jobs to Dixon—Lemons himself; Roy Dickey, the former Vernon mayor and president of the institution; and King. The other seven were "outside" directors—or ones who didn't work at Vernon Savings. They ran music stores, funeral parlors, and ranches.

For his part, Dixon used money and fun to influence the board members. Many still owned stock in the institution, and dividends under Dixon had soared. He treated them well, too. Since 1983, the trip to California had become an annual event for the male members of the board.

"These people were from a typical Southern, Baptist town. They never got to let their hair down," said one Vernon officer.

> We'd pick them up in the plane. It was first class all of the way. We had lobster and shrimp. A lot to drink. When we got to California, the stretch limos would pick us up, and we'd go to Solana Beach. We'd throw a big party. We'd have girls come. They weren't all pros. We'd have the pros mixed in with straight girls that were just escorts. We would take the girls aside and point out which director to get. Two or three of them would go over and start chatting him up. They were all smiles. These people are from Vernon, Texas. That kind of stuff just isn't done here. When you know something that private about someone, you've really kind of got them in your corner.

On occasion the directors said they questioned some of the deals that were brought before the board, but they were no match for Dixon and his cohorts. "There were all of these bright, talented young men who would fly up from Dallas and make a presentation to us," said Speer. "They had maps and we would question them. I would ask how much money of their own are these people putting in this, and they would give me the right answer. Actually, we had a conservative loan policy; people will laugh at that today. But they never told us what they were doing. I wasn't suspicious of the loan volume. I just thought it was a new angle."

None of the board members seemed to understand exactly how Vernon operated under the new regime. The staff covered up any troubles in Vernon's condo projects or risky loans with doctored reports. The directors didn't even get suspicious when Dixon split with Herman Beebe. Speer and others would later tell the FBI that the board didn't even know about Vernon's interest in airplanes, artwork, or beach houses. "We all thought the art, the planes, and the house belonged to Dixon," said Speer. "We didn't know Vernon's funds were involved."

But subsequent events suggest otherwise. Each time the directors sat down to discuss the thrift's affairs, a tape recorder caught their every word. The tapes were supposed to have been destroyed. But they weren't. As King started briefing the board members at the airport about Dixon's plan to have a Vernon subsidiary acquire the California car dealerships, the tape recorder turned slowly, preserving every word.

"Don has formed Symbol Cars West," said King as the meeting got under way. (Actually, the name was Symbolic Motors West.) Lemons had decided to defer to King on this presentation. The car dealerships were a sensitive subject; the directors were about to find out why. It was better to have a former state regulator such as Pat King explain Dixon's plans. King spoke with a deadpan drawl: "Symbol Cars West is under Vernon Capital Corp. So Vernon Capital Corp., through Symbol Cars, now owns three automobile dealerships in California. One is a Rolls-Royce dealership, one is a Ferrari dealership, and the other is a classic-car dealership."

For a brief moment there was silence. A chair shuffled slightly, and one board member coughed. But no one could keep a straight face. King's proposal soon brought the house down. A few seconds later, the room erupted in laughter. It's hard to determine who said what next over the din of hooting, howling, and gut-busting laughter. "I wonder whose idea this was," shouted one director as the volume of guffaws intensified. "Let me tell you," shouted another. "Pat said Don got real interested in it. It didn't take Pat and Woody long to get interested." Everyone in the room laughed a little harder—the Hawaiian shirts were shaking.

In the directors' minds, Vernon Savings was on a roll. Earnings were at a record level, and projections for 1985 suggested Vernon would repeat 1984's year of snappy growth. They knew of no problems in the condo operation or in Vernon's rapidly growing loan portfolio. The Rolls dealership seemed like just another Dixon deal, one of those wacky, wonderful things that always seemed to make money. With the initial disclosure out of the way, Lemons stepped forward to speak.

Woody was an expert at cajoling the board toward decisions. Also captured on the Vernon Savings tapes was a December 1984 presentation in which Lemons had advocated Vernon's acquisition of a luxurious beach house in Del Mar, California, in which Dixon and his wife would live. The beach-house presentation was a salesman's symphony—a revealing moment that showed how easily the board would approve exotic investments for one of their own. Lemons had warmed them up with a detailed briefing about one of Vernon's highly successful California real estate investments that the thrift had just sold at a profit. He could talk to the board members as if they were all sitting around the pinochle table at the local gas station. He used dramatic pauses, simplistic comparisons, and homespun humor to cast his spells.

"We thought we'd make one million five on this northern California deal, but we're only gonna make six hundred thousand," Lemons had told the board. A few seconds passed before he continued:

> Now we want to ask you to approve the purchase of another piece of property, and it is totally for speculation. We have to rely on Don. I looked at the property and it's got pretty good stats. I'll tell you all about it, because you have to rely on Don's ability to trade. It's a distress situation on a very large home right on the beach in Del Mar, California. The house has been through a divorce and a big fight, a long battle in the courts. We made an offer, subject to board approval and several other things, to buy the house. It's been sitting vacant for two years. We think we can let Dana go in and decorate it and freshen it up. The numbers are steep. We've offered two million dollars for the house. It's a lot for anybody, and they came back and accepted the offer. We've got till Monday to close it. So Vernon Savings would be the purchaser. Within the last two years, there's been a cash offer for this house, an all-cash offer, between three million two and four million. It didn't go. The sellers want out of it; they want to get rid of it. There are several appraisals, none of them less than four to five million five. This is a Johnny Carson—type house that's right on the beach in Del Mar. It's about a three wood from the Del Mar racetrack. You remember when we were out there eating at a place named Jake's. It's right near there.

Lemons had made his beach-house pitch on a gray winter day in late 1984. Once he had laid out the proposal, the board-room in Vernon's home office fell so silent that one could almost hear the tape recorder spinning. Directors shifted in the high-backed brown leather chairs. Dixon's flashy investments and lifestyle surrounded them. A chandelier made of deer antlers cast light on the long, oak boardroom table. Western art acquired by Vernon adorned the boardroom walls. The *Watcher of the Plains* statue squatted firmly in the lobby. But $2 million for a beach house in Del Mar, California, was pretty hard to swallow, particularly for people in Vernon, where you could still buy a three-bedroom house for under $50,000.

"There are only five homes there," Woody had told the board as he resumed his sales pitch.

> The houses on each side of it went for over four million. You have a private gate. You go in the rock gate and there is a parking area for about seven or eight cars. As I said, there are five homes there. They are probably the finest homes in San Diego or Los Angeles. I don't think it will take much time to sell it. Two million dollars sounds like a crazy number. But, I mean, you never know. Did you see what Johnny Carson just paid for another home? Did you see that? About nine million six somewhere along the coast. There are plenty of buyers out there with plenty of money.

Lemons had hammered home his confidence in Dixon's ability to sell the place. "I suspect we'll sell it as fast as we can," he had said. "Honest to gosh, that is one thing we ought to do. We ought to take advantage of the fact that we do have cash. There are bargains, and we ought to see if we can bargain-hunt. We might decide later we're lucky to make a couple of hundred thousand dollars. I don't know, but I suspect not."

Lemons had paused once again, and the boardroom fell silent one more time. A few directors had asked some questions, but decision time had arrived. Finally the tape recording picked up a telling comment by one of Vernon's independent board members. "I'd hate to tie Don's hands," he said. No one disagreed. Vernon Savings had acquired a $2-million beach house.

As Lemons started making his pitch for the car dealership

at the airport a few months later, he used many of the same techniques. By this time, Dixon and his wife had renovated the beach house and moved in. The directors had heard about the stunning view of the surf and had been promised a visit to the place on their upcoming trip. They would leave for California in less than an hour, and Lemons capitalized on his past success, telling the board members that the automobile dealership proposal was just a real estate deal with another name:

"The bottom line is when we started this, we bought a piece of real estate for about five million and that's all we've got in it," he said as the laughter died down in the airport meeting room.

> We bought a location. It's in La Jolla, California, near San Diego. I'll be honest with you, I think what's going to happen is that within five or six months, Don will ask the regulators to let him acquire that personally from the savings and loan. Pat's already taken this thing to the savings and loan commissioner for approval, and they've okayed it. But they said the Federal Home Loan Bank is getting really fussy about subsidiary activity. This is probably too small, but they will probably object anyway. So Bowman said why don't I approve it and why don't you see if Dixon can find—in six months or a year—another person to go in there. We don't know if it will make money or lose money or what. My guess is it will lose money. But Don has a way of making money out there, so the jury's still out.

Lemon's appeal to logic failed to quell the jokes, though. The absurdity of a savings and loan in Vernon, Texas, population 12,500, owning a La Jolla Rolls dealership was too much for the board members to take. It was like opening a Saks in Seymour, a tiny little town down the highway. "Do you think this means we'll get to see his car collection?" one board member quipped.

Lemons joined in the fun, mixing business with his folksy style of humor and ability to tell a story of opportunity lost. He remarked that he had seen an increasing number of Rollses in Dallas. "I'm gonna tell you what. I had an opportunity to buy one," Lemons told the directors. "It was about a '76 or '77, and it looked like a brand-new one, and it didn't seem like much money. It was gorgeous. It was green with a black vinyl top. They was wantin' thirty-five thousand dollars for it. I mean it was a cream puff and probably was a good deal, you know it? And I let it get away." Then he gave the directors that personal twist—a good ol' Lemons yarn:

> I'm gonna tell you a funny story. Awhile back, I went to a deal—it was a dinner up there at the governor's home with Mark White. We flew on the Citation down there to Austin, like on a Saturday night. We arranged to have a limo pick us up. So we get there and it's a Rolls-Royce limousine sittin' there with a guy in it. And we start off drivin' down the road, and he's talkin' kind of French or somethin'. We can hardly understand him, you know. And somethin' was said by somebody, and he suddenly turned around and said, "Y'all from Vernon?" We said yeah, and he said, "Hell, man, I'm from Seymour."

The room erupted with laughter once again. Regulators like Ed Gray might not have thought the situation too funny. By this time Gray was about to launch a crackdown on many savings and loans for outlandish business practices, such as one that had invested federally insured deposits in a windmill farm. But this was funny stuff. Rolls-Royce dealerships in Vernon and Seymour natives with French accents. It was simply too much.

Everyone was in good spirits; that sense of comfort from being around those of your own filled the room as Lemons brought the board back to the business at hand. "Well, we need a resolution to adopt the organization of a new subsidiary, Symbol Cars West." There was no shortage of volunteers. The motion was made and seconded. "I'll tell Don you made the motion," Lemons told one director, "and that everyone seconded it." The guffaws drowned out Lemons's request for any further discussion, and the directors took turns with wisecracks. "Talk about windmill factories," yelled one. Dixon's plane had roared out of the Addison airport just north of Dallas and had just landed in Vernon. It was waiting to take the directors, minus Yvonne Robinson, to California for a good time with some real Mrs. Robinsons. They would return in a few days carrying cartons of California strawberries that the Vernon's staff always sent back home with the board. "He came back and told me he'd been out there picking wild strawberries," one of the directors' wives would later say. "But I told him that's not what the paper said he was doing." Before they left, the board passed the car dealership resolution, and a pleased Woody Lemons couldn't resist one more joke. The directors filed from the rooms and the tape recorder caught Lemons's last wisecrack over the sound of shoes shuffling across the wooden floor. Said Lemons with a laugh: "Ed Gray won't mind."

12 The Daisy Chain

T he ad first popped onto the TV screens across north Texas in mid-1985. "Boy, Vern, this sure is a dull game," said Ernest P. Worrell, the corny, slapstick comedian whose career had not yet blossomed into his kids' TV show *Hey Vern, It's Ernest*. Ernest stared at his unseen pal, Vern, across a chess board and winked into the TV camera. "Vern, your old buddy Ern, noted entremanure, has moved his whole fortune to Vernon Savings and Loan, you know? I'm going to earn a whole bunch of that filthy lucre, knowhutImean?" As the Vernon Savings and Federal Savings and Loan Insurance Corp. logos popped onto the screen, Ernest P. Worrell moved his checker across the board quickly, looked into the camera, affected a grotesque grin, and mouthed the words: "Crown me."

For thousands of Texans and other Americans, Vernon's public image in 1985 was as innocent and upbeat as Ernest P. Worrell. Not everyone, of course, was drawn to the thrift by its prize-winning "Hey, Vern, it's Ernest" ads. Vernon had set up a money desk so government agencies, pension funds, other S&Ls, and banks could bypass money brokers and invest their spare funds directly with Vernon Savings via a simple phone call. The consistently high interest rates it offered savers drew huge deposits from money brokers and well-heeled investors in New York, California, Florida, and Washington, D.C.

123

In Texas, though, the hokey ad campaign was so popular with savers that Vernon Savings started an Ernest P. Worrell fan club, inviting Ernest, an actor whose real name was Jim Varney, to Texas for personal appearances. The response was terrific. Customers flocked into Vernon's home office and its new branch in Wichita Falls to get a glimpse of Varney, who wore a cap, a T-shirt, a denim vest, and a contorted smile. Ernest stood around, gave a little talk, made some funny faces, and posed for pictures with little old ladies who stuffed their savings into Vernon's vaults. Other promotions included banking courses that Vernon sponsored in local high schools, the purchase of animals in livestock shows, contributions to community fund-raising drives, support for local athletic teams, and a Valentine's Day questionnaire asking recipients for their comments regarding the thrift's services.

"I like the homelike atmosphere—not like walking into a mausoleum," said a Carrollton, Texas, customer. "The people are the nicest I've ever experienced in the banking industry. Don't change your philosophy regarding your customer and you'll continue to enjoy much success," said another.

Indeed, by the summer of 1985, Vernon's techniques in Texas and nationwide had propelled it to the top of the heap. The lead story in an August 1985 *National Thrift News*, the S&L industry's trade paper, carried a stunning headline: "Vernon, Tex., Tops ROAA at Big S&Ls."

Dixon's thrift had reported the top return on assets among billion-dollar savings and loans around the country during the year ending in June 1985, the paper reported. In fact, Vernon's financial performance was almost twice as good as the next most profitable thrift in the U.S., according to the figures compiled by Kaplan, Smith and Associates, whose survey was like the Academy Awards of the S&L industry. Not bad for a savings and loan in a town of 12,500 people.

The trouble was Vernon's financial report was a joke. Even as the *National Thrift News* went to print, Bowman's examiners had given Vernon a confidential supervisory letter saying that the thrift's profits were suspect. It was the old quality-of-earnings argument. The $12-million loans to developers were coming due, and Vernon's borrowers couldn't repay them. Some of the projects were incomplete and generating no rents; some were burdened by cost overruns; some couldn't attract sufficient rents because of soft real estate markets; and some were ill-designed fiascos that should never have made it off the drawing boards.

Instead of foreclosing and taking over the properties, though, Dixon kept the developers afloat with the Vernon shuffle—he would simply refinance the loan and lend them more money. A developer with a troubled $12-million loan would borrow an additional $2 million in federally insured deposits from Vernon, including about $400,000 in loan fees or points that Vernon would deduct from the proceeds and book as income. The loan also included enough money for interest to keep the loan trouble-free for another year.

The thrift—in short—was borrowing its earnings from depositors. Thanks to the Vernon shuffle, it now had $14 million of its depositors' money loaned on a project of dubious value in a sinking real estate market instead of just $12 million. If the market didn't turn around and rise in value pretty soon, Vernon would one day have to foreclose and sell the property securing the loan at a loss. If it would fetch only $10 million in a foreclosure sale, Vernon would face a shortfall of $4 million. That's the amount of money it would have to raise above and beyond the sale proceeds to cover the $14 million in deposits it had originally used to fund the loan. If the property sold for less, the gap would be wider.

Of course few of Vernon's loans were as simple as that. Most were enormously complex transactions that baffled state examiners who had spent their careers checking out loans on bungalows. Moreover, thanks to federal deposit insurance, Vernon could perpetuate the problem indefinitely. If the original depositors walked into Vernon and wanted to withdraw their $14 million, Vernon wouldn't even have to foreclose and sell the property. It could simply raise its interest rates, lure $14 million in new deposits into its vaults, and use the money from the new depositors to take care of the old ones. With the government guaranteeing the safety of the deposits, the new customers assumed no risk, even though they got a higher interest rate. The risk fell totally upon the Federal Savings and Loan Insurance Corp., otherwise known as FSLIC (pronounced "fizzlick"), the taxpayer-backed government agency that guaranteed the deposits would be repaid. It was a "Heads I win, tails FSLIC loses" situation.

By mid-1985, thanks to Dixon and his team, Vernon had put

scores of those $14-million loans on its books. Overall, the thrift reported it had taken in about $910 million in deposits and invested the money in assets that Vernon valued at $1.03 billion. During the year ending in June, Vernon reported that its assets had generated about $28 million in income, justifying the $7.2 million in dividends paid out to Dixon's Dondi Financial Corp. and about $2 million in bonuses for Vernon's top brass.

But the state examiners and Dixon's own auditors had questioned the accuracy of the financial report. No one doubted that Vernon owed depositors $910 million. That much was clear. But there was considerable skepticism that its assets were actually worth $1.03 billion. About 80 percent of the money Vernon had taken in from depositors had been invested in risky assets, such as commercial loans or loans to developers, including several big ones who had gone to Dixon to get their loans refinanced several times. When the loans came due and the developers couldn't repay them, Vernon merely lent them more money, gambling that the thrift would recoup its money when the real estate markets rallied.

But no one really knew how much money Vernon would get if it had to foreclose on the developers and dump the projects in a forced sale. Vernon maintained the projects would still bring in just over $1 billion, or more than the total the borrowers owed. But few knowledgeable people believed that. Perhaps the deals would have fetched enough to cover the $910 million Vernon owed depositors. But that was doubtful, too. Some of the loans— such as the ones to the hunt club or the beach house—seemed designed to do little more than generate fees and perks for Dixon and his developer pals. In the inflationary economy that existed prior to 1985, the economic lunacy at Vernon and dozens of other thrifts had been covered up by rising land values. But by June 1985, Vernon's markets were characterized by falling oil prices, a softening economy, and overbuilt construction markets.

Asset values weren't Vernon's only problem. The $28 million in earnings that Vernon had reported were equally suspect. More than half the money was generated by points and fees generated by the Vernon shuffle, and the other half came from a single, shady transaction in Vernon's troubled condo operation.

Despite their concerns, the state regulators didn't act against the thrift. They sent Vernon one of those CYA letters that expressed regulatory concerns but meant nothing. Vernon's outside auditors from Arthur Young & Co. also signed off on the thrift's financial statement for fiscal 1985, which ended in June. Accountants who persisted with too many questions would simply lose S&L business. Their clients would go elsewhere, looking for an auditor who interpreted the rules more liberally. "In the trade it was called accountant shopping," said William Black, a former deputy director of the FSLIC, "and the K Mart Blue Light Special among accountants was Arthur Young and Co.'s Dallas office."

As a result, by mid-1985 Vernon Savings remained able to cover up its problems and report record earnings, prompting investors to shove even more money into its vaults and vastly increasing the cost of eventually shutting down the place.

Exactly how Dixon brought it all off was evident in his treatment of the most serious problem he faced—the continuing troubles with Rick Ramsey's old condo operation.

Ever since Ramsey had walked out the door, Vernon had been unable to find a buyer for the unsold condo projects that the thrift was trying to unload. Dixon's Dondi Residential Properties, Inc. which was dubbed the Drippie subsidiary, had originally borrowed much of the money to build the units from other S&Ls. Vernon Savings inherited the problem when Dixon merged his condo building operation into the thrift. But the loans had not been repaid by the time the Empire scandal hit and the condo markets slumped. Vernon was like the proverbial homeowner who rented out his house when he couldn't sell it in a bad real estate market. Instead of cutting the sales price and taking a loss, Vernon converted many of the condo units to rental property and waited for a better sales market. The trouble was, inadequate rents, low occupancy, and the anemic market didn't generate enough income to cover the monthly costs of the condos. They soon became a drag on Vernon's earnings, because the thrift was covering the losses on the units owned by its subsidiary.

Nevertheless, Dixon insisted that the troubled assets continue to be valued at or near the total amount of money that had been invested in the condos. It was like saying a house was worth $300,000 simply because that's how much some fool had paid for it.

Auditors from Arthur Young & Co. had started raising questions about the values that Vernon had on the condos in mid-1984 when they looked at the books of the S&L's Drippie subsidiary. Like Ramsey, the auditors scrutinizing Vernon's financial statement for fiscal 1984 argued that Vernon should write down the value of the units, or set aside some money in a reserve to cover any potential losses and reflect the lower prices that the condominiums would no doubt fetch in the existing market.

But Dixon objected vigorously. Setting up a reserve was the equivalent of slapping a lower value on the condominiums. The money placed in reserve would have to be deducted from the Drippie unit's income. That would lower Dixon's financial batting average; force Vernon to declare lower earnings; inhibit its ability to pay dividends; and erode its net worth, the Key yardstick watched by regulators.

In 1984, the auditors had backed off when Dixon successfully argued that the right investor would pay the higher prices for the Drippie condos to get his hands on the growing tax losses that the units would generate. It was a dubious argument. But Arthur Young's auditors went along with him—for that year, anyway. As soon as they went out the door, though, Dixon knew he had to do something before Arthur Young & Co. showed up for a repeat performance.

"Arthur Young's auditors had really hammered hard on those assets during their 1984 audit," said Greg McCormick, who worked extensively on the condos at Vernon. "That gave management the idea that since they had loaded their gun so to speak, they would really have a good argument for potential writedowns at next year's audit."

By early 1985, Dixon had ordered a hard-nosed review of the Drippie deals to assess the true extent of the damage. Shock waves rippled throughout Vernon when McCormick's figures emerged. The Drippie condos, McCormick reported, were not only losing money each month; the value of the condos had plunged by $15 million to $22 million because of the deteriorating real estate markets in Texas. Recording the loss of value and taking a hit on Vernon's bottom line would wipe out half the thrift's net worth—a stroke of the accountant's pen that would trigger prohibitions on dividends and drive the company's finances to a hair-raising level for federal and state regulators.

The estimates on the Drippie deals didn't sit well with Dixon. "A mandate came down from Dixon that these assets were to be sold at all costs," said McCormick. In other words, Dixon wanted the Drippie deals off Vernon's books—pronto.

On paper, the events that would unfold over the next several months looked as harmless as Ernest P. Worrell's hat. To the uninitiated, it would appear that Dixon, by the end of the year, had once again displayed his Midas touch. Despite the dreadful markets, the Vernon Savings subsidiary miraculously sold each and every one of its ailing condo projects to another developer at a fat profit that boosted the thrift's income, increased its net worth, and enabled Vernon to declare a $2.5-million fourth-quarter dividend to Dondi Financial, up from the $1.5 million in the previous quarter.

Actually, Dixon didn't wave any magic wands. He and his executive team were an imaginative group. When pushed, they could be terribly creative. Their flair for originality was usually evident in the names they chose for special committees. The thrift once set up a committee to handle fatally troubled loans. They called it the Assets in the Ditch (or the AIDS) Committee. When faced with the problems posed by the Drippie deals, their imaginations simply worked overtime.

Within days, a "Drippie swat team" went to work deep in the bowels of Vernon Savings and Loan on a plan to implement Dixon's orders. The idea was to come up with a marketing plan to get the Drippie condos off Vernon's books at a profit. Dixon's old partner from Raldon, Raleigh Blakely, who had come to work as a top officer at Vernon Savings, was the team leader. Another member was Dixon's son-in-law, Bruce Stoodard. Although he was no major player at Vernon, McCormick was a key member of the team. Described by one former Vernon executive as a "nervous, jumpy kind of guy who easily caved when pressured," McCormick, an accountant, was the numbers man. "Unfortunately," he said, "I was forced to live, eat, breathe, sleep, and make love to those numbers over fourteen to sixteen months."

The team's primary link to a happy ending was the daisy chain. Even before he had met Herman Beebe, Dixon understood the principle behind a daisy chain. In its simplest form, a daisy-chain deal was based upon a time-honored "you scratch my back, I'll scratch yours" arrangement. If, for example, Vernon Savings wanted to get a $10-million bum loan to a developer off its books, the thrift would get another friendly S&L to lend the guy enough money to pay off the loan from Vernon. Vernon would then reciprocate with a similar loan made to one of the friendly S&L's troubled borrowers. The S&Ls in the deal would usually include in the loan enough money for points, upfront interest, and a developer's fee so the thrift could book profits from the deal, and the borrower could get some money to tide him over. The deals could be arranged in such a way to boost the earnings and net worth of both institutions and keep the examiners off everyone's back, as long as no one got caught. In short they were sham sales of deals. When bank and thrift regulators first stumbled upon these transactions in the early 1980s, they described them as a "daisy chain," borrowing a slang term for a group of people having sex simultaneously. It was a fitting metaphor for what was about to occur.

In early 1985, Vernon's Drippie swat team swung into action and took the daisy-chain scheme into new directions. McCormick started things off by gathering the numbers needed to determine how much money the troubled condo properties would have to fetch in a sale to wipe out any potential losses on Vernon's financial statement—a massive job that covered more than 600 unsold condominium units, 148 acres of land, and scores of condos that had been converted to rental units. It was as if he added up all of the money someone had spent buying, fixing up, maintaining, and carrying a house to then arrive at a sales price.

Once the costs were calculated, McCormick said, Blakely shuffled the numbers around to make everything look a little better: "Blakely, I would have to say, massaged or allocated them around whereby a certain parcel of land would come up to be twenty-two thousand dollars per dwelling unit cost. He'd say that's outrageous, let's move five thousand dollars per dwelling; you net that over to this and try to spread the cost."

Once the swat team determined the sales price needed to get the project off Vernon's books at a profit, the thrift hired a real estate appraiser to produce a financial assessment that would justify the price tag. Normally an appraiser looks at the sales price of surrounding properties, the square footage, and the condition of the property to come up with an estimate of the value. Vernon's appraiser used *The Price Is Right* approach. "He was given a list of target numbers that management would like to see," said McCormick. If the appraiser came back with a number that was too low, said John Hill, Vernon's former chief lending officer, "he was told to go back and get a higher one."

"I voiced some concern as to how much scrutiny the ap-

praisals could stand up to, but that never seemed to be a problem," said McCormick. "I was told, don't worry about it. Your
job is just to do what we tell you to do. You just gather the
numbers and we'll get the damn thing closed."

Armed with fresh appraisals, the swat team then added a
new link to the daisy chain. Instead of turning to a friendly S&L
for a back-scratching deal, Dixon and the top brass at Vernon
developed a list of anointed borrowers who regularly relied upon
Vernon for big loans. "These were the potential candidates to
approach—the guys that are going to sit up and do the favor of
buying these assets at Dondi's price," said McCormick.

Within days, a plane carrying Blakely and McCormick came
to a halt in Houston and the two officials headed for the offices
of John Riddle, a Houston developer and big borrower from
Vernon. Blakely laid out the terms of the deal to Riddle: Vernon
would lend him enough money to buy seventy-nine to eighty-
nine condos plus 5.4 acres of dirt at a Texas condo project called
Ridgemar. The loan would include enough money to cover any
points, closing costs, or other fees. Riddle could keep any rents
that came in and wouldn't have to come up with a dime of his
own. Dixon and Vernon officials would verbally guarantee that
Riddle wouldn't have to pay any losses on the project. And once
the so-called sale had passed muster with auditors and examiners, a Vernon partnership would take the whole deal off Riddle's
hands. The only catch was that Riddle would temporarily have
"to go on the hook fully" with a personal guarantee that the loan
would be repaid so the whole transaction could be papered as a
heads-up deal for auditors and regulators.

Riddle's attorney was astonished at the presentation. As
McCormick remembered the session, the lawyer turned to Riddle
once Blakely had finished. "John," he said, "this is not kosher,
something is wrong here." But Riddle replied, "Relax. It's a
friendly deal. It's a Dixon deal. You know, it's one of those."

Closing a Drippie deal wasn't always that easy. Back in
Dallas, Dixon needed someone to take Beau Rivage, a Drippie
deal in Louisiana, off his hands for a while. Harvey McLean, the
owner of the Paris, Texas, Savings & Loan and a major Vernon
borrower, seemed as well qualified as anyone; he was from
Shreveport.

At first, Dixon casually raised the subject with McLean
during a meeting. "He explained that they had a number of

[deals] in Dondi Residential Properties that they needed to get out of the savings and loan, and that since I was from Louisiana, they thought Beau Rivage should be placed with me. The understanding was that shortly after the end of Vernon's fiscal year, I would sell [it] to [another] entity."

McLean balked. "I told him I'd rather not do that, and I hoped that they would work out another method for getting rid of the properties."

But Dixon kept up the pressure. Over the next few months, McLean had several discussions involving Beau Rivage with Dixon and Woody Lemons. "I protested that I did not want to take the property, but they pointed out to me that I had been required to do this before and that everything had worked out." In fact, on three occasions, McLean had temporarily taken deals off Vernon's hands, and everything had worked out all right. Yet he remained uneasy about the Beau Rivage project; it was a real dog and he continued to resist.

One day, McLean, a soft-spoken Harvard graduate who wore monogrammed shirts, found himself in a meeting with Woody Lemons, the blunt, good-old country boy and Vernon chairman.

As Woody's eyes danced around his office in Vernon's Dallas branch, he told McLean that Vernon officials were having a hard time getting borrowers to acquire the Drippie deals. He looked everywhere but at his guest. Lemons talked about how it had been a frustrating experience, never mentioning any of the foot-draggers by name. Suddenly he turned in his chair and stared directly at McLean, who resembles an inquisitive graduate student.

Then McLean heard Lemons's real message: Vernon had a simple solution for any who wouldn't play ball. It would call all of their loans. McLean, who at one point owed Vernon Savings more than $30 million, got the point. Later that month, he planned to refinance a huge loan, and it contained a provision that Vernon could use to call all of his debts. In case he missed Woody's hint, McLean got another clue from Dixon while sitting in Don's office talking about some other deals: "Mr. Dixon was significantly more subtle than Mr. Lemons, but the message was nevertheless very clear. If you did not take the Drippie deal, your relationship with Vernon would go to hell."

McLean acquired the fifty-six condominium units at Beau Rivage from Dondi Residential Properties, Inc., at a price that was far more than the units were worth. In all, he borrowed about $7 million from Vernon to complete the deal—a debt that would have required rents of about three dollars per square foot just to pay the principal and interest. At the time, Beau Rivage condos were fetching rents of only thirty-five cents per square foot and nearly half were empty.

McLean and Riddle, of course, weren't the only Drippie borrowers. The process was repeated time and again across Texas over the next few weeks. At times the deals were structured to bail out the borrowers, too. Vernon, James, and Paul Smith were Dallas developers, friends of Dixon's, and extensive borrowers at Vernon Savings. In 1985, their company was in deep trouble. In fact, one of their loans—an $11-million borrowing at Guardian Savings and Loan of Houston—was one year overdue, and several of their loans at Vernon Savings obviously were in jeopardy. Yet Dixon's thrift lent the Smiths an additional $5.5 million in mid-1985 so they could acquire a Drippie deal.

A number of unwritten understandings accompanied the Smiths' $5.5-million loan. There were the normal suspensions of interest payments and maturity dates. But James Smith got a Drippie bonus. Dixon and Vernon Savings agreed to lend Smith an additional $8 million so he could refinance his troubled loan at Guardian Savings, even though Vernon's underwriter, loan officer, and case supervisor had recommended the new loan be rejected. The $8-million deal was included in a larger borrowing by Smith, who used some of the proceeds to cover his cash needs and his own salary, which ran more than $200,000 a year despite his financial troubles.

Not all of the Drippie shenanigans went off without a hitch. Accounting rules prohibited Vernon from booking a profit on the deals if the borrower didn't put up a down payment. But Vernon found a way around that. Federal savings and loan regulations said no cash down payment would be needed if Vernon could sell off a portion of the loan to another savings and loan.

Vernon rattled the daisy chain. Pretty soon the swat team had a list of friendly savings and loans to approach, including Sandia Federal Savings and Loan, an Albuquerque, New Mexico, institution partially owned by two Dallas-area real estate developers. Sandia eventually acquired a 20-percent interest in many of the loans, satisfying the down-payment test and clearing the way to close the deals. About the same time, two of Sandia's major stockholders, Delwin Morton and Chuck Wilson, got large loans from Vernon secured by their Sandia stock.

McCormick discovered another problem with some of the loans. By the time the points, fees, and other costs were added up, the sales prices on some units exceeded the Alice in Wonderland appraisals that Vernon had acquired. "They were estimates of the amounts that were needed to get up to total recoup of the sales price Dondi Residential was seeking," McCormick said. If, for example, the appraisal on the first one, Cedar Springs, was $661,000, the loan from Vernon might have been bumped to $700,000 to cover closing costs and pay points and the like. McCormick, who easily got carried away in the anxiety of the moment, flagged the excessive loan amounts with his accountant's pencil. But he was soon instructed to use his eraser. McCormick recalled that upon seeing the notations, Blakely barked, "You know goddamn well we can't lend in excess of the appraisal." In the vernacular of the times, Vernon officials put a "mustache" on the problem loans; the excessive amounts were reclassified as unrelated working-capital loans to the buyer; they appeared to have nothing to do with the Drippie project.

Once the problem loans were restructured into Drippie deals, Vernon's lawyers papered them and the swat team started processing the sales. "The price tags that ultimately ended up on the closing statements were in fact just numbers that they had arrived at mainly because they thought they had a captive borrower, and they could jam these things down their throat. The sales price also allowed Dondi Residential to book a gain on the sale of all this stuff. It was artificial," said McCormick.

Dixon's name never really appeared in any of this. But as those who worked at Vernon can attest, not much went on there that Don didn't approve. "Everyone who worked at Vernon worked for Don Dixon," John Hill once said. Dixon was the one who could work dozens of deals in his head and watch them fall together simultaneously. It was as if he were finally the musician he had yearned to be as a youngster. Just as composers create a symphony from the competing sounds of violins, oboes, French horns, and flutes, Dixon shaped his deals from the clashing interests of bankers, lawyers, fellow developers, and wheeler-dealers.

Before the fiscal year ended, Vernon closed forty-seven loans totaling more than $98 million to the twenty lucky recipients of the Drippie swat team's largess. It was music to Dixon's ears. Instead of losing the $15 to $22 million that McCormick had estimated, Vernon booked a $13-million profit on the deals, about half of its earnings for the year. The deals once again passed the accountants' muster, and McCormick went off to a new assignment in another Vernon subsidiary in Florida. Ernest P. Worrell cut a new series of ads, only to be let go a few months later when the ad campaign ended. He made the cover of *Roundup*, Vernon's employee publication, though. "So Long, Ern," said the headline, "Golly Bob Howdy—It's Been Great!"

13 Mr. Inside, Mr. Outside, and Mr. Inside Out

F
riends packed the cavernous Senate Caucus Room across the street from the U.S. Capitol building. Normally senators reserve the huge chamber for special hearings or events that draw TV cameras, klieg lights, and overflow crowds. The nation learned details about Watergate and the Iran-contra scandal from hearings in the caucus room. But the throng of senators, congressmen, and legislative aides that gathered there on a Saturday morning in August 1982 didn't show up for anything of historic importance. They had come to a memorial service for Glenwood S. Troop, who had died a few days before, at age fifty-eight. He had been a lobbyist for the U.S. League of Savings Institutions.

Prior to his death, Troop had never heard of Donald R. Dixon or of Vernon Savings, and he didn't dream the survival of the industry he represented would be threatened by financial deregulation. He died the very month that the lawmakers passed the Garn–St. Germain bill, which lifted the burden of government regulation from the industry's shoulders. Yet Troop's legacy would have an enormous impact on Dixon, Vernon Savings, and the crisis that was about to engulf savings and loans. More than any other person, he was responsible for the S&L industry's Washington lobbying machine—a political juggernaut that drove the cost of the S&L crisis through the financial stratosphere and allowed the Dixons of the world to survive.

The memorial service on that hot summer day in Washington symbolized the depth of the ties that Troop had sown between the industry and the nation's political power structure. The U.S. Senate is the clubbiest of clubs; it doesn't open its ornate caucus chambers to just anyone. Senators must pass special resolutions if their offices are to be used for nonofficial purposes. Troop clearly was a special case. The lofty eulogies that echoed through the chamber made it seem as if the senators were burying one of their own, and the praise didn't stop at the caucus room door.

When the leadership gaveled the Senate into session the following Monday, Majority Leader Howard Baker of Tennessee rose and in an ironic twist, dedicated the Senate's weekly poem—"World Breaking Apart"—to the memory of Troop. Baker's colleague across the aisle, Senate Minority Leader Robert Byrd of West Virginia, also expressed his grief at Troop's passing. But Sen. Donald Riegle, a Michigan Democrat who would chair the Senate Banking Committee just six years later, said it best:

> Late last Wednesday Glen Troop, a personal friend and one of Washington's premier lobbyists, died of a heart attack at his home in suburban Alexandria. To many in this town, he was a Washington institution. On numerous occasions, I sought his counsel in considering legislation that might benefit Americans in their dream of home ownership. I respected and shared his belief that the American people deserved to have a system of financial institutions specializing in home finance. For as long as I am in the Senate, I believe that each time we consider financial institutions or housing legislation, I will think of and miss Glen Troop.

A hard-drinking Massachusetts native who hated to wear a tie, Troop had arrived in Washington fresh out of the University of Maryland in 1952. He resembled the actor Robert Young, minus the *Father Knows Best* smile, and his career blossomed along with the industry he represented. A decade later, he would quietly slip through an unmarked door next to a newsstand at the old Carroll Arms Hotel and enter the Quorum Club, a Capitol Hill enclave founded by Bobby Baker, the Lyndon Johnson protégé who would be driven from his job as secretary of the Senate by financial scandals. Troop was president of the club, which featured small luncheon tables and an elegant bar where congressmen and lobbyists could gather for lunch and discuss business amidst masculine decor. The club had smoky rooms, leather chairs, and deeply stained paneled walls adorned with paintings of nudes. Troop worked Washington like a maestro.

"He knew everybody—congressmen, other lobbyists, key aides, secretaries, even the clerks," recalls a lobbyist. "The stories of his contacts are legendary. He used to show up at the House clerk's office. Everyone else would be standing in line waiting for the first printing of a bill, and Glen would walk up to the clerk and say hello. He was real friendly with the help. He'd give them little Christmas presents, stuff like that. She'd hand him a large manila envelope. It was the bill we were all waiting for, but he had it first."

Troop quickly discovered what his successors would learn years later—it was money that really greased the wheels of influence in Washington. He capitalized on the League's ability to raise political contributions from thrifts around the country and solidified his contacts in Congress.

Troop's tenure was tainted by scandal. He set up a 1962 meeting in which a California insurance executive said he handed Bobby Baker an envelope stuffed with cash—part of $100,000 the industry contributed to politicians when fighting a $10-million federal tax proposed by the Kennedy administration.

Troop also introduced Baker to Max Karl, a Milwaukee tycoon who ran MGIC, a home-mortgage insurance company with a board of directors that included four former presidents of the U.S. League. Baker soon acquired MGIC stock for $3.27 a share, just seventeen days before the stock was registered for sale to the public. He and some associates sold it shortly thereafter for more than $22 a share. Baker was eventually forced to resign from his $20,000-a-year job as secretary of the Senate.

But the scandals and bold headlines didn't stop Troop, who ignored Washington's parochial press corps. By the time he suffered his fatal heart attack in 1982, Troop had built an astonishingly successful full-service lobby that would survive him. The U.S. League functioned like a big business from its headquarters in Chicago, where it provided legal, research, insurance, and investment services to three thousand or more members, or about 98 percent of the nation's savings and loans. But its true power rested in Troop's office. Indeed, the League's Washington operation had become so influential with congressmen and regulators in the nation's capital that little S&L business could be done—or undone—without it.

"It was a good old boy network," said Ed Gray. "The good old boys came up to Washington and got their instructions and everybody fell in. I was in Freddy St. Germain's office one day. I got to know him well; he was pretty supportive of me when he ran the House Banking Committee. I showed him some of my regulatory proposals and he said, 'Ed, don't bring that stuff to me unless you can get the U.S. League to support it. Forget it. It's all good, but forget it.' "

Gray said he also groused about the League's sway over its regulators with William Seidman, his counterpart who regulated commercial bankers. But Seidman told Gray that the bank board had long been a captive of the industry. "Bill told me, 'Ed, we trained our lions a long time ago. You still haven't trained yours.' "

Troop's death couldn't have come at a worse time for the savings and loan industry. Prior to 1982, the U.S. League had represented a homogeneous group. Members would split over arcane insider issues. But they would set aside their differences on key legislative issues. Troop worked Capitol Hill buoyed by the unanimous support of thrift owners, whom he could enlist to contact lawmakers. "They didn't have just anybody walk in," said one congressman. "The guy coming through your door was often on your campaign finance committee. Don't forget, there aren't many congressional districts that don't have a friendly S&L."

Nevertheless, once Troop died, the unity started to crack. The fissure started when a fight erupted between traditional thrift owners and new entrants to the industry such as Dixon.

At first, the dispute focused on the dwindling reserves in the FSLIC, the fund that the government maintained to insure deposits placed into savings and loans by ordinary working folks. Passage of the Garn–St. Germain bill had opened the doors to a new generation of lucrative investments and opportunities for thrift institutions. But it also exposed them to huge potential losses and rampant fraud.

Empire Savings was the first major thrift to show that deregulation had a downside. When Faulkner's financial follies proved too much for the institution, state and federal regulators swept in, closed the place, and dipped into the FSLIC fund to pay off the insured depositors. The regulators then tried to recoup the FSLIC outlays by slapping for-sale signs on the assets that FSLIC had taken over. The result: a stunning $165-million loss.

Later in 1984, five federally insured savings and loans in Tennessee with assets of $300 million failed after the empire of a local banking entrepreneur named Jake Butcher collapsed. Then came San Marino Savings and Loan in California, which went under with $812 million in assets. Each failure represented trouble for the FSLIC. By year-end 1984, the assets that FSLIC had inherited from busted S&Ls in the previous twelve months exceeded the total for the previous fifty years combined.

The closings took a toll on the deposit insurance fund. The health of the FSLIC was maintained by fees and assessments from savings and loans who proudly displayed its sticker on their windows. As the roster of insolvent savings and loans grew, its reserves, or the financial cushion of the fund, deteriorated rapidly. Traditional savings and loan owners who had stuck to home loans objected vigorously when Gray suggested they pay higher fees and assessments to restore the FSLIC's reserves. They were being penalized for problems that were caused by high-flying thrifts such as Vernon. Nevertheless, the skimpy level of cash in the fund convinced Gray to propose an industry-wide special assessment that drove the cost of deposit insurance for S&Ls far higher than their competitors in banks.

"I just wanted to turn off the spigot because every week, I'd get this briefing, and things were getting worse," said Gray. "This might sound like a bit of an exaggeration, but it was true. When I would go up to Capitol Hill to testify, I'd ask for an executive session and I'd tell them I was concerned that disclosing the problems of FSLIC publicly would cause a run. I told them we had a disaster on the way. But hey, nobody wanted to hear this. They'd say, 'Why do you bring us this sad news?' "

The FSLIC fund was only one element of the problem,

though. To fend off their financial troubles, Dixon and other go-go S&Ls also raised the interest rates they paid savers, luring into their vaults the fresh cash they needed to stay alive and fund their salaries and dividends. Soon traditional S&Ls complained once again to Gray, arguing that Dixon and his ilk were also driving up the cost of their funds. Savers who wanted a higher rate on their money could get higher returns at Vernon simply by reading its ads in the *Wall Street Journal*. The combination of higher interest and insurance expenses squeezed their bottom lines, propelling other marginally healthy S&Ls toward insolvency. If something didn't happen soon, the problems would get worse.

The traditional operators inundated Gray and the League with complaints that the bank board wasn't cracking down on the new entrants to stop their abusive practices. But the old guard soon discovered that their free-market friends in the Reagan administration had made life much easier for operators such as Dixon. By mid-1985, David Stockman, the head of Reagan's Office of Management and Budget, had slashed the bank board's already low-paid staff of examiners to 747 for the entire nation. The cuts came at the very time the industry expanded rapidly. Some S&Ls had not been examined in years. Yet every time Gray tried to get a staff increase, OMB would oppose him, even though the examiners were paid by the industry.

"Stockman was busy doing other things," Gray said. "I had to talk about this with his associate director, Carol Crawford," who was called Dragon Lady by industry lobbyists. Gray said it was a frustrating experience: "How are you supposed to be able to deal with this when OMB says screw you. Because in effect they don't want to give you any more people. So you do the transferring, try to do the best you can yourself. Because you know you're not going to get any help."

Eventually, Gray did an end run on OMB by transferring the entire examination staff from Washington to the district home loan banks. That put the staffs under the regional banks, whose budgets were not controlled by OMB, and the examination staff started growing again.

But the problems with examiners took a long time to solve, and the resolution didn't erase the bitter feelings. The rift in the industry deepened, and William O'Connell, the U.S. League's Chicago-based president, stepped in to referee the dispute.

When Troop was alive, he and O'Connell had worked Washington as a Mr. Inside and Mr. Outside team reminiscent of Doc Blanchard and Glenn Davis, the two infamous backs on the Army's 1940-era football team. Comfortable out of the spotlight, Troop twisted congressional arms and made campaign pledges in the confines of places like the Quorum Club. O'Connell was different. A small man with thin gray hair, O'Connell was the League's public face—the guy the industry would trot out to make public statements and speeches. He looked as if he belonged in a savings and loan—serious, businesslike, and aging. But O'Connell was the new breed of Washington lobbyist—the Reagan-era man who worked the media as hard as he worked Congress. He quickly realized that when working with Congress and the financial markets, perceptions were as important—actually more important—than reality.

To work the media, O'Connell would swoop into Washington from Chicago for lunch with journalists at the old Sans Souci restaurant. He had an Irishman's knack for inflating journalistic and political egos in a town where egos were as big as the Pentagon. And he had organized the U.S. League as if it were a Chicago political ward.

But O'Connell faced incredible obstacles when he had to wrestle with the feuding elements of the S&L industry. Gray's decision to increase the deposit insurance premium for FSLIC angered many in the industry. The League's membership got even madder, though, when a frustrated Gray started airing the industry's troubles in public to justify his action. In June 1984, Gray issued an official paper publicly expressing concerns over the dwindling insurance-fund reserves. Industry leaders who had pushed Gray's candidacy didn't know what to think. Publicly discussing the industry's problems wasn't good for business. After being humiliated by the disaster at Empire, Gray also started talking as if more regulation was needed—a position that ran counter to the policies of the industry and the Reagan administration.

Gray said the industry and Congress ignored him when he talked in private. So he began discussing the problem publicly because the FSLIC's problems were glaringly apparent anyway. "They got tired of hearing me," he said. "I mean, I was called up to the Hill every two weeks to testify. I don't know what else I was supposed to talk about. I'm sure everyone wanted me to talk about the profitability of the industry, which I did. But the fact is, we did have a problem.

By 1985, the industry's friends on Capitol Hill began wondering what was going on. Gray was ramming through the bank board new regulations designed to crack down on the Don Dixons of the industry. He was also talking of seeking authority from Congress to raise billions of dollars more through an industry-financed scheme designed to replenish the FSLIC fund's reserves. The new money would give Gray the resources he needed to close more savings and loans.

O'Connell tried to forge an industry consensus on the issues raised by the bank board chairman, but he couldn't do it. Each solution seemed to generate as much opposition as support. Pretty soon lawmakers who had originally voted for the deregulation bill began to wonder what was going on. They wondered about talk of fresh injection of capital and the need for more legislation. Knowledgeable, friendly lawmakers questioned whether the situation facing the industry was as bad as Gray said. But when they turned to O'Connell, they got Mr. Outside's official response: Don't worry—the industry's problems were manageable. The League would see that they stayed that way.

O'Connell's response was the kind of thing that the industry's friends on Capitol Hill wanted to hear. Savings and loans may seem like simple organizations to average Americans. But speeches on FSLIC, interest spreads, and bad assets are not the kind of subjects that get politicians on the six-o'clock news. Congressmen rely heavily upon the industry and its lobbyists to tell them when serious problems exist and to respond to their questions.

William McKenna was the man who stepped forward with some answers. While Troop was Mr. Inside and O'Connell Mr. Outside, McKenna was Mr. Inside Out. A California lawyer known as the patriarch of the S&L industry, McKenna, in the words of House Banking Committee chairman Fernand St. Germain, had been around the industry since he was knee high to a grasshopper. A survivor of Republican and Democratic administrations, McKenna reveled in the mystique of the power broker, preferring to operate in the shadows. He was chairman of the Federal Savings and Loan Advisory Council—an influential, low-profile group of industry powers who advised the bank board chairman on key issues. And he rose to become chairman of the

Federal Home Loan Bank of San Francisco, the most influential district bank in the system.

McKenna would show up at League conventions in Hawaii but stay out of the sunlight because of his extremely fair skin. His thin red hair and slightly disheveled look suggested he was an absentminded man. But he had a razor-sharp mind and zeal for gamesmanship. When an industry leader once dropped by a table where McKenna was having lunch with a reporter, McKenna purposely avoided introducing the S&L man to his guest. After the intruder walked away, McKenna chuckled and said to the reporter, "He'll spend all afternoon trying to find out who you are."

McKenna knew O'Connell's soothing message to Congress was pure bunk. The industry was sliding into deeper troubles, and both he and O'Connell knew it. Early in 1985, the advisory council McKenna chaired had ordered a confidential report from industry insiders that documented the extent of the industry's troubles.

The authors had concluded that the expanded powers given thrifts under deregulation had created a monster. Go-go savings and loans such as Vernon had shifted emphasis from home loans to riskier commercial mortgages and real estate development. The changing investment strategy had unleashed too many investment dollars that were chasing too few good projects.

Deregulation hadn't really changed the management structure of the S&L industry much. The same people who had been running S&Ls before the Garn–St. Germain bill passed ran them afterward. McKenna knew most of them. They were perfectly capable of understanding the home loan business, but they were not sophisticated financiers. Commercial lending and development loans were far more complex undertakings. They required a much higher level of financial sophistication, skill, training, and most of all, experience.

Unfortunately, many of the thrift industry's traditional managers had plunged into the commercial end of the market, hoping to match the strong performances reported by the Don Dixons in the industry and to recoup the capital they had lost prior to deregulation. Copying Vernon, weakly capitalized S&Ls also jacked up the interest rates offered depositors so they, too, could invest in get-rich-quick real estate deals.

Well-meaning but uninformed managers thought the high-yielding loans would restore their net worths. But they didn't know what they were doing. They had invested in the real estate industry's equivalent of junk bonds. In 1982, three-fourths of all thrift failures had been caused by an interest-rate squeeze. The rates that savings and loans paid to get new deposits were higher than the returns they earned when they invested the funds in fixed-rated home mortgages. By 1985, three-fourths of the industry's problems stemmed from a more vexing problem—bad assets put on the industry's books by greedy managers and developers like Don Dixon. In a plummeting real estate market, the investments were like a ticking time bomb in the balance sheets of hundreds of American S&Ls.

It didn't take much imagination to determine where the industry and its deposit-insurance fund were headed. By 1985, the confidential report said that some 329 federally insured savings and loans—just over 10 percent of the industry—had failed since the government started deregulating S&Ls. Almost half of the failures had occurred in the time since Gray took office in 1983. Many more troubled S&Ls were being kept alive by accounting gimmickry and financial sleight of hand because the industry didn't have enough money in its deposit-insurance fund to shut them down.

The situation in the deposit-insurance fund was particularly alarming. Just two years earlier, the insurance fund had $6.4 billion set aside in reserves to cover potential failures at savings and loans with $667 billion in insured deposits. That wasn't good; it meant the government had about one dollar set aside for each $100 in insured deposits compared to $2.07 per $100 in 1970, an all-time high.

By 1985, FSLIC-insured deposits had risen 26 percent to $844 billion, mainly because so many troubled S&Ls were jacking up interest rates to lure new money into their vaults. But the insurance fund reserves had fallen nearly 30 percent because of the huge losses incurred covering failures such as Empire. The agency had only fifty cents in reserve for each $100 in federally insured deposits. If the FSLIC had to pay off depositors because of a few more large insolvencies like Empire, the fund could run out of cash. The system that had successfully stood behind S&L deposits since the Great Depression was threatened with bankruptcy.

Equally disturbing was the mountain of unsold real estate

that was piling up because of the FSLIC's activities. The agency was severely understaffed. As it took over troubled S&Ls, it had inherited the homes, apartment buildings, office towers, and condo projects underlying thousands of loans in default. But the overburdened staff couldn't unload the property quickly. As a result, FSLIC's inventory of unsold real estate soared. If the agency were forced to dump the property on the market suddenly, McKenna feared it would create a fire-sale atmosphere in which prices would plummet, undermining the industry's financial prospects and hurting its stock prices. Something clearly had to be done.

McKenna and his colleagues kicked around several ideas. One obvious option was to unleash Gray and his staff on the Vernons of the world. Gray could close the thrifts, pay off their depositors, and face up to the losses. But that approach posed several problems, the main one being money. Financing such an undertaking and restoring the fund would cost the industry a bundle—about $15 to $20 billion in fees and assessments. That wouldn't go over well with thrift operators already struggling to compete with banks, which paid far lower deposit-insurance premiums.

McKenna soon came up with a solution that was far more palatable: Why not create a new organization that the industry could use to rig the real estate markets and borrow its way out of the problem?

McKenna couldn't have picked a more obscure and arcane name for the new organization. He called it the Federal Asset Disposition Association, otherwise known as FADA. Under McKenna's scenario, Gray could move against a thrift such as Vernon, take it over, throw out the old managers, and replace them with some hired by the government. The new managers would then separate the good assets from the bad and sell the junk to FADA, which was really a huge savings and loan capitalized by government guaranteed loans. FADA would then manage the troubled real estate and hold it off the market until it could be sold in an orderly manner. Presto, the industry's problems would be solved.

A powerful force in the California S&L industry, McKenna didn't have to twist any arms to convince Gray to try the FADA approach. The bank board chairman was desperate for help. Besides, he owed his job to the California thrifts. In November

1985, Gray unveiled the new plan at the 93rd annual convention of the U.S. League in Dallas.

"The chartering of FADA does not constitute a panacea for the difficulties of the FSLIC," Gray told the thousands of S&L executives from the podium. "It is one element in a much larger mosaic of actions to strengthen the FSLIC's hand in meeting its obligations now and in the future."

Many of the S&L executives gathered in the Dallas Convention Center didn't know what to think. Gray had hinted such an organization might be formed a few weeks earlier during congressional hearings. Most of the thrift owners were still seething about Gray's January 1985 decision to increase their FSLIC insurance premiums to about two-tenths of one percent of their deposits, or more than twice what their competitors in the banking industry paid.

But the high-flying S&L owners from Texas didn't like the sound of the new organization at all. When combined with new regulations being pushed by Gray, FADA gave Durward Curlee, the lobbyist for thrifts such as Vernon and Lamar Savings in Austin, something to worry about. The Texans suspected that the new organization might be used against them. Industry powers such as McKenna could pressure Gray to move against rapidly growing competitors, force them into receivership, and pass on their assets to the FADA. Politically savvy members of the FADA board could then vote to sell the assets to their cronies in the industry at bargain prices and hide any losses in the budgetary nether world of a quasi-government agency.

Their fears were only reinforced when Gray announced that the chairman of the new organization would be McKenna, who proceeded to organize a board that read like a Who's Who of the U.S. League.

A new organization with vague goals and a powerful board dominated by the U.S. League was something for Vernon Savings to fear. Another team of federal examiners from the Federal Home Loan Bank Board had already moved into Vernon during August for another look at the books. If the industry kept up the heat on Ed Gray, Vernon could be in trouble.

Within weeks of Gray's speech, T. W. (Tibby) Weston, a Houston real estate consultant, proposed a competing private-sector organization preferred by the go-go S&Ls such as Vernon and Lamar Savings of Austin. Called the READY Association

(Real Estate Acquisition, Development, and Yield) and backed by a $1-million loan from Lamar, the new organization would be set up to sell zero-coupon bonds. The proceeds of the bond sales would then be used to acquire troubled assets from ailing S&Ls. True to the spirit of the times, no government money would be involved. It was a "private-sector initiative" designed to warm the icy veins of the Reagan administration's Office of Management and Budget. It was owned by good old private investors such as Vernon Smith, one of the borrowers in Dixon's daisy chain. The new organization would need an okay from some people in Washington. But that didn't matter.

READY had its roots in Texas, and Texans had a lot of friends in Congress.

14 Dixons Outdo Dallas

I t was a few weeks before Christmas 1985 in Del Mar. Guests at the political fundraiser at Dixon's beach home passed through two iron gates and a long colonnade before entering a courtyard that resembled a fairyland. Three beautifully lighted Christmas trees floated in an enormous pool. A well-stocked bar, three life-sized antique wooden horses, and tables crammed with delicacies converted the poolside expanse into a dramatic stage for entertaining. A small hall a few steps away led to a huge deck with a stunning view of the Pacific waves that pounded the beach about two hundred feet below.

"What a wonderful setting," thought Peggy Freeman, a gossip columnist for *Ranch and Coast*, a local magazine, as she stepped on the deck and scanned the crowd for a familiar face. Her eyes soon fell upon Dixon.

As he mingled with his guests, he cradled in his arm one of those tiny, fashionable Shih Tzus that seemed incapable of a bark. "How strange," thought Freeman. "I haven't seen anything like that in a hundred years. It's something women from Hollywood used to do when they went to Saks."

To Freeman and to many others, Dixon seemed a man at the pinnacle. If his financial empire was beset with problems, he didn't show it. He moved through the crowd with an air of superiority—above the pedestrian concerns of gossip columnists

149

who thought he looked silly. He greeted his guests with a genial grin and barely audible Texas drawl. The traces of gray in his long, curly hair and mustache belied his boyish mischievous streak. His open-collared shirt, sport coat, friendly plump face, and inquisitive brown eyes portrayed a man of confidence.

The guest list alone showed that Dixon had traveled more than miles from Vernon, Texas. In one corner, Freeman saw Rep. Bill Lowery, the local Republican congressman, chatting with contributors. In another, a photographer's strobe flashed as a knot of elegantly dressed women posed for pictures with Philippe Junot and his father, Michael, the deputy mayor of Paris. Del Mar mayor Arlene Carson and her husband, Al, mingled with the guests, sipping champagne and plucking chunks of lobster from trays borne by smartly dressed waiters. A jazz combo on the balcony reached for the right note as Barbara and Roy Wieghorst, son of Olaf, one of Dixon's favorite Western artists, moved through the crowd. People talked Republican talk, recommended bond funds, and passed gossip along to Richard Rosenblatt, the publisher of *Ranch and Coast*, who said he was there out of curiosity: "We went to the party basically to see this lavish, talked-about house. Anybody who was anybody was there. One of his henchman later called me and said you crashed that party. I said, 'What are you talking about?' I was invited by the PR head of the Lowery campaign; the other side of the family so to speak."

For Dixon the party was a celebration of his success. His efforts to ingratiate himself with San Diego society had started back in 1984. Using the services of the city's infamous madam may have been a good way to wow Texans. But that wouldn't do for local residents in heavily Catholic San Diego, where befriending a bishop was better than knowing an alderman. Dixon was a Protestant who didn't know a high mass from a menorah. He soon remedied that, though, by hiring Ernie Osuna, who came from an old-line San Diego Catholic family that had strong ties to the Catholic church and the local bishop, the Right Reverend Leo T. Maher. Before long, Dixon's second wife back in Dallas was flabbergasted to learn that he was taking their daughters to a Catholic mass on Sundays. The church fathers were equally stunned with the generosity of Vernon's prodigal son.

It doesn't take long for someone with deep pockets and a savings and loan full of money to become well loved in the

Catholic Church. Bishop Maher soon recognized Dixon's interest in the church with a seat on the board of trustees at the University of San Diego, a local Catholic college. Dixon responded by making a contribution to the bishop's efforts to build a student union at the school. He gave the bishop a chunk of Dondi Financial stock, which Dixon valued at $3 million, with the proviso that he—or someone else he found—would buy it for cash in the near future. It was the single largest charitable contribution in the school's history, and an appreciative bishop wanted to name the thing the Donald R. Dixon Student Union. But Dixon demurred. He already had what he wanted. The noncash contribution of stock, which Dixon's accountants promptly deducted from Dondi's taxable income, opened the doors to Dixon's promised land. The bishop introduced him to the cream of San Diego's society—people such as Congressman Lowery and fellow university trustee Douglas Manchester, a local real estate man and developer of the Intercontinental Hotel, a fixture on San Diego's skyline.

Freeman was quite taken with Dixon and his soiree. The party that night was dazzling. The Dixons had organized a true holiday extravaganza. For $250 each, the guests got more than an elegantly catered dinner. Everywhere that Rosenblatt looked, he saw prominent businessmen, politicians, and community leaders sipping fine wine or marveling over the festive cotton-candy decorations on the peach and raspberry desserts. "You came in through these lavish gates," he said. "It was right on the water, gorgeous. It had that fantastic reflecting pool. The party was all over the house with great mounds of everything, all kinds of special effects, you know, carved-ice buildings, that sort of thing."

Rosenblatt and other guests wandered through the compound. Up the circular staircase on the second floor was an impressive display of Western art from Vernon's collection, which was then valued at about $5 million. Several Olaf Wieghorst originals adorned the walls. A lone cowboy against a sunset background by W. Herbert Dunton hung above the fireplace in the Dixons' bedroom. Freeman and Rosenblatt were impressed.

So was Lowery. Politicians spend a lot of time raising money for the next campaign, and a day with Dixon could seem like a month on the campaign trail. In all, a hundred or more guests showed up for the $250-a-plate dinner. That's $25,000. And that wasn't all. Within weeks, Lowery would be whisked to Dallas in Vernon's jet for another Dixon fund-raiser where he would meet some Texans with silver buckles on their belts and silver dollars in their pockets. The Dixons were the kind of friends that a congressman with a struggling campaign fund needed. Freeman soon found herself snapping a picture of a smiling Bill Lowery with a carnation in his lapel, Dana Dixon in one arm, and her sister in another. Freeman used it to accompany her *Ranch and Coast* article on the party. It was titled "Dixons Outdo Dallas." It was too bad that the Dixons hadn't moved there earlier. They were good copy.

Dixon started flirting with the idea of living in California when he was a youngster. He fell in love with the area around San Diego almost instantly and returned there time and again over the years. By the mid-1980s, he had started investing Vernon's funds in the state's sizzling real estate market and had made the area around Del Mar his second home.

The beach house, about a twenty-minute drive north of San Diego, was a perfect spot for someone with Dixon's interests. An enclave of the rich and famous on California's celebrated Gold Coast, Del Mar was one of those places where cocktail parties were a blood sport and people sort of made themselves up as they went along. The town was just down the road from Los Angeles and was home to movie stars and business moguls. A Saturday guest at the Turf Club at the Del Mar racetrack might bump into Elizabeth Taylor, Pete Rose, or Milton Berle. People played polo, collected art, called themselves equestrians, drove antique Mercedeses, and read articles about acupuncture in their saunas. Being idle rich was nothing new in Del Mar.

But sun, fun, and glitter were not the only features that attracted Dixon to Del Mar. By late 1985, Vernon Savings was in trouble, and Del Mar was full of the kind of people with whom Dixon could do business. Don and Dana took to the task like pros. "They were very socially and politically aggressive," said Rosenblatt. "My wife and I were suspicious; they just came on too strong."

Dixon didn't hesitate to use the financial wherewithal provided by Vernon Savings to speed things along. The house in Del Mar had been acquired and remodeled just as the Vernon board had been told. Contrary to past promises, though, no one slapped a for-sale sign on the lawn. Instead Dixon and Dana moved in months before the Lowery fund-raiser and used the place as a weekend hideaway for well over a year.

The upper crust was impressed. Even in Del Mar, people coveted the beach house. Private property close to the beach is rare and expensive. The Pacific was literally a stone's throw from the lavish house that surrounded a huge pool. Dana furnished the place with a Southwestern decor from the Vernon-owned interior-design gallery she ran in nearby Rancho Santa Fe. She spared no expense.

Besides housing major pieces from Vernon's impressive art collection, the house was also decorated sumptuously with Indian dhurrie rugs, antiques, chaise longues upholstered in hand-painted canvas, giant beehive terra-cotta-colored jars, antique kilims, wooden marionettes, original Victorian bamboo pieces, and a collection of expensive ceramics. The place even had a mascot—a peachy-white cockatoo that barked and answered to the name of Seaweed. The carpet, bleached woods, washed-magnolia couch, and antiqued furniture gave the place a glowing sand and sunset palette to complement the stunning view of the Pacific through the floor-to-ceiling, bronze-tinted windows. One visitor compared the Dixons' huge bedroom to a cloud that seemed to float above the sea and sand. For parties and other special occasions, Dixon would park four of his antique classic cars in the garage, converting a car park into an impressive automobile showroom. "Dana did her own decorating so perfectly, she fell in love with the place and decided to keep it," Freeman told her readers.

But the beach house wasn't enough. Even as the construction crews were finishing up in Del Mar, Ray Schooley broke ground for Dixon's dream house in nearby Rancho Santa Fe. The project was financed through a Vernon subsidiary named Lenders Corp., which lined up a construction loan from Sandia Savings, the New Mexico thrift in which Dixon's Dallas friends were major stockholders. The furnishings were financed by Vernon's design subsidiary. The estate, called Los Torres, was a celebration of excess that awed the celebrities and millionaires who would be Dixon's neighbors. When Dixon ordered the $1.5 million worth of landscaping work for the seventeen-acre compound, Schooley thought he was about to start work on a crowning achievement in his career as a builder for the rich and famous.

He transplanted boulders as big as Volkswagens and acres of grass to the area to serve as lush surroundings for the three large Maui ponds with man-made waterfalls that Dixon ordered. Schooley also broke ground for the 10,000-square-foot main house with a thirty-foot-high canterra-stone entry of Moorish design. Everything in the place was unbelievable. The garage (3,200 square feet) was big enough for thirteen cars, a wet bar, and a mechanics' pit for Dixon's antique-car collection. The stable had ten padded stalls and a three-bedroom apartment. The tennis courts had a viewing stand. The main house had five bedrooms, six and a half baths, eight fireplaces, five wet bars, two kitchens, two family rooms, a blue mosaic-tile pool, a spa, a gazebo, and a huge Roman bath surrounded by four white columns that reached to a skylight. Schooley had never built anything like it:

"They never knew what they wanted. They'd go off on some trip and come back with new ideas. They had a touch of Mexico in this room, Spain in another. France over here. Texas there. Rome in the bathroom. The place looked like the goddamn League of Nations." Gary Roth was stunned when he picked up the racks for Dixon's temperature-controlled wine cellar; they cost $38,000. But Schooley wasn't surprised:

> He'd come back from Europe and call me and change something. He'd tell you to tear out a whole room. He'd just say, "Don't worry, we're rich; we've got the money." He found doors from a castle in Spain and wanted them on the front. One time he had this wine-tasting table that he found in a castle. He probably paid a fortune for it; it's a piece of junk. The wine cellar wasn't big enough for it. So he tells me to make the wine cellar bigger. It was already built! You know what we had to do? We took up this floor above the ceiling and lowered the table into it. And her? She had everything painted salmon and pink. This place was designed to be a party house. None of the guest bedrooms even had closets. No one would be here that long.

Soon Dixon and his wife were grist for the local rumor mill. Ever since its founding, Rancho Santa Fe, which locals call The

Ranch, had been a special place. Some four thousand acres of land was originally acquired from Ernie Osuna's family by the Santa Fe Railroad, which planted 3 million eucalyptus trees there to be forested and used as railroad ties. Santa Fe officials discovered the wood was too soft, though, and made board members buy ranches at the site instead, creating one of the most exclusive, closely knit communities in America. In a town where the garden club made news, Dixon was a hot topic. Bertrand Hug, the chef at Mille Fleurs, the pricey French restaurant in the heart of Rancho Santa Fe where the Dixons dined regularly, soon got all sorts of questions about the Texan:

> People wanted to know more about him. They were fascinated. They would come in and say, "You know him, tell me what's he like." He was a party animal. He had great parties, the kind that you just had to be there. He sponsored the Del Mar Jazz Festival. He sponsored the Concours de Élégance—you know, one of those fancy antique-car shows where the women dress up and walk their dogs. You know how you say he is full of shit. Well, he was full of shit with a smile. He'd smile and say, "Can it get any better than this?" He was good to me, a big spender, a very good customer. I liked him a lot.

Van Boxtel, Dixon's old friend and business associate, marveled at how quickly Dixon made connections in the community. Dixon used Symbolic Motors, the Vernon Rolls dealership that the board had approved, to cement his ties in the area. "He had a way of getting to know powerful people," said Van Boxtel. "We had lived here for seven years. He was here no time and knew more people than we did. Everyone thought he was wonderful. He'd put his antique cars on the soccer field, charge admission, and donate the proceeds to the school. He singlehandedly created a new market for classic cars in this area. He had a fantastic collection. He had a Duesenberg. He owned Eva Braun's Mercedes. The Concours he sponsored rapidly became a place to exhibit cars and win a trophy. It was amazing."

The Dixons and their Texas friends spared no expense, according to Van Boxtel:

We went on this hunting trip with him and some other couples from Texas—all Vernon borrowers, I guess—in late 1985. He called and wanted us to go, but I think he was just trying to fill a billet. We hunted pheasant in Denmark, red-legged partridge in England and Spain. It wasn't hunting. It was shooting. It was like shooting clay ducks; they were all coming at you. We were flabbergasted at the shopping sprees they took. I had an old jacket and some rubber boots like I used to wear to hunt around here. They would go out and buy thousand-dollar outfits—knickers and derbies with a feather; jackets; suede skirts; boots; the whole thing. They would go out into a field and if they got their boots dirty, they'd go buy a whole new outfit and come out the next day strutting around like peacocks. It was unbelievable. We couldn't get over the flamboyance; it was too much for us. Don hunted with twelve- to four-teen-thousand-dollar shotguns. Dana ordered a complete shipping container full of antiques for her new house. We didn't have much to do with them after we came home from the trip.

Others in the area didn't react that way, though. Dixon made a good political connection in Lowery. The California Republican was a member of the House Banking Committee at the time, and Dixon and his pals were trying to bring some of their problems with regulators to the attention of officials in Washington.

He made business connections, too. Douglas Manchester, the developer Dixon had met through Bishop Maher, soon became involved in a deal to acquire and syndicate a whole slew of the Drippie projects held by Harvey McLean, John Riddle, and the other Texas developers. By late 1985, they were getting anxious for Dixon to fulfill his promises that he would take the unsold condo projects off their hands.

Dixon started plans for a new company to finance a wide range of other development loans like the ailing deals on Vernon's books. He planned to raise some $550 million through stock and bond sales and bank borrowings. The idea was to create a California investment company that would operate similarly to Vernon without the savings and loan regulations that were starting to crimp his style.

Not everyone was mesmerized by Dixon's charm or ideas. Rosenblatt said he was approached by a real estate salesman who asked him if he wanted to swap some real estate he owned in the area for some of Dixon's condos in Texas. "I asked, why would I want to do that? The land here is worth far more than some Texas condominiums."

But Rosenblatt was a haughty publisher who merely dabbled in real estate. Dixon knew the path to success was to aim at the social stratosphere.

A special guest at his lavish party for Lowery was the man at the pinnacle—Bishop Maher. By then, Dixon and the Right Reverend had become good friends. Maher and his sidekick, Monsignor I. Brent Eagen, pastor of the Mission San Diego de Alcala, had just returned from quite a trip to Europe with the Dixons, courtesy of Vernon Savings.

It had been first class all the way: the flight over in Vernon's jet; the Grosvenor House in London; the Bristol in Paris; the Hotel Ritz in Madrid; stops at the Gucci and Bulgari boutiques in Rome; a side trip to the Relais de Margaux in Bordeaux, a château that Dixon and some partners were converting into a hotel and restaurant.

Maher was so thankful for Dixon's kindness that he introduced him to his boss, which was about as high on the pecking order as Don Dixon would ever aim. A throng of thousands gathered in front of St. Peter's Basilica in the Vatican one sunny day for Pope John Paul II's weekly address. The Pope, dressed in white, descended the steps to greet the special visitors. He approached a six-foot, slightly overweight man from Texas with a petite blond wife on his arm and a painting in his hand. Bishop Maher had arranged the private audience for Dixon and Dana. "I was very well aware of everything I said and that I was in the presence of someone very special," Dixon later recalled. Dana was speechless. The trip had cost Vernon Savings $17,000, not counting the cost of the jet. But this surely was a special moment. In gratitude for the special honor, Dixon handed the Pope an Olaf Wieghorst original—an oil painting of an Indian on horseback called Night Sentry. It was valued at $40,000 and belonged to Vernon Savings. It was hung in the Vatican.

15 Politics

D on Dixon sat behind his desk on the elevated platform shuffling papers. Woody Lemons and Pat King seemed engrossed in another conversation at a conference table nearby as Pat Malone walked into the room and stopped before Dixon's desk. Dixon looked up and issued some marching orders: "There was a firmness to his tone," Malone said. "He spoke directly. I knew that he meant what he said. He explained to me that he had made commitments to political candidates, that he needed the money, and that I should tell the officers they could voucher it."

It was January 1986 and Dixon had discovered that his problems with regulators were not limited to the ones from Bowman's office. Thanks to Ed Gray's expanding staff of bank board examiners, federal regulators from the deposit-insurance agency had been scrutinizing the books at Vernon Savings since August, and it didn't seem as if they would ever leave.

At first Dixon had tried to get next to Ed Gray and explain Vernon's problems the old-fashioned way. "It was in August of 1985. I went to the Jewel Ball, which is the main charity fundraiser in San Diego," said Gray, who often traveled to his hometown for the weekend.

Tawfiq Khoury, a big homebuilder in San Diego, had invited me and my wife to sit at his table in the

158

Diamond Circle, where the largest donors sat. It was a round table with about ten seats, and two of the people at the table were Don Dixon and his wife. Tawfy introduced us and said something about Dixon's being involved in an S&L in Texas. My wife started talking to his wife, and later Mrs. Dixon said something to the effect that they had a beach house in Del Mar and wanted us to come up for dinner. I didn't know anything about it. A couple of weeks later, my wife told me we were going out to dinner that night at the home of the two people we had met at Tawfy Khoury's table. I remembered just enough to recall that he had something to do with a Texas S&L, and I told my wife I didn't want to go. She was furious; wouldn't speak to me. But she eventually called Mrs. Dixon and canceled. Thank God I didn't do it. If I had, I would never have been able to explain it. It would have been "Sayonara, Gray."

Dixon wasn't one to be discouraged by a cold shoulder, though. When Gray rebuffed his dinner invitation, Dixon merely intensified Vernon's efforts to wield political leverage on the bank board through campaign contributions to politicians from both parties. If Ed Gray didn't want to sit down for a chat about the impact of his policies on Vernon and other go-go thrifts, then maybe he'd listen to the people who controlled his purse strings—congressmen in Washington, a town where money really talked.

Ever since he had acquired Vernon Savings in 1982, Dixon had grown increasingly frustrated with government regulators. As a general proposition, he considered them obstacles—dumb people who got in his way. Reports from Durward Curlee suggested that Ed Gray was a special case, though. Gray seemed abrasive, insecure, and totally dependent upon his staff. He appeared to hate Texas S&Ls, and it was hard to believe he knew what he was doing.

The last thing Dixon needed was any more trouble with regulators. Things were already bad enough with the economy. Oil prices stood at $25 per barrel in December 1985—$7 per barrel below their 1981 peak. By early 1986, they were starting to fall even more and the worst was yet to come. Real estate markets in the Southwest were hurting, too. The oil-price decline coincided with a property glut that aggravated his problems in the condo operation. Dixon was already scrambling to find someone to take the Drippie deals off the hands of his special borrowers at Vernon. The proliferation of for-sale signs simply gave him another headache.

Vernon's earnings relied heavily on the profit participations it had demanded in return for making its multimillion-dollar loans to developers such as Harvey McLean and Jack Atkinson. Some of the developers' deals were ill conceived and some were potentially lucrative. But many were slated for completion in the coming months. If the developers couldn't profitably rent or sell their projects because of a slumping economy, they'd be unable to repay hundreds of millions in construction loans or refinance them with another lender. Vernon would have to refinance the deals itself or face steep losses. Even worse, to maximize its fee income, Vernon had structured the loans so they would come up for renewal every six months, generating a constant demand for new funding.

Dixon didn't mind lending the developers more money. He'd just lure in some new deposits and lend the developers enough to stay afloat for another six months or a year. Hanging tough with developers was what Vernon Savings was all about. It was a real estate developers' bank. The alternative—foreclosure—would simply trigger a senseless disaster that would be equally costly to Vernon Savings and the government's deposit-insurance fund.

But that meant Vernon needed a constant stream of fresh deposits flowing into its vaults. Otherwise it would run short of the cash it needed to fund renegotiated loans, meet demands for withdrawals, and cover other items, such as salaries, dividends, and so on.

But Gray was interrupting the flow of deposits into Vernon and dozens of other thrifts with a barrage of new rules and regulations at the bank board. Worse yet, he planned even more drastic steps in the future. He had to be stopped.

"This guy didn't understand economics," said Durward Curlee, a lobbyist for Dixon and other Texas thrift operators.

You saw what Alan Greenspan did when the stock market went to hell in 1987. He stepped in and said he would make as much credit available to the banks as they needed. He saved everyone and was the hero. Our stock market was oil prices. They started falling, and what did Ed Gray do? Exactly the opposite of what Greenspan did. He cut off our source of credit. The rules he wanted were all well and good if they had been passed back in 1982 when everything was good. Hell, they should have been passed. But putting them into effect in the middle of 1985 was just asking for a goddamn disaster.

The rules and regulations grew from Gray's frustration with Congress and the industry, two institutions that lacked the political guts to grapple with the problems looming on the horizon. Gray's new batch of examiners had barely started their exams when dire warnings of trouble started flowing back to Washington. The alarming tone of the reports wasn't spawned by the shocking disclosures involving individual S&Ls that would come within a few months. The initial reports simply suggested that the rapid growth of deposits in states such as Texas with liberal regulations and economic troubles spelled trouble, particularly given the poor financial health of the deposit-insurance fund. Its reserves were strained and it couldn't take many more hits.

Gray was singularly ill-equipped to deal with the situation. He wasn't an economist, financier, or even a very good politician. But he was smart enough to realize that he was an inviting target for the Congress and the industry to use as a scapegoat for their inaction. Congress didn't know what to do, and the industry had urged him to crack down on the highfliers one by one, which was impossible, given the size and talent of his agency. So he adopted a two-phase strategy that succeeded in angering everyone.

Gray already had implemented phase one of his solution over opposition by the industry and the highfliers. He had rammed through the bank board new rules and regulations designed to inhibit the ability of thrifts such as Vernon to grow rapidly and invest government-insured deposits in crummy deals. Ideally, the regulations would limit the exposure of the deposit-insurance fund by preventing rapidly growing S&Ls from taking on too many deposits. Gray's phase two would come when—and if—the Congress, under pressure to do something about the growing losses, passed legislation to inject new capital into the troubled deposit-insurance fund. That would give Gray the money he needed to close down the Dixons of the world, pay off their depositors, seize their assets, and ease the upward pressure they had exerted on interest rates.

To Dixon, the most immediate problem was Gray's growth regulation, a set of rules that required bank board approval for annual asset growth of more than 25 percent. Gray had figured the rules wouldn't bother well-run thrifts; about three-fourths of the industry grew at rates of 25 percent or less. But he thought the regulations would hurt the guys he was after; the new rules restrained deposit growth at go-go outfits such as Vernon, whose deposits had soared by an average 300 percent a year since Dixon had taken over.

Unfortunately, though, there was a loophole in the regulations passed by the bank board. Savings and loans routinely sell loan participations—or a piece of the action—to other institutions. Vernon could originate ten $5-million loans, collect its up-front fees, bundle them into one $50-million package, and sell the whole thing to a thrift from Iowa. There were plenty of rural S&Ls that took in more deposits from farmers than they could prudently invest in small-town America. Loan participations sold to others were exempt from the growth targets. In other words, if the loans were originated and sold quickly, they didn't count against the 25-percent growth ceiling. Vernon could thus originate loans, collect its huge fees and points, and then sell them to someone else.

It didn't take Dixon long to discover the loophole. "When the feds first came out with all of the new regulations," recalled one former Vernon executive, "we had a meeting in Del Mar, and Dixon said he figured we could still do about four hundred million dollars in loans a year as long as we sold some. That meant we had to sell about a hundred fifty million dollars a year to other institutions."

Sometimes the loan participations were sold to a friendly S&L in the daisy chain. In other cases, Vernon executed secret illicit side deals in which it promised to buy back the loan if any repayment problems later surfaced. Regardless of where the loans ended up, though, the regulation that prompted the loan sales helped spread the cancer. Vernon's risky loans were put on the books of other weak institutions who wanted the deals for their lofty interest rates and promised profits. Blinded by greed, the weak thrifts hoped to grow out of their problems by putting more lucrative loans on their books.

Gary Roth said selling the loans to others was easy. Loan brokers made fortunes peddling the deals. Gipp Dupree, a Dallas loan broker, said he made more than $1 million in fees through deals he negotiated for Vernon in December 1985 alone. Roth said people working for other thrifts almost volunteered to buy the packages.

Sometimes Vernon officials used the California approach: "Let's say someone from a savings and loan in the Midwest or the East got invited out here to look at the deals," said Roth. "You'd take him to dinner at a restaurant with an ocean view. Back home it's winter; out here the weather is perfect. He'd look out the window at the surf pounding the beach and he'd talk about how nice it would be if he could work out here. You'd smile a lot and say, 'Let's talk about these loans,' and he'd buy them."

On other occasions, Vernon used the Dallas approach: "You'd get some guy from Hutchinson, Kansas, down here," said a former high-ranking officer at Vernon.

> We had this gal workin' here, you know. We called her Rowdy. God, she was beautiful. She was tall, blond, absolutely gorgeous. When she first came to work, Woody called her in. He wrote this note on a piece of paper and folded it and told her to take it on in to Don. She came walkin' in Dixon's office when we were havin' this meetin'. The conversation just stopped dead and we all watched her when she came walkin' in across the room and handed the note to Dixon. He opened it up and smiled. It said, "Eat your heart out." When these guys from Hutchinson, Kansas, came to town, we'd have Rowdy take 'em out for a night on the town in a limo. She'd wine and dine 'em. Nothin' else would go on. She'd just pour 'em into their rooms that night. The next day they'd go home with a bunch of loans.

Another regulation enacted by the bank board accelerated the spread of the disease; it required heavier investment in residential mortgages if an S&L wanted to retain its tax advantages. One top Vernon officer recalled:

> A lot of Vernon's apartment and condo loans qualified as residential investments. Suddenly there was a big market for these loans from other S&Ls. We were always scrambling to stay under the growth regulations. So we had the desire to sell. They wanted to keep their tax breaks. So they had the desire to buy. We got to the point where at the end of a quarter, I would get on a plane and fly to Kansas City to get some loans off the books by the end of the day. The trouble was we sold off our best stuff, and the more we sold, the more we were left with the junk that nobody wanted to buy. Eventually we lost credibility in the market.

Even Dixon could see that the participation loophole only provided a temporary respite from the regulations, though. If the economy didn't turn around soon, he knew he faced real trouble. Meanwhile, Gray was also seeking more money from the Congress to recapitalize the insurance fund, and that would spell disaster for Vernon and dozens of other high-flying thrifts. Gray was already mad at the way the highfliers in Texas had thumbed their noses at him. No one doubted what he would do if he got some additional resources. He'd use it to pay off their depositors and close them down once their problems were exposed.

Dixon was lucky in one respect. Gray had been able to overcome industry opposition to his new rules and regulations. But his legislative packages seeking more money for the insurance fund were opposed by the powerful U.S. League. Gray's initial proposals for raising the cash called for a one-percent fee on deposits. Another measure suggested that the FSLIC float a huge bond issue to raise the money. But both proposals had one critical ingredient that engendered fierce industry opposition: They required that recapitalization of the FSLIC be financed by the thrift industry, not the American taxpayer.

The U.S. League opposed the one-percent fee vehemently. "I really think that the bank board tried to anticipate the worst scenario," the League's O'Connell told reporters at the time. "We have to be careful that we don't do anything to impose additional costs on those institutions that are struggling to make it." He announced the League's opposition almost immediately. Behind the scenes, the League also opposed a developing administration plan to float a $15-billion bond issue to be repaid by a continuation of the special assessments Gray had already imposed on the industry.

Gray had a few supporters on Capitol Hill, such as Rep. Henry Gonzalez, a maverick Texas Democrat, and an Iowa Republican congressman named Jim Leach. But most members of the House Banking Committee took their lead from the powerful U.S. League. If Dixon and his cohorts simply joined the opposition, they could at least stop Ed Gray. And if Gray couldn't get any money, he couldn't close any S&Ls. Vernon had to get involved in politics.

At first the political activities launched by Dixon seemed old hat for Malone, who was in charge of Vernon's government relations. Prior to joining Vernon, Malone had spent several years with the Texas League in Austin, where money mixes with politics as freely as bourbon blends with branch water. Vernon had also retained the services of his former boss at the Texas League, Curlee, who had set up a consulting company to advise about fifteen or twenty thrifts such as Vernon. Malone was Vernon's liaison to the organization.

Curlee had started off back in 1984 setting up regular meetings of his clients in Austin, Dallas, or Washington to discuss a common strategy to deal with bank board regulations. At times, the sessions were like a Hall of Fame of the Texas S&L crisis. Curlee's list of clients included the larger-than-life Texans who ran some of the fastest-growing S&Ls around. They were people who got things done, even if they had to bend a few rules along the way.

Dixon would sometimes attend the sessions. So would Stanley Adams, a mysterious hulk of a man who ran Lamar Savings Association, often worked into the early morning hours, and tooled around Austin in a Maserati. "There was nothing wrong with Stanley except he's crazy," said Curlee.

Adams had once applied with Bowman's office to open a branch on the moon. He even specified a location—Cayley Crater in the Sea of Tranquility. "What the hell," Adams told Bowman when they met to talk about the application, "they laughed at Da Vinci, too."

Curlee also represented Sunbelt Savings, a Dallas S&L run by Ed McBirney, who liked to watch kung-fu movies as he flew around the country on one of Sunbelt's seven planes. McBirney was renowned for his lavish parties. He once spent $1.3 million of the thrift's funds on Halloween and Christmas parties, including one at his home with a safari motif. Byron Harris, a Texas television journalist who reported extensively on the S&L crisis, captured the essence of the soiree in a story in *Texas Monthly*: "Hundreds of guests arrived at his palatial North Dallas home to find a feast of lion, antelope, and pheasant. In the backyard, smoke machines provided an eerie, supernatural fog. A magician performed feats of levitation while two huge disco singers, Two Tons of Fun, supplied the music." Competitors nicknamed McBirney's Sunbelt Savings "Gunbelt S&L."

Other Curlee clients included fast-track operators such as Harvey McLean, who had purchased Paris Savings and Loan in Paris, Texas. The savings and loans these men owned eventually would account for billions of dollars in losses to the deposit-insurance fund.

Curlee set up a Washington office to give the group a presence in the nation's capital. Initially, he said his clients tried to reason with Gray. But he soon discovered that he was involved in a clash of cultures. A hard-rock conservative and street-smart political operative, Curlee felt comfortable with the back-room politics of the Texas statehouse. Gray was the loquacious PR man from California who courted reporters and whispered in their ears. Curlee soon came to view Gray as an errand boy for the huge California savings and loans. Gray was equally skeptical about the Texans.

"We were forced to get involved in the politics," said Curlee. "We couldn't talk to Gray. He was one of these guys who you'd talk to and he'd blab everything to the press. He didn't have time to talk to us. He was too busy making speeches. We had nowhere else to go but to get involved in the politics."

Curlee recognized almost immediately that Washington was a company town. "Conventional thinking—not conventional wisdom—but conventional thinking dominates the place," said Curlee. "And where does conventional thinking come from—

from the staffs, the think tanks, the study groups, those kind of things. I figured it would take four years for an idea to gestate into conventional thinking. So you hire yourself a think tank and buy a study on what you want to do. It [the idea] gets into the agency, then to the staff, people start talking about it and it gets in the press, and then everyone thinks, 'Okay, that's it.' "

But an ideal opportunity to curry favor and get things done surfaced in the spring of 1985. Just after Reagan's landslide victory over Walter Mondale, Sen. Phil Gramm, a Texas Democrat-turned-Republican, urged Reagan to appoint Rep. Sam Hall, a Democrat in Texas's First Congressional District, to a federal judgeship. Gramm felt Reagan's popularity in Texas would help the GOP win an election to replace Hall in a district that had been represented by Democrats since Reconstruction. A victory could be hailed as the first step in a major party realignment in the New South.

The Democratic leadership rightly considered the ploy a major challenge to its long-standing dominance in the House. Hall's district was in the backyard of House Majority Leader James Wright, a Fort Worth Democrat and prime candidate as the next Speaker of the House. He wasn't about to be humiliated by some Democratic turncoat. A bitter and hard-fought campaign ensued as both parties started hitting contributors with deep pockets to finance their efforts.

On the Democratic side, Rep. Tony Coelho of California ran the show. Tough, aggressive, and smart, Coelho was one of Congress's Young Turks. He had seen Republicans and President Reagan rack up astonishing gains at the polls because of their ability to raise huge amounts of campaign money from businessmen. Unwilling to cede these contributions to Republicans, Coelho launched a determined drive to provide a Democratic alternative to the Reagan touch. He took over the Democratic Congressional Campaign Committee—a traditional stepping-stone to power in the House—in 1982 when it was $300,000 in debt and had raised less than $2 million in the last election cycle.

A politician with a fierce and partisan personality, Coelho believed in the infamous statement of Jesse Unruh, a former speaker of the California Assembly: Money is the mother's milk of politics. He raised more than $6 million in his first term as the DCCC chairman, mainly by making it clear to businessmen that Democrats—and not Republicans—controlled the U.S. House of Representatives. Coelho's finance committee chairman was Tom Gaubert, the former power behind Independent American Savings of Irving, Texas, a friend of Dixon's and no friend of the Federal Home Loan Bank Board. Soon Curlee and his clients heard about the political facts of life from Coelho.

"Coelho was a master," said Curlee. "He'd never make a promise. On business issues, he told us most Democrats are neither liberals or conservatives. He said we'd find out in D.C. that we'd have our biggest problems fighting big business. They're all Republicans. He said we'd get more help from Democrats because they are for medium-size businesses. It made a lot of sense and it worked."

Gaubert set up the East Texas First Political Action Committee. "Actually I set it up before we even had a Democratic candidate in the First District race," he said. "I started raising money for whoever would run because I figured we would need it. By the time the primary was over, we didn't have much time."

Encourged by Coelho and enlisted by Gaubert, S&L operators such as Dixon poured thousands of dollars into the First District campaign on behalf of the Democrats. Employees at Vernon were soon writing checks to the East Texas First PAC. One day John Hill looked up from his desk and saw Malone there with his hand out. "He wanted a thousand-dollar political contribution for a political action committee known as East Texas First." Hill knew nothing about East Texas First but gave Malone $1,000 anyway.

The campaign wasn't limited to Vernon Savings. When David Farmer went to work as a senior vice president and chief financial officer at Commodore Savings, another Curlee client, he was told he would receive a premium above his starting salary and that he was expected to contribute the premium to a political action committee. That was illegal.

Farmer, too, soon heard of the East Texas First PAC. One day he said he was talking with John Harrell in the Commodore president's office when the subject of the East Texas First PAC contributions came up.

> I was told there was a piece of legislation pending
> in Congress that was detrimental to the S&L industry in
> the state of Texas. And that there were ten savings and

loans in the state contributing equal twenty-five-thou-
sand-dollar amounts for a total of two hundred fifty
thousand dollars specifically to this East Texas First
PAC. In return, I was told, Jim Wright guaranteed that
the legislation would not get out of committee. I remember John and I discussing it, and we both were somewhat
amazed at the process. But we guessed that if anyone
could keep a bill locked up in a committee, it would be
the future Speaker of the House.

The June 1985 conversation related by Farmer came three
months after Gray had asked for congressional approval of his
hotly contested proposal to inject $8.5 billion into the deposit-
insurance fund before a House Appropriations subcommittee
and just months before he floated the idea of a bond issue. By
August, though, the special election occurred and the S&L executives could breathe a little easier; their man—and Wright's—
had won.

Jim Chapman, a conservative Democrat and former prosecutor, narrowly won the seat in Texas's First Congressional
district in a multimillion-dollar race that had attracted national
attention. The East Texas First PAC had contributed just over
$100,000 to Chapman's race. Included in the contributions was
a $1,000 check to East Texas First from Mrs. Robert H. Hopkins,
the wife of Commodore's chairman. She had written Jim Wright's
name in the bottom left-hand corner of her check. But Gaubert
insisted that the contributions were not linked to any promises
by Wright.

Back in Washington, Gray continued to push for his legislation, arguing that the deposit-insurance fund would soon be
broke. But the bill would become tied up in the House Banking
Committee. No legislation of any kind would emerge for months.
Meanwhile, Gray's drive to require higher capital standards for
the industry and his hiring of additional examiners made powerful enemies in the industry and in the Reagan administration.
News stories obviously leaked by Regan and his minions at the
Treasury Department soon appeared in major papers such as the
Wall Street Journal and the *Los Angeles Times* suggesting that
Gray would soon step down because of industry opposition to
his FSLIC recapitalization proposal. The stories were obviously
designed to undermine Gray. The Texas industry didn't even

bother to cloak its feelings in anonymity. When asked in October 1985 about rumors that Gray might be among several senior staff members leaving the bank board, Tom King, the executive vice president of the Texas League of Savings and Loan Associations, said he thought that Gray's departure wouldn't be all bad. "Personally I think the priorities Ed Gray has set are not in the best interest of FSLIC. Maybe it's time for someone to come in and restructure those priorities," he told the *American Banker*. Gray was furious, particularly with the leaks sprung by Regan, who had not forgotten the bank board chairman's efforts to limit brokered deposits.

By year-end 1985, it was obvious that Gray was vulnerable. S&L operators across the political spectrum started complaining about him. Charles Keating, a well-known and politically influential Arizona developer who ran a California thrift, engaged Gray and the bank board in a nasty public fight over new regulations. Back in Dallas, Dixon intensified his efforts to raise money for politicians perceived as friends of thrifts like Vernon, and by extension, enemies of Gray. At first he tried the legal way—through a political action committee or PAC that Vernon had set up. After a few months, though, Vernon's employees had voluntarily contributed a measly $10,000 to the PAC. Federal laws limited individual contributions to $1,000 per candidate per election, PACs to $5,000, and total spending to $25,000 per election. That wouldn't do at Vernon Savings. So Dixon called Malone in and told him to raise the money from officers who could recoup the contributions on their expense accounts.

Malone felt uneasy about his conversation with Dixon. He had come to work at Vernon Savings in the summer of 1984. Most of the time, Dixon had been a dream boss—the kind of guy who would send key employees a liter of Dom Pérignon for Christmas. After going to work at Vernon, Malone enjoyed a six-figure income at an S&L that had become the talk of the industry.

But Malone also knew that Dixon could be harsh with people who gave him the wrong answers. When Rick Ramsey— a man with seniority, rank, and long-standing ties to Dixon— insisted that the Drippie projects be written down, Dixon got rid of him. So much for seniority, rank, and loyalty to an old friend. When things took a bad turn with Herman Beebe, Dixon shoved his mentor out of the picture, too. When the company's outside auditors challenged his optimistic condo-project forecasts,

Dixon showed them he could teach Julia Child a thing or two when it came to cooking the books. If Dixon asked an employee to do something, he didn't want to hear that it couldn't be done. "If you complained to Don about something, he'd tell you, 'If it were easy, I'd get a Girl Scout to do it. You go get it done. That's what you are paid for.' He didn't want to hear about your problems," said one former Vernon executive.

Malone wasn't disturbed that Dixon had asked him to solicit Vernon officers for political contributions. He'd already done that. But he felt queasy about the second part of Dixon's message: "He told me to tell the officers that they could expense it, if need be." Creating fake expense accounts to cover political contributions was illegal and Malone knew it: "I knew what Don said was wrong and I knew that he wanted the money." Malone didn't say yes or no; he simply went out and did the dirty deed, no questions asked. To refuse Dixon's request would have been suicidal to his career and six-figure income: "The alternative was not inviting. I was subject to becoming one of the outcasts or perhaps losing my position at Vernon. Don wanted the political contributions collected and I was going to go and collect them."

Employees soon came to dread Malone's visits. Dixon didn't ask Malone to do something he wouldn't do. Dixon pitched in to help raise the money, too. One day Malone would show up asking for money. The next time it would be Dixon. After Malone hit him up for $1,000, Hill recalled Dixon showed up. "Don came in and told me to give him a check for four hundred dollars for Martin Frost. And when I said, 'Who's Martin Frost?' he said, 'He's a congressman friendly to the S&L industry. Get it back out of your expense account.' "

Dixon didn't limit the political footsie to Democrats. Republicans were involved, too. One day Malone approached Roy Dickey, who had been made a vice president in the Dallas office by then, and asked for $500 for Sen. Jake Garn, a Utah Republican who was chairman of the Senate Banking Committee at the time. "Pat said Don was raising more money and needed me to contribute." A month later, Pat King, Vernon's president, solicited Dickey for another $500—this time for Senator Alan Cranston, a California Democrat on the Senate Banking Committee. When Dickey asked about being reimbursed for the donations, he was told to expense it.

The campaign contributions bought access to some powerful people. One day Dixon wandered into Hill's office with a guest— Tom Loeffler, the former Republican congressman who had just lost a bid to become the governor of Texas.

"He introduced me and said Tom was going to be assisting us in our legislative liaison. He left and then came back shortly thereafter without Loeffler and asked me for a check for a thousand dollars.

" 'Jesus, Don, you know this is adding up,' I said. Dixon replied, 'Well, you can get it back.' "

Malone later provided a more compelling reason for the Loeffler contribution:

> Don told me that Mr. Loeffler had told him that if we could get some people to attend a luncheon, Tom Loeffler would bring Treasury Secretary Jim Baker to Dallas to make an appearance and create a forum for some S&L executives to talk with him about industry problems. I think that the fact that he could bring Mr. Baker sort of denoted a premium on that particular luncheon. And Mr. Loeffler definitely needed all the help he could get in paying off his gubernatorial expenses.

16 Garden City

J oy Love was worried about the weather. Blair Davis looked across the small table. It was unbelievable. He'd been sent to Jason's to have lunch with this woman, talk to her about spending the weekend in Kansas with a bunch of strange men. All she could talk about was what she would wear. None of those "Tell me about this trip" or "What's expected of me and my friends?" kind of questions. She was worried it would be cold in Garden City; that she would need some warm clothes. But Blair knew Joy wouldn't be getting cold. Neither would her friends. Joy was a smart girl; she knew why she was going pheasant hunting without a gun. Davis concluded she was just trying to hit him up for some more money. He wouldn't fall for it.

It was February 1986, and Davis, a twenty-seven-year-old native of a small west Texas town named Floydada, had worked at Vernon's Dallas office as an associate loan underwriter for only a few months. It was like no place he'd ever seen. The thrift clearly had political problems. Financial troubles seemed likely, too. But nothing seemed to stop the fun. Soon after he had signed on, his boss, John Hill, called him in and outlined some duties that weren't in the job description. The next thing Davis knew, he and Hill were heading down Greenville Avenue in Dallas. Hill pulled into the parking lot of a windowless, two-story building with a metal plaque near the door offering a $100,000

173

reward for information on a local murder. The victim was the former owner of the place. What an epitaph; what a place—they didn't have anything like the Million Dollar Saloon in Floydada.

Green, red, blue, and orange lights seemed to streak through neon tubes and dart across the flat-black ceiling, reflecting off the mirrored walls. On the right night, the Lady in Leather would dance through plumes of smoke and pulsating strobes, thrusting her firm, bare breasts toward an audience of plump little men in golf hats and cowboys in Stetsons. Her voice would moan the lewd lyrics of her song, "Dr. Longjohn," a suggestive ditty about a dentist who used his drill to fill a cavity. There was a homogeneous quality to the dancers who performed on the three stages and two bars; all were white, most had long blond hair. You'd swear they were mannequins, except for the sinuous, lusty twists their bodies took to the honky-tonk tunes. Their bosoms had been enhanced by silicone into firm, round, sculptured breasts that had the natural beauty of a plastic rose. Some would smile as they danced; some closed their eyes; some would stare at customers. Some would just stand at the bar talking about things like their bowling scores.

Hill's contact at the saloon was Valerie, a waitress who wasn't much of a looker. He had met her on an earlier sojourn down Greenville Avenue searching for women to take a trip or to attend parties with Vernon executives. Hill described the process as if he were hiring girl Fridays:

> The procedure was for me to go to the Million Dollar Saloon and contact one or more of the waitresses that I had become acquainted with. Initially, I worked with Valerie. I would ask if she or one of the dancers would like to go either to a dinner party or on a trip to Florida. Then she'd ask around and recruit the girls that wanted to go. I usually compensated them on the order of a hundred dollars a day for missing work. If they had special expenses like baby-sitting or something like that, normally we added that to their compensation.

By late 1985, though, Hill had become terribly busy with other chores at Vernon. He'd been promoted and needed someone he could trust to take over the duties of Vernon's social director. He turned to Davis, the young underwriter who had just been hired. He was perfect for the job. Tall and lanky with short blond hair and a boyish look, the well-spoken Davis came off as a clean-cut kid from west Texas, not the kind who looked as if he would cavort with dancers who did more than the two-step.

Davis took to the job like a real pro. Once Hill introduced him to Valerie, Davis's first test-run went as smoothly as a Drippie deal. In mid-December, Hill called Davis into his office, gave him a few thousand dollars in cash, and told him to set up a party at a local hotel for Dixon and some other Vernon executives. Davis promptly headed for a rendezvous with Valerie and hired eight girls for a party that night at the Sheraton Park Central, where he had booked two rooms.

About six P.M., a stretch limousine carrying Davis pulled into the parking lot of the Million Dollar Saloon and picked up the eight girls. Davis thought of everything. He had the driver stop at the Sound Warehouse for a stereo and some cassette tapes. Dancers needed good music. He stopped at Centennial Liquor, where he got a good price for some booze. Then he told the limo driver to head for the Sheraton:

"Hill had indicated I should go to the hotel, set up the liquor, and make sure everyone was comfortable and had a drink. When Hill and some other men showed up at the party, John requested that I leave." Davis then departed without asking any questions. A few days later Hill called Davis in and told him he had passed muster. The thing had gone off without a hitch. Hill told Davis to cover the cost of the bash by putting it on his expense account. Vernon Savings would pay for the party, and Davis would have plenty of future opportunities for repeat performances.

Actually, Vernon could ill afford the fun by then. The thrift was getting hit with one potential disaster after another. The most devastating was a collapse in oil prices triggered by developments in a faraway land. Iran had opened its oil spigots to earn revenue so it could finance its war with neighboring Iraq. The Iranian decision backfired, though; it prompted OPEC's largest oil supplier, Saudi Arabia, to increase production, too. The Saudis had sided with the Iraqis in the war. By increasing production, the Saudis flooded the market and prices plunged, depriving the Iranians of easy revenue. The huge stores of oil flowing out of the Middle East sent prices sharply downward in Texas, too. Between 1985 and 1986, oil prices fell 50 percent to

$12 per barrel. Texas's oil-based economy was devastated just as hundreds of new office buildings were coming onto the sales market.

In Washington, the situation wasn't much better. The FSLIC was rapidly sliding toward financial disaster, forcing the Congress to take up legislation that would give federal regulators some money to close sick savings and loans. Federal and state examiners were already crawling all over Vernon Savings. And Roy Green, Gray's handpicked head of the Dallas Federal Home Loan Bank, had made it clear he meant business. Rumor had it he was in the market for a new enforcement chief to spearhead a crackdown on Texas S&Ls once regulators got more money from Capitol Hill.

Some of Vernon's most immediate problems surfaced out in California. In late 1985, Greg McCormick had been ordered to report back to Dallas from Florida. "I first met with Ray Jeter when I got back, and he said I was going to stay there until I lost my tan or got as white as everyone else." Dixon was trying to honor his agreements with the Drippie borrowers. An attempt to sell the money-losing condos through a tax-sheltered real estate syndication scheme had fallen through, and Dixon was trying to get Doug Manchester in San Diego to help him dump the projects.

McCormick soon found himself knee-deep in the paperwork for a Dixon-Manchester deal. The upshot was that a Vernon subsidiary would invest $20 million in Transwest—a Manchester partnership—and it would then help dispose of the money-losing condo projects by capitalizing on the tax benefits they could bestow on well-heeled investors. It was a typical Dixon, convoluted deal. Transwest would take the projects off the hands of the Drippie borrowers at prices that would allow McLean, Riddle, and the others to repay their loans to Vernon and get the Drippie deals off the thrift's books. Accountants were supposed to paper the whole deal as a legit transaction and fool the examiners by portraying the money shuffles as a Vernon investment in California.

Midway through the complex negotiations, though, lawyers for Harvey McLean and several other Drippie borrowers got suspicious. "They were starting to raise questions like 'Who is Transwest?' and 'What is this mirror game that is being played?' " said McCormick. Some of the Drippie borrowers wanted indemnity agreements absolving them from any liability if Transwest failed, if the Dondi Group failed, or even if the unspeakable happened and Vernon Savings failed.

But Vernon couldn't really indemnify anyone; a letter to that effect would expose the thrift's continuing involvement in the deals and negate the transactions that had been used to fool Vernon's auditors. McCormick was instructed to have a local law firm prepare a "very blanket, plain vanilla indemnity letter" that could be given to a Drippie investor who wanted indemnity agreements. The letter was sent to several Drippie investors, including Riddle and McLean.

"Riddle's attorney came back with a red-lined copy with more of his pencil-writing than there were typewritten words on the indemnity, trying to fully protect Mr. Riddle's interest. I don't think it was ever executed to his satisfaction," said McCormick. "McLean drafted one that was sent to me that was not even for a corporate indemnification by either Dondi Group or Vernon or Transwest. It was a personal indemnification to be executed by Woody Lemons. When confronted with that, Woody laughed and said, 'There's no way. You guys are crazy.' "

The letters were really a ruse, though. McCormick said John Smith, Vernon's president, gave him instructions that under no circumstances would true indemnities be given. "I think, and I can't be certain, that possibly two got out, and they were referred to as 'bottom desk drawer, deep-freeze letters' where the assurance was given that unless there's ten ticks of the clock till the world ends, we won't bring this letter out."

But the paper game didn't work. Vernon's auditors balked at the deal, and Manchester backed out at the last minute when Vernon failed to send him the paperwork and documentation he wanted. Vernon and Dixon remained honor bound to help out the old Drippie investors just as state and federal regulators started combing through the thrift's records with unusual zeal.

In many businesses, such doings might cause heads to fall, sweeping corporate reorganizations, or budget cuts. At Vernon Savings, they just had another party. Davis got another call summoning him to Hill's office. Linn Bowman's examiners had issued a nasty letter to Vernon's board, criticizing the thrift for shoddy loans. Dixon had decided that the commissioner needed another hunting trip—this one with some female companionship. King issued an invitation to his old friend, and Bowman,

the Sherlock Holmes of the savings and loan set, figured that
duty called. When Blair Davis arrived in Hill's office, he got his
orders: Help Pat Malone line up some girls for a pheasant-
hunting trip to Kansas.

The trip to the Million Dollar Saloon was a maiden voyage
for Malone. "It was the first and only time I have ever been
there," he said. Davis introduced him to Valerie and they hired
girls to accompany Malone, Woody Lemons, Pat King, Dixon,
and Linn Bowman to Kansas.

Like everything else that was happening, the trip didn't
come off too well. Davis gave Malone $1,500 for the trip, picked
up the girls in a limo, and took them to Love Field in Dallas,
where they boarded a Kitty Hawk Airlines charter flight for
Garden City, Kansas. The flight went well. When the girls landed
in Kansas, they wrote "Good flight!" on the manifest and com-
plimented the pilot, adding: "Bobby is a super guy." But things
deteriorated after that. Malone recalled the frustrations of the
trip:

> Hill told me I was to pass out funds to these women
> that would be coming on this trip. He told me to just
> pass it out a little bit at a time to the women when they
> were there in Kansas. Lemons, King, I, and Dixon, I
> think, flew to Austin, picked up Bowman, and then flew
> directly to Garden City, Kansas. Later on in the evening,
> the ladies arrived. The room configuration was that
> everybody stayed at the Wheatlands Motor Inn, and
> there was a room that was sort of a hospitality suite in
> the middle where we had drinks before going to dinner
> that night. We came back and stayed long into the night
> in the hospitality room.

Once the evening had ended, Malone's escort said she was
sick. It must have been the mountain air. So Dixon, Bowman,
and Lemons went off with their escorts and Malone's room
doubled as a sick ward. The next day, Malone learned that he
wasn't the only one who had had a bad night. During the
pheasant hunt, Lemons and King complained about one of the
girls. "As I recall the conversation," Malone said, "Mr. King and
Mr. Lemons said to me, 'Don't pay that woman any more money.'

Mr. Lemons appeared more annoyed than Mr. King." But Malone had already parceled out the entire $1,500.

The girls were still around the next day when everyone sat down for dinner. But the same girl who had been sick the night before became ill again. Soon the boys learned the disease was spreading. "The woman who was with Mr. Lemons the evening before went with the woman that was ill. I slept in the hospitality room," said Malone. The next day, the boys went hunting, and the girls went back to Dallas. When Pat Malone returned to Vernon's offices on Monday, he had a call from Blair Davis. It was unbelievable! "Blair told me that the women on the trip felt like there was a problem; that they were not paid a sufficient amount of money."

Not one to be discouraged by a little bad luck, Hill scheduled another hunting trip about a week later—this time without that snoop Bowman. John Hill would show them how to have some fun. A large group of Vernon executives, including Hill, would make the trip, and no one wanted anything to go wrong. There would be none of those Million Dollar Saloon girls, either. Hill had personally selected Joy Love to take care of the girls on this trip.

Hill had instructed Davis to meet Joy for lunch. He had even picked the restaurant—Jason's. Although Joy was a familiar name to several executives at Vernon, it was the first time Davis had ever seen her. She was a pro—no doubt about that. Slender with light brown hair that came down to her shoulders, she appeared in her late twenties or early thirties. She was a local girl who spoke with a drawl and stood about five foot six. To those who bothered to notice, she was pretty. But her most dominant feature was her body, and her most pronounced skill was the way she used it. She wasn't named Joy because she posed for Christmas cards.

Joy wasn't the only girl who would make the trip. Davis met her for lunch to iron out the details of transporting Joy and a group of her friends to Garden City. Lunch lasted about one hour and they had a pretty businesslike discussion. Both knew why they were there and there wasn't much small talk. The girls would meet at the Addison airport and be flown to Garden City aboard a charter.

"We discussed when we would get together and where I

would meet," said Davis. The next day Davis looked like a tour guide leading the escorts to the airport in Addison: "They actually all had their own cars, or they were carpooling with one another. I escorted them in my car over to Aviall Aviation where they would board the plane." Joy was a good businesswoman; she wanted the cash for the trip up-front. After Davis gave it to her, though, he panicked. The other girls that emerged from the cars weren't what he was expecting.

"Mr. Hill had been accustomed to girls who were professional dancers. These girls were ordinary working girls. They weren't unattractive. But the other girls had been outstanding in terms of physical attributes, and I felt like John might have some objections."

Davis quietly found a telephone and dialed the number of the hotel in Garden City so he could talk with Hill, who had already flown to Kansas with several other Vernon executives. "Mike Maples, who was an accountant at Vernon, picked up the phone in Garden City and then I spoke to John shortly after that."

"We've got a problem," said Davis as he described the physical attributes of the working girls whom Joy had lined up. But Hill told him not to worry: "He said something like just cull the herd." Unfortunately, this trip didn't go much better than the prior one, though. Davis later learned that weeding the less statuesque girls from the group was just the beginning of the problems. A number of the girls just didn't get it. They thought they were going to Kansas for the ambience—you know, stay at the hotel, have some nice meals, check out the French restaurant in Sublette. It wasn't the kind of reaction the boys from Vernon expected. The hunting trips were supposed to be like Texas toga parties—not a safari.

"I remember how we would come in there to the airport in Vernon's planes," said a former Vernon executive who made the trip.

We went there for some hunting. We all wore those camouflage hunting clothes and had our guns out. We must have looked like the contras. But we went there to have some fun, too. That particular trip Charlie Bazarian went along. He was big, fat, and disgusting—weighed about three hundred pounds. I'll never forget seeing him standing in front of Vernon's office in Dallas wearing all the hunting clothes he had just bought, sweating like hell and holding a shotgun in his hand. He wasn't going to Kansas to go hunting. I can tell you that.

Once some of the girls figured out that the guys had more than pheasants on their minds, a few became angry and stalked off on their own like spoilsports. They said there had been a "failure of communication" and sulked in the bar or restaurant or sat around by themselves for most of the weekend. The Vernon bunch couldn't believe it. A "failure of communication?" Where did they think they were—divorce court?

Davis got a rash of complaints when the hunters returned to Dallas. But by that time, a lonely weekend was the least of their worries. Federal regulators had descended on Vernon in force, poking through everything from loan ledgers to expense accounts. If they unearthed some of the expense accounts used to cover hunting trips, political fund-raisers, and late-night parties, the fallout would be as bad as the experiences themselves.

Hill had told Davis to recover any of his own money he had spent by creating false entries on his expense account. If Davis had used $200 of his own money to hire girls, he was supposed to hide the outlay in his expense account by charging Vernon for meals he never ate or for personal expenses that he simply billed to the thrift.

But the Vernon executives had spent so much money on political contributions and prostitutes, it was hard to come up with enough bogus receipts. Money that Davis had spent hiring girls for the party at the Sheraton showed up on his expense report as outlays at Wolff Nursery or Keller Feeds.

Hill was even more daring. His expense accounts included relatively large outlays at the C&S Hardware in Dallas, where Hill purchased hammers, pliers, and lawn equipment he needed around his house. No one seemed to check them too carefully. At one point he submitted an expense account claiming a $192 reimbursement for a Weed Eater. Sometimes even Hill was embarrassed at the claims. "I had one expense voucher that I was bringing to Pat King for approval. It was a particularly large one. I don't recall the amount. It was over five thousand dollars. And

I said, 'Don't look at that too close. Remember, it's got some politicians in there.' He indicated that he understood."

Some of the guys had complained to Dixon, but he wasn't too sympathetic. After Dixon had asked Hill for $1,000 for the Loeffler campaign in early 1986, Hill said he complained that the checks to the politicians and girls were adding up. Dixon replied that he could charge everything to his expense account, but Hill responded, "I'm out thousands of dollars. Is there some way you can figure out to do something different to reimburse me? Can you give me a bonus—something? He said check with John Smith."

Malone gave people some pointers. When Ray Jeter, an asset manager at Vernon, started complaining about the burden of the contributions, Malone told him to use his imagination. "He used an example that there were several bars in the office. If I chose to restock my liquor cabinet at home, I could just keep the ticket and put on there that it was for restocking the bar in my department." When Jeter took up the matter with King, he had a similar reply:

"Pat Malone's briefcase."

Jeter said he got the message. "From that, I gathered certain implications. Mr. Malone had a very unusual briefcase that was made of exotic skins, an attaché-type case. I was in need of a larger briefcase because of the traveling I was doing. So I purchased another quite expensive briefcase."

Davis at one point filed an honest expense report. The reaction wasn't too good, though. Pat King stalked into a meeting between Jeter and Hill carrying one of Davis's expense vouchers, and Jeter recalls: "As he came in the door, he said, 'One of you two need to get your boy under control and explain the rules to him. John and I looked quizzically at each other, and King said, 'Blair Davis. Tell him I didn't literally mean put broads on his expense account.' John turned to me and said, 'Handle it.' And Pat started to hand me the expense account and John said, 'No, I will.'"

King didn't take it personally, though. A few weeks later, Davis said he got a call from King summoning him to the Vernon president's office. Once Davis entered, he said, King shut the door and asked him to get two girls to serve as dinner companions for himself and a friend. Davis said he complied. It was the same old drill—the girls got picked up in a limo and taken to a Sheraton near the Dallas–Fort Worth airport. "We walked in and looked at the sunken area, which had a bar off to one side. And we sat down and had a drink. We were there a short while, maybe five or ten minutes, and Pat King came walking up to us. I introduced him to the young ladies, and he said his friend, Mr. Bowman, was waiting in the other room."

17 The Alamo

R.B. Tanner caught him off guard. Dixon had no warning that Tanner would march unannounced into his office in May 1986 with wife, family, and lawyer in tow. Don looked different from the last time Tanner had seen him: "He had a blue-and-white-striped cotton shirt on with the collar open. He didn't have that leather vest or a Western shirt. When he saw us, he said, 'I must have done something to get the whole family after me.'"

Just months before, Tanner's son, Ray, who had become a savings and loan examiner for the state of Texas, had phoned his father to tell him about State Savings and Loan, a Lubbock thrift owned by Dixon's friend Terry Barker. Young Tanner went into State Savings to examine the books and was stunned. He called R.B. to tell him about the extent of the problems and to seek some advice. Tanner told his son to report everything to federal officials immediately. Once the conversation ended, though, Tanner thought about his son's tale of rapid growth, risky loans, and huge potential losses at State Savings; it sounded a lot like the rumors he had heard about Vernon Savings in recent months. He was worried: Dixon still owed Tanner and his family around $2 million on the notes they had taken as payment when they sold the thrift in 1981. The notes accounted for more than half of the sales proceeds. He decided he'd better deal with the situation in the good old Texas way—an eyeball-to-eyeball confrontation.

Tanner stopped just short of Dixon's desk and got a good fix on his eyes. He spoke bluntly: "Don, we know your planes have been leaving the airport pretty often for Europe. Are you taking money out of the country?" At first, Dixon didn't utter a word. He didn't blink or seem at all shocked by the question. Then he leaned back in his chair and put his hands behind his head. Everyone noticed the large circles of sweat that darkened his blue-and-white shirt under the arms. But his voice was calm; he flatly denied that anything was wrong and reassured the Tanners that they would be paid around $2 million that Dondi Financial Corp. owed them. The notes were personally guaranteed by Don R. Dixon and this was Texas, where a look in the eye was better than a lawyer and a handshake better than a judge.

The meeting was over almost as quickly as it had started. Tanner had gone into Vernon's offices with an uneasy feeling in his guts about Dixon. R.B. had spent a lifetime approving loans to all sorts of people; he had never failed to spot a liar or a fraud. But Dixon had looked Tanner square in the eye and guaranteed that he would be repaid. For one of the few times in his life, Tanner ignored his instincts. He dismissed his doubts. But Tanner had overlooked one thing: In the past, he had had more information about the people with whom he was dealing. This time it was different.

By the spring of 1986, the savings and loan system that Tanner had supported so strongly over a lifetime was working against him, the regulators, and the rest of the American public. Even under the best of circumstances, the official doings inside a savings and loan or a bank were secretive business. Depression-era bank runs had sunk hundreds of banks once depositors suspected financial troubles. Federal laws enacted after the debacle cloaked the nation's financial system in secrecy to prevent a repeat performance. Federal law prohibited regulators and examiners from discussing any elements of a bank exam, even after the institution had been closed. Even if board members knew what was going on in Vernon Savings, they weren't supposed to tell people like Tanner, even though the thrift's owners owed him a lot of money. Most of the directors at Vernon didn't seem to care enough to find out what was really going on anyway.

Tanner knew Vernon Savings was growing too fast; he told his wife that all the time. But he had no idea how bad things really were.

Tanner wasn't alone. Back in Washington, Ed Gray, the man responsible for regulating savings and loans for the federal government, didn't know much more than Tanner. Federal examiners had entered Vernon months before—for the first exam in two years. But their report wouldn't reach his desk until November 1986, which was several months away. Their record in dozens of other Texas S&Ls wasn't much better. The places were such a mess, and there were so many in trouble, that exams were taking forever. Thanks to his Washington staff, Gray had a general idea that big trouble loomed on the horizon; he constantly warned almost anyone who would listen of an impending disaster. But no one wanted to hear it.

It was no wonder. At times, even Gray's supporters on his staff thought he had lost it. Tensions had increased between Gray and the industry. The U.S. League didn't like his running around the country telling everyone the industry's deposit-insurance fund was broke. Gray was expected to solve the problem, not complain about it. As the bad feelings intensified, Gray acted paranoid. He ordered guards stationed at the fifth-floor elevator of the Federal Home Loan Bank Board offices to stop intruders. He bickered endlessly over policy details with his two fellow board members, who were more sympathetic to the industry views.

At one point, he even locked his door and refused to admit Donald Hovde, a Wisconsin real estate developer and fellow board member, who was reduced to slipping notes to the chairman under the door. The other board member, Mary Grigsby, a Texas thrift executive with enduring ties to her home state, was so uncomfortable with her role that she jokingly donned a Groucho Marx disguise during a visit home. Gray spent most of his time endlessly going over his speeches and public statements; he seemed to be building a historical record so he wouldn't be blamed for the mess he envisioned. It didn't help when Durward Curlee and his clients leaked details of his antics to the press. The stories didn't exactly portray the image of confidence and stability that Tanner and others had come to expect of the nation's thrift regulators.

Even as Gray's examiners moved into Vernon for their exam,

they didn't know what to expect. Criticism leveled by the state examiners had seemed to shock the Vernon board members. But the thrift's managers had dismissed it as nit-picking. Yet the state had inadvertently stumbled across a startling disclosure—the percentage of loans classified as troubled by state examiners was four times as high as the percentage that Vernon had disclosed in routine reports to the federal government.

The federal regulators quickly concluded that Vernon was rife with potential conflicts of interest, dubious loans, inside deals, and risky investments. But examiners can't close savings and loans merely because they suspect problems. Federal laws require that they build a strong case. Unfortunately, though, the financial deregulation laws pushed by the Reagan administration and the Congress had changed all of the rules. Federal thrift examiners hadn't been trained to analyze Dixon's complex deals. Even if they had, deregulation had weakened rules so much that it was hard to determine exactly what was allowed and what wasn't. It would take time—months and months—to build a case. Meanwhile, Vernon Savings kept luring more government-insured deposits into its vaults.

Vernon's spectacular growth in deposits was no secret. Thrifts don't soar from $78 million in deposits to $1.3 billion in four years without attracting some attention. The regulators had made Vernon promise to limit its growth when the thrift signed its supervisory agreement in August 1984. It had quite obviously ignored the deal, for it had grown rapidly since then. But the real question was what Vernon had done with the depositors' money. If $1.3 billion in deposits had been invested in deals that were worth only $800 million, someone would have to figure out where the thrift could get $500 million to eventually repay depositors. As they began checking the loans and projects in which the deposits had been invested, Bill Churchill, Art Martin, and other federal examiners got a sinking feeling in their stomachs. Practically every loan that they looked at had some sort of a problem.

Part of the reason was the way Dixon and Vernon structured their loans. To maximize fee income, Vernon typically extended its loans for six months instead of a year so it could charge renewal fees twice a year instead of once. But that meant the loans rolled due faster and increased Vernon's default rate when borrowers were unable to pay off. A lot of the problems were due to more suspicious transactions. Vernon had lent $36.6 million in insured deposits to a developer who had used the money to acquire ninety-nine acres of land, including thirty-one acres under water. From most indications, it looked as if the only thing you could do with the land was park submarines. An appraiser said the ninety-nine acres were worth only $12 million. But Vernon had approved the $36-million loan assuming that the land would rise in value once the developer used it for a lake and a resort that would include 170 condominiums and a hotel. The $36-million loan earned Vernon huge fees. But it was like lending someone $300,000 on a house worth $100,000 and gambling that the thing would more than triple in value once it was remodeled.

The examiners concluded that some transactions were merely a subterfuge designed to inflate Vernon's earnings and support the huge dividends, bonuses, and salaries for Dixon and Vernon's officers. On December 31, 1985, for instance, Vernon sold 7.1 acres of foreclosed real estate to a company controlled by Harvey McLean's Paris Savings and Loan. The transaction generated a $2.8-million gain, which helped boost Vernon's profits to a level where it could justify dividends. But the loan included a key provision that said Vernon would repurchase the property later on. Two days after Vernon logged the profit generated by the loan, it declared a $1.6-million dividend to Dixon's Dondi Financial.

There were loans made to big Vernon borrowers who used the proceeds to make interest or principal payments on other Vernon loans. There were loans to ventures in which Dixon or some of his cronies had a financial interest. Examiners were particularly disturbed by Vernon's relationships with other savings and loans. Included in its loan portfolio was nearly $30 million in loans secured by the stock of other savings and loans, such as Sandia Federal Savings and Loan Association in New Mexico, where Dixon was a major borrower; Key Savings and Loan Association, which was controlled by Dixon's lawyer, Larry Vineyard; and McLean's Paris Savings and Loan and Shamrock Federal Savings and Loan in Shamrock, Texas. Sitting right before the examiners' eyes was the daisy chain that Dixon and the other owners used to purge their books of bum deals.

Equally disturbing were the slices of Vernon loans that had been sold to other thrifts, including some that were known to

have problems on their own. Vernon routinely collected payments from borrowers and passed the money on to the participating thrift. If the borrower didn't have the money, Vernon
would often make the payment for him and cover up the fact
that the loan was in default. Thus by moving against Vernon, the
examiners would jeopardize the loan income flowing to other
weak thrifts. They would risk creating even more severe problems for the cash-strapped FSLIC.

As new deposits flowed in and were shuffled around within
Vernon, the number of examiners grew. Vernon's board members
were puzzled. Not much had changed at the meetings in Vernon
boardrooms. According to the staff, Vernon's problems were
easing. In fact, at the January meeting, Larry Landrum, Vernon's
chief financial officer, told the board that in December 1985
alone, Vernon had a net profit of $3.1 million, an extremely good
month. Vernon had been criticized for relying too heavily on
brokered deposits, which still represented about 20 to 30 percent
of Vernon's deposits. But they were down from about 65 percent.
Vernon had been criticized for making too many acquisition and
development loans, but the regulators wouldn't detail what was
an acceptable level.

Yet the place was crawling with examiners. At one point,
twenty-three were there from both federal and state offices, and
the atmosphere was getting more hostile by the day. The examiners complained that high-ranking officers such as Lemons,
King, and Landrum were impeding their work, withholding
documents and giving the regulators a hard time. When directors
asked the examiners if they were finding anything wrong, they
got no answer. King told the other directors:

> Last year, if you'll recall, we had Mike Lee as the
> examiner in charge. Mike was a guy that would meet
> with you every day. He would tell you everything that
> he found that day that he didn't like. And I used to get
> so aggravated with him because I thought this guy
> doesn't like anything. He just loved to tell you about the
> things he didn't like. On the other hand, [this year] you
> have Art Martin, who will tell you absolutely nothing.
> I've sat right here in this room with him on numerous
> occasions over the last six, eight months, whatever it
> has been, and I'd ask him, 'Art, are you finding anything

wrong? Are there any problems?' And he'd tell me, no—
no problems. Everything going fine. And then—boom—
they drop a bomb on us. In retrospect, I'd prefer to deal
with someone like Mike Lee. At least you have no
doubts about where you stand.

Yvonne Robinson said she had asked Martin if he would
stay on Vernon's board were he a director; Martin replied that he
would because he thought Vernon was a very good association
and would work its way out of its problems. But another director
said he had an unusual phone call from Martin. "He called me
and asked me if I had any back copies of the minutes. I told him
I might have three or four. And he said, why don't you have
some more? I felt like he wanted to see if things had been
changed. That was what I first thought about—that he thinks
somebody had changed some of the minutes, left out a page or
something. I didn't think examiners were supposed to call the
board of directors."

The examiners were far more forthcoming to the bank board
offices. Gray went ballistic at the initial reports flowing in from
Vernon and other thrifts in Texas. The declining economy could
create a disaster. New regulations at the bank board revamped
the loan classification procedures. His supervisors' reports were
bleak. He wanted to discover the true dimensions of the problem
and see if he could limit the damage. He called a meeting of his
twelve regional bank presidents and asked ten of them to contribute some examiners to a force of 250 who would launch a six-
week examination blitz in Texas starting in March 1986.

Word of Gray's "get Texas squad" spread rapidly throughout
the state. S&L executives who had made honest mistakes in a
bad economy became as concerned as the unscrupulous operators. "They called them Gray's carpetbaggers," said Gray. The
idea of some examiner from Boston or Chicago poking his nose
into their thrifts was unsettling. What was Gray trying to do—
form a posse? None of this seemed to make any sense to them.
Gray didn't have enough money to shut down anyone. Congressional auditors at the General Accounting Office (GAO) had just
reported that the insurance fund needed a $22-billion injection
of capital. What would he do once he found out that a thrift had
problems? Shoot the owner? Opposition to Gray's legislative
initiatives spread throughout the industry and extended to S&L

lawyers, appraisers, real estate agents, and dozens of others, who started complaining to their congressmen about regulators.

By April, the examiners at Vernon had enough evidence of foul play to demand some changes. John Hill got a call from Richard Hewitt, Vernon's appraisal consultant who had just left the bank board to start his own firm after a decade as the government's top authority on appraisals. According to Hill, there was a note of hysteria in the voice of Hewitt, who had just heard some bad news from his former colleagues with the government: "He was quite alarmed. Richard told me he'd been contacted by the Federal Home Loan Bank Board and that they were going to start removal and prohibition actions against a number of Vernon officers."

The officials at Vernon weren't the only ones with worries. Hewitt, who was the author of the government's appraisal standards, had just started Hewitt, Olson, Smoker and Associates, Inc., a firm that was on its way to becoming a nationally known real estate appraiser. Vernon was one of its major clients. But Hill had put him in a potentially embarrassing situation just a month before. While in California at a real estate seminar, Hewitt, a car buff, had stopped by Vernon's classic-car subsidiary, Symbolic Motors, and had admired an older Corvette in the showroom. A few weeks later, after he'd returned to his home in Florida, Hewitt, who reviewed Vernon appraisals for accuracy, got a little present from his major client—a 1967 red Corvette that cost Vernon Savings $19,500. Hewitt said that he didn't think Hill or the others at Vernon were trying to compromise him. The gift, he said, came as a complete surprise.

"I was on a trip, and when I got home, there was this red Corvette in the driveway. It had a price—I forget what it was— written on the window in shoe polish or whatever it is that car dealers use. I asked my wife what it was doing there. She said she didn't know. She said some guy had come by with the car on a trailer and dropped it off. It sat there all weekend. The last thing I needed was another Corvette—I was already restoring one. When I went into my office on Monday, my secretary said that John Hill of Vernon Savings has called while I was gone and had asked for my home address."

Although Vernon's records clearly suggest that the car was to be a gift, Hewitt said he thought that Vernon officials were trying to get him to buy.

"We were a small firm and Vernon was a major client. We didn't want to lose their business. I even talked with my partners about it and said we have to buy a car to keep the business."

Eventually, he said, he gave the car back. But he also decided he had better do some damage control for his client before anyone started hauling Vernon officials before the bank board.

After the phone conversation, Hewitt and Hill showed up in Washington—fast. At the bank board offices near the White House, Hewitt conferred with the people who had informed him that several of Vernon's top officers were about to be canned. The message to the bank board staff was simple: Vernon would replace the officers voluntarily if the bank board backed off on a formal action.

Early the next week, Hill met with Dixon and King: "I told Dixon that the bank board wanted the resignations of Woody Lemons, Pat Malone, Pat King, and Larry Landrum, and if they didn't get the resignations, they were going to seek removal and prohibition. King advised Don not to capitulate."

Lemons wasn't surprised when Dixon summoned him to the beach house in Del Mar over the weekend. With the value of the real estate underlying Vernon's commercial-loan portfolio spiraling downward, everyone knew the end was near. King and Hill were there, too. Dixon told Woody that the regulators had criticized Vernon's philosophy of rapid growth and brokered deposits and that the four top officers, including Lemons, had to go. Hill took care of giving the bad news to Malone and Landrum.

On Monday, the staff got official confirmation of the news. Lemons and Malone would resign. The bank board had approved the plan; no removal and prohibition charges would be filed. Hewitt's intercession with his colleagues had paid off: The bank board had gone along with a proposal that Hill would replace King as Vernon's president. Hill later sat in on a meeting called to tell everyone he would be in charge. As he looked around the table, Malone heard his cryptic comment: "This is like the fox guarding the chicken house."

The directors were stunned when they got the news, particularly the word of Lemons's resignation. Although King resigned as president, he was allowed to replace Lemons as chairman of the board for a few months. He immediately tried to smooth things over after the regular business at the April 24 board meeting:

Woody told me in December that he was getting
ready to hang 'em up. He's been fighting this for ten to
twelve years. Quite honestly he was tired and he wanted
to put himself in a position that he wasn't on the
treadmill quite as fast. The second thing we need to
keep in mind is that Woody's not really going away. I
mean, he's still gonna be here and he's unofficially
gonna be involved and we're gonna be calling on him to
do things for us maybe on a consulting basis or whatever. So it's not like he's going away and we'll never
hear from him again. Pat Malone won't go away either.
He's going to work for Durward Curlee. I was a little bit
afraid that some of you that have been here as long as
you have might say if Woody's going to hang 'em up,
maybe I'm ready to hang' em up, too. You know it's
better than it was a year ago and it's gonna be better a
year from now, and I just think things will continue to
get better and better. I guess what I'm doing is that I'm
appealing to you all to hang in there and stay with us
because we need every one of you.

The directors at the meeting agreed that it was no time to do
anything radical. They decided to get Woody a plaque memori-
alizing his service to Vernon Savings. But they were troubled
about Vernon's lack of directors' liability insurance, which had
not been renewed when it expired, and by the bank board's move
to block the regular quarterly dividend. Another unsettling prospect was the meeting they were to have with federal regulators
in Dallas the following Wednesday. King warned them of a
change in atmosphere that had occurred because of some new
faces in the Dallas Federal Home Loan Bank:
"They said that Bill Churchill will be chairing the meeting,
and of course, you all know Bill. I think the thing I would like
you to be aware of is that if Walter Faulk is there, I just want to
prepare you because he is a new guy they brought in from
somewhere, and boy, he's a real sweetheart. He stands up and
yells and sways his arms in the air. And you know, I don't know
what this guy will do if he is there. He talks a whole lot but
doesn't say very much." The board was briefed that they'd
probably be told that Vernon had violated its supervisory agreement on twenty-seven counts, and that they might be asked to

sign a cease-and-desist order that would chastise the thrift. Hill said he would try to brief the board members before the meeting to tell them what would go on. "I think Dr. Hewitt will be there. I think they'll temper their remarks in front of him. We need to have our hand slapped and do what we need to do to correct their image of Vernon Savings. Probably the best way to do it is to stop making money, and that's a hell of a charge for a new president."

But the directors soon learned that the executive team had once again misread the situation. Churchill presented the board with a draft of a cease-and-desist order and told them there was no room for negotiation. "As you'll recall," King later told the board members, "he said what you see is what you get." But the C&D proposed by Churchill was watered down by Gray's staff in Washington. "After we appealed to the Washington level, there have been considerable changes made," King later told the board, adding, "Everything that is in the current proposed cease-and-desist order are things we can live with."

The demands from Selby's staff in Dallas kept coming as quickly as deposits flowed into Vernon, though. They demanded new lists of all Vernon subsidiaries and their officers or new conflict-of-interest policies that merely duplicated those that Vernon had already ignored. Regulators wanted things such as schedules of all loans made in 1984 and 1985 by type, by state, or any changes in ownership since the exam began. A move to establish a loan loss reserve, a bookkeeping entry that could lead to a declaration of insolvency and a government takeover, signaled that the end might be near. King resigned from the board and Dixon finally decided he had to do something.

He would say good-bye to Vernon's faithful in the hangar where he kept the jets. Raylan Loggins said the farewell was vintage Dixon:

It was in the summer of 1986 and it was hot as hell in the hangar. All employees got a memo to go to the hangar after work. They had all the planes taxied out. Two of Dixon's Rollses were parked in the next hangar over. Everybody went. There were about two hundred people there after work. At first Dixon wasn't there. They had a couple of bars set up and some hors d'oeuvres. We were all hot in suits and ties from work and no air-conditioning in the hangar. We went in and had a couple of drinks. Then Dixon showed up. They cleared out a circle in the center of the crowd. This was around seven or seven-thirty. Dixon was in the center of the circle with a microphone in his hand. He began walking around the circle talking and looking everyone in the face. He talked about the troubled state of the industry, the economy, the problems with the regulators at Vernon. He told us it would require a political solution. He would step down and go to Washington to launch a political drive to resolve the problems of the entire industry. He came off as selfless. Then he introduced everyone in the new ruling triumvirate. John Hill was drunk. He tried to give a speech, but he was stuttering words. Dixon said he was going to leave on his mission and leave us here to continue running Vernon.

Another Vernon executive said Dixon rode off like the Lone Ranger. "He told us he would go off to Washington—blaze new trails. That was the last time any of us saw him. He blazed new trails all right. He got so far ahead of us, we couldn't find his trail." Loggins added that Dixon's words were prophetic: "He compared everyone there to the defenders of the Alamo, and then he got into his plane and took off. I looked at the guy standing next to me and said, 'Hey, didn't everyone who stayed behind at the Alamo die?' "

18 *High Spirits*

The yacht *High Spirits* slipped gracefully into a berth at the Washington harbor. Launched as the *Maemere* in 1929 just before the start of the Great Depression, the luxurious 110-foot motor yacht was an opulent symbol of a bygone era. Dixon first heard of the *High Spirits* in 1982 from John Hill's cousin, Rosswell Harbort Westmoreland III, a fellow Dallas real estate developer. Friends in a Florida brokerage firm in which he was involved told Westmoreland that the *High Spirits* was for sale. "I had seen a brochure on the yacht and thought it might be of interest to Dixon. I told him of its existence and its heritage."

Dixon looked at it that evening and liked what he saw. The *High Spirits* wasn't just any yacht. Originally designed by John Trehpy, an Annapolis, Maryland, shipbuilder famous for his elegant yachts, the boat had gone through several names and owners before a South Carolina real estate developer acquired it. It was a sister ship to the presidential yacht, *Sequoia*, which had been sold by President Carter in an economy move, and it was just what Dixon needed. It could comfortably accommodate eight for intimate cruises. But its twenty-by-twenty-seven-foot enclosed fantail and spacious dining salon could handle larger parties of thirty or forty. A partnership composed of a Vernon subsidiary and several other developers such as Harvey McLean acquired the yacht after borrowing $1.3 million from Vernon Savings. In addition to its air force, Vernon now had a navy.

Even as Vernon's jet cleared the runway in Addison kicking off Dixon's industry crusade, the *High Spirits* had glided into a slip at the Washington harbor. Dixon had ordered it there, figuring that the yacht would be a perfect place to stay and entertain the high and mighty when he was in the nation's capital.

Dixon got to Washington just in time. His speech to Vernon's employees was no exaggeration. The savings and loan industry definitely had a thorny political problem that was growing more serious by the day.

The main trouble was rooted in the government's FSLIC deposit-insurance fund. Between its inception in 1934 and 1979, the FSLIC had been forced to help only 124 savings institutions, mainly by quietly merging troubled S&Ls into healthy ones. In that forty-five-year stretch, only 13 of the 124 sick institutions had actually been closed—the action that triggered a depositor payoff. By contrast, in just six years ending in 1986, the FSLIC rescued 166 S&Ls and closed 49. The industry had never seen anything like it, and the worst was yet to come.

As the FSLIC closed sick institutions and paid off depositors to honor its $100,000-per-account guarantee, its reserves continued to plummet. Ed Gray had tested the patience of his most ardent supporters in the industry by running around the country saying the fund was broke. The FSLIC, after all, was the backbone of the S&L system; admitting that it was insolvent risked a well-justified loss of public confidence. But few depositors had been hurt, thanks to Gray's jerry-rigged solutions. So everyone ignored him.

Government officials had engaged in all sorts of flimflam during the 1980s to stave off the appearance of bankruptcy. At one point, the FSLIC issued paper notes called "income capital" or "net worth" certificates to troubled savings and loans rather than close the institutions and pay off depositors. But that was a cosmetic solution to keep the troubled S&Ls off the FSLIC's beleaguered financial statement and put off a day of reckoning.

In April 1985, Gray tried something called the management consignment program, or the MCP. Under an MCP, bank board officials fired corrupt or inept managers of troubled institutions and replaced them with executives hired from other S&Ls. The new managers ran the sick institution for a fat fee under a management contract and tried to reverse the thrift's fortunes. But the MCP program functioned more like an employment agency for the industry's good-old-boy network. Most of the thrifts in the MCP eventually went broke anyway; it just took a little longer.

At times, it seemed as if everyone had a different plan to rescue the deposit-insurance fund. But no one really knew what to do, particularly Ed Gray.

Gray had attempted to get congressional approval of one recapitalization plan—an $8.5-billion injection into the FSLIC. But he had been clobbered by opponents. In desperation, he'd turned to McKenna and the U.S. League when he endorsed the FADA asset disposal agency. At least McKenna understood the problem plaguing the industry was far different from the interest-rate-spread troubles of the early 1980s. S&Ls now had billions of dollars in bad assets on their books. The best thing he could do with sick institutions was force them into the MCP program, fire the old managers, hire new ones, and get the bum assets off the books by moving them into FADA.

Thanks to the miracles of government accounting, the transaction could be papered as a sale by FSLIC. The deposit-insurance fund's insolvency would thus be hidden in FADA, which would have years to hold on to the property or dispose of it. All FADA needed was a line of credit from the Treasury.

The industry, of course, loved the FADA idea. This was true accounting smoke and mirrors. The transfers into FADA didn't solve any of the problems. It was simply an accounting gimmick. But the financial gymnastics would make the deposit-insurance fund look solvent to the public. Meanwhile, FADA's ability to rig the market by holding on to billions of dollars in junk property propped up the price of real estate, which was the collateral for most of the industry's loans. The industry, particularly the big stockholder-owned S&Ls in California, wouldn't face any big real estate write-downs that would hurt stock prices.

Actually the McKenna plan—if properly executed—wasn't such a bad idea. It would have created a government-sanctioned shell game. At least it might have limited the damage, though. McKenna's plan might have cost the American taxpayer $15 to $20 billion eventually. But that would have been far better than the $400 to $500 billion of the S&L bailout that would come within a few years. Nevertheless, the free marketers in the Reagan administration's Office of Management and Budget and the Treasury opposed it. McKenna had structured FADA along the lines of the old Reconstruction Finance Corp., which President Roosevelt created to help rescue the banks during the Depression. It smacked of Big Government, something that gave the Reagan OMB ulcers. Besides, no one in the administration or on Wall Street wanted some quasi-government agency borrowing billions of dollars in a massive recapitalization of the FSLIC.

The Treasury Department backed a better idea. It wanted the Congress to authorize the creation of a special agency to sell $15 billion worth of government-backed bonds that would be repaid by the S&L industry. The $15 billion could then be given to the FSLIC so it could afford to close sick S&Ls, pay off depositors, and take over their assets. The Treasury-backed plan was much more to OMB's liking; it would get the job done plus it had political appeal. Congress would have to get its fingerprints on the mess, because legislation would be needed to authorize the plan. If the scheme worked, Reagan could take credit for it; if it failed, Reagan could blame Congress. Had the Congress passed this plan, the cost of the crisis would have been minimized, too. But the U.S. League opposed the idea. It didn't think its members should be forced to pay special assessments for the decade or more it would take to pay off the bonds.

Ed Gray got caught in the cross fire. He tried to support some elements of both plans. But supporting one side merely angered the other. The U.S. League and other elements of the industry became particularly critical of the bank board chairman. After hearing of the $15-billion plan, one executive of a healthy California institution said he would not contribute "one more nickel" to help the FSLIC.

When Gray had two officials of the Dallas Federal Home Loan Bank preview the idea before a high-powered U.S. League legislative conference, Gerald Levy, a Milwaukee S&L owner and newly installed League president, reflected the frustration of the members. He had just looked at computer printouts documenting rapid growth at many Texas institutions, despite new bank board regulations designed to stop such expansion. Now Levy had regulators from the Dallas bank coming before him with the gall to propose drastic nationwide solutions when they couldn't stop the troubles in their own backyard. Levy vowed to "drive a stake into the heart" of the plan.

By the time Durward Curlee started popping corks on bottles of Jordan cabernet out on the *High Spirits* in Washington Harbor, even Gray's best friends thought the chairman was losing it. Aides noticed that Gray's hands often trembled. He stayed at his office late into the night, chain-smoking and writing defensive speeches, stopping only long enough to order out dinner or run up the street to the local McDonald's.

"The pressure was incredible," recalled Gray. "Each week I could see things getting worse and I knew we faced a tragedy. But it didn't seem like we could get anything done." Gray could envision being set up as a scapegoat if depositors staged a run on savings and loans. He had carried McKenna's water and created the FADA, but OMB and Treasury had stripped the agency of any power. It ended up being a property manager for the FSLIC and not much else. The administration had proposed its $15-billion plan, but the U.S. League was gearing up to oppose it in Congress. The League had come around to support a modified bond issue of $5 billion to recapitalize the FSLIC. But everyone knew the League was just posturing. A real legislative brouhaha was shaping up, and no one knew who would win.

Out on the *High Spirits*, Curlee and his clients smelled opportunity. If the administration won the fight, Curlee knew that Gray would use the $15 billion in fresh resources for his campaign against Texas thrifts. He'd close down half the S&Ls in Texas, starting with highfliers such as Vernon Savings. The fate of Vernon and his other clients probably wouldn't be much better if the U.S. League prevailed. But a stalemate might evolve if his clients helped the League oppose the Treasury. Curlee and his clients would then have enough time to call on their new-found political friends and weaken whatever bill that emerged so it wouldn't hurt them.

As the administration prepared legislation that would be needed for its plan, a loose confederation of high-flying S&Ls and their supporters developed around the issue. Thrift executives and Vernon insiders insist that no one plotted to set up a cabal to oppose the $15-billion plan. The opposition, they say, was the spontaneous reaction of several institutions and owners like Dixon. But that misses the point. The alliance didn't have to be a tightly coordinated effort. Within months, a flood of well-timed campaign contributions and political favors emanated from Vernon and other thrifts, such as Charlie Keating's Lincoln Savings and Loan. The contributions sent a clear message to Capitol Hill: There were a lot of people with deep, deep pockets who wanted the Treasury's FSLIC bill stopped at all costs.

The use of the *High Spirits* was a stroke of genius. Dixon didn't know any more about politics than most people. He couldn't explain why the chairman of an appropriations subcommittee was more powerful than the leader of the Joint Economic Committee. But he understood money. The campaign finance scandals of the Watergate era had been caused by corrupt individuals. But the system that Congress had set up to correct the problems had corrupted entire institutions, such as the Congress itself. Bagmen and plain brown envelopes stuffed with cash had been replaced by political action committees and campaign finance consultants who made a mockery of the Watergate reforms. Only a handful of legislators, such as Jim Leach of Iowa and William Proxmire of Wisconsin, relied upon individual contributors. Most spent as much time raising campaign money from interest groups such as the thrifts as they did on their official duties. A yacht moored in the shadow of the Washington Monument would be a great fund-raising gimmick. The boat was just a floating tax shelter for investors anyway. Why not use it for parties for the people who passed the laws that made it all possible?

Dana made sure the *High Spirits* looked nice. She had already redecorated the thing thanks to Vernon Savings. She loaded it with so many flowers that it looked as if it were from the Rose Bowl. Vernon Savings picked up a $3,000 floral bill for the month of May alone. The Washington harbor was only a few blocks from the Capitol, and the *High Spirits* soon became the talk of the town.

One night it would slip quietly into the Potomac for a midnight cruise and sit-down dinner for sixteen in the spacious dining salon, where the rich and mighty of yesteryear had enjoyed elegant dinners. The next night it was hors d'oeuvres and Edna Valley chardonnay for a handful of guests.

Dixon's new friend Rep. Tony Coelho used the *High Spirits* for Democratic Congressional Campaign Committee fund-raisers eight times between May and September of 1986. Although he later said he wouldn't recognize Don Dixon if he walked through his door, former House Speaker Jim Wright joined Dixon on the *High Spirits,* too. Just days before Wright was elected Speaker, Dixon got a note from Coelho on the campaign committee's letterhead:

Dear Don:

Enclosed are photographs which were taken on the *High Spirits* yacht. I thought you might be interested in having the photos. Don, please feel free to contact me if I may be of assistance.

The photo showed Wright and Dixon aboard the yacht and was inscribed: "For Don Dixon, with very best personal regards, Jim Wright."

Rep. Bill Lowery, Dixon's congressman in California, used the *High Spirits* a couple of times, including once for a press party. Texas Democrats such as Rep. J. J. Pickle and Rep. Jim Chapman used the boat, and bigwig Republicans came aboard, too. "I was there staying on the boat once," said Tom Gaubert, a onetime member of the *High Spirits* partnership, "and they asked me to get off because Ed Meese was coming aboard."

Dixon and his chums used the yacht for legislative conferences, strategy sessions, and just plain fun. Tibby Weston, the Houston real estate man, said he met Dixon on the *High Spirits* to discuss the READY, asset-disposal organization. And the yacht was used to spread the word. The congressmen and administration officials who were guests not only heard about the evils of the Treasury plan, they also started hearing about READY, a private-enterprise solution to the problem that didn't involve any government money.

Dixon, Curlee, and the others entertained ashore, too. There were receptions at the Jockey Club, where the chardonnay went for $45 a bottle and the strawberry sabayon cost $48.50 a head. They did personal favors. Dixon made Vernon's jet available to Coelho, the DCCC's champion fund-raiser. Coelho could hopscotch around the nation raising money on a schedule that would have been impossible with commercial flights. Coelho wasn't the only one who got rides. When he was flying off to the coast, Dixon would sometimes take along an important political guest. Sen. Pete Wilson, a California Republican, rode on the plane, as did former president Gerald Ford and Sen. Paul Laxalt,

President Reagan's closest friend. God knows what they talked about.

But the parties and the plane rides paled in comparison to the highfliers' fund-raising efforts. As the Congress prepared to take up legislation that would give Ed Gray the resources he needed, Dixon spread contributions around Washington and leaned hard on employees and fellow S&L executives to do likewise. Besides the money raised from Vernon's employees, contributions flowed into select campaigns from Danny Faulkner, whom the government accused of looting Empire Savings; Ed McBirney of Sunbelt Savings; Del Morton, a Texas real estate man and big stockholder at Sandia Savings; Tom Gaubert, the onetime power at Independent American Savings; John Harrell of Commodore Savings; Harvey McLean of Paris Savings; Billy Williams of First City Savings in Irving; Jarret Woods of Western Savings; and more.

The sudden abundance of charity wasn't limited to S&L executives. Candidates also got money from big Vernon borrowers such as Jack Atkinson, Vernon Smith, Tommy Stone, and Ron Finley, all Texas developers who'd borrowed millions from Vernon Savings. Loan brokers found that requests for contributions accompanied the large fees they earned for selling off Vernon's loans to other institutions. Gipp Dupree said he contributed $5,000 each to Rep. Jack Kemp, Bill Lowery, and Tom Loeffler, and $2,500 to Sen. Alan Cranston, at Vernon's request. But he later deducted the $17,500 from a $250,000 kickback that Woody Lemons demanded after Dupree earned a $1.5-million fee on a Vernon deal.

Texas savings and loans weren't the only ones overwhelmed by generosity. Officials at Silverado Savings, a highflier in Denver where then Vice President Bush's son Neil was a director, became actively involved in fund-raising efforts. The involvement of the Vice President's son would later generate investigations and charges that regulators held off closing the place because of young Bush's position on the board.

The contributions by the owner of a rapidly growing California thrift would later make Charles Keating's name a household word. An aggressive Arizona thrift executive, Keating contributed nearly $2 million to politicians, including five U.S. senators who would later rue the day that they took his money. So would Keating, who was indicted by a grand jury on charges relating to his handling of the thrift. Executives at Columbia Savings, a California thrift that had heavily invested in junk bonds, gave money to politicians at about the same time. So did Michael Milken, the Drexel Burnham Lambert genius who pioneered the junk bonds Keating used to finance his entry into the S&L business. Years later the House Banking Committee and U.S. Securities and Exchange Commission would investigate Milken's plans to use his junk bond operation to help out thrifts such as Vernon and Keating's Lincoln Savings.

Few really know the breadth of the fund-raising operation. Officials at Vernon and the other S&Ls viewed campaign finance laws with the same disdain they reserved for federal thrift regulations. To get around campaign spending limits and avoid detection, they engaged in secretive fund-raising drives similar to the daisy-chain deals that kept their institutions afloat.

At Commodore Savings in Dallas, board chairman Robert Hopkins came up to his secretary one day and told her to give him two $12,000 checks from a custodial account that contained Commodore funds. The two checks were then taken to Vernon Savings, where they were cashed and converted into twenty-four $1,000 cashier's checks that ended up in the political campaigns of Lowery and former representative Jack Kemp, the New York Republican, erstwhile presidential candidate, and current secretary of Housing and Urban Development. U.S. law prohibits an individual from giving more than $1,000 per election to federal candidates. So the twenty-four $1,000 checks showed up as contributions from Hopkins and members of his family, many of whom had nothing to do with the S&L industry. Kemp got $12,000, and Lowery, a member of the House Banking Committee, got the other half during a Dallas fund-raiser that Dixon had organized. Lowery later told a San Diego reporter that he and Kemp had netted about $50,000 each on the trip.

There is ample evidence to suggest that the legislative melee over the S&L funding plan turned into a political bonanza for Republicans and Democrats alike. Money flowed in from friends, political action committees, employees, and customers of thrifts. Some of the documented contributions suggest that big money was involved. Besides the $2 million that Keating dumped into campaigns, the U.S. League's political education committee donated nearly $1 million to candidates during the 1985–1986 period, including contributions to virtually every member of the

Senate and House banking committees. Common Cause, the self-styled citizens' lobby, documented $11.7 million in campaign contributions to congressional candidates in both parties from S&L political-action committees during the 1980s. And that is just what could be documented. Memos unearthed by federal prosecutors suggest that politicians kept up the pressure once the money rolled in. "We have $890,000," said one telegram to Commodore Savings's Hopkins from Texas attorney general Jim Mattox, a Democrat who recently lost the gubernatorial primary in Texas. "Within striking distance of $1 million. Today is the day. Let's go for it. Send five thousand now."

Dixon seemed to concentrate on the House side of things while Keating focused on the Senate. A former Navy Hellcat pilot turned land developer and antipornography crusader, Keating had acquired Lincoln Savings and Loan in Irvine, California, and turned it into a cash cow for his land development business. Keating was unbelievable. He and his employees would donate more than $1.8 million to politicians between 1984 and 1988. On one day in March 1986, Keating, his family, and associates made fifty-one contributions to Sen. John McCain, a Republican from Keating's home state of Arizona, who received $112,000 from Keating. That's the advantage of an extended family.

Keating contributed an astonishing $850,000 to Senator Cranston, the ranking Democrat on the Senate Banking Committee, and to voter registration drives that helped Cranston win a close election. He pumped $200,000 into a foundation set up for Sen. John Glenn, the former astronaut, Ohio Democrat, and national hero. Glenn used the money to pay off his 1984 campaign debts. Keating gave $76,000 to Sen. Donald Riegle, the Michigan Democrat who became chairman of the Senate Banking Committee, and $55,000 to Senator Dennis DeConcini of Arizona.

On the House side, the spending was much more diffuse and is harder to track. It went into all sorts of individual campaigns. Keating got involved there, too. He and his associates donated $20,000 to Rep. Doug Barnard, who chairs the bank board oversight subcommittee. But Dixon was most active on the House side. He constantly pressured employees, customers, friends, and others to donate to political campaigns. He told Vernon officials he had made pledges to politicians and he intended to keep them. When Vernon president John Smith and a group of employees groused about the contributions in front of Dixon, he reiterated his instructions to expense them and got defensive. "Don responded by saying it was the responsibility of Vernon Savings to grease the wheels of political America," Smith said.

A lot of money went into Coelho's DCCC. More than $200,000 flowed in between early 1985 and mid-1986 from Vernon, other high-flying thrifts, and their supporters. The contributions to senators and House members came in as the donors were having trouble with regulators and felt threatened by pending legislation. The political body also added to the S&L losses, meaning that half the American taxpayers eventually picked up the tab by funding a massive government bailout designed to restore solvency to thrifts such as Vernon.

Of course, Lowery, Kemp, Wright, Coelho, DeConcini, Riegle, Cranston, Glenn, McCain, and many others say they did nothing wrong. If contributions were somehow illegal, they say they didn't know it. Some, such as DeConcini and Riegle, have given the money back. Coelho's campaign committee repaid Vernon Savings for the use of the *High Spirits*.

But none of these public-spirited refunds came until the lawmakers got caught. Also no one bothered to explain why a group of real estate developers from Dallas would pour tens of thousands of dollars into the political campaign of some congressman from San Diego or some senator from Utah.

Indeed, when he was asked whether he thought the campaign money influenced any of the lawmakers, Keating replied, "I certainly hope so."

Keating was right. The S&L executives did get something for their money. Barnard held hearings and gave Keating a forum from which he could criticize the bank board. The Treasury legislation that the industry and the highfliers opposed went nowhere, either. When powerful congressmen such as Majority Leader Wright and senators such as Cranston want a bill passed, they can get the job done. Obstacles don't stop the Congress when powerful leaders want legislation. The administration's bill started working its way through the bureaucracy in mid-1985. It was introduced into the Congress in early 1986, just before the start of the primary season for midsession elections. As all House members and a third of the Senate, including Cranston, prepared to face voters, House Banking Committee chairman Fernand St. Germain, himself a large beneficiary of S&L contributions, canceled four straight markup sessions that had been scheduled to move the bill out of the committee. It remained in the House Banking Committee until the fall, when it was finally reported to the floor with several provisions that made it next to impossible for Gray to start closing savings and loans willy-nilly. The House eventually passed the $15-billion bill complete with restrictions that would hamstring Ed Gray, but a last-minute version that contained only $3 billion in funding emerged from the Senate. The lawmakers decided they didn't have enough time to work out any differences in the legislation. So it died as the last piece of business in the 99th Congress.

Although both the Senate and House played a role in blocking the legislation, the House Democratic leadership played a crucial role in the developments that led to the abandonment of the legislation. During the same time frame in which the Democratic leaders stalled the bill, Dixon, Vernon employees, and the thrift's major borrowers gave Coelho's DCCC $48,000. Another $62,500 flowed in from other high-flying S&Ls and developers in Texas. An additional $56,500 landed at the DCCC courtesy of Michael Milken and his company, Drexel Burnham, and $29,100 flowed in from Columbia Savings and Loan, the California thrift and big advocate of Milken's junk bonds. Keating and his employees chipped in another $8,000, and people associated with Silverado gave $4,000. The total take to be parceled out to Democratic campaigns by the leadership exceeded $200,000. What a coincidence.

To ordinary working folks, the contributions may seem like a lot of money. But to the Dixons and Keatings of the world, it was peanuts. What were a few hundred thousand dollars in political contributions if the money bought access to politicians who helped protect S&Ls with billions of dollars in federally insured savings deposits? Vernon had assets of close to $2 billion; Lincoln more than $3.5 billion.

As the S&Ls tossed money around in Washington, the impact of their influence peddling fell unevenly on their customers. In most cases, depositors probably benefited from the legislative inaction. As long as Vernon Savings and other thrifts remained open, they kept bidding up the interest rates offered to savers to keep the money flowing in. Since the funds were insured by

Uncle Sam and the high-flying thrifts usually operated on the national money markets, Dixon and Keating helped keep upward pressure on certificates of deposit and daily passbook rates around the country. Savers got higher rates on their money and put little pressure on congressmen to do anything. Borrowers didn't fare so well, though. High rates on CDs also translated into high rates on loans. And not all depositors did as well as those at Vernon. The high interest rates shoved S&Ls without political clout into insolvency, spawning sorry stories like the one about a seventy-two-year-old retired railroad worker in New Orleans. He lost $60,000 when the Crescent Federal Savings Bank failed, and he discovered a clerk hadn't set up his account properly. More common was the small businessman who faced a loss of credit midway through a project because his S&L had gone broke.

But the parties that really paid the price were the American taxpayer and the honest S&L operator. By delaying the legislation, the Congress and the Reagan-Bush administrations simply increased the cost of eventually resolving the industry's problems. Deposit-insurance premiums remained high for the honest and dishonest segments of the industry alike. Good thrift operators, who were the majority of the industry, paid for the insolvencies generated by the bad. Pretty soon the price grew so high that American taxpayers had to step in; the industry couldn't afford to repair the damage, and the taxpayer couldn't afford to ignore it.

The political contributions and influence allowed Vernon and Keating's Lincoln Savings to remain open for months longer than they might have. Closing them and hundreds of other S&Ls could have saved American taxpayers billions of dollars. The losses at thrifts such as Vernon widened every day as they took in more federally insured deposits to compensate for the plunging value of their assets. Yet when regulators tried to crack down, the taxpayers' representatives not only denied Ed Gray's request for money, they also intervened on behalf of their campaign benefactors.

Reagan's White House displayed an astonishing tone of indifference to the problems. Donald Hovde's October 1986 resignation from his $72,500-a-year job as a board member left Gray without any authority to take any kind of official action. Mary Grigsby had resigned from the three-member board two

months earlier, and Gray couldn't act unless he had at least one
other board member. Yet the White House left him alone and
without power for nearly a month as more and more S&Ls hit
trouble. In November, at the request of Sen. Mack Mattingly, a
Georgia Republican who had received more than $10,000 in
campaign funds from Keating and his associates, Reagan filled
one of the bank board vacancies with Lee Henkel, an Atlanta
attorney and real estate developer who had done more than $60
million worth of business with Keating's S&L. Another person
whose name had been put forward for the job was Durward
Curlee. But he didn't have a chance.

Henkel wasted no time showing the flag. Reagan made
Henkel a recess appointment after Congress had adjourned,
meaning he could take his seat immediately. Once the Senate
reconvened, Henkel would have to be confirmed. In one of his
first actions in December, though, he proposed a rule that would
have immunized Lincoln Savings from any enforcement actions
in a dispute with the bank board over $615 million worth of
direct investments that Lincoln had made in real estate and
other risky deals. By January, incoming Senate Banking Committee chairman William Proxmire of Wisconsin announced that he
would oppose the Henkel nomination when it came before the
Senate. Proxmire also asked for a Justice Department investigation of Henkel's actions. Henkel asked Reagan to withdraw his
nomination a few months later.

But that didn't stop others from rushing to Lincoln's aid.
When the Federal Home Loan Bank of San Francisco in early
1987 accused Keating of unsafe and unsound banking practices
similar to those at Vernon, Senators McCain, Glenn, Cranston,
DeConcini, and Riegle set up a meeting with federal regulators
and spent more than two hours grilling them on their treatment
of Keating's S&L, which was eventually closed at an estimated
cost of $2.5 billion. Dixon and the Texas S&Ls wouldn't be
treated any differently. None other than Jim Wright personally
took up Vernon's case with Ed Gray. Texas attorney general Jim
Mattox in early 1987 threatened to file suit against the bank
board, alleging that the feds were discriminating against his
Texas benefactors. Bowman criticized Gray for his Rambo mentality.

When Dixon and his friends wanted to complain about Ed
Gray and his regulators to someone who really counted, former

representative Tom Loeffler, a Texas Republican and beneficiary of S&L contributions, came through. He staged a Dallas fund-raiser. Who was the main draw? None other than James Baker, a Texan who had replaced Regan as Treasury secretary and the man whom George Bush later tapped as secretary of state. Loeffler brought Baker to the fashionable Crescent Club to listen to the complaints from thirty to forty-five thrift executives about the board and FSLIC legislation. From most indications, Baker didn't waver from his support of the Treasury plan. But the Treasury later went along with a watered-down version of the bill that significantly weakened the regulators' hands.

"Baker was taken pretty much by surprise," said Weston, the Houston real estate man who attended the fund-raiser. "He wasn't prepared for all of the complaints." There was no question that he got an earful. Seated next to Baker at the main table was Donald R. Dixon of Vernon Savings and Loan.

19 High Noon

When Harry Joe Selby walked through the doors of the Federal Home Loan Bank of Dallas to start his new job in May 1986, he didn't exactly resemble some character out of *High Noon*. Small and plump with white hair and pink cheeks and an avid bird-watcher, Selby appeared the antithesis of the grim, gray, iron-fisted bank examiner sent to Dallas for a showdown with the Don Dixons of the world. Yet Joe Selby had personally been recruited to take the chief thrift regulator's job at the Dallas bank by Ed Gray and Roy Green. "I went out and asked everyone who was the best and toughest regulator in the country, and Joe's name kept coming up," said Gray.

A thirty-two-year veteran of the federal agency that regulates national banks, Selby enjoyed impeccable credentials as a tough, experienced bank regulator. Although Selby didn't know it, Texas S&L executives had already complained about his selection for the job to Treasury Secretary James Baker during Tom Loeffler's luncheon in the Crescent Club. Baker, according to one executive present, expressed shock that someone such as Selby had been hired at the Dallas bank; he told the audience that Selby almost brought down the entire banking system by his overzealous reaction to the Penn Square Bank failure in Oklahoma City during 1983.

But Selby had been in hostile situations before; he figured

211

he could capitalize on his reputation as a regulatory gunslinger to restore some order and discipline to the fast-growing thrifts in Texas and four Southwestern states of District Nine. Besides, the salary—$165,000 a year—was good and he liked the idea of moving back to his native state. He had grown up in Ganado, a tiny town in the heart of Texas's oil and cattle country.

Selby is the first to admit he wasn't prepared for the culture that faced a thrift regulator in Texas. As he settled into his temporary office on the third floor of the bank building, the fifty-five-year-old regulator was shocked at the primitive nature of the place. The building itself was packed with workmen adding a new wing with features such as a day care center and a health club. But what really needed updating were the examination procedures. Examiners still used pencils and notepads during an exam and brought their handwritten notes back to a typing pool, where secretaries turned them into final reports. Every process he encountered seemed the same—long and tedious. Like the cars zooming down the John Carpenter Freeway in front of the building, the age of computer technology had passed right by the Dallas Federal Home Loan Bank. You'd think the place was still in Little Rock.

What bothered Selby most was the cozy relationship between the regulator and the regulated. Banking regulators weren't exactly known for their hostile attitudes toward bankers. But this was unbelievable. Regulators routinely got jobs at institutions they supervised, or they got mortgage loans while exams were under way. Selby fired off some conflict-of-interest letters to former regulators now working for S&Ls. He also took a critical step by merging the bank's examination and supervision staffs, and he set up a system of priorities so the sickest thrifts in the state would be examined first. Under the old system, the examiners might as well have been conducting exams by alphabetical order. He stunned the S&Ls in the district by forming an investigative unit to work with the U.S. attorney and the FBI on bank board referrals to the Justice Department for criminal prosecutions. But the industry's jitters didn't bother Selby; he wanted everyone on notice that the cozy relationship in Dallas was history.

When Selby moved to Texas in mid-1986, he brought with him a wealth of knowledge about the banking industry. But Selby knew little about savings and loans. Ironically, the only

Texas S&L he had ever heard of was Vernon Savings. A friend in the banking industry had told him about a thrift from Vernon, Texas, that had been in Taiwan soliciting deposits. "Frankly," he recalled, "I was flabbergasted. I knew where Vernon, Texas, was. I didn't even know it had an office in Dallas." When Selby arrived in Dallas during April to attend the district bank's board meeting, he learned more. One examiner told him the bank had just called in Vernon's Don Dixon and asked him to sign an agreement restricting Vernon's activities. Dixon had refused.

Within weeks, Selby started a crash course on the history of this notorious thrift. When talking with Vernon's board members, the regulators at the district bank may have kept to themselves their thoughts about Vernon Savings. But Selby discovered they didn't hold back around the office. Vernon was known to the staff as "Vermin." Everyone seemed to think it was headed for big trouble. Yet from what Selby could determine, everyone had sat around for four years watching Vernon grow like a prairie fire and had done next to nothing about it.

Even a cursory look at some past exams showed that the state and federal examiners who actually went into the institution had reported suspicious transactions. As far back as 1982, examiners had noted violations, including one that raised a conflict-of-interest question and numerous instances of loan-documentation violations. In 1983, state examiners noted another troubling sign—more than 80 percent of Vernon's assets were concentrated in interim construction and land development loans. That seemed dangerous. The examiners pointed out that Vernon had financed the cost of the land, the closing costs, and interest charges in 95 percent of the cases—creating the kind of economics that made the thrift precariously dependent on perpetual inflation in land values.

Federal examiners, too, had zeroed in on the soaring growth of brokered deposits during 1983; brokered funds were up nearly 1,000 percent, a sure sign of trouble. They reported significant regulatory violations; unsafe and unsound banking practices; lending deficiencies; inadequate books and records; incomplete financial statements on borrowers; violations of loans-to-one-borrower regulations; and conflicts of interest.

If any S&L customer had done anything nearly as egregious involving a mortgage loan, the regulators would have suggested a public flogging. But the top guns in Austin, Dallas, and Washington didn't move forcefully against Vernon Savings. In mid-1984, the district bank summoned the board members to Dallas and requested that they sign a "Supervisory Agreement." That was like giving Ivan Boesky a rosary for penance. The board members, who had been told that the agreement was needed to make the regulators feel better about their silly rules, signed the thing, promising not to do any of that terrible stuff again and to develop a new business plan. They then returned to Vernon and approved Dixon's acquisition of a $2-million beach house and a Rolls dealership.

In 1985, state examiners went into Vernon again. As usual, a copy of the letter on the exam that the state sent to Vernon in July ended up in federal files. It said that Vernon's troubled loans equaled 7.8 percent of its assets. At the time, Vernon's reports to the feds put that percentage at 1.6 percent. If true, the state's figures suggested that Vernon faced a disaster; its troubled assets were twice as large as its net worth. Again, no action was taken.

A month later, the feds came back in and conducted an exam that concluded Vernon was "out of control." The exam uncovered sham transactions such as the Drippie deals designed to boost profits artificially and put off a day of reckoning; numerous loans to other troubled S&Ls in the daisy chain; huge unsecured loans to Dixon pals such as Jack Atkinson; and glaring conflicts of interest. In one deal, Vernon, through a subsidiary, lent $3.2 million for land deals to two partnerships in which Vernon attorney Frank DeMarco and another man were involved. Just months after the loans were approved, the partnerships got some new members, including Dixon, his right-hand man, Richard Little, and another Vernon executive.

After reviewing Vernon's history under Dixon, Selby couldn't believe his eyes. "I've been in supervision for thirty-four years," Selby would later say, "and this was the most egregious case of poor management, self-dealing, conflicts of interest, and abuse that I had ever seen."

Yet by May 1986, Vernon Savings still was in operation, taking in deposits. Gray says that he didn't even remember knowing much about Vernon at the time, other than that it had been placed on a problem list. Bowman hoped the problems would go away for obvious reasons. But Selby wondered how big the problem might be. In the year that had just passed, Vernon had lured an additional $400 million to $500 million of insured deposits into its vaults. If the money had been invested in a bunch of bum deals, the FSLIC might be faced with another headache—this time a migraine.

Selby started asking some hard questions, but the answers he got were soft. "The only real answer I ever got was that we didn't have a very good examination staff," he said.

To Joe Selby, that was no excuse. He started bearing down on Vernon Savings about the same time that Don Dixon summoned employees to the hangar party to announce his imminent departure. As Dixon left for Washington, the Vernon board was called to Dallas for a meeting. The board members soon discovered why Dixon had headed east. Things were going to get real hot around Vernon Savings. Joe Selby was going to see to that.

If Vernon Savings had been Selby's only problem, the savings and loan crisis might have been contained to one city or at the worst, one state. But Vernon, unfortunately, was one of many. Problem institutions had started to surface in a number of states, but the situation was particularly bad in California and Texas. Go-go S&L owners such as Dixon, Ed McBirney, Terry Barker, Stanley Adams, and dozens of others had driven up interest rates when luring brokered and jumbo deposits to finance their rapid growth. In doing so, they unleashed a tremendous building boom, particularly in Texas and other Southwestern states. They lent money on sound and shaky deals alike so they could book the fees and paper profits needed to bleed S&Ls through dividends, bonuses, perks, and side deals. Most of the Texans told Selby their current problems stemmed from the temporary collapse of the oil economy and the glutted real estate markets. In truth, the economic decline merely exposed what they had been doing. Selby started wondering just how big a mess he had gotten into.

A closer look at Vernon gave him some insights into why the situation had been allowed to fester. Examination reports on financial institutions resemble police reports about arrests. They contain subjective evaluations of the cop on the street. In many cases, the examiners' gut instincts are correct. But federal officials can't shut down a state-chartered S&L based upon intuition. They need proof that can withstand a court challenge. In the chummy atmosphere that existed between the regulator and regulated, few supervisors had the guts to build a solid case. Even if they had mustered some courage, getting the records needed to document abuses was not as easy as it might seem.

Not only did the move from Little Rock to Dallas strip the Dallas bank of legal and supervisory talent at a crucial time; thrift managers also frustrated the regulators' efforts at every turn. At the initial sign of trouble at Vernon, the regulators had forced the thrift's management to sign the supervisory agreement in mid-1984. That might have been an adequate step in the past, but it meant next to nothing in the deregulated culture of the 1980s. At first Dixon and Lemons simply ignored the agreement. When state examiners moved in to inspect Vernon's books about six months later, though, Vernon's top brass took precautionary steps.

Nancy Horne, the assistant corporate secretary who kept the minutes of board meetings in Vernon, received instructions to rewrite the minutes dating back to July 1984 and make them conform to the supervisory agreement that had been signed that year. Horne didn't resign in protest, blow the whistle on her bosses, or anything else. In fact, Horne probably wasn't aware that there was anything improper in the request. Vernon executives were always adding or deleting loans to the board minutes after the meetings. Sometimes the revisions involved loans that board members knew of but simply didn't have time to discuss. On other occasions, Horne was told to insert in the minutes big loans that the board never discussed or knew about. She wasn't too worried; she had a record of what actually transpired at the meetings. They had been recorded on tape ever since she started in her job. In mid-1986, though, that changed, too.

"John Hill asked that the meetings not be recorded in the future. At the next meeting, Pat King stopped me during a recess of the meeting and told me not to bring the recorder to the meetings anymore. He did not give me a reason. John Hill then directed that I destroy all previous tapes. I did not. I turned the tapes over to Roy Dickey, who was the corporate secretary at the time." Future meetings were not recorded.

Had logic prevailed, the huge salaries, dividends, and bonuses should have set off alarm bells in Austin, Dallas, or Washington. Collectively, Vernon declared $22.9 million in dividends between 1982 and mid-1986, including $22 million to Dixon's Dondi Financial Corp. In addition, Dixon and his key

executives earned six-figure salaries and about $15 million more
in bonuses between 1983 and 1986. More of the bonus money
went into Dixon's company that might have met the eye. Dixon
required top executives to buy some Dondi Financial stock when
they joined the company. The anointed few used their bonuses
to pay for the shares.

But the big dollar payouts were not as flagrant as they
seemed to be. All dividends had been approved by state and
federal regulators, who believed they were based on Vernon's
record profits. Although examiners were suspicious of Dixon's
earnings, they couldn't prove that the fat bottom lines were
based upon sham transactions until the deals fell apart. And
then it was too late. Salaries at Vernon were big, but not that big.
By 1986, Lemons earned $157,500 a year; Pat King earned
$140,000—not huge salaries for running a company with $1
billion in assets. Dixon got paid $272,500, but his salary came
from Dondi Financial, not Vernon Savings and Loan.

The salaries didn't include the huge bonuses. In addition to
his salary, Lemons's bonus in 1986 was $347,300. King's was
$177,000. But the examiners and board members didn't even
know about the big bonuses. The bonus program had not been
authorized by the board; it was a secret.

"I was told that these accounts were to be kept secret," said
Brenda Bryant, a Vernon employee who set up the accounts.
"They did not want any employees except those that were
participating in the bonus program to have knowledge of the
accounts. It was my idea to number them because I didn't know
of another way that would be easier. That would be a code."
Bryant could see why the accounts were so hush-hush. If other
employees knew the size of the bonuses, they'd probably resent
not being a part of the plan. She did. After three and a half years
at Vernon, she asked her boss, Pat Malone, why she was excluded
from the program. "He told me, 'Brenda, Don Dixon determines
who is on the bonus program.' He let me know that I wasn't
important enough."

Selby had the advantage of hindsight, though. By mid-1986,
several of Vernon's loans were obviously in trouble, suggesting
that the thrift's dividends might have been based on phantom
profits. Nervous employees were starting to talk, too. Vernon was
a state-chartered thrift, and Selby was dumbfounded that Bowman hadn't acted. It looked like the Texas commissioner had

obviously been easy on Vernon because of his personal and business relationship with King. But even Bowman must have seen that Vernon could cause the state far bigger troubles if it wasn't stopped. As a state official, Bowman could have moved against Vernon far more swiftly than the feds. Yet he didn't act. Selby didn't know about Bowman's hunting trips or his under-cover work as a sleuth.

As Selby reviewed the history of Vernon, the only disciplin-ary action that seemed to carry any sting was the removal of King, Lemons, and the others a few months back. But the feds—and not the state—had done the pushing. The bank board had leverage over Vernon because of federal deposit insurance. And Lemons still acted as a consultant to Vernon, while King had been allowed to stay on as chairman of the board, even though he had been forced out as president. Selby wasn't going to let up so easily. "We were trying to get control of it," said Selby. "We knew how bad things were. Our examiners were in there, the state was in there telling us how bad things were, uncovering the abuse. We all knew Vernon was down the tubes. We wanted to get control of it and see if we could limit the damage to the FSLIC."

By July, Selby had forced Vernon to sign a cease-and-desist order based upon the results of an exam that had been conducted in 1985. The order required the thrift to adopt prudent lending and underwriting practices and imposed stiff lending restric-tions that made it all but impossible for Vernon to renew loans to its favorite family of borrowers. A month later, Selby initiated another exam—this time a special investigation that included subpoena powers to look into possible criminal actions by the management of Vernon.

The pressure from Selby didn't go over well in the executive suites at Vernon and Dondi Financial. From the perspective of Dixon and others, Selby's crackdown smacked of gestapo tactics. Texas, after all, was part of America, where a man was presumed innocent until proven guilty. Besides, Dixon and his team still had a lot of money sitting in Vernon Savings.

Ever since the secret bonus plan had been implemented in 1983, Dixon and his key employees had received two types of bonus payments each year. One was a cash bonus that was paid out quickly, and the other was a deferred bonus that sat in an account for months. Vernon initially put part of the yearly bonus into a deferred account to keep executives involved in the company. A key employee thinks twice about leaving if a large chunk of his earnings has been deferred and placed in an account that he will lose if he quits.

When Lemons, King, and the others were forced out by the bank board, they still had more than $1 million sitting in their deferred-bonus accounts. If past policies stood, they would forfeit their bonuses since they left the company. But Dixon and others at Vernon didn't think that was fair. After all, Lemons and the others didn't quit; they had been kicked out by the feds. So the rules were suddenly changed.

An unsigned memo soon appeared in the personnel files of Vernon Saving executives. "Deferred compensation [of bonus] accounts for individuals who attain the level of executive vice president or above are hereby fully vested. Payments from these vested accounts will continue until the account balances are exhausted," the memo said. In other words, regardless of what they were doing, Lemons, King, and all other Vernon executives in the plan would get a partial bonus payment every three months until there was nothing left in the accounts.

Big money was involved. Richard Little had $591,000 in his numbered account; Lemons, $550,000; King, $391,000; Hill, $299,000; Smith, $211,000; and Malone, $137,000. In all, Vernon executives had $2.1 million in deferred bonuses, not counting $900,000 set aside for Dixon.

Lemons and Malone got the good news in a letter from John Smith, Vernon's senior executive vice president. The decision was made in time for Lemons, who had been fired in April, to get a $52,276 bonus check in July 1986. Other Vernon executives got their payments, too, including Malone, who was by now working for Durward Curlee.

But what would happen if bank board regulators with subpoena powers got wind of the secret bonus accounts? Selby was bearing down too hard. Something had to be done.

The new batch of FSLIC examiners had hardly passed through Vernon's doors when Brenda Bryant got a phone call from John Smith. "He asked what kind of loan we could do against the deferred-bonus accounts that would not require loan committee." Bryant grew more uneasy about the discussion with Smith the longer it lasted. He had inquired whether Pat King, without loan-committee authorization, could borrow the money in his numbered account instead of waiting months to receive it in the regular quarterly payments. The way things were going, King and the others were clearly worried that the accounts might be frozen if Selby learned of them.

"I told him a share loan was the only loan that we could do without a loan-committee authorization and he said, 'All right, we want to do some.' He knew the exact balance in King's deferred-bonus account, and he wanted to do a hundred-percent loan. I said we couldn't do that. A share loan against an account can only be for up to ninety percent. He was not aware of that and he said, 'All right, we'll do it for ninety percent.' "

Bryant didn't like the idea. "I told him I was concerned about the transactions. I was nervous and I felt they were illegal. Previous employees who had left Vernon had never received any of the money in the accounts. They were always liquidated and zeroed out. I also felt it looked like they were all running off with the money." Smith didn't respond. Instead, he had an aide later deliver Bryant memos from King documenting that the accounts were fully vested, and she started paperwork on the loans.

Over the next month, Vernon executives, one by one, took out loans against their deferred-bonus accounts or arranged to have their money transferred to individual accounts at the Republic National Bank in Dallas. Bryant recalled when Richard Little came into her office to sign the loan documents in August 1986: "He stayed and chatted with me awhile and told me he would be leaving Vernon, that he was asked to leave. He was upset. He said it had to do with a savings and loan that Vernon did business with in California. He had personal loans at this savings and loan, and federal people, as he called them, thought that was a conflict of interest. He said he had done nothing wrong." In a sense, Bryant expected to hear from Little and the others when the first payments on the share loans were due on October 16. She didn't hear from anyone.

Dixon had already removed himself from the savings and loan's affairs. But he still maintained an office across the pond in Dondi Financial's offices, and he didn't like this business with the regulators. Not being men of the financial world, they simply didn't understand how a real estate development operation worked. The regulators had panicked. Cooler heads would simply have waited until the real estate market rebounded. Prices would rise and inflation would take care of everything.

Instead the feds had sent Dudley Do-Right to Texas and everything was falling apart.

By August the pressure being applied by Selby was starting to hit Dixon and others right where it hurt—in the perks. Dixon had been forced to cancel his hunting trip to Denmark and England with Bruce West, Atkinson, and several other large Vernon customers. Here he wasn't even technically working for the place, yet he was prepared to take some of its major borrowers hunting. Calling off the trip was too bad; a Vernon subsidiary had already made the commitment for everyone to go. Vernon Savings would just have to eat the commitment fee. Times were tough. Forfeiture of the fee cost Vernon Savings $150,000.

Dixon wasn't the only one who felt the heat. Others in the industry didn't like Selby's heavy-handed techniques, either. Rumors soon started to spread that Selby wasn't susceptible to the normal weaknesses of male regulators. In other words, there was no Joy Love in this guy's future; he was gay. Word had it that the only way to get on his good side was to hire lawyers from a ring of homosexual attorneys that the Texans dubbed the Fruit Loop.

Selby began to realize he was involved in something far bigger than he had thought. The stakes were enormous; billions of dollars were involved. For that kind of money, men do desperate things. The rumors were vicious. Friends passed on one about a plot to kidnap him. One afternoon, the phone at the home of supervisory agent Bill Churchill went dead. A repairman found the problem—a little black box called a bug.

Unbeknownst to Selby and Gray, the complaints went all the way to the White House. In August 1986, Larry Taggart, the former California S&L commissioner who had gone to work consulting for Dixon and Keating, sat down and wrote a seven-page letter to Donald Regan, then White House chief of staff. Reminding Regan of his family's ties to the Republican Party, Taggart said:

> I am writing because of a genuine concern for the thrift industry in this country and the fact that a number of actions have been taken recently which will cause irreparable harm to savings and loan associations. Additionally, these actions being done to the industry by the current chief regulator of the Federal Home Loan

Bank Board are likely to have a very adverse impact on the ability of our Party to raise needed campaign funds in the upcoming elections. Many who have been very supportive of the Administration are involved with savings and loan associations which are either being closed by the FHLBB or threatened with closure.

One week later Taggart joined Dixon for wine and spirits on the *High Spirits*. But his letter to Regan was too little, too late. As Selby increased the pressure, Bowman finally moved against Vernon. He later said he was motivated by the discovery of some side deals involving Dixon and Lemons that his examiners unearthed at other S&Ls. But many people felt he acted to preempt Selby. People might get the wrong idea if they found out about his detective work.

In September 1986, Bowman dispatched a team headed by Deputy Commissioner Earl Hall to literally assume control of Vernon Savings and Loan and make a statement about who was in charge. Hall boldly moved into Dixon's office and commandeered Woody Lemons's old company Cadillac. He became Vernon's chief executive officer by state fiat and summoned all of the remaining top officers into Dixon's office for a meeting.

"We were all sitting around, and Earl was saying we'll have to do something about these delinquent loans," said one former Vernon executive at the meeting. "I wasn't paying much attention. I knew there was nothing anyone could do with them. By this time, we had the Bad Attitude Club. We'd go up to the Million Dollar Saloon and have long lunches. Earl didn't know what he was doing. All he could do was take away credit cards and reject expense reports."

In the meeting, Hall took a hard line on the delinquent loans, encouraging the officers to lean on recalcitrant borrowers. Suddenly he had to go to the bathroom. As he walked across the room, he kept talking, but no one watched him. Suddenly everyone heard a crash. As they turned in their chairs, they saw Hall sprawled on the floor.

He had tripped on a step by the bar near Dixon's private bathroom. He had a broken ankle and would spend the next several months at Vernon limping around with a cast on his foot.

20 The Wright Stuff

R ep. Jim Wright and two of his key aides sat in the offices of George Mallick, a Fort Worth real estate developer and a Wright confidant. The Democratic Caucus had just elected Wright Speaker of the House, one of the most powerful positions in the nation. Election by the full House was a formality. The Democrats had just regained control of the Senate for the first time in six years. There was much work to be done when the 100th Congress convened in January of 1987, which was less than a month away. Wright and his aides were plotting strategy in Mallick's modern burgundy-and-gray offices when the phone call came in from Tony Coelho, who would serve as House whip under Wright. Wright's top aide, John Mack, took the call in another room.

Mack picked up the phone and listened to Coelho's complaint that one of their contributors had a problem: "He said there was a problem with his bank, that the FSLIC was going to shut it down that day. This banker was trying to find other methods of financing to keep his bank alive, and was there something we could do to give him a grace period."

The bank, of course, was Vernon Savings and Loan, and the banker was Don Dixon, who had helped with fund-raising for the Democratic Congressional Campaign Committee. After state officials had moved in on Vernon in September, Dixon tried to salvage the situation by convincing Bowman and other regulators to approve a recapitalization plan. Dixon told Bowman and the feds that he could convince some new investors to inject fresh capital into the beleaguered institution and rescue it from insolvency. But Selby and the feds were pressing hard for a federal takeover at Vernon—a step that would wipe out stockholders such as Dixon. The feds wanted the thrift out of Dixon's hands and time was running short.

Mack soon hung up and returned to the meeting. When he got a chance, he told Wright of the conversation: "Tony Coelho says that Don Dixon of Vernon Savings and Loan is trying to get a hold of you on the phone and you have not answered his call. Tony claims it is a crisis and that this guy is going to lose his whole career, his life's work, and his whole business if you don't talk to him and find out what you can do." Wright agreed to make a phone call. Although Wright didn't know it, that one simple call would help drive the cost of the savings and loan crisis skyward. He dreaded the probable conversation, too. If the past was any indication, it would be one more complaint about Ed Gray and the regulators at the Federal Home Loan Bank Board.

It was nearly Christmas, 1986, and Jim Wright was getting a little sick of S&L horror stories. Dixon wasn't the first to complain. Gripes about Ed Gray and his regulators had been going on since the guy took office. Businessmen always complain about government bureaucrats. Wright was used to it. But the frequency and intensity of the complaints about Ed Gray and the bank board were unusual. The tenor of the attacks had really picked up the prior spring when Gray's carpetbaggers hit Texas and the administration introduced its bill seeking $15 billion to replenish the deposit-insurance fund called the FSLIC.

In Washington, the whole thing was like a joke. Reporters at the daily sessions in the Speaker's chamber mocked the arcane nature of the agency that few knew anything about. "Mr. Speaker," they'd say after peppering Wright's predecessor, Thomas P. (Tip) O'Neill, with questions about more familiar matters like aid to the contras, "what about the FSLIC bill?" The old pros would chuckle; O'Neill didn't know much more about it than they did.

But the legislation had set off alarm bells in Texas. The state's congressional delegation had been swamped with calls. Democrats and Republicans alike heard warnings that the Federal Home Loan Bank Board would use the FSLIC money to shut down Texas S&Ls willy-nilly.

The accusations didn't come from chronic whiners. People of substance placed the calls—financiers, S&L executives, lawyers, realtors, big-time land developers, big-time political contributors. Durward Curlee, the former director of the Texas Savings and Loan League, complained. If bank board chairman Ed Gray got his hands on $15 billion, Wright and his colleagues in the delegation had been told, he'd shut down half the savings and loans in Texas, merely because the oil market was bad. Somebody had to do something.

It wasn't hard to see where Gray was coming from. He had just addressed the American Bankers Association convention in California and had blasted deregulation-minded thrifts. "Thrift deregulation has been misused and severely abused by some savings and loan operators," Gray told the bankers. "The daredevils, the high rollers, those who have neither the expertise nor the management skills to run thrift institutions—and yes, the crooks, driven by greed—have cost and will cost the FSLIC billions and billions of dollars in losses." Gray didn't mention any names, but everyone knew whom he meant.

A New Deal liberal by temperament and persuasion, Wright usually wasn't sympathetic to the complaints of most businessmen, particularly big tycoons like those in Reagan's kitchen cabinet. They already had plenty of friends in the White House. But Jim Wright was a booster back home, and many of the complaints came from Texans or medium-sized businessmen— the ones Coelho was trying to court for Democratic campaign money.

At first Wright had treated the complaints the usual way— they were referred to aides who made phone calls on his behalf. But the Fort Worth Democrat became personally involved in the FSLIC flap when it became apparent that the grievances weren't isolated complaints. There was a pattern of abuse that seemed to be emanating from the bank board, an agency run amok.

For Wright it had all started in August 1986 when he got a call from a Fort Worth friend of thirty years asking the then House majority leader to meet with Craig Hall, a Dallas S&L owner and big real estate syndicator.

Hall, the caller said, had been having trouble with a government agency. Wright had no trouble guessing which one—the Federal Home Loan Bank Board. At a September 2 meeting in his office a few weeks later, though, Wright was surprised at Hall's story. He was aghast to think that things had gotten so far out of hand.

Craig Hall was no small fry. He ran a company that operated 65,000 apartments and 4 million square feet of office space. His company—Hall Financial—and his extensive network of investors were some of the largest real estate owners in Texas and the surrounding states. Hall told Wright that the downturn in the regional oil economy had jeopardized his ability to remain current on the financial obligations of his business. He had dumped millions of his own money into the firm and was trying to restructure all of Hall Financial's loans with his lenders.

But Ed Gray's bank board was standing in his way. One of his largest lenders was a California savings and loan that had been taken over by the FSLIC, and the agency wouldn't go along with a debt restructuring proposal Hall had made. Instead, Scott Schultz, a young man who had been appointed conservator by the bank board to safeguard the thrift's assets, wanted to foreclose on Hall's loans, an action that would have a domino effect on the company's extensive real estate holdings. Hall explained that Schultz's action could trigger a "financial disaster that would have extreme ramifications, not only on Dallas and Texas but also nationally." Hall said he had written to Ed Gray seven times trying to explain that Schultz's action would be harmful to the bank board's interests. Hall would be forced into bankruptcy court and would default on numerous loans that would probably shove other weak S&Ls insured by the FSLIC over the edge. Going along with Hall's plan would definitely benefit the Dallas entrepreneur. But Hall argued that the FSLIC had much more to lose by not going along with the plan. The S&Ls that would topple because of a Hall bankruptcy could cost the deposit-insurance fund $700 million and wreak havoc on the already depressed Texas economy. But Hall said he couldn't even get a hearing from Gray. The only response he'd received was a letter from the bank board chairman saying he could not meet with him because of some arcane federal rule.

The story angered Wright. He'd been a boy during the Depression. He knew how bad things could get. Now he had some Washington bureaucrats threatening to push Texas's beleaguered real estate markets deeper in the hole. With Hall still in the room, Wright grabbed the phone and made two calls.

The first was to Freddy St. Germain, whose House Banking Committee controlled the $15-billion FSLIC bill pending before the Congress. Hall saw real power at work before his very eyes. Wright told St. Germain, "This just doesn't seem right. Something has got to be done." Wright asked St. Germain to look into the situation and said he would contact him when he got back to Washington.

Wright then made a second call to Coelho. Hall knew something of him. Although Hall said he was a Republican, he and some of his employees had given Coelho's DCCC fund-raising committee just over $5,000 a few weeks before. Hall said he didn't know why Wright called the California legislator. But one thing was clear: Wright wanted Hall to know that the Democrats' champion fund-raiser was in the leadership loop. After a long discussion with Coelho in which he repeated Hall's story. Wright hung up and peppered Hall with questions about Scott Schultz. The meeting had been scheduled for fifteen minutes; it had lasted for an hour and a half. Before Hall left, Wright asked him to forward more information about the dispute to his office. Hall returned to his office and prepared a thick briefing book.

Early the next week, Wright returned to the nation's capital. St. Germain already had the FSLIC bill bottled up in his committee, and Wright was armed with information from Hall. Within days, Wright requested Ed Gray to meet with him in his office on Capitol Hill. By several accounts, Hall's name didn't even come up during the two-hour meeting on September 15. Wright passed along numerous complaints he had heard about the bank board, and had to leave unexpectedly after about twenty minutes. The rest of the time Gray listened to similar complaints from other lawmakers whom Wright had invited to the meeting—Rep. Steve Bartlett, a Republican from Dallas, and two other Texas Democrats, Rep. John Bryant and Rep. Martin Frost, all of whom had received political contributions from the Curlee group or other S&Ls. No one would name names. They said their constituents feared reprisals from regulators. Nevertheless, Gray promised to look into the complaints.

Four days later, the legislative logjam that had stalled Gray's FSLIC bill in the House Banking Committee broke. On a 47-to-1 vote, St. Germain's banking committee reported to the House

floor a massive banking bill that included the $15-billion FSLIC
recapitalization plan. Gray thought he might get his $15 billion
after all. He could then start shutting down some S&Ls and limit
the deposit-insurance fund's exposure to another year of huge
losses.

But Wright was a canny legislator who knew the ways of the
House as well as the road to his hometown of Weatherford.
Within days, he had sprung his trap. Soon after the September
15 meeting, Gray's phone rang. His secretary announced that the
caller was House Majority Leader Jim Wright, and the bank board
chairman soon heard Wright's seasoned Texas drawl on the other
end of the line. He talked in detail of Craig Hall this time and of
Hall's nemesis, Scott Schultz. Said Gray:

"I mean he knows Scott Schultz's name. Can you imagine?
One of the most powerful men in the United States knowing all
about Scott Schultz!"

Wright didn't threaten Gray or anything; he didn't have to.
This was Washington, the seat of power politics. Gray knew what
was going on. Wright simply asked Gray to see if there was
anything he could do. A few days later, Wright exercised his vast
powers over legislation as the majority leader of the House and
blocked further consideration of the FSLIC recapitalization bill,
which had been scheduled for floor action on September 29.

It was a classic Washington power play by a man who really
knew how to pull the levers. Republicans such as Rep. Stan
Parris of Virginia complained that Wright's move was irrespon-
sible. But their complaints were ignored. All eyes were on Ed
Gray. The bank board chairman had hung all of his hope on the
FSLIC legislation to rescue him from the mushrooming crisis.
The deposit-insurance fund was already broke. Without more
money, Gray couldn't shut down high-flying S&Ls such as
Vernon—the ones who were bidding up interest rates and hurt-
ing everyone.

"Put yourself in our shoes," Gray later recalled. "You see
your legislation, which is in the public interest, being held
hostage. You know it. You know nothing's going to happen. I
mean my staff is talking to the House Banking Committee staff.
So there are no secrets here. We all know what's going on. The
big point is that Jim Wright, the most powerful man in the House,
was saying you better learn how to play ball with me, or you can
forget FSLIC recap. I mean this was hardball politics."

Wright's action triggered some soul-searching at the bank board. Gray had a long discussion with his staff and finally decided to dump Scott Schultz. The bill was too important to sacrifice for some overzealous young regulator out in California. Someone would just have to tell Schultz, "Welcome to the NFL." To make the move more palatable, Gray transferred Schultz to another job and replaced him with a highly regarded regulator from New York, Angelo Vigna.

"I called Angelo. I said, 'Angelo, we've got a problem. We've got to get somebody else in here, a new face.'" Gray quickly called Wright and gave him the good news. "I told him we've brought in a new man named Angelo Vigna, and I told him who he was and he seemed pleased by that." Gray then told Vigna to find a way to build a responsible economic case for renegotiating Hall's loans.

In Gray's view, he didn't cave in to Wright. He had shuffled Schultz out of the way—no question about that. But he had replaced him with one of the most respected regulators in the industry—one who also eventually resolved the troubles to Hall's satisfaction. A week later, the St. Germain version of the FSLIC recap bill passed the House by a voice vote. But the specter of the chairman of the bank board's backing down before the future Speaker of the House had an impact within the S&L industry and on the staff of the bank board. In the waning days of the 99th Congress a month later, the Senate passed a recapitalization plan that contained only $3 billion in funding. The bill in the Senate, where Keating had dumped most of his contributions, was different from the House version. A conference committee would have to be appointed to iron out the differences. After conferring with the House leadership, St. Germain rejected the smaller bill and said there was no time to work out the differences. The FSLIC recap bill was the last matter taken up by the 99th Congress, and the lawmakers went home without passing a conference report that would have worked out a difference in the two versions. "They passed those bills just to cover their asses," said Gray. "They knew they wouldn't have time to work out any differences."

Gray's capitulation on the Hall matter didn't really satisfy Wright. The complaints that Wright had received troubled him. If Jim Wright had wanted the FSLIC bill passed, it would have become law. But he didn't. Even before the session had ended,

Wright had asked his friend and business partner, Mallick, to set up a meeting with some of their friends in the Texas real estate business once he returned to Fort Worth. He wanted to learn more about Gray and the bank board; he'd heard allegations that some of the board's supervisory actions were aimed at Democrats like Tom Gaubert, the Texas S&L owner who was also treasurer of the DCCC. Wright suspected a partisan attack on a big Democratic fund-raiser.

Back in Texas, Mallick had no trouble setting up the meeting. A swarthy, plump man of Lebanese ancestry who was also a real estate developer, Mallick had a keen interest in savings and loans. He spread the word in Texas real estate circles that Wright wanted to know more, and set up a luncheon at the Ridgelea Country Club in Fort Worth for October 21, three days after the 99th Congress had adjourned. Wright requested that Rep. Carroll Hubbard, a Kentucky Democrat who chaired the banking committee's oversight and investigations subcommittee, attend, too. Wright had expected only a few friends. When he arrived at the luncheon, he found 150 people from the real estate, savings and loan, and housing-finance industries.

Wright and Hubbard heard horror story after horror story about the capricious and arbitrary way that the bank board was treating savings and loans in the Southwest. One particular regulator singled out for heavy criticism was the new man in Dallas—Joe Selby. At the end of the session, Wright publicly asked Mallick to prepare a study of the savings and loan problems in the district. He returned to Washington with stories of demonic regulators ringing in his ears.

Wright didn't like this talk of picking on Democrats. Within a month, he was back on the phone with Ed Gray, who faced another grueling run at trying to get his bill through the upcoming 100th Congress. This time the discussion centered around Wright's friend Tom Gaubert, a cigar-chomping Texas S&L operator whom the bank board had forced out of a suburban Dallas thrift called Independent American. Wright was particularly concerned about the political overtones involved in taking action against a prominent DCCC fund-raiser. Gaubert had also raised $100,000 for Wright in 1985. "He insisted that Gaubert was getting a raw deal and that I had to talk with him," said Gray.

Gray didn't like the idea. He never talked with people who had issues before the board. Gaubert, who had been accused of unsafe and unsound banking practices by the bank board staff, had already agreed to leave the management of Independent American. But Gaubert had been allowed to retain a financial interest valued at $20 million to $30 million in Independent American. The new management that the regulators put into the S&L had done such a bad job that Gaubert's entire investment was in jeopardy. When the Dallas Federal Home Loan Bank recommended a complete takeover of Independent American, Gaubert tried to get his previous agreement overturned. He wanted to regain control of the thrift and protect his investment. After listening to Wright, Gray finally agreed to see Gaubert. "I made an exception for Jim Wright," said Gray, who figured the review would put him in the Speaker's good graces and improve the chances for his legislation in the upcoming session of Congress.

About five o'clock in the afternoon a few days later, Gaubert walked into Gray's office. He was an affable man with big shoulders, a bigger belly, and a square, open face. He could talk the hide off an armadillo, and Gray soon fell under his spell:

"I had Shannon Fairbanks, my chief of staff, in there. So I have a witness to this. He starts by telling me what a wonderful guy I am. I kid you not. He says, 'I don't agree with you on everything, Mr. Chairman. But by gosh you understand the problem. You've been trying to deal with them. We've got a lot of bad people in this business.' So he takes a lot of time trying to butter me up."

Gray said that Gaubert then told him that most of the problems at Independent American had been caused by the staff and not Tom Gaubert. "He says he was disturbed by the staff. In effect, they were a bunch of devils. He is riding a white horse. But they were all bad—almost evil. If you have been with him all this time, these people start to take on a worse and worse cast. They're just terrible by the time he finishes. He made an impression on me, and I went back to my staff about it again. Finally I said, all right, I've got a hell of a problem here. So I'm going to deal with it."

In an unprecedented step, Gray hired an outside lawyer to review his own staff's handling of the Gaubert case. The outside lawyer eventually criticized the way the staff handled the case, but didn't disagree with the final decision.

Gray immediately let Wright know about his decision to

review the Gaubert case, but the majority leader was on the phone to Gray again within weeks. Gray said he would never forget the call; it came late in the evening in November and he had Fairbanks once again listen in to his side of the conversation:

It was basically another call about the treatment of Texas S and L institutions. And then he said he understood Selby was a homosexual. And he understood from people that he believed and trusted that Selby had established a ring of homosexual lawyers in Texas at various law firms. People needing to talk with the Federal Home Loan Bank supervision people would have to deal with this ring of homosexual lawyers. Being very concerned about the reputation of a man like Selby, I had no idea what his sexual preference was. I told Wright at the time that it didn't make any difference. But then he said to me, "Isn't there anything you can do to get rid of Selby or ask him to leave or something?" And I said, "No, I was the one who recruited him. I think very highly of him. He is doing what I want him to do. He is being a tough regulator."

The call had lasted seven and one-half minutes. Wright would later call Gray a liar and say he never asked that Selby be fired. He said he merely relayed complaints about the regulator to Gray. But Gray said he double-checked Selby's former supervisors at the Comptroller's office about the allegations and found them to be without foundation. He felt sick and went home to San Diego for the Christmas holidays.

Back in Fort Worth, the call to Wright from Tony Coelho had revived the whole sordid S&L mess for the powerful Texas Democrat. It wasn't Wright's favorite topic. It was almost Christmas. Within a few weeks, the House would vote to establish a committee to investigate the White House's role in the Iran-contra fiasco. That was the scandal dominating the headlines. But this S&L thing wouldn't seem to go away. He picked up the phone and got Don Dixon on the other end of the line.

To Wright, Dixon's complaint had that familiar ring. "Look," Wright heard Dixon say, "they are getting ready to put me out of business. They are going to wipe out me and all of the stockholders. They are going to take our business away from us. If I can be given a week, I have located a source of income, a source of loans, financing in Louisiana, a person who will take over all the nonperforming notes and provide capital to continue and redo our operation here."

Wright said Dixon told him the problem was in the Federal Home Loan Bank in Dallas. Regulators there would not give him any time: "They said not one week, not one day." Dixon asked him to talk to Ed Gray.

Wright placed a call to Gray about eight A.M. shortly after Christmas. A bank board employee patched the call through to Gray's home in San Diego, where he had gone for the Christmas break. As Wright recalled the conversation, he said: "Ed, I don't know anything about Vernon Savings and Loan. I don't know if it's a valid operation or not. I don't know if it's meritorious. But this man, Dixon, claims so and so. He's being kicked out of business. He's got a week or three or four days that he can save it and avoid foreclosure. Why don't you look into it?"

Gray said he told Wright that his information was bad: "I told Jim Wright we're not going to close down Vernon Savings because I'm the one who calls the meetings, and I don't know anything about it." Gray said he would clarify what was going on and get back to the Speaker. But Wright responded that he was about to get on a plane back to Washington and Gray should phone John Mack with any information.

After Wright hung up, Gray got right on the phone to Roy Green in Dallas and asked about the status of Vernon Savings. Green started briefing Gray on what he knew about Vernon. Gray said he wasn't too shocked at the gory details. "You have to remember," he said, "we had hundreds of these things by now." Dallas supervisory agents had asked the Vernon board to sign a consent-to-merge agreement, a preliminary step to a federal takeover, but no one had plans to close Vernon that day, the next day, or even the next week, mainly because FSLIC didn't have enough money to shut the place down. Gray hung up, got John Mack on the phone, and asked him to assure the Speaker that no one would be closing down Vernon Savings. Gray explained there were negotiations under way over a consent-to-merge agreement, but that was far different from closing someone down. Mack seemed to accept the response and told Gray a delay was important because Dixon had an investor in Louisiana who wanted to recapitalize the institution.

"I said, hey, be our guest if he has someone with money to pour into Vernon Savings," Gray said. "John didn't say who the guy from Louisiana was. But I said, whoever these people are, John, they've got to be insane to want to recapitalize an institution like that. He seemed to be satisfied with that and I hung up."

Within forty-five minutes, though, Mack was back on the phone. Gray said he was very angry. Mack said he had talked to his source, which was Don Dixon, and that the consent-to-merge action was tantamount to closing him down. Gray insisted that Mack's sources were mistaken, and the bank board would not be taking action of any kind until after the Christmas break. Mack was not satisfied.

This was bad news. Getting on the wrong side of John Mack was as bad as being in trouble with Wright. As the Speaker's top aide, Mack wielded enormous influence on Capitol Hill. He was extremely close to Wright. The two went back more than twenty years when Congressman Jim Wright rescued Mack from a long prison term. A nineteen-year-old manager of a Virginia discount import store in 1973, Mack had nearly murdered a young woman who had entered the store just before it closed. It was a brutal attack. For no apparent reason, Mack had pounded the twenty-year-old college student repeatedly with a hammer, exposing her skull in five places. He then grabbed a steak knife, stabbed her five times in the left breast and shoulder near her heart, slashed her repeatedly across the throat, and drove her away in her car, leaving her for dead in an alley behind the store. He then went to the movies.

The girl miraculously survived, though, got to a hospital, and Mack was arrested the next day, eventually pleading guilty to malicious wounding. He was sentenced to fifteen years in the Virginia State Penitentiary, but he only served twenty-seven months in the less oppressive confines of the Fairfax County jail before being paroled to take a job as a staff assistant in Wright's office. At the time, Wright's daughter was married to Mack's brother. Mack had remained with Wright ever since, rising to become the most powerful staff member on Capitol Hill, despite his record as a convicted felon. Other lawmakers were vaguely aware of his background and praised Wright for giving a young man who had made a mistake another chance.

Now Ed Gray would need another chance, but he wouldn't be so lucky.

Just after the first of the year, the Federal Home Loan Bank in Dallas received four proposals regarding Vernon Savings. The bank supervisors had heard that Vernon was contemplating a stock sale. But none of the plans represented a viable plan for solving Vernon's problems. All four were rejected.

The regulators were still in charge at Vernon as the 100th Congress convened a few days later. One of the first pieces of legislation to surface was the $15-billion FSLIC recapitalization bill that was introduced into the House. The legislation was a top administration priority; the deposit-insurance fund lacked the funds to shut down sick S&Ls. Over the course of the next year, they would lure millions in federally insured deposits into their vaults, keeping themselves alive but increasing the exposure of the FSLIC to massive losses.

But the chances for quick action on the bill had diminished significantly. Wright was furious at Ed Gray. So was John Mack. Both thought the bank board chairman had double-crossed them and moved against Dixon the very day he had promised otherwise. Opposition to the bill also intensified in the industry. Curlee's group opposed the legislation, saying it unfairly discriminated against Texas and states facing an economic depression. The powerful U.S. League was against it, too. Its leadership said the League would back only a $5-billion plan with forbearance provisions that required regulators to ease up on what the League euphemistically referred to as "well-managed institutions in trouble due to local economic conditions." It was the kind of thing that the highfliers wanted.

No less an authority than Joe Morris, then chairman of the U.S. League, issued a statement that said savings and loans in economically depressed regions of the nation needed special dispensation from the rules so they could work out their problems. "We are keeping to a minimum the eventual cost to the FSLIC," he said, arguing that a failure to stretch the regulations would force the closing of many institutions that were well managed and provided a needed service to the community.

Gray was livid. He later complained that the U.S. League catered to the Don Dixons of the industry at the expense of its other members: "You bet they did. Everything was put in simple terms. We've got to protect the industry. They're all dues-paying members. Why else would you have the League if you weren't there to protect the dues-paying members? All they cared about was the weak sisters. And trying to lift the weak sisters, everybody drowns.''

The House Banking Committee held hearings on the legislation three weeks later. As Roy Green and Joe Selby sat down in the cavernous banking-committee hearing room, Green spotted a familiar figure sitting nearby. "Joe," Green said to Selby, "have you met Durward Curlee?"

"Oh, yeah," Curlee replied, shaking Selby's hand. "I've heard of you through a mutual friend. From what I understand, he's the only friend you've got."

After the morning testimony, Wright met for lunch with some of the thrift industry's powerhouses—W. W. (Bo) McAllister of the San Antonio Savings Association, Texas Savings and Loan League president Tom King, and U.S. League president William O'Connell. "Speaker Wright indicated to us that he was considering slowing up the FSLIC recap until he was satisfied with efforts toward forbearance," McAllister later wrote in the Texas League's magazine. "We encouraged him to take this action and that is exactly what happened."

By February, bank board officials could see the recap legislation was stuck again. Wright, who had an infamous temper, remained furious with Gray. At best Wright considered Gray an incompetent—ignorant of the actions of his own bureaucrats. At worst he was a liar. With the FSLIC legislation in limbo, the bank board regulators' hands were tied. The situation simply got worse. Money-losing S&Ls took on more deposits to cover their losses, and the cost of resolving the overall problem escalated rapidly. Finally, Selby suggested that they arrange a meeting with Wright to explain why the Dallas district bank had increased its emphasis on regulation and supervision and to emphasize the need for the legislation. Robert Strauss, the former Democratic National Committee chairman and Washington lawyer, and Livingston Cosberg, a wealthy Houston S&L operator, set up the session.

At three-thirty on February 10, Selby, Green, William Black, a bank board lawyer, and another regulator walked into Wright's office. They were apprehensive. Complaints about federal regulators were pouring in from all corners of Capitol Hill by now. But few lawmakers had Wright's power to block critical legislation. "It seemed like there was nothing we could give Wright," Black told John M. Barry, an author allowed to attend the meeting because he was doing a book on the Speaker. "We gave him the conservator's head for Craig Hall. He still comes after you. Gray met with Gaubert. He still comes after us. He asks for Selby's head. Gray couldn't look himself in the mirror if he fired Selby. Then he tried to help Dixon. From Gray's perspective and mine, we were being blackmailed. We paid and the price kept going up."

The regulators were ready to bolster their case by showing Wright some unflattering confidential reports about Vernon and Dixon, but they changed their minds when they walked into the Speaker's office. Wright sat at his desk flanked by his aides, John Mack and Marshall Lyman. Author John Barry was in the meeting, too. That didn't bother the regulators. But they were stunned to see the other two men present—George Mallick and his son, Michael, private citizens who had just presented the Speaker with a slanted report on the savings and loan situation that was highly critical of the federal regulators. Black said that the presence of the Mallicks had a chilling effect on the entire discussion.

Green, a Southerner, began the presentation, explaining the role of the Dallas bank, what the regulators were trying to do, and telling the Speaker that the sickest S&Ls had to be closed to limit the damage and to save the healthy ones. He went on for about a half hour.

After he finished, Selby turned to the Speaker and said, "We just wanted to show you we didn't have horns."

Wright eyed Selby suspiciously, according to Barry's account of the meeting. "People are afraid. Solid businessmen are frightened of you," Wright said. "They tell me you've been punitive. They say, 'If Joe Selby heard me say this, I'd be out of business.'"

Green tried to smooth things over, but Wright kept it up. "They worry that if FSLIC gets this fifteen billion dollars, they'll put people out of business willy-nilly. Seems to me that's what you were doing."

Green figured the Speaker's remarks referred to Dixon and

Vernon Savings and raised the subject to clear the air. Green argued that the bank board was unaware that anyone was really interested in buying Vernon.

Wright countered that Dixon had said he had a interested buyer.

Green was on the defensive, trying to explain that there was a difference between a consent to merge, a conservator, and actually closing an institution.

"They didn't want any of those things," Wright fired back. "They wanted a week. Dixon said he had a buyer and needed a week. Mr. Gray told me there was no way he would not have that opportunity. You're talking semantics now, you're talking words."

Black, a red-bearded, gutsy lawyer who likes to cut right to the issue, had had enough. He challenged Wright aggressively, saying "those aren't just words." Gray, said Black, had not tried to mislead the speaker. Some attending the meeting interpreted Black's remarks as an attempt to bait Wright. Others said he was simply trying to correct the record. By all accounts, though, he angered Wright, and the Speaker's legendary temper, complete with the arching of his bushy eyebrows, flared. He leaned across his desk: "Now just a goddamn minute," he said to Black. "I listened to you. Now you listen to me."

The room fell silent for one of those awkward moments that seem to last for hours. Green tried to smooth things over once again. But the meeting ended soon afterward. Black didn't forget about the exchange. Jim Wright didn't either.

21 The Cops Come

Raylan Loggins says he'll never forget the day the feds closed Vernon Savings and Loan.

The takeover came as no surprise to Loggins, a thin man of medium height with short dark hair, dark glasses, and a dry wit. He knew that Vernon had serious problems from the day he joined the staff in February 1986. Loggins had been hired as a workout specialist—someone who takes bad loans and tries to work them out with borrowers so they become good loans. He had worked at several S&Ls and finance companies over the past ten years before he landed at Vernon.

"I had researched the place. Vernon had a reputation of being a lender of last resort for people. But it was still listed as the third-highest return on equity in the state. I talked with Ray Jeter about a job and he made the great financial understatement of the year. He told me, 'I think we have a few problems here, but you can work them out in six months.' "

Loggins got a flavor of the problems after working for Vernon less than twenty-four hours. "Financial institutions keep a daily ledger and mark a trial balance every day," he explains. "That's how you keep track of what's going on. I asked to be put on the list to receive the daily ledger. I was told that they didn't keep one. They said they tried to, but they could never make it balance so they'd quit and hadn't kept one for fifteen months."

239

Loggins's career at Vernon blossomed. Within three months he was made a vice president. He got on the bonus plan. As regulators forced Lemons, King, Malone, and the others to quit, Loggins's star rose. Yet anyone could see that the place had big troubles. Just seven months after he had signed on, the state of Texas moved in and put Earl Hall in charge. That's when things really started to deteriorate.

Loggins and other Vernon employees portrayed Hall as a "nice little man" who tried to do his job but was woefully ill equipped to handle the huge problem that had been dumped in his lap. Bowman, who was Hall's boss, said he was never supposed to go into Vernon and run the place for any length of time. The state had seized control of Vernon because it could act more quickly than the feds, Bowman said, adding that someone had to stop Vernon before it crippled other thrifts in the state:

> We hired some consultants to do a study of their salaries and to do an operations analysis. The FSLIC was supposed to be in there to take over within ninety days. But the FSLIC didn't have any money. Every time you turned around, it had a different director. It just wouldn't get going. You could have had Jesus Christ go in there and he couldn't have done any better. Earl effectively became the CEO and tried to preserve whatever integrity Vernon Savings had. But with the situation he had and with the economy so bad, the hole was just going to get deeper.

Hall's ill-fated commandeering of Dixon's office was only his first misstep. Once in control, he limped around the office and quickly learned what a mess he had on his hands. Vernon's books and records were in disarray. By the time that the state had intervened in September 1986, state and federal examiners had been in the institution for months, combing through documents and unearthing astonishing items. They had never seen anything like it. Vernon's fleet of aircraft had grown to six, including the Falcon 50 and a jet-black helicopter in San Diego that looked more suitable for combat in Cambodia than commerce in California. Examiners showed Hall one of Philippe Junot's expense accounts; it was for $12,000. Vernon had ordered another airplane—a $13.5-million "Star Wars" model. Then came documentation of abuses by Vernon's management—the huge bonuses, the exclusive use of nonearning assets such as beach houses, the yacht, the hunting lodge, the luxury cars, and the art collection. There was the travel; Dixon had billed Vernon Savings for $17,319 to cover "business expenses" for the trip to Europe that included his visit with the Pope and side trips to the Gucci and Bulgari spas. And the appraisals used to assign values to the collateral on some loans were often done months after the actual loan was approved.

In some cases, Hall knew what to do. He grounded the fleet of airplanes, canceled the order for the new jet, and refused to pay Junot any money. Dixon had purchased dozens of paintings for Vernon's portfolio, such as George Phippen's *Brush with the Hostiles* and Clark Hulings's *Mule with a Plaid Blanket*. He had paid $125,000 for the two oil-on-canvas westerns. Hall had them appraised to determine how much they would fetch in a sale: only about $45,000. So much for the art collection valued at $5 million.

Out in Carlsbad, California, a government investigator found a huge shipping container with more than $500,000 worth of antiques in a warehouse for Dondi Designs, the Vernon subsidiary that owned the antique store Dana operated in Rancho Santa Fe. The array of goods in the container, which had been hauled there by truck, baffled investigators. There was a seventeenth-century coconut cup bearing the coat of arms of the Duke of Lennox; a Byzantine monastic cistern; sixteen antique Spanish chairs; two finely carved walking-stick stands in the form of grizzly bears; a Gothic refectory table; a cast-iron coat of arms of the Borough of Lowestoft in Suffolk; a pair of large brass-and-iron firedogs; an Indian bronze caldron with cow heads; and dozens of other items.

The government checked out the value of the container's contents with James Hepworth, a London art dealer who had originally assisted the Dixons with the purchases. But the investigators just came back with more bad news for Hall. Although the antiques had been financed by Vernon's Dondi Designs subsidiary, Hepworth told the government that Dixon and his wife planned to use the stuff.

"Hepworth acknowledged that Don and Dana Dixon had

purchased the container of antiques for their own private residence in Rancho Santa Fe," a report on the interview said,
adding:

> Hepworth said Dixon wanted the Spanish-castle
> look and he bought heavily carved oak furniture to
> achieve this decor. All items were to the Dixons' per-
> sonal taste. The southern-Italian stone well with origi-
> nal ironwork valued at about $17,000 was an item that
> the Dixons loved and had to buy. These items were not
> for commercial sale, and Hepworth stated they would
> be difficult to sell on that basis. He added that individ-
> uals in Europe generally did not buy heavily carved
> Spanish furnishings, and he was not certain about the
> clientele in the U.S. He said he thought it would take an
> extremely long time to sell the items.

Hall reported his findings to Bowman, Selby, and other
federal officials, who began making investigation referrals to the
criminal division of the U.S. Justice Department. He also hired a
consultant to study the bonus plan at Vernon, only to discover
that the board had never really authorized it. He started seeking
more resignations and firing some senior officers. But there were
some problems at Vernon that no one could resolve.

Before the state had assumed control in the fall of 1986, the
thrift's officers had said the value of Vernon's assets ($1.418
billion) exceeded the amount it owed depositors and other
creditors ($1.362 billion) by $55 million, which was the net
worth it had reported on its June 1986 financial statement. It had
also reported a steady string of profits from its operations. A
thrift with a net worth of $55 million was solvent—a status that
insulates it from a government takeover. The government can
take over a thrift only if it is insolvent. After its examiners
unearthed some suspect transactions in routine exams during
July, though, the bank board had launched a more thorough
exam of Vernon and had started questioning its financial stability. By August, preliminary indications suggested Vernon's solvency seemed to rest on its ability to overstate its net worth by
hiding financial losses. By the time Hall took control, the examiners from the bank board and FSLIC were thoroughly examining
individual loans to determine if there were hidden problems. If

the true value of the thrift's assets was lower than the total Vernon owed its depositors and other creditors, Vernon would be considered insolvent and therefore be eligible for federal takeover.

But by seizing the thrift, the regulators created an even bigger mess. As examiners moved in to pore over Vernon's loans and investments and document the extent of its problems, the thrift's normal operations came to a halt. With Hall in charge, no one seemed to have any authority to renew loans, deal with problems, or make fundamental decisions. Vernon's loan portfolio had been structured to maximize fees by rolling loans over every six months. Soon loans started lapsing into default rapidly as borrowers encountered due dates and couldn't get their loans extended. The borrowers started screaming, but it didn't do much good. The cease-and-desist order the board of directors signed the past August had sharply restricted Vernon's ability to make renewals. Even if Hall had wanted to renew the loans, the federal cease-and-desist order made it next to impossible. Hall didn't know what course to take.

"We used to have a game at my offices," said Jack Atkinson, who was listed as Vernon's largest borrower. "I'd come in first thing in the morning and call Earl Hall and ask him to call me. Then we'd take bets if he'd ever call back. I never did talk to him. I've never even seen him."

Some former Vernon employees said Hall wasn't really to blame. "The feds were running the show," said a former Vernon executive who worked at Vernon under Hall. "We had loans out that would come due. The feds would say collect. These guys couldn't pay; they were real estate developers; they operated on no cash. You couldn't get a decision out of anyone. No payments, no decisions. Pretty soon the guy would go into Chapter Eleven bankruptcy and tie up the property. If they would have restructured the loans, they would have lost money. But nothing like what eventually happened."

By November, just two months after Hall had taken over, the inaction had clearly made the situation worse. Vernon's income from loans literally dropped off the chart. Many of the borrowers unquestionably deserved to have their loans called. The only reason they wanted renewals was to rip off more money, keep their high-flying lifestyles intact, and hide their ill-gotten gains in some annuity they could shield from their creditors in bankruptcy court. But the best interest of the party that stood behind the deposits—the American taxpayer—wasn't served, either. A lender who faces a loan in default wants to keep in close contact with the borrower. He can encourage him to make whatever loan payments he can afford and take any steps necessary to protect the collateral on a loan against seizure by another creditor.

"In real estate development, I don't care what you do," said Atkinson, who later went to jail for his financial shenanigans, "but you have to do something. The worst thing you can do is nothing, and that is exactly what the government did."

As the examiners combed through Vernon's loan portfolio, Loggins said workouts became nearly impossible. He agreed that the thrift's already dubious assets started to deteriorate further once the state took over. Vernon's financial reports at the bank board suddenly showed plunging income. In the three months ending in December 1986, Vernon reported no income from its operations. Even Selby agreed that the government had never faced anything quite like Vernon. No one really knew what to do, and Hall didn't appear capable of handling the situation.

Said Loggins:

> Earl looked like he was in his sixties. He was a chain-smoker and he had a heart condition or something. One day I was talking to him and his hands started shaking, then his body started shaking. He's holding on to the desk and the desk started shaking, and he grabs for the drawer and takes a pill to stop it. He'd show up about nine or nine-thirty, take a couple of hours for lunch, and leave about four or four-thirty. Looked like a little old lady driving out of the parking lot in Woody's big ol' Cadillac. He brought some people in with him. There were a couple that were pretty smart. But they didn't do anything, either. One guy was named Lou. He's pretty smart and I figure he might do something. He takes this desk and the in-box starts filling up with stuff. I'm watching it and I say to myself he's got to do something pretty soon because his in-box is full. He did. He got another in-box.

A lot of employees and borrowers think the government officials did nothing on purpose; they wanted the loans to deteriorate and give them an excuse to take over Vernon on the grounds of insolvency. Actually, though, the government simply made a bad situation worse. No matter what they might have done, nothing could save Vernon Savings.

Of the $1.5 billion Vernon had raked in and still owed depositors when Hall took over, only about 15 percent had been invested in home loans. The rest had been stuffed into other kinds of loans, mainly high-risk, speculative investments. Upon closer inspection, the examiners found that Vernon had dozens of big loans that had been delinquent for months.

Under government rules, a thrift with delinquent loans was supposed to have set up a reserve to account for the fact that it might not get repaid. If Vernon had $10 million worth of delinquent loans, it should have set up a $10-million loan-loss reserve that would have highlighted the dubious nature of its assets. The reserve would have triggered a corresponding decline in its net worth. But the examiners that Hall had authorized to scrutinize the books soon discovered that Vernon officials had engaged in all sorts of flimflam to hide the delinquent loans from examiners. As a result, Vernon had not been forced to take a hit on its net worth, which was the crucial number that the regulators had been watching.

Vernon had used several tricks to avoid the reality of its bad loans.

The easiest one had been to replace the overdue note with a new loan—one that included an unwritten understanding that the borrower would use the proceeds of the new loan to pay the interest on the old one. That bought everyone a little time and provided an insight into why all the developers were frantically calling Earl Hall.

Vernon had also activated the daisy chain and had swapped bum loans with another thrift. One variant was called trading a dead horse for a dead cow. Vernon had lent developers enough money to pay off their troubled loans at another thrift, and the other thrift had reciprocated by lending one of Vernon's developers enough money to pay off his bum loan at Vernon.

Vernon had also sold the bad loans to other greedy S&Ls with an unwritten understanding that Vernon would buy back the loan if the borrower defaulted. Under the deal, Vernon had continued servicing the loan, collecting monthly interest payments from the borrower, and passing them along to the institution that acquired the loan. When some of the borrowers had failed to meet the monthly payments, though, Vernon hadn't paid off the loans. The thrift had simply raised its interest rates to lure some fresh deposits and had made the payments to cover up the default.

Obviously all of these tricks would have been apparent to examiners months before had Vernon kept accurate records. But the team that went into the thrift after Hall took over discovered that the records were as phony as the daisy chain. Once every month, someone had to butcher the delinquency report to cover up any problem loans. Just months before the state had taken over at Vernon, the officer in charge of the overdue-loan list—Roy Dickey—had ordered an accountant to prepare an accurate delinquency report so he could see how bad things really were.

When Chris Barker called Dickey with his conclusions, Dickey was stunned. "He had no idea [the number of overdue loans] would be that large," Barker said, "and I remember one of the first things he said was, what can we do to make that number smaller?"

The loans weren't the only problems. Bank board examiners were shocked to discover that nearly three-fourths of Vernon's income was self-generated. In other words, Vernon got 75 percent of its earnings from the fees and points it got through the old Vernon shuffle.

Had the Texas economy turned around and had oil prices boomed as everyone had hoped they would, the whole mess would probably have been covered up. But the economy didn't go along with the sham, and within two months of the state takeover, federal officials were thinking about closing Vernon down. "By this time, the state was looking for a way to say we were insolvent," said Loggins. "They were trying to strangle us slowly—to cut us off by stopping any more loans. They started getting rid of more guys. The turnover was quite high. Every day you would look up and wonder who was in charge or do I have my job. Everybody had a bunker mentality. Nothing was getting done."

By early 1987, a review of only 60 percent of Vernon's outstanding loans and investments showed that the thrift would have to write down its assets by $300 million. That meant the value of Vernon's assets had slipped below its liabilities to depositors and creditors. It had no capital to fall back upon, and the situation would just deteriorate the longer the thrift remained open. Vernon had to keep deposits flowing in; that was the only way it could pay salaries and other bills. But 80 percent of its loans were high-risk deals; they continued to slip into default and lose value. More than $1 billion in loans was sixty days or more overdue. More operating losses loomed on the horizon. The thrift was broke. There was no doubt about it. By allowing Vernon to remain open from June to December of 1986, the government had already exposed the FSLIC to an additional $200 million in liabilities. Government officials estimated that Vernon would need an additional $400 million in high-cost deposits guaranteed by the FSLIC simply to meet its existing commitments during 1987.

Dixon continued his efforts to raise money. At one point, Dondi Financial Corp. filed a statement with the Securities and Exchange Commission to sell some stock in a private sale. Rocky Crocker, a onetime Vernon general counsel, said Dixon wasn't trying to bail out of the situation. He wanted to sell Dondi Financial stock so he could raise capital to put into the thrift, Crocker said. But it wasn't enough. Dixon started selling some of his personal assets, too, such as his car collection. But the money didn't go into Vernon Savings. It went into bank accounts under Dixon's personal control.

Despite Vernon Savings's gloomy finances, the government concluded that it couldn't close the thrift. The lobbying campaign launched by Dixon, Keating, Curlee, and the others had created a legislative impasse back in Washington. The FSLIC didn't have enough money to shut anybody down. The bank board would have to take a more creative approach.

The meeting on what to do about Vernon convened in the sixth-floor boardroom of the Federal Home Loan Bank Board in Washington at 9:20 A.M. on Friday, March 20, 1987. It was a typical hush-hush deal. Tom Melo, a bank board staffer, gave an overview, tracing Vernon's history from a traditional thrift concentrating on home loans to Don Dixon's daisy chain. "The association," he said, "reported one point three billion dollars in delinquent loans on twelve/thirty-one/'eighty-six."

"One point three billion dollars?" said an incredulous Gray, who was in California and attending the meeting via telephone hookup.

"Yes," replied Melo. He continued to recite Vernon's problems—poor lending practices, loans to buddies, excessive dividends, big salaries, and significant losses. When he was done, Gray asked if Vernon was the same thrift that he had recently seen as the institution with the highest return on assets in the *National Thrift News* survey. "I think it would be instructive for all of us if you could explain how it could have such a high return and what happened."

Melo told the board members how Vernon had operated. Soon Bowman joined in by phone from Austin. "The biggest problem that we encountered after we got in there," Bowman said, "was the way they had generated their profits internally." Bowman estimated that about 90 percent of Vernon's income during 1984 and 1985 had been created by interest payments and assessments that the institution had included in its loans to developers so the borrowers could turn around and pay the money to Vernon as points and loan fees.

There was no doubt that Vernon's condition had deteriorated badly. A big part of the reason was Dixon's leadership of the institution. But the government's mismanagement had made the situation worse than any of the bureaucrats were willing to admit. In an ideal world, the bank board would have voted to shut the place down, take over its assets, and pay off depositors. Government estimates suggested that Vernon was losing $10 million a month, and federally insured deposits were being used to cover those losses. But thanks to Jim Wright and his pals on Capitol Hill, the board couldn't afford to take such a step.

So the bank board took up a plan to take over Vernon Savings and place it in the management consigment program (MCP) for ailing thrifts, an action that would wipe out Vernon's stockholders and place the thrift under the control of new managers appointed by the government. It was the kind of thing that the bank board had been doing with increasing frequency until it could get some more money from Congress.

In effect, the bank board would vote to put Vernon Savings in a holding pattern and acquire its assets by government fiat. Uncle Sam was responsible for the repayment of all deposits of up to $100,000. It was a big step. Assuming such a large burden exposed the beleaguered FSLIC fund to a potential payout of $1.7 billion. No one knew what Vernon's assets were worth, but they would clearly not cover the $1.7-billion debt to depositors that FSLIC had assumed. If luck held out, the bank board's consumer-affairs officers would be able to sooth the jittery nerves of depositors the following Monday so that hordes of savers wouldn't ask for their money back right away. Through press releases and the stationing of bank board employees in Vernon's branches, the government could try to assure frightened savers that Uncle Sam—or the FSLIC fund—still stood behind every dollar in insured deposits and that there was no reason to withdraw their money. Despite Gray's warnings about the insolvency of the FSLIC, most Americans didn't have the foggiest notion that the deposit-insurance fund was broke. "Nobody here went running over there to get their money out," said Vernon resident Jack Eure. "They felt like as long as there was a sugar daddy, then things were all right with the insurance; they didn't have anything to worry about. The smart people probably knew the insurance fund was in trouble. But the ordinary person didn't. They just kept their money in there because they were paying that high interest." As long as they believed the government would take care of them, there would be no run on deposits and FSLIC wouldn't have to honor its guarantee for months, if at all.

Meanwhile, FSLIC and the local Dallas bank would provide Vernon with any emergency funds it might need and keep the thrift open to see if the government-appointed management team could reverse Vernon's fortunes. Outright liquidation remained a future option, but Bowman asked that it not be considered anytime soon. He feared an actual closing of Vernon would trigger severe problems on the already depressed Dallas real estate markets, and in seventy-five other savings and loans that had been heavily involved in buying loan participations from Vernon.

The bank board next turned to a discussion of who would be hired to run the place. The staff recommended San Antonio Savings Association (SASA), which was run by a good Republican, Bo McAllister in San Antonio. SASA would get an initial fee of up to $35,000 to recoup any expenses incurred in preparation for a takeover; a monthly management fee of $25,000 per month for the first three months; $15,000 for each subsequent month; plus 135 percent of SASA salaries and benefits. Before voting to approve the takeover, bank board member Larry White remarked that "this is indeed a sorry tale. Are we satisfied that today we have enough procedures and enough controls in place so this couldn't happen again?"

Raylan Loggins was sitting at his desk in Vernon's Dallas branch. It was another Friday Watch—a Miller time of sorts for Vernon employees, who wandered into Loggins's office to drink a few beers before everyone quit for the week. A gallows humor dominated the Friday sessions. The employees knew federal regulators always closed thrifts after business hours on a Friday afternoon. Loggins and his colleagues gathered at the end of the work week to drink beer and place bets on whether that Friday would be their last.

Dixon was long gone. By early 1987, he was living in California, selling off assets and parrying inquiries from the government. He was living in a rented house. His castle at Rancho Santa Fe had not been completed; builder Ray Schooley had even accused him of absconding with the Spanish-castle doors, which were missing from the front entry. R. B. Tanner had moved to Denton, Texas, and was wondering if he would ever see any of his money again. Many of the other members of the Vernon team had scattered around the state and the nation.

Around three-thirty P.M., Loggins's phone rang. It was a lawyer friend from the other end of Vernon's building. "You want to have a laugh," the friend told Loggins, "just look out in the parking lot." Vernon's two-story offices had large plate-glass windows with a view of the asphalt parking lot that ran the length of the building. Loggins couldn't see very well from his office. So he wandered over to his friend's desk on the second floor of the building. The closing wasn't exactly a stealth operation:

> There was this white Dodge with blackwalls out in the parking lot. It was obviously a security guard's car. This woman got out and started walking around. Then another white Dodge with blackwalls pulled in the lot. A man got out. They had big pistols on their belts, looked like .357 magnums or something. They walked around, trying to figure out what to do. We were looking out the window laughing at them. They obviously didn't know where to go. They went to the west door; it

was locked. Then they went to the center door. They
looked in but then went back to their cars. We were
laughing. By now a lot of people are looking out the
windows. Then another white Dodge with blackwalls
pulls into the parking lot and six guys get out. They're
all wearing black suits, white shirts, red ties, and cheap
shoes. They all had attaché cases and marched in lock-
step toward the door. It was like an MTV video. We
were all looking out the window laughing. By this time
everyone had started drinking, too, which didn't help.

The Friday Watch was over. Vernon Savings was about to be
taken over by the federal government. The people from SASA
accompanied the government officials who marched across Vernon's parking lot and into the building. They stood by all of the
doors, asking employees not to leave. "They broke us up in about
two or three groups and took us out on the patio," said Loggins.

They told us what was going on and asked for our
cooperation. They said we wouldn't be able to leave for
a while and not to take anything out of our desks. People
had removed everything they didn't want them to see
six months ago anyway. They said we couldn't take
anything out of the building, either, and that the security guards would stop anyone at the doors. We were
allowed to make one phone call. It was silly, like the
gestapo or something. Then we all sat around and
watched them search Dick Veteto's car out in the parking lot. Some of the clerks and the lower-ranking people
got kind of scared. I just went back to my office and had
another beer.
    They started to call everyone in. Later in the eve-
ning after a lot of people had left, they came into my
office and said I was needed upstairs. I went up to the
second floor and there were a bunch of FSLIC people in
a room eating pizza and drinking beer. They offered me
some pizza and a beer and asked me what I knew about
Don Dixon. I said, "What do you want to know?"

22 The Black Hole

Vernon Savings survived the Federal Home Loan Bank Board longer than Ed Gray did. Gray had returned to Washington from his San Diego home a troubled man. House Speaker Jim Wright had misunderstood what had happened with Vernon Savings. He remained furious. Soon after arriving back at his office, though, Gray discovered he had other problems—lots of them. The knives were out for him in Washington. The signs were everywhere.

His first clue came in early January when a long letter landed on his desk from Rep. John Dingell, a Michigan Democrat, confidant of the House leadership, and one of the toughest men on Capitol Hill. Dingell, the chairman of the House Energy and Commerce Committee, was notorious for using his oversight subcommittee to investigate anything remotely concerned with commerce and energy. He cut a wide swath in Washington and had focused his sights on the FSLIC, using the pretense that it involved accounting and securities issues.

His staff had received anonymous tips in October 1986—the same month that Jim Wright heard the complaints at the country club in Fort Worth—about conflicts of interest and fraud at a resort that FSLIC had acquired during an S&L rescue in Lake Placid, New York. Dingell's investigations subcommittee was looking into the situation.

252

This was trouble. Gray would have to play a key role in the administration's new drive for a $15-billion FSLIC recap bill. The last thing he needed was another attack on Capitol Hill. His critics had just finished one assault. Thrift executives opposed to Gray's policies had leaked expense reports suggesting that Gray lived like royalty during his extensive travels. Newspaper headlines such as one in the *Washington Post*—"Bank Board Lived Well Off S&Ls"—detailed how Gray and other bank board members had racked up expenses like a $649-a-night room in the Waldorf-Astoria, a $4,000 limousine bill in Dallas, and a $5,000 hotel bill in California, all paid for by the industry through its support of the district banks. In the rough-and-tumble political world of Washington, the headlines were like having your name in neon on a pornographic bookstore marquee. Gray had been humiliated, his credibility shattered. Friends and enemies on Capitol Hill blasted his profligate ways.

Stunned and hurt, Gray fought back, slamming the industry for unauthorized disclosure of private reports. But he knew he'd been had by his opponents and he hated it. If Ed Gray was susceptible to anything, it was bad judgment, and his enemies had just landed a solid punch. Finally he wrote to St. Germain apologizing for his flawed judgment. It was vintage Gray. After admitting he erred in the first sentence, he went on for two single-spaced pages, defending his travel and documenting the financial strains under which he operated. Ed Gray was paid $75,000 a year, far less than many of the thrift executives who opposed him. He lived in a $500-a-month flat, worked dawn-to-dusk hours, mailed his paycheck to his family in California, and had even raided his daughter's college tuition fund to get by. He was $80,000 in debt. Yet in his obsession to prove his honor, he pledged to repay $28,000 in expenses and tried to put the ugly mess behind him.

Now he had Dingell crawling up his back. Congressional hearings staged by the towering Michigan Democrat usually resembled public floggings. Dingell's letter presented Gray with a long list of questions and told him that a "lack of cooperation is not helpful."

Gray had just started answering some of the questions when another bombshell hit. Someone leaked a Booz Allen & Hamilton report to the *Post* that blasted the bank board's operation of FSLIC. Staffers on Dingell's subcommittee soon started leaking investigative memos comparing Ed Gray unfavorably to Pentagon contractors.

Then came Rep. Carroll Hubbard, the Kentucky Democrat who had been summoned to Fort Worth by Wright to attend the country club meeting. Although the public didn't know it, he had more than one reason to haul Gray before his House banking oversight committee for hearings. Just a few months before, he had written Gray a letter asking for financial assistance for First Federal Savings and Loan of Mayfield, Kentucky, Hubbard's hometown.

The institution had gotten into financial trouble and was heading toward insolvency. Hubbard told Gray the thrift was special to him: "I don't own any interest in the institution," he said in his letter. "To be open and candid with my friend, Ed Gray, I want you to know that before I was elected to Congress in 1974, I did substantial legal work for First Federal. Some of my closest friends in my hometown are on the board of directors." Included in his plea for federal assistance and special treatment for the thrift was one sentence written all in capital letters: "THE ONLY SOLUTION IS THAT FIRST FEDERAL NEEDS WORKOUT TIME AND FINANCIAL ASSISTANCE TO GET OVER THE RE-STRUCTURING HUMP THEY ARE HAVING TO ABSORB."

The letter was like many Gray received from congressmen who would later express outrage about the delays that drove up the cost of the savings and loan scandal. Gray didn't even see it; he routinely had such letters referred to his office of congressional relations.

About six months later, though, Hubbard called Gray before his oversight subcommittee and demanded to know why the FSLIC had hired an accountant with no resort-management experience for $97,000 a year to manage the Lake Placid resort. When Gray responded that it was hard to get anyone for the job in that area of the country, things got nasty. Hubbard shot back: "What about the fact that he might have been hired on the recommendations of his brother, who was working as a lawyer for the FSLIC? Am I way off base, or am I hitting a home run on that one?" Those guys from Kentucky were sure subtle.

Meanwhile, Gray's FSLIC recap bill hadn't fared much better than the chairman. In the one month since the bill had been introduced, St. Germain had canceled two subcommittee sessions scheduled to prepare the legislation for full committee consideration. Speaker Wright had come out for a measure that would give the FSLIC only $10 billion and bind its hands with rules designed to protect ailing thrifts from overzealous regulators. Rep. Steve Bartlett, a Texas Republican who had the staunch support of the Curlee group and other Texas S&Ls, had prepared a list of amendments to weaken the administration bill, and the U.S. League supported the weakest version around.

When Congress's own auditors from the General Accounting Office (GAO) told a House subcommittee that the $15 billion was the minimum needed and that the FSLIC itself was hopelessly insolvent, the League's O'Connell publicly accused the agency of trying to frighten Congress into passing a bloated bill. His arguments sounded like the same ones advanced by Curlee's clients.

"We do not think that it is proper for Congress and the public at large to be misled about the true condition of the FSLIC," O'Connell wrote to Senate Banking Committee chairman William Proxmire. "We contend that the problems facing the FSLIC have been aggravated by the Bank Board's refusal up to now to take into account the difficulties facing institutions in the dozen or so states with serious economic problems and the board's insistence on using unrealistic standards for determining the quality and value of assets held by institutions in these areas. It is clear to us that the information from the GAO is part of an effort to justify the huge $15-billion FSLIC funding program."

By the time the bank board voted to take over Vernon Savings and place it in the MCP, the legislation had come to a head in Washington. Late in March 1987, the Senate passed the Competitive Equality Banking Act, providing only $7.5 billion for the FSLIC, far short of what would be needed. If the bank board and the administration were going to get more money, it would have to come from the Democratically controlled House.

Things looked bleak for Ed Gray. Under attack by Democrats, Republicans, and the U.S. League, Gray was reeling. A House banking subcommittee gave him a brief victory when it voted 42 to 1 in favor of giving the FSLIC an additional $15 billion. But the full committee soon reversed the vote and approved a plan providing only $5 billion, which is exactly what the U.S. League said it would support. As the bill headed toward the House floor for a vote in April, Gray knew he was history. His term was set to expire in June, just a few months away. He had told the administration he didn't want to be reappointed. But even if he had, it was clear that the White House had other things in mind. Treasury Secretary Baker had traveled to Texas to assure Wright that Gray was out.

With little else to lose and the end near, Gray and his staff finally struck back. In late April, Gray appeared before Dingell's subcommittee and blasted the industry. He accused "some elements" of the industry of secretly plotting to make American taxpayers underwrite a bailout of the deposit-insurance fund. By opposing the $15-billion version of the legislation, Gray said, his opponents hoped to frustrate the board's efforts to close insolvent thrifts, thereby allowing the potential bill facing the FSLIC fund to grow so large that taxpayers would have to come to the rescue. It was an extraordinary charge from a bank board chairman—an office that had always been considered a toady of the industry. But Gray's attack was ignored as the ramblings of a desperate and unstable man.

He got everyone's attention a few days later, though. The FSLIC lawsuit filed in Dallas's U.S. district court against Dixon, King, Lemons, Malone, and the others rattled the presses at the *Dallas Morning News*. It sought $350 million in damages and etched into the public record for the first time the charges of fraud, looting, and waste—the cars, the beach houses, the jets, and the European extravaganzas enjoyed by the institution and the man Wright wanted to protect. Wright couldn't have done it better himself. The Speaker was humiliated. The full House was preparing to vote on the $5-billion FSLIC plan. Capitol Hill was crawling with S&L executives the League had brought to Washington to stump for the $5-billion plan. Calls flowed in from other areas of the country. Yet one day after the FSLIC lawsuit was filed, House Speaker Jim Wright and House Banking Committee chairman Fernand St. Germain reversed their opposition and came out for the $15-billion plan.

It was one of those face-saving moves that occurs all the time in Washington. "Why not appear on the side of the angels?" said George Gould, then the undersecretary for finance at Treasury and a key figure in the legislative battle. "Wright made a speech on the floor of the House for the fifteen-billion-dollar bill. But Tony Coelho was running around the floor telling everyone the Speaker didn't care how they voted." Coelho, of course, backed the $5-billion version.

When the lawmakers finished recording the votes, Wright, who had pushed controversial legislation through the House over the opposition of an extremely popular president, lost 258 to 153. The $15 billion got voted down. A version of the legislation by Rep. Jim Leach, an Iowa Republican whose bill was also opposed by the industry, went down even worse—391 to 17. The $5-billion plan supported by the entire industry passed overwhelmingly—402 to 6. It was an incredible display of the U.S. League's legislative clout. On the three votes, Democrats went with the League overwhelmingly each time. But even Republicans voted against their own president and backed the legislation sought by the League. Virtually every congressman who received money from the high-flying and traditional thrifts voted the way the industry wanted on at least two of the three votes. And when one or two of the lawmakers strayed from the League's path, it was usually a face-saving move like Wright's. "This was one of the great scams of the S&L crisis," Gray said later. "Wright and Freddy St. Germain were taking some heat, so they come out for my plan. Yet Coelho, the closest guy to Wright, the guy who counts the votes, he tells everyone to vote no, not to worry about what Wright says. It was so transparent, even at the time. It shows how absolutely cynical they all were."

The House sent the $5-billion bill to a conference committee, where lawmakers were to meet for months trying to work out their differences. Ed Gray had suffered a suffocating defeat. "I felt about as low as you can get, as low as a human being can feel," he'd later explain. Gray spent the remaining months at the bank board gathering his papers into blue-bound volumes that would preserve his actions and positions for posterity. He had come to his job as a darling of the industry. He was leaving as a deserter from a hostile force. Ed Gray was no genius. Of all people, he understood that. He had made plenty of mistakes, too. The genesis of the savings and loan crisis occurred under his tenure. Yet in the end, perhaps because he didn't know what else to do, Ed Gray had done the right thing. He didn't buckle under to the industry. On his last day, June 30, he had to be dragged from his typewriter where he was documenting the disaster he could see looming on the horizon. He would become obsessed with exposing the whole story, with avoiding the fate of a scapegoat. But when his chief of staff, Shannon Fairbanks, led him into the second-floor bank board auditorium that day, he found the room packed with some seven hundred members of the staff who had gathered to bid him farewell. The *Washington Post* described his departure poignantly:

"As Ed Gray, his clothes rumpled, his soul tormented, walked through the throng, Kenny Rogers's 'The Gambler' pounded through a set of giant stereo speakers: 'You got to know when to hold 'em, know when to fold 'em, know when to walk away, and know when to run.' "

Vernon Federal Savings and Loan—the name of the new government-operated institution created by the government take-over—hadn't fared much better than Ed Gray. By July, it was still alive, but the SASA managers who had been sent to Dallas by Bo McAllister were having just as hard a time with the thrift as the government officials they had replaced.

Part of the problem was inherited. The government had placed some fifty-three other S&Ls in the MCP program, the formal name for all of the seized thrifts being run under the supervision of the bank board. As originally envisioned, the program would allow the bank board to get rid of crooked or inept managers and replace them with a new team who could either revive the thrifts' fortunes or close the places down once FSLIC got some more money. The only trouble was that the MCP program was a joke.

The new managers at Vernon immediately faced the hidden losses they had inherited from Dixon and his team. "The government didn't really realize how bad the loans were. We were the ones who figured that out. Once we started digging into the loans, we told them they had big problems," said one of the SASA managers.

But the FSLIC also imposed a cumbersome management system on the MCPs that often was as bad as the institutions themselves. The new managers actually managed to drive up the cost of closing Vernon Savings for a second time, often by following some of the same techniques used by Dixon and his crew.

Back in Vernon's offices, Raylan Loggins started seeing some familiar sights. "It was the same old story," said Loggins. "SASA sent people in here who had been hired because of family ties or some other reason. They moved into Dixon's corner office and found the repossessed Cadillac. They were people that SASA didn't know what to do with. So they sent them to Vernon."

SASA, like almost every other Texas thrift, faced some troubles of its own at the time. McAllister wasn't about to turn down a risk-free fee for managing a sick S&L. But he also wasn't about to send his first team over to Vernon to manage a competing thrift. He had one of his best people, John Scaramozi, oversee the operation from San Antonio. But the rest of the management sent to Dallas was weak. SASA's Roger Clark took over at Vernon, commandeered Dixon's office, ordered thousands of dollars in landscaping and remodeling on the company condo in which he lived, and joined the usual clubs in Dallas. Upon learning of the outlays, an embarrassed Scaramozi cracked down. But Clark's management of the thrift didn't reverse the tide at all.

Over the next several months, Vernon continued to lose money. When it approved the MCP, the bank board had guaranteed that it would advance funds to Vernon to cover its cash needs. But it faced severe financial problems, too. So it also said that FSLIC could authorize the thrift to raise cash by luring fresh deposits from the marketplace. That was precisely the problem the regulators were trying to correct. Clark had the same experience as Dixon's team. He had to bid up the interest rates to savers to stem the loss of deposits to his equally troubled competitors. Otherwise he would run short of cash. Deposits at Vernon actually fell between June and September of 1987 from $1.5 billion to $1.4 billion. But the thrift's cost of funds went up from $31.2 million to $33.4 million.

The losses from daily operations continued, too. Vernon Federal would lose another $60 million to $70 million as an MCP because income from its loans and investments had slowed to a trickle while expenses continued. Loggins said the place was an administrative nightmare.

In its effort to please all elements of the industry, the bank board had not only hired SASA to manage the place, it had also hired McKenna's brainchild, FADA, as the asset manager. The trouble was no one spelled out exactly who had authority to do what. Turf fights between competing bureaucracies broke out almost immediately.

Hired by FADA to manage Vernon assets, Loggins and his colleagues squared off with SASA officials over money. "I had the authority to manage an asset or a piece of property but not to dispose of it. An electric bill came due on an office tower and I said, 'Pay it.' At least we'd keep the tenant in there and keep some cash coming in. But the SASA people would say, 'You don't have the authority to do that; we're the managers. Don't pay it.' So we'd refer the thing to the board and they'd argue over it. Pretty soon the tenant would get mad and move out, and the developer would quit sending whatever payments he'd been making."

The bank board had also adopted a salary system that guaranteed friction. As an employee of FADA, Loggins's salary wasn't covered by government pay ceilings. FADA had been set up to lure property managers and real estate specialists from private industry and paid higher wages than SASA, which paid the going rate for employees in the Texas market. To make matters worse, the employees from the FSLIC, which actually owned the institution, got paid even less because they were limited by civil service ceilings. "FADA was a boondoggle," said Vaughn Mitchell, a Texas mortgage-loan specialist hired by the agency to investigate several Vernon loans. "I got paid sixty thousand dollars a year. That was more than some of the people I was working for." The three-tiered salary structure poisoned the atmosphere with jealousy and bitterness.

Clark, who would later be criticized for incompetency in running savings and loans for the government, started complaining about the inadequacy of his $90,000-a-year salary soon after he got his job. SASA officials, with the approval of the government, bumped him to $120,000 and finally to $150,000 a year.

By the time Gary Bowser and Jim Deveney, two investigators from the House Banking Committee, showed up in Dallas to investigate the downfall of Vernon Western and Sunbelt Savings, SASA and FSLIC employees were complaining bitterly about the huge fees FADA charged the busted S&L for its services. Bowser and Deveney learned that FADA, by September of 1987, had billed the FSLIC $10.7 million for asset management and legal services at Vernon, including $1.5 million for subcontractors, even though it had dozens of employees at the thrift. Fees for consultants hired at hourly rates of up to $150 an hour and for lawyers had quadrupled within a year at Vernon.

"We had forty-eight single-family homes that were owned by Vernon," said one SASA employee who asked not to be identified by name. "FADA hired some company to do forty-eight separate business plans on how we would sell them at a thousand dollars a pop. The whole sale could have been handled with one plan for a thousand dollars."

SASA and FSLIC employees' outrage escalated when the FADA board voted a $75,000 bonus in addition to the $250,000-a-year salary for McKenna's handpicked CEO at FADA, Roslyn Payne. Bowser and Deveney quickly focused their investigation on the FADA as Vernon languished in confusion.

Back in Washington, word of Vernon's management problems plagued Gray's replacement, M. Danny Wall, a former Salt Lake City urban planner who had worked for Sen. Jake Garn until Reagan tapped him for the bank board job. Wall wore dark, three-piece suits, had a combative personality, and almost never smiled. He viewed Vernon as the "government's black hole," but he already had his hands full helping Treasury Secretary James Baker fashion a compromise between the two versions of the FSLIC recapitalization bill that had been passed by the House and the Senate. Fearing Wall Street's reaction to more delay, Baker finally prodded the conferees to approve $10.8 billion in new capital for the FSLIC, which was higher than both houses had voted. The money would come from government-guaranteed bond issues that would be retired by industry assessments. Once the bill was signed by President Reagan a few weeks later, the FSLIC had some more money, and one of the first things the new chairman did was to consider shutting down Vernon Federal Savings—again.

By November 1987, Vernon Savings had been under the control of the government or government-controlled managers for fifteen months. During that period, it had suffered an additional $144 million in operating losses. Regardless of who was at fault, the FSLIC would have to pick up the bill.

Unfortunately, Vernon's losses were just part of the problem. Its loan portfolio resembled a financial Lebanon. In all, the government and SASA had written off as a loss $700 million of the $1.8 billion that Vernon had lent developers and other customers, leaving it with assets valued at about $1.1 billion. If those assets could have been sold for $1.1 billion in the open market, Vernon would have been about $200 million short of covering the $1.3 billion it owed depositors.

But the figures didn't tell the whole story. Included in the $1.1 billion worth of assets was $565 million that ten real estate developers such as Harvey McLean and Jack Atkinson had borrowed from Vernon Savings. The concentration of loans to just ten borrowers staggered the government.

Even if the ten developers' projects had started out as good deals, they were dead meat by late 1987. The government wouldn't have been able to sell them for anywhere near $565 million. Most were hopelessly ensnarled in bankruptcy proceedings that wouldn't be resolved for years. Moreover, even if the government could have gotten its hands on the property, it couldn't sell it. Dumping that much real estate on the market would create a fire-sale atmosphere and undercut the value of collateral held by other marginally healthy savings and loans. FSLIC faced a dismal prospect. By taking control of Vernon it had assumed debts of $1.3 billion to depositors. It wouldn't get anything near $1.3 billion by selling the assets it had acquired in the deal. But no one could really say what the assets were worth. FSLIC simply couldn't put them up for sale yet.

For Danny Wall, Vernon Federal's financial condition was just the start of the problems. The thrift had also sold at least $500 million worth of loans to about seventy-five other savings and loans around the country and had lent $44 million to seven other S&Ls. The majority of the S&L participants and borrowers had trouble, too. Regulators were reluctant to take any action that would have a domino effect on the other thrifts, particularly since about half of them were being operated under regulatory supervision anyway.

The most efficient thing that Wall could have done was to close Vernon Federal Savings on the spot. By November 1987, it would have cost him about $1.3 billion, minus whatever he would eventually get for the assets he sold. But a payout of $1.3 billion from the FSLIC represented more than 10 percent of the $10.8 billion that the Congress had just approved to take care of the entire industry. Even under the most conservative measure, some three hundred to four hundred thrifts thoughout the U.S. faced problems similar to Vernon's.

A deregulation advocate with a keen faith in free markets, Wall decided to rely on the free enterprise system for help. He'd handle the problem by using the same techniques as his soul mates in private industry—he'd borrow his way out.

Wall's plan to put an end to Vernon—for the second time— would be repeated, in one form or another, and with increasing sophistication, in dozens of other cases in the coming months. Vernon Federal was to be busted up into two organizations.

One would be named Monfort Savings after the street where Vernon's offices were located in Dallas. The FSLIC would give Monfort $200 million in cash and issue the thrift a interest-paying note. The note permitted Monfort to borrow an additional $1.1 billion from the FSLIC if it was needed to cover Vernon Federal's $1.3 billion in deposits, which were transferred to the new thrift. If Vernon's old depositors stormed the place and demanded their money, the FSLIC would have all of the money it needed. Hopefully, that wouldn't happen, though. By emphasizing to depositors that the safety of their savings was still guaranteed by Uncle Sam, the pace of withdrawals would be slowed. Eventually the government would have to pay depositors the $1.3 billion. But if the government could keep withdrawals to a minimum, the FSLIC wouldn't have to come up with the full amount for years. Wall's staff figured that Monfort could probably get by with the $200 million in cash plus the interest that FSLIC paid on the note. Giving Monfort $200 million might seem like a lot, but it was better than paying out $1.3 billion right away. In keeping with the administration's free enterprise theme, the same managers—SASA—would be hired to run Monfort exclusively.

The second organization to be formed would exist on paper only and would be called Old Vernon. It consisted of virtually all of Vernon's troubled assets. FADA would be hired to manage those apartment projects, office buildings, Italian stone wells, planes, paintings, and yachts as best it could until they could be sold. The proceeds would then be used to settle some of the five hundred lawsuits that had been filed against Vernon by borrowers, other S&Ls, and a wide range of creditors seeking billions of dollars in damages. If any money was left over—and few thought there would be—it could be used to repay the FSLIC for the $1.3 billion in cash and notes it had stuffed into Monfort to ensure that depositors were made whole. Stockholders such as Dixon would be wiped out. In effect, the government would absorb the costs of the prostitutes, the planes, the art, and all the rest.

As Wall and his team sketched it out, it would be the second-costliest bailout of a financial institution in the history of the U.S. But it was early in the savings and loan crisis. Big things were still to come. It was also something new. In effect, FSLIC, a quasi-governmental agency, was creating new government debt by issuing its notes, which had not been authorized by Congress. In financial lingo they called Wall's technique leveraging the FSLIC fund. In plain English he was plunging the agency so deeply into debt that only the taxpayer would be able to bail it out. But it was an ingenious way to stretch FSLIC's limited resources. After all, it was the age of the leveraged buyout. Debt and Carl Icahn were in. None of this financial quackery was counted in the budget deficit, either. The government just didn't figure things that way. The bank board approved the plan in secret. Vernon Savings was about to become history. Said one Washington lawyer who attended the session:

> We had the meeting in the board room here. We went over the numbers and figured out how we would staff the closing. It was the first closing under Wall with the new money. Everything was to be kept secret until after we took it over. People had made hotel reservations in Dallas. After a while, I walked back to my office and I almost died. The envelope with the press release announcing the closing had disappeared from my desk. It had been mailed by mistake to a Reuters reporter. I ran back upstairs. Everyone was still in the room. I told them what happened and we tried to stop the release. But it got out and we had to move a half day early.

The FSLIC stealth team once again moved quickly. Federal officials swooped in on Vernon Federal Savings offices on November 19, 1987. "We all knew they were coming," said Loggins. "The tip-off was the lawyers. They all suddenly wanted to be paid in full by Friday." A casual customer who happened by Vernon's main office on the town square in Vernon on that gray fall day probably didn't even notice anything unusual, except for the extra people around after working hours. The bronze *Watcher of the Plains* statue still sat in the lobby like a vigilant guardian frozen in time. The name on the door hadn't been changed yet and the FSLIC sticker remained on the window like the government's Good Housekeeping seal of approval.

But word soon started to spread and a photographer from the *Vernon Daily Record* showed up to snap pictures of Pat Swindall twisting his screwdriver as he changed the locks on the front door of Vernon Savings and Loan. The next day's headline spread across the top of page one in the paper that had once published W. D. Dixon's column told the story: "Federal Regulators Take Control of Vernon Savings." Something momentous had happened. For all practical purposes, Vernon Savings and Loan, the little thrift started by R. B. Tanner so many years ago, was dead. The name was changed to Monfort.

Local townsfolk expressed shock and relief at the news. Vernon employees told reporters they were glad it was over. Rumors that the government planned dire actions had swirled within Vernon Savings for months. Local bankers were relieved that the feds had finally acted, too. Vernon had driven up everyone's cost of deposits by offering premium interest rates to savers. But many residents expressed shock that the federal government swallowed the local S&L whole.

Despite its high-flying reputation in Dallas, Austin, and Washington, Vernon Savings had remained a source of local pride. Vernon's meteoric growth, fueled by hometown boys such as Don Dixon, Woody Lemons, Roy Dickey, and Pat King, had become a Vernon, Texas, success story. Local news stories about Vernon Savings had always emphasized the positive. Less than two years before, the *Vernon Daily Record* ran a glowing story on the thrift's silver anniversary. There had been rumors for well over a year about troubles at Vernon Savings among the townsfolk. But few had any idea of how bad things were. Vernon resident Jack Eure explains: "They were paying high dividends and people were wondering how they could keep it up. But when stories came out in the paper about what had really gone on, the women and all that, people were shocked. Some of the directors were thought of as clean people. This was a real shock. You know this is a small town—everyone knows everyone."

Tanner was saddened by the news for more reasons than

one. Just ten months earlier, Dixon had missed Dondi Financial's quarterly payment on his notes to Tanner and his family. R.B.'s lawyer notified Dixon that he still owed Tanner and his family nearly $2 million, which would become due in one month if Dondi Financial didn't repay the notes. R.B. filed suit a month later, but Dixon soon filed for protection from his creditors in bankruptcy court in southern California. In subsequent court filings, Dixon promised to repay all of his debts, but the bankruptcy petition ensnarled Tanner and his family in a legal fight from which they would emerge without their money.

By the time the FSLIC moved to close Vernon the second time, Tanner had lost more than the institution he had founded. He feared he had also lost the nearly $2 million that Dixon owed him. "I'm devastated by this," he said. "After all, this represents about sixty-five percent of my life's work and I can't start over." Tanner was almost as disgusted with the government lawyers who had seized Vernon's assets as he was with Dixon. The government had helped create the problem through lax regulation. "I can't answer why the state and federal regulators allowed it to go as far as it did," Tanner would later say. But government lawyers would also fight Tanner's efforts to get his money back, arguing that anything left in Vernon or in Dixon's bankruptcy case belonged to the deposit-insurance fund. The fight would continue for years.

Tanner wouldn't lose hope, though. Every morning, usually at nine A.M., he would sit at his kitchen table, grasp his wife's hand, and pray for the man who owes him so much money. "Don Dixon needs to know the Lord," he would say, bowing his head in prayer. "Dear Father, we all sin and come up short in the glory of God. But we ask for your forgiveness."

23 Laguna Beach

D ixon looked puzzled. The stranger who walked into his small office one floor below the Regata Hair Salon in Laguna Beach wasn't a familiar face. Dixon's business quarters differed from the spacious office with stained-glass doors and elevated desk on the second floor of the Vernon Savings building in Dallas. He had a few remnants of his past—an antique blunderbuss rested on the heavily carved Old English desk that once graced the master bedroom of his oceanside house at Del Mar. But his new surroundings were far more modest. High-pitched hair dryers whined in the beauty shop one floor above; tourists wandered by looking for the small art gallery nearby; and the closest thing he had to a secretary was an answering machine.

"I'm looking for Don Dixon," the stranger said.

"You got him," said Dixon without hesitation.

The stranger, a newspaper reporter, plopped down in the chair sitting in front of the desk. Dixon had a puzzled look on his face. The reporter pulled out a *Chicago Tribune* business card, tossed it on Dixon's desk, and said, "Damn, Dixon, you're a hard man to find." The onetime Vernon chief smiled. He hadn't talked to a newspaper reporter in recent years, and he didn't think he had missed much. He hadn't had any good press lately, that much was for sure. But Dixon was polite and friendly. "What can I do for you?" he said.

It was August 1988, and the sun was bright. Dixon sat behind his desk wearing tan slacks and an open-collared shirt. There were no gold chains or flashy medallions; aviator sunglasses shielded his eyes from the sun in this beach community about one hour south of Los Angeles. He was relaxed, tanned, and curious. His lawyer had said Dixon wasn't in hiding. But he wasn't advertising his presence, either. There were no Donald R. Dixons in the Laguna Beach phone listings, no names on his office window, and few friends who could—or would—tell of his whereabouts. The reporter had tracked him down by getting a forwarding address from the post office and talking to someone at his home, who inadvertently pointed him toward the office.

The news from Washington and New York was full of leveraged buyouts, financial skulduggery, and scandals on Wall Street. But sitting in his Laguna Beach office, Dixon was a headline for a different story. He was the Ivan Boesky of Main Street.

Vernon Savings was not one of Dixon's favorite topics. He had started putting the savings and loan behind him even before he bid farewell to the thrift's employees in the airplane hangar in Addison. The first thing that went was the $2-million beach house in Del Mar. Dixon and Dana had lived there off and on rent-free for about a year after it was remodeled and had racked up $560,000 in living expenses. It was the usual stuff—$36,780 for flowers, $37,000 in telephone bills, and $23,000 for car service. They handled the expenses in the usual way, too; Vernon Savings paid them. But Dixon had a friend willing to pay about $2.8 million for the house and furnishings, which meant that Vernon Savings would just about break even.

So, in June 1986, Vernon Savings sold the place to Lawton, Inc., a company owned by Bruce West, Sr., a fellow Texan who was also a major borrower at Vernon Savings. It didn't take Dixon long to conclude that this West was a sharp guy. Dixon could keep hundreds of intricate details about complex deals in his head. His former wife said she thought they had two bank accounts when they got divorced. "I found out we had about twenty-five." Yet West got the best of Dixon and Vernon Savings in the house sale. The $2.8-million sales price included about $1 million worth of Vernon artwork that had been hung on the walls. When West claimed the artwork weeks later, Dixon said he was stunned.

"He told me he'd acquired the investment art along with the

furnishings in the purchase of the Del Mar beach house. And I told him at that time that had not been my understanding. Of course, I was not involved, for the most part, in the sale from Vernon to Lawton. So it came as a complete shock to me," Dixon testified later in a deposition. He subsequently signed an affidavit acknowledging that West had acquired the art in the deal. West got a tremendous buy and Vernon lost money.

Dixon was impressed. This West was a man with whom he could do business. Dixon continued living in the house, paying rent to West's firm for another six months. He and his landlord had some discussions about their common business interests, past and present. Finally they formed a partnership in December 1986, just about the time the beach house was sold once again. West's company sold the place to Sid and Jenny Craig of Jenny Craig Diet fame just six months after he'd acquired it. The Craigs paid $3.2 million for the house, giving Dixon's new partner a fat profit of about $400,000. It was easy to see why he and Dixon joined forces. Because of the way the transactions had been financed, West's company also walked away from the Del Mar house deal with $2.2 million, which was transferred into the new partnership he formed with Dixon.

The next thing to go was some of the cars. Antique-car buffs at the Fourth Annual Rancho Santa Fe Concours d'Élégance in July 1986 marveled at the 1930 Cadillac V-16 Madame X Imperial Landaulet parked on the Fairbanks Ranch soccer field. But the General Motors classic was nothing compared to some of the beauties that were auctioned off afterward at the showroom of the Concours sponsor, Symbolic Motors, the La Jolla subsidiary of Vernon Savings. It was an unusual sale. Symbolic Motors didn't come out too well. It took in only $132,202 in the auction. That was hardly enough to offset the $336,750 the Vernon subsidiary spent on advertising, food, beverages, auction fees, and other expenses designed to lure well-heeled bidders such as Ralph Engelstatt, owner of the Imperial Hotel in Las Vegas. The loss of $200,000 was absorbed by the Vernon subsidiary.

But Dixon, the motivating force behind the auction, didn't come out so badly. Of the nineteen cars that fetched $2.3 million in the auction, eight belonged to Dixon, who took in $1.8 million of the total sales proceeds. He sold his 1931 Duesenberg dual-cowl phaeton for $600,000. Once he paid off the liens, Dixon walked away from the sale with about $600,000 cash. Another sale a few months later netted Dixon an additional $400,000. The money was promptly transferred into personal investments or into trust accounts at his attorneys' offices. He used $100,000 as a partial payment on a $350,000 retainer for William Ravkind, a Dallas criminal attorney Dixon hired to be on call in case he was needed.

Dixon spent several more months severing his ties with Vernon Savings and selling or trading his personal assets in business deals, including several with West. "When Don's problems started, he got real close with Bruce West," said Van Boxtel. It was complex stuff. He had to flip around a $600,000 loan against a deferred-bonus account in Vernon Savings. He sold land in Texas, the Moonlight Beach Club property, and more. After state and federal regulators started sucking the blood out of Vernon Savings, Dixon moved to Laguna Beach and tried to make a go of it with a BMW dealership he had acquired. But that didn't work.

A week before the federal government filed its April 1987 civil suit against Dixon and several others, Don and Dana filed their bankruptcy petitions, buying some time until they could come up with a reorganization plan to pay off their staggering debts. The bankruptcy filing was a brilliant stroke; it gave the creditors a stake in Dixon's success at working out his problems, blunted their criticism, and ensnarled their lawyers in Dixon's complex business dealings. There were a lot of nice assets listed in his bankruptcy filings—a pair of Fabri twelve-gauge shotguns worth $25,000, three Honda motorcycles, a whopping $438,000 federal income tax refund for 1986, and much more. In all, the assets totaled about $9 million. But the creditors' lawyers suspected that the knot of new corporations, partnerships, bank accounts, and trusts Dixon had formed obscured some hidden assets. Vernon Savings had paid Dixon and Dondi Financial dividends and salaries of between $20 million to $30 million over the years, not counting any of his side deals. Everyone wanted to know where the rest of the money went. Just as their lawyers started scrutinizing Dixon's business ties, though, the Justice Department stepped in and made it clear that Dixon's association with Vernon wasn't a thing of the past. Prosecutors put a hold on all of the legal maneuvering until they made more progress on the Justice Department's top priority—a sweeping criminal investigation of Dixon and several other Vernon Savings officials back in Dallas.

As he leaned back in the chair behind his antique desk, Dixon didn't exactly personify an attitude of remorse. Even before the government officially took over Vernon, Dixon had started drawing an $18,000-a-month consulting fee from the Wedgewood Group, the partnership he had started with West. That may sound like a lot of money to the average person, but it wasn't much for Dixon. He estimated his annual expenses at $600,000 in 1986, a year in which he had cut back on travel and entertainment. Wedgewood gave him a company car—a BMW. He rented his house from his business partners and shared the small office with one of several lawyers he had retained.

His cavalier attitude toward the past surfaced at a June 1987 creditors' meeting crammed with people who said he owed them millions of dollars. One of the lawyers present asked Dixon why he drove a Ferrari as a company car at Dondi Financial, the parent company of an insolvent savings and loan. Dixon explained he got the Ferrari after he had totaled the company Mercedes: "It was a family Ferrari, four seater, automatic transmission." The questioner was Frank Arnold, an attorney, and son-in-law to R. B. Tanner.

From Dixon's perspective, Arnold's question was one more cheap shot implying that Vernon Savings had failed because Dixon blew all of the thrift's money on cars, trips, jets, and the good life. People who held that opinion didn't understand. In his mind, Don Dixon didn't cause the downfall of Vernon Savings; the regulators did.

In court proceedings, Dixon's lawyers had already told everyone that Vernon was like the Chase Manhattan Bank, Bank of America, or Citicorp—the financial giants that had burdened the world with an international debt crisis by investing in Third World countries at a time when they thought the loans were good. Vernon—and Don Dixon—thought real estate development was the way to go. That's why he invested Vernon's deposits in land, sticks, and bricks. He was just like the bankers. Economic problems beyond anyone's control changed the landscape in both cases. It was that simple. But bank regulators didn't panic, sweep in on Chase Manhattan, hamstring the place, and close it. No pack of federal prosecutors hounded big, powerful banks.

Things were far different when it came to Vernon Savings, though. So what if events had proven Dixon wrong in 1986. And so what if Vernon's loan portfolio resembled postwar Dresden. Everything would have been okay if the government had not panicked. All he and his pals in the daisy chain needed was some time so they could scratch up the money they needed to keep their projects afloat. Once the real estate market recovered, everything would have been okay. "I had a plan that would have been financed by Drexel Burnham," Dixon said. No government money would even have been involved. Vernon lost millions, Dixon and his cohorts readily agree, because of Dixon's ill-timed real estate investments. But it would go on to lose $1 billion or more because of the way a bungling pack of inept regulators mishandled the situation.

Actually, there is some truth to Dixon's version of events. Don Dixon created the problem at Vernon Savings. As he sat in his Laguna Beach office, even Dixon admitted that. But the regulators who assumed control of the institution made it far worse. By August 1988, it was in the government's best interest to make Dixon and his cohorts appear even worse than they were to cover up how badly the bank board had handled Vernon Federal and its successor, Monfort. The managers whom the bank board brought in to run Monfort Savings managed to lose more money, even though all of the bad assets had been stripped from the S&L.

From the day that Monfort rose from Vernon's ashes, its assets were $200 million in cash and the interest-paying $1.1 billion note that the FSLIC gave the thrift to keep it afloat. Theoretically, all the new managers had to do was sit back, collect interest on the note, and pay depositors enough to prevent a run at the newly created S&L. Once Monfort got rid of some old high-cost deposits, FSLIC, under Danny Wall's game plan, was supposed to replace its notes with good assets from other S&Ls. Eventually Monfort was to be sold to private investors or merged into another institution.

But that's not what happened. Instead Montfort lost an additional $20 million in the first nine months of 1988. One reason was interest expense. The interest that FSLIC paid to Monfort on its $1.1-billion bailout note was far below the interest Monfort officials had to pay to keep depositors from deserting the thrift en masse. By early 1988, there were hundreds of other troubled S&Ls in FSLIC's sick ward. The government couldn't afford to close them, either. So government-appointed managers continued to bid up interest rates to keep federally insured deposits flowing into their vaults. Otherwise they wouldn't have enough cash to pay the bills. As a result, they all lost money.

The bank board compounded the losses from the interest-rate squeeze. Instead of replacing the FSLIC notes in Monfort with good assets, the bank board used the thrift to warehouse junk assets taken out of other S&Ls it was trying to sell. By late 1988, the bank board had dumped around $200 million to $300 million in real estate investments made by another insolvent Dallas S&L into Monfort. The bank board, in fact, was in the heat of its campaign to sell hundreds of sick S&Ls to some of the nation's richest families and biggest political campaign contributors at bargain prices. By flushing bum assets into Monfort, Wall dressed up other troubled S&Ls he was trying to peddle. He complicated Monfort's problems, but that didn't matter. Dixon and the government had already made such a mess that Vernon's name was synonymous with disaster. By swapping the assets around, Wall simply sweetened the pot for the big-money barracudas swirling around the other sick S&Ls, hid some of his troubles in Monfort, and blamed the whole mess on the problems inherited from Dixon.

Indeed, by mid-1988, Wall was comparing Dixon unfavorably to Keating, the antipornography crusader who made "S&L" a dirty word. "It seems to me," Wall said, while arguing for lenient treatment of Keating, who also gave the Bush campaign $100,000, "that Dixon's emergence and crashing was a very short-lived exercise from start to finish. It seems to me that Mr. Keating, to my own knowledge, has been a very active and a very entrepreneurial businessman for at least the last thirteen years that I've known him. He is clearly not a flash in the pan and he's not a Don Dixon."

Nevertheless, Dixon can hardly blame the government for all of his problems. Charges that he and his executive team looted Vernon Savings were not the figment of someone's imagination. The government couldn't have mucked up Vernon Savings as much as it did had he not ruined it first. As he leaned back in his chair and adjusted his glasses, Dixon bristled at such suggestions; his detractors, he said, staring straight at his visitor, made misleading allegations about his flamboyant lifestyle, such as disclosures about the "gastronomie fantastique" tour of France. "Sure we traveled to Europe," he said. "Vernon had an office in Switzerland. We went on a trip there. On the way, we stopped in France and ate at three-star restaurants two times a day, six days a week, because we were looking for a chef as a consultant for a restaurant Vernon was going to start." But his critics weren't even worldly enough to understand that eating and drinking your way across France can be hard work: "You think it's easy eating in three-star restaurants two times a day, six days a week?" he asked. "By the time it is over, you want to spit it out."

Dixon also correctly argued that economic problems beyond his control—the downturn in the oil economy—played a role in his downfall. But Vernon didn't fail because oil prices declined. The plunge in prices merely exposed the shoddy deals, conflicts of interest, and the daisy chain in which he was involved. Dixon told his visitor that he hadn't launched his full defense. In his view, the fall of Vernon primarily remained a story of government malfeasance, plain and simple: "I've got one hell of a story to tell. I just am not ready to tell it yet."

By that time, several of Dixon's colleagues had told their story to the FBI, to juries, and to judges, and the audience wasn't too impressed.

John Hill had pleaded guilty to charges of making illegal campaign contributions to politicians and procuring sexual favors for Vernon board members. Dallas U.S. district court judge Barefoot Sanders gave him a lecture:

> You know, Mr. Hill, I went through your pre-sentence report with a great deal of amazement. You are a person of obvious talent and a great academic record in high school and college. You got high honors. You have a very supportive family. But I will have to say you were a participant. Maybe you were led, maybe you were pushed, but you were a participant in what seems to be a monumental and pervasive fraud. You pleaded guilty to it and I can't attribute it to anything except the highly contagious thing called greed, which is permeating the entire society, particularly in this part of the country, the consequences of which we are all going to carry.

Hill was sentenced to a few months in a minimum security prison and has been a government witness against several of his former colleagues.

Hill's former helper, Blair Davis, got immunity from prosecution if he would testify against other Vernon officials charged with crimes. Davis decided to head for the real action—he entered law school in Houston.

Pat Malone went to work at a funeral parlor in Cleveland, Texas, after pleading guilty to a federal conspiracy charge in connection with his activities at Vernon Savings. He is a cooperating government witness after a prison term that lasted several months.

Jack Atkinson pleaded guilty to diversion of loan proceeds and was sentenced to a prison term of up to eighteen months and fined. Said Atkinson just before leaving for his jail cell: "I'd just like to know one thing about Don Dixon. Who in the hell did he piss off? Just who in the hell did he piss off?"

Pat King was found guilty of federal charges after a long trial in Dallas. He got a five-year prison term.

After a long delay, Woody Lemons went on trial in Dallas and was convicted of collecting a $200,000 kickback generated by a Vernon loan made after he left the institution. Lemons had all sorts of people come forward and plead with the judge not to sentence him to jail.

"Well, Mr. Lemons," U.S. district court judge Robert Maloney told Woody, "the court has received what I believe is probably a record number of letters of personal recommendation sent to me on your behalf from family and friends. They all praise your community contributions and dedication to your church. Also as a somewhat unusual circumstance, I have received some correspondence from others who definitely have a different opinion of you and of what sentence I should set today." One of the other letters was from William Seidman, a federal banking regulator who urged Lemons be given a stiff sentence. The judge continued:

> A common thread runs through these letters which ask lenient treatment for you. These people know you to be honest and seem to express the belief that you are a victim of the savings and loan failure rather than

someone who has committed a crime. I sympathize with your friends. But they are wrong about you. You are not a religious person. Your friends who see you in church and at Sunday school don't know that, even though you are present, you are not listening. You would have heard that it is neither loyal or charitable to cheat those who trust you. You would have heard that greed is not a virtue. And greedy you were. I do not believe the oath you took to tell the truth meant anything to you.That's an indication to me that you have no real moral values. You are a thief in every sense of the word, and you must be punished accordingly.

Woody got thirty years.

Not everyone associated with the Vernon Savings story was accused of crimes. Federal prosecutors have not leveled charges at Durward Curlee, who is now a lobbyist in Austin, Texas, or Linn Bowman, who works in Austin as a savings and loan consultant. There have been no charges publicly made against others, either, such as Raleigh Blakely, Greg McCormick, or lower-ranking employees of Vernon Savings. Indictments are pending against Danny Faulkner and Charles Keating as of this writing. And not everyone thinks the financial collapse was their biggest mistake. Dixon said his biggest mistake was getting involved in politics. The yacht, the plane rides, and the high profile made him too tempting a target for politically motivated prosecutors: "That was my mistake," he said. "I went to Washington."

Soon after the interview, Dixon moved from Laguna Beach back to Dallas. Some friends said he was involved in a Bahamian insurance deal. Others said they don't know what he is doing. One close friend says Dixon has gotten religion. Tim Timmons, Dixon's preacher friend in California, said that Dixon has seen the error in some of his ways, particularly those involving the women hired for Vernon Savings parties. Timmons said Dixon has repented and has taken to helping others. He has even pitched in to help Timmons's church. He is giving the church financial advice.

24 The Savings and Loan Crisis

I t was a bright, sunny day in Dallas. A group of reporters gathered near the FBI headquarters in the city's trendy West End. All of the major papers were there. So were the TV cameras. They were waiting for Don Dixon.

Just a day before, federal prosecutors had filed a thirty-eight-count indictment charging Dixon with a variety of crimes. The Justice Department charges made a big splash; stories about Dixon appeared on TV news and in the nation's major newspapers. He even made the front page of the *New York Times*. But it wasn't the kind of press he wanted. The government said Dixon had used Vernon's money illegally for hunting trips, prostitutes, political contributions, cruises, antique cars, and the house at Solana Beach. "If convicted on all 38 counts in the indictment," wrote *Dallas Morning News* reporter Tracy Everbach, "Dixon could receive a maximum 190-year prison sentence and be fined as much as $9.5 million." And federal prosecutors implied that more charges might be added later.

Dixon had shown up at the FBI headquarters to surrender to authorities at around nine A.M. But a picture of Dixon walking into the building wasn't what the photographers and cameramen wanted. Justice Department sources had tipped them that a better

277

shot was in the offing, and they soon seized the opportunity. A door swung open and Dixon emerged, flanked by two FBI agents in their I'm-gonna-be-on-TV-today blue suits. Dixon walked briskly toward the government car that would take him to a hearing before a federal magistrate. A temple from his eyeglasses jutted carelessly from the jacket pocket of his gray suit. His hands were behind his back—in handcuffs.

The strobe lights flashed and the TV cameras whirred as the agents led Dixon to the U.S. district court a few blocks away. U.S. Magistrate John Tolle initially set bail for Dixon at $100,000. But Dixon's attorney, Billy Ravkind, said his client didn't have the money; he was unemployed. After a brief discussion, Tolle released Dixon; no cash bond was required. The Justice Department didn't object, either. As Dixon emerged from the courtroom, he approached Everbach and the other reporters.

"He didn't appear upset or anything," she said. "He was really pretty cool, calm. You didn't see any beads of sweat." Dixon told the reporters that the government was using him as a scapegoat. "So far," said Dixon, "the government has been successful in hiding behind the so-called crooks. We are the easy target. All the stories you've heard about the millions of dollars the savings and loans crooks took—it's totally dead wrong. The true villains are the politicians, the regulators. The whole system of deregulation was improperly handled."

In an exchange that lasted about ten minutes, Dixon also gave the journalists a hint of his defense. It would be impossible, he said, to get a fair trial: "It's hard for any individual to face the U.S. government in trial and hope to win. The only chance anyone has is to get a fair and impartial jury. Thanks to the media, that's going to be impossible for Don Dixon. I've been tried and convicted in the press." He pleaded not guilty a few days later.

It was June 14, 1990, and Dixon had clearly become ensnarled in something far bigger than he had ever imagined. When he acquired Vernon Savings back in 1982, he figured he was just a good ol' Texas boy doing what good ol' Texas boys had always done—makin' some money and havin' a little fun. But Dixon wasn't alone when he went to Little Rock seeking government approval to buy R. B. Tanner's savings and loan.

Other real estate developers, dentists, pilots, and entrepreneurs repeated the ritual in bank board offices and state capitals across the U.S. At first they made buckets of money through loans to their buddies, to themselves, or to cronies. It was Don Dixon multiplied by 100 or 200. The regulators welcomed them with open arms as the saviors of a sick industry, and they lived high, lending each other federally insured deposits in complex daisy-chain deals that were like initiation rituals for a fraternity of high finance. Thanks to the advanced financial alchemy practiced by their accountants, they reported enviable leaps in paper profits and dipped into pools of federally insured deposits to pay themselves fat dividends, bonuses, and salaries.

To a man, Dixon and his fellow entrepreneurs probably didn't set out to destroy and plunder the savings and loans they had acquired. That wouldn't have made any sense. Keeping the thrifts alive was the only way they could keep their pockets full. They were simply agents of avarice who operated on the financial margin and got carried away. They had absolutely no business owning savings institutions that relied upon federally insured deposits for their lifeblood.

Amazingly, they were not a big group. Even at the peak, the losses that would eventually propel the industry toward a crisis could be traced to a few hundred S&Ls like Vernon. Most of the trouble also occurred in just two states—Texas, where Linn Bowman was state commissioner, and California, where Larry Taggart had run things. In fact Vernon and nineteen other Texas thrifts accounted for about one-third of the entire S&L industry's losses in 1987.

Yet they had an impact far beyond Dallas, Austin, or Sacramento. The premium interest rates they offered customers perpetuated a devious scheme. Money poured in from all corners of the nation as greedy savers, investors, government agencies— even other S&Ls and banks—responded to Wall Street Journal ads that offered savers top interest rates on certificates of deposit.

The economies in states such as Texas and California, already overheated by strong oil prices and the Reagan administration's huge defense budgets, got an additional dose of inflation as high-flying S&Ls engaged their undercapitalized competitors in a feeding frenzy for deposits and loans. Federally insured deposits were stuffed into crooked or dubious deals built upon foundations of inflation, high hopes, and low standards. Thinly capitalized thrifts hoping to strike it rich aped the techniques practiced by the Vernons of the world. Nearly every S&L paid more for its deposits, and many slashed rates on their loans to get an edge on competitors. Buildings and condo projects sprouted across the landscape.

But the premium rates paid to savers also drove up the cost of funds for other S&Ls on the national money markets, squeezed profit margins, and exposed hundreds of weaker thrifts to a downturn in the economy. Indeed, when the artificial boom and plunging oil prices triggered an inevitable slump, the number of troubled S&Ls mushroomed to a thousand, or about a third of the industry. A new danger developed. An obscure little federal agency had to step in and manage the situation. If regulators from the Federal Home Loan Bank Board failed to handle the situation properly, the nation and its taxpayers would face a disaster, which is exactly what they got.

For Donald R. Dixon, the S&L debacle would evolve into a crisis in more ways than one. On one level, Dixon's loss of control over Vernon Savings triggered defaults, severe financial trouble, and scores of bankruptcies for the Vernon native and his cronies. But the financial troubles became a minor part of his problems. Thanks to the U.S. Congress and the bungling pack of inept government-appointed managers who took over Vernon and hundreds of other floundering institutions, a bad situation became far worse.

As they stalled, vacillated, and did almost anything to avoid facing the true problem, the cost of closing the thrifts and paying off their depositors soared. Pretty soon the price tag was so high that the entire S&L industry would have gone under trying to pay it. American taxpayers would have to step in, honor the guarantee, and bail out the deposit-insurance fund to prevent a loss of confidence similar to the one that caused the Great Depression.

As economists, analysts, and politicians started estimating the projected cost of the bailout, they were shocked at the price tag. It started at $10 to $15 billion but soon soared beyond $100 billion. "The bailout to come will be the largest ever in the history of the U.S. It will be far bigger than the cost of the assistance given to Chrysler, Lockheed, and New York City combined," Senator William Proxmire thundered in a speech on the Senate floor.

Confused at how such a debacle could occur, and understandably irate, American taxpayers started demanding some scalps, and the politicians who had willingly taken all of that campaign money graciously offered Dixon's. A vigilante atmosphere evolved in which demagoguery and demands for harsh punishment flourished. Dixon faced an unsettling prospect: He might become a victim of the very scandal he helped create. Government prosecutors and lawyers scoured Dixon's finances looking for secret ill-gotten gains. "There are no hidden bank accounts, no millions," a defensive Dixon countered in the courthouse corridor. "There are not even any thousands or even any dollars." He added in a later TV interview:

"Is there a book somewhere that says it's illegal to take perks?"

Whether Dixon illegally looted Vernon Savings is a question that may never be answered. After being indicted, he was tried in late 1990 on federal charges involving illegal political campaign contributions and misappropriation of Vernon funds to pay for parties, prostitutes and rent on the Solana Beach house. In its criminal case, the government never raised Dixon's leadership of Vernon or any Daisy Chain deals. Those issues will be dealt with in the federal civil suit still pending in court. Government criminal prosecutors wanted to limit their case to simple issues that wouldn't confuse a jury. As of this writing, the Dixon jury couldn't reach a verdict in the criminal case after a week of deliberations, raising the prospect that the case may be tried by a new jury.

Far more important is a question that he raised in his defense. Dixon and his ilk unquestionably caused a big problem. If they didn't loot the savings and loan, they surely looted the public trust and undermined confidence in a system that has generated decades of prosperity for generations of Americans. But Dixon and his pals didn't cause on their own a crisis that will cost $400 billion to $500 billion.

The willingness of Democrats and Republicans in Congress to ignore the evolving scandal while they raked in political contributions is already well known. But the Bush administration and its man on the spot, M. Danny Wall, helped drive up the cost, too, in a far more obscure and complex way. Once he took over from Gray in 1987, Wall, with the support of officials who would occupy key positions in the Bush administration, continued the inept, indecisive, and vacillating policies that kept Vernon Savings alive far longer than necessary and drove up the cost of resolving the problem even more.

From the day he took office, Wall knew how the game would be played. A Capitol Hill insider who had spent more than a decade working for Utah Republican Sen. Jake Garn, Wall came to the bank board chairman's job after six years as the chief of staff on the Senate Banking Committee. He knew how Congress worked. Soon after he took office, the bank board dealt with the guy who had caused House Speaker Jim Wright his problems. Joe Selby was forced out of his job in Dallas and dismissed.

Wall also knew what happened to guys who bucked the powers in the S&L industry. In the end, Ed Gray had refused to cave in to industry demands and had committed the cardinal sin—he told the public how bad things really were. Perhaps Gray did the right thing because he had no other choice. Perhaps he did it for some other reason. But Gray's fate didn't escape an ambitious man such as Wall. After Gray left the bank board, he found it next to impossible to get another job.

"Ed Gray had a lot of guts," said George Gould, a U.S. Treasury official in the Reagan era. "I tried to help him get a job with some financial firms on Wall Street after he left the administration. But each time he'd have an interview, someone from the U.S. League would call and say, 'You won't get much mortgage bond business from us if you hire him.' The League did a lot of mortgage bond business and that would be the end of it for Ed." After months, Gray finally got a job in a small S&L in Miami.

Wall wouldn't make the same mistake.

From the outset, Wall faced the same problems as Gray. The deposit-insurance fund contained only about $600 million, down from $6.8 billion in 1983. The thrift industry was in the midst of the worst year it had ever experienced; it was about to post a record yearly loss of $7.6 billion. And dozens of sick thrifts were waiting in the wings to be taken over.

Danny talked tough. "We are not going to regulate to the lowest common denominator," he said in an early speech at the National Press Club. "We don't need to tie the capable hands of the industry leaders to protect depositors from the actions of the small fringe group that has misused their thrift charters. We can, and believe me, we will, rid the industry of those who have violated their duty."

But Danny Wall knew he couldn't close all of the S&Ls that should have been put out of their misery. Like Gray, he didn't have enough money to pay off their depositors. And he knew something else. The people who put him there didn't want him to shut down S&Ls willy-nilly. It wouldn't look good that close to an election.

Wall took office in mid-1987. Ronald Reagan was still in the White House, basking in the enormous popularity he hoped to transfer to his vice president, George Bush, then a candidate for the Oval Office in the November 1988 elections. No one wanted some ugly, complex mess in the savings and loan industry ruining the campaign. After all, Reagan was the prime force behind the policies that had created the troubles; he brought to Washington the economic zealots behind the drive for deregulation. George Bush, too, had presided over a White House task force that had advocated taking the wraps off the financial industry for some bare-knuckled competition. It was a no-win situation, and the last thing the administration wanted was some guy at the bank board blabbing about how bad things were with an election coming up. Wall's job was to contain the problem until after the polls closed—period.

He got some help right away from James Baker, the Treasury chief who would leave within months to run Bush's White House campaign. Baker had watched the S&L problem fester. Like many others, he knew the industry faced some troubles; he heard complaints all the time from the people in his native state, Texas. That's why he had been roped into the fund-raiser where he sat next to Dixon. But Baker already had his hands full trying to correct another Reagan administration disaster—Don Regan's inept handling of U.S. trade policy and the dollar.

By the time Bush's election campaign drew near, Baker could see the S&L crisis as an embarrassing and potentially dangerous situation looming on the political horizon. Congress had caved in to the pressure from the U.S. League and passed legislation that would inject $5 billion to $7.5 billion into the FSLIC, far short of the $15 billion the administration had sought. Even worse, House and Senate negotiators were mired in disagreement over their respective versions of the bill. Concerns were rising that the industry would get hit with a disastrous run on deposits any day.

A consummate politican and pragmatist, Baker stepped into

the fray and soon got both sides to agree to a deal that would provide the deposit-insurance fund with $10.8 billion, or a total higher than either side had voted. That would at least forestall the problem until after the election campaign. If Bush won, the new president could say, with some degree of accuracy, that he inherited a problem created by his predecessor and a Democratic Congress. If the Democrats won—well, welcome to the NFL.

Wall took to his job like a real pro. Critics of the administration's handling of the S&L situation, such as Bert Ely, an Alexandria, Virginia, financial analyst, almost immediately attacked the $10.8-billion bill as too little too late. Ely correctly argued that the problem was far worse than the administration wanted to admit. He called upon the government to face up to the bad news, level with taxpayers, appropriate some money, close the money-losing S&Ls, pay off depositors, and cut its losses. Under Ely's logic, the faster the administration acted, the less it would eventually cost.

Honest and frank lawmakers such as Congressman Jim Leach, a Republican from Iowa, and Senator William Proxmire, a Democrat from Wisconsin, agreed. "It is with reluctance but profound conviction that I rise to state that the FSLIC's crisis has grown beyond industry resources," said Proxmire, a fiscal scrooge, in a speech to the Senate. "The taxpayers must help. We know that the problem is serious. We also know that it needs to be addressed urgently. Witnesses before the Senate Banking Committee have testified that the cleanup cost is growing at a rate of fifteen percent a year. That's one billion dollars a month. Delaying a real resolution increases the final bill that will have to be paid by the taxpayer."

But Danny Wall would have none of that. As the election campaign heated up in late 1987 and early 1988, he argued that the $10.8 billion was adequate. Just months after his confirmation, Wall unveiled a new plan in which he would take over sick thrifts, merge them into new institutions, and sell them to private investors. No tax money would be involved. Wall labeled the idea the Southwest Plan, named after the area of the nation with the most troubled institutions. But Proxmire called it the garbage plan: "Lacking the money to do the job right, the bank board has resorted to garbage deals with garbage thrifts."

On paper, the idea sounded great. The bank board would sweep in and take over an institution such as Vernon, strip it of some bad assets, prop it up with government IOUs and loan guarantees, and try to sell it to a private investor. A prime feature of Wall's plan was the mouth-watering tax breaks, subsidies, and guarantees against losses that Wall would use to lure potential purchasers.

It was a clever trick, too. The government could avoid using its resources on expensive liquidations in which depositors would have to be paid off immediately. With only $10 billion to $11 billion available, Wall wouldn't have been able to close many thrifts like Vernon, which would eventually cost more than $1 billion. Under his plan, he could put a mere $200 million cash into an institution and guarantee the safety of the remaining deposits with promissory notes or IOUs. They wouldn't have to be repaid for years, if at all. As long as depositors didn't rush in en masse and demand their savings, Wall's plan would work. Best of all, he would obscure the extent of the problem in the deposit-insurance fund, deferring the true cost of the troubles years into the future.

Unfortunately, the plan encountered a couple of significant snags right away. By early 1988, Wall had taken over an increasing number of troubled savings and loans, appointing government managers to run them until he could find a buyer. But he had a hard time coming up with interested private investors. Despite the juicy tax breaks and subsidies, investors were reluctant to stuff their money into institutions with such troubled histories.

The first problem soon fathered a second one. Uncle Sam's inventory of troubled savings and loans grew into a significant force in the industry, pitting government-subsidized institutions against their privately owned brethren. Ideally the government managers were supposed to slash the high-cost deposits in the sick S&Ls by lowering interest rates paid to savers. The result would be a more salable and stable thrift that wouldn't be a threat to the rest of the industry.

But that's not always what happened. Ely surveyed several thrifts that had been rescued by the bank board plan, including Monfort Savings, and found they were actually paying savers higher interest rates than the industry average. Like Dixon and the other highfliers, the government-run S&Ls had to use some of their deposits to cover losses; the cash-short FSLIC hadn't provided them enough money.

Meanwhile, the caseload of troubled thrifts kept growing at the FSLIC. Instead of being driven to the wall by Dixon and his pals, other marginally profitable thrifts were now being hurt by Wall's zombie thrifts and the fees they had to pay FSLIC to support them. One thrift owner, Theo Pitt, described the process as "vampire economics."

The policy spread the problem like a cancer. Savings and loans routinely engage in complex loan participation sales just like those that Dixon had used to circumvent growth limits. When Vernon Savings first went down, shocked bank board officials discovered it had sold interests in about half of its loans to seventy other S&Ls in Kansas, California, Massachusetts, Florida, Nebraska, Wisconsin, Illinois, Colorado, New York, Utah, and Texas. Many of them eventually went under because of problems spawned by loans they had acquired at Vernon. As they fell, a ripple effect flowed through the industry; S&Ls with which they did business started failing, too.

By mid-1988, Wall's Southwest Plan had come under vicious attack for its lack of results. Yet he continued to defend it and argued that tax money would never be needed. Wall bristled at the suggestion that he got his bank board job to get the administration past the election.

He vowed he would lure private capital into the industry and resolve the troubles.

To this day no one knows the extent of what happened in the pressure-cooker atmosphere and secrecy that came to characterize the incredible S&L sales that Wall would engender over the next several months.

Vernon Savings was not the only thrift to become a repository for bad assets stripped from another S&L with a for-sale sign on the door. The same thing happened at dozens of others. "The bank board people were playing all kinds of games; shuffling things around. No one knew what was going on," said the manager of one troubled thrift. All anyone knew was that Wall wanted to get the troubled thrifts off the government's hands so that he and his mentors couldn't be accused of a federal bailout.

As the pace of the sales quickened, some of the President's largest campaign contributors stepped forward to acquire government-owned S&Ls in incredible deals. Wall engineered the sale of American Savings and Loan Association, then the nation's largest troubled S&L, in Stockton, California, to the billionaire Robert M. Bass of Fort Worth, a member of George Bush's Team 100, the 249 individual contributors who had given Bush's campaign at least $100,000 each, a total of $25 million. The Bass interests put up $350 million as part of its deal with the bank board, but got government assistance valued at nearly $2 billion. The entire negotiation took place in secrecy, and bank board officials have never released all of the records in the deal. A year later, the thrift reported earnings of $214 million.

James Fail, an Arizona insurance executive, hired Robert Thompson, a Washington lobbyist who had been congressional liaison for Bush when he was vice president, and acquired fifteen bankrupt Texas S&Ls, putting up only $1,000 in his own money and borrowing the rest. Thompson, who had no background in the banking business, later said he had been hired because he knew how Washington worked. There was no question about that. In return for Fail's $1,000 investment, Thompson negotiated a deal with Wall for his client that generated $1.8 billion in federal subsidies for the thrifts acquired by Fail, who had pleaded guilty to a fraud charge in Alabama during 1976. The 15 S&Ls acquired by Fail were consolidated into Bluebonnet Savings and Loan, which became one of the nation's more profitable thrifts thanks to the government handout.

As spring turned to summer and summer to the fall of 1988, Wall's office churned out press releases touting the latest S&L resolution. Bush was elected President in November, but the victory at the polls didn't stop Danny. Indeed as year-end 1988 approached, Wall alerted investors to quicken the pace of the deals that they had negotiated and close them before the end of the year. The tax breaks that made the acquisitions such sweet deals were about to expire. Under new provisions in the law, the tax benefits would be cut in half. If someone wanted a government-owned S&L, he'd better beat a path to the offices of the bank board before midnight 1988.

In the last five days of 1988 alone, Wall sold thirty-four institutions with almost $62 billion in assets to a handful of rich investors. The bank board's offices were in a state of pandemonium. Papers littered the floors, and Wall's staff had adopted the garbage rule. Any paper on the floor was garbage; any on a table—important. Another Team 100 member, Ronald Perelman, the leveraged-buyout artist and chairman of Revlon, Inc., picked up the remnants of Vernon Savings in an astonishing deal.

For just $315 million, he acquired Monfort and four other S&Ls with assets of $12 billion. Even if things didn't work out, he'd get his money back within two years. The tax benefits incorporated in the deal would save Perelman's other ventures $500 million in income taxes. A taxpayer bailout was already under way; Americans simply didn't know it yet. Perelman also got a government aid package valued at $5.1 billion. It was a fitting end for Vernon; its successor, Monfort Savings, was sold to a guy who ran a cosmetics company.

Los Angeles economist Benjamin Stein said the S&L sales such as the one to Perelman were among "the best deals that a free society ever offered its richest and most powerful citizens— truly staggering opportunities for a few extremely wealthy persons to effect a government-sponsored, no-risk, leveraged buyout on a heroic scale financed with money taken from the ordinary taxpayer." They weren't a bad deal for people like Roger Clark, Monfort's CEO, either. He lost his job. But the government soon hired him to run Keating's Lincoln Savings once it failed. He got a raise to a salary of $300,000 a year. But he didn't do much better than he did at Vernon. At one point the conservator at Lincoln criticized him for incompetence.

Journalists started comparing Wall to midnight-madness stereo salesmen with names such as Crazy Eddie. The taunts didn't bother Wall, though. He brushed aside criticism from experts and his own staff and continued to cater to the industry. At one point, he even cut an unprecedented deal with Keating, another Bush Team 100 member, that allowed Keating's Lincoln Savings and Loan to move to a more friendly regulatory environment.

But the nation would discover in a few months that Wall's sales were simply a daisy chain of the government's own making—an expensive, devious paper shuffle designed to defer a day of reckoning until after the polls closed.

Bush started facing up to the crisis soon after he took office. The President knew how bad things were even before the election. Instead of explaining his position on the issue to voters, though, Bush and his Democratic opponent squared off on issues such as whether they believed in the pledge of allegiance. Bush's close friend and confidant, Treasury Secretary Nicholas Brady, had already started a Treasury Department study of the S&L problem. And soon after he was seated in the Oval Office, Bush unveiled a plan to bail out the S&L deposit-insurance fund. The administration suddenly admitted the crisis would cost American taxpayers money—about $50 billion over the next ten years.

When unveiling his plan to the public, the President was expansive. He allowed how the problem had been developing for years, but he didn't explain why he wouldn't even mention the subject until after his inauguration.

"Economic conditions have played a major role in this situation," the President said. "But unconscionable risk-taking, fraud, and outright criminality have also been factors. While the issues are complex and the difficulties manifold, we will make the hard choices, not run from them," said Bush.

He also vowed that those responsible for the mess would be punished: "I make a solemn pledge that we will make every effort to recover assets diverted from these institutions, and to place behind bars those who have caused losses through criminal behavior. Let those who would take advantage of the public trust and put at risk the savings of American families anticipate that we will seek them out, pursue them relentlessly, and demand the most severe penalties."

The President's comments, of course, were aimed squarely at Dixon and his fellow highfliers. By the time Dixon faced reporters in the courthouse hall in Dallas during June 1990, a financial crime that would have drawn six months to three years in a country-club prison like Allenwood looked like a one-way ticket to Alcatraz.

But Bush didn't comment on Dixon's partners in crime. Jim Wright, Tony Coelho, Ronald Reagan, Danny Wall, the United States Congress, the U.S. League, and dozens of others, including the President himself, helped drive up the cost of the thrift crisis. They played politics with the public interest and put at risk the savings of American families for their own petty political interests.

Dixon started the problem at Vernon Savings. That can't be disputed. But Reagan and Congress created the system that let him through the front door. Some of the schemes that have drawn the sharpest criticism of Dixon and his buddies may be entirely legal, thanks to deregulation. "I suppose bad members of the industry are at fault, but they are at fault because the government allowed them in," said William Seidman, the FDIC chairman who led the initial Bush bailout effort.

"The government said here's the candy and you can have all you want. What they didn't realize is that if you combine a credit card on the United States with no limits, the chance to invest that money just about any way you wanted, and then call off supervision because you decide you have deregulated the industry, you create almost an entrapment—a fatal attraction of whatever they call it in the law. It's like Mayor Marion Barry. They provided him with a fatal attraction."

Even after it had opened the door, the government failed to seize control at the first sign of trouble. The cost of closing Vernon and paying off depositors might have been limited to $100 or $200 million had someone acted sooner. But no one moved against Dixon. Instead they waited and stalled and refused to face up to the problem for years. By the time anything was done, the cost had soared to more than $1 billion.

But what happened to the people who helped him stall legislation in Congress? When Dixon was indicted on charges of making political contributions to Wright, Coelho, Bill Lowery, Jack Kemp, and others, the Justice Department said there was no evidence that the politicians knew the contributions were illegal. What a cop-out. When it came to making a case against Dixon's legislative "partners in crime," the Justice Department hid behind a legal technicality. The nation's elected representatives had literally mugged the American worker and taxpayer, sentencing them with a costly bailout that sapped the U.S. economy of vital resources. You can bet America's industrial competitors—Japan and Germany—aren't spending billions of taxpayer dollars on a financial bailout inflated by the actions of their legislators. Yet the U.S. Justice Department took the easy way out, going after Dixon, whose blatant greed made him an easy target.

Multiply Vernon Savings by hundreds of other thrifts and you have the savings and loan crisis. Members of Congress now call it the greatest financial scandal in the history of the country. But that is just one more instance of how little they understand what is really at work.

The S&L debacle is far more than a financial crisis; it is a political crisis of the first order. It represents what happens when a nation's political system becomes rotten with self-interest, when raising money to stay in office becomes more impor-

tant than the common trust, and when the average citizen becomes insulated from reality, be it by deposit insurance,
ignorance, or indifference.

The crisis isn't over, either. President Bush may think he
can end it with lofty rhetoric, a multibillion-dollar bailout, and
indictments against people like Dixon. But the future could
prove to be more challenging. The potential cost of the crisis is
staggering. By the time the government finally closes the books
on Vernon, bailing out the S&L, it will probably have cost around
$1 billion to $1.3 billion. It would take 150 S&Ls like Vernon to
make a $150-billion problem, which is the administration's
original estimate of the damage. But 150 S&Ls represent only
about 5 to 10 percent of the industry. By some estimates, about
1,000 savings and loans—or about one-third of the industry—are
broke, another 1,000 are nearly broke, and the remaining 1,000
are healthy. Of course, not all of the troubled thrifts will be as
costly as Vernon. But it won't take many to escalate the cost
beyond $150 billion. The numbers are already rising. The cost
of raising that much money is burdening an economy already
threatened with recession.

The government is not just sitting on its hands. Thanks to
the Bush rescue plan, America now has another federal agency
to help the taxpayer out of this mess. Called the Resolution Trust
Corp., the new agency has an organization chart that looks like a
wiring diagram for a nuclear reactor. The Bush administration's
high hopes for the RTC have a familiar ring; it will move in, take
over sick S&Ls, clean them up, and sell them. This time the
government admits tax money will be involved, but the RTC is
supposed to resolve the ugly mess once and for all.

Don't bet on it though, and be prepared for a huge price tag.
Even people who helped set up the RTC have their doubts about
whether it will work. "I had as much to do with setting it up as
anybody," said Seidman, just after he announced that he would
step down as the leader of the Bush administration bailout effort
last year. "When we were initially looking at it, the S&L crisis
was, let's say, a fifteen-billion-dollar problem. Then you can
prescribe a plan to get those institutions out of there, close them
down, and liquidate them and get this minor cancer out of the
system. Back then it was about a golf-ball-size problem. Now it's
the size of a basketball and still growing. I'm not sure you can

use the same treatment." When asked if the RTC might not work, Seidman replied:

"I don't know the answer to that. I ran the White House policy-making office for President Ford, and I can assure you that we would have convened all hands and said, 'What can we do to keep these avalanches from occurring, from the institutions having to be sold, the real estate put on the market, and from raising the money to finance it?' "

At this juncture, no one really knows how much it will eventually cost to resolve the problem. If the RTC could close all of the insolvent savings and loans around the country tomorrow, use $150 billion to pay off depositors, and then sell the assets it took over for $50 billion, then $150 billion would take care of the problem. The total cost would be $100 billion, or the difference between the total amount paid to depositors and the amount earned from the assets that had been taken over.

But the RTC can't close all of the insolvent savings and loans around the country at once and pay off their depositors. It is too big a job to do simultaneously. Even if it could seize all of the S&Ls, it couldn't sell their assets. The RTC faces the same problem that confronted government regulators when Vernon fell. Selling hundreds of millions of dollars' worth of property quickly would wreak havoc in the nation's real estate markets. The excess supply of property would knock down sales prices and appraisals and undermine other S&Ls, whose real estate portfolios would have to be marked down to reflect market conditions. The action would just create more troubled S&Ls and heighten the government's problems. Seidman said that the property the government will acquire and sell from sick S&Ls represents the largest liquidation of real estate in the history of the U.S. It will take a decade or more to resolve the problems, and no one knows what the future will bring.

The biggest threat remains the same as the one posed by Vernon Savings. The longer sick thrifts remain open, the more it will cost to close them. Rising oil prices triggered by Iraq's invasion of Kuwait have helped somewhat. The higher price of crude has stopped the decline in land prices in the Southwest, where the economy is still tied to oil. But the S&L crisis has also driven up the government's true budget deficit. And soft real estate markets elsewhere aren't helping matters. The danger is that the government will be unwilling to face up to the escalating cost, and the Bush plan will become one more daisy chain designed to put the problem off to another day. It is heading that way already.

At the RTC, the government's inventory of assets from failed savings and loans is growing faster than the agency can sell the property. Between August 1989 and June 1990, federal officials sold some 13,000 office buildings, homes, condos, and house trailers that it had acquired by taking over savings and loans that went broke. Yet the total register of RTC assets still grew by 14 percent. The problem? So many savings and loans had failed that the government can't sell off the property fast enough. Some of the property may prove hard to sell, too. The latest list includes everything from a Houston pool hall to two uranium mines. Overall, the RTC is sitting on a hodgepodge of real estate, junk bonds, mortgages, and securities that covers about $200 billion worth of loans. And it is just getting started.

The situation isn't much better at the White House. To its credit, the Bush administration has a plan; that is an improvement over the Reagan team. But the administration is mishandling the S&L bailout, creating a second phase of the scandal that could prove as damaging as the first. Initially hobbled by infighting and a lack of direction, the RTC resembles a dumping ground for the politically unemployed. The pace of the administration's rescue effort is incredibly slow, too, forcing the White House to increase reluctantly its estimates of the bailout's total cost. Like Ed Gray, Seidman has angered the administration with his candor about the true dimensions of the problem. Few Bush loyalists were sorry to hear him say he would leave office before his term expires.

The fall of Vernon Savings and the rise of the savings and loan crisis did claim a few official scalps. Some of the politicians who capitalized on the situation fell from grace. The voters of Rhode Island had enough sense to defeat House Banking Committee chairman Fernand St. Germain. He soon resurfaced in Washington as a lobbyist for an S&L. Jim Wright and Tony Coelho were driven from office by financial controversies. In purging Wright from power, though, the Congress studiously avoided allowing his role in the S&L scandal to become a prime issue. Although the S&L issue played a large role in Wright's downfall, he was actually driven from office because the House Ethics Committee concluded he used royalties from a book he published to circumvent campaign finance limits. Coehlo stepped down because of a junk bond investment. But he quit his congressional seat before his broader role in the scandal became an issue.

Danny Wall finally got his comeuppance. Rep. Henry Gonzalez, perhaps the only member of the Texas congressional delegation who had the guts to oppose the bailout, forced Wall to resign in a blistering set of hearings that focused on his handling of Keating. Keating was indicted last year on forty-two counts of allegedly defrauding investors through the sale of junk bonds to customers of Lincoln Savings and Loan. He pleaded "absolutely not guilty" to the charges.

Senators such as Donald Riegle, Dennis DeConcini, John Glenn, and John McCain must also face voters and explain why they took all of that money from Keating. The members of the so-called Keating Five have another problem. After ignoring the S&L crisis for years, the Washington press corps finally stopped looking in the mirror and discovered something was up. The mighty corps is focusing its guns on the senators.

The added scrutiny is not limited to the normal practice where one of the nation's esteemed political reporters writes a story and everyone else repeats it. The nation's Capitol press corps also made Keating and his Senate pals the target of a skit in the spring 1989 Gridiron Dinner. The President, captains of industry, movie stars, and "important" people gathered for the show, where the cream of the corps dresses up in funny outfits and acts silly for the people they are supposed to cover.

Suddenly three newsmen and three professional singers danced out onto the stage. Lee Bandy, a reporter from Columbia newspapers, played Keating. He was dressed in a white robe with angel wings, carried a harp, and wore a halo. The other five played the senators who had intervened with regulators on Keating's behalf after receiving hefty campaign contributions from the Arizona thrift executive. With a burst of enthusiasm and showmanship, they then sang "What a Friend We Have in Keating" to the tune of "What a Friend We Have in Jesus." It was official. The Washington press corps was on the story.

How much good the added attention will do is anybody's guess. Cranston already announced he won't seek re-election because of health problems. None of the other senators are up for re-election for a couple of years. But politicians driven from office because of complex financial scandals are the exception and not the rule. Under the system that gave America the savings and loan crisis, incumbents are reelected 90 percent of the time. It actually pays to take the money. The real crisis is that most of the senators and congressmen who created the policies responsible for the S&L scandal remain comfortably in office. Public apathy keeps them alive.

Congressional Democrats are capitalizing on the President's problems, sensing that voter outrage over the cost of the bailout will give them a potent issue in 1992. The politics is mean. Democrats have focused their guns on the role of the President's son, Neil, who was dumb and unethical enough to help his business partners get huge loans from Silverado Savings, a failed Denver thrift where he was a director.

But the Democrats are just as culpable as the President in the S&L scandal. Four of the five recipients of Mr. Keating's largesse were Democrats. Moreover, some of the Democrats leading the charge have just as poor a record as the Republicans. Rep. Frank Annunzio, an Illinois Democrat who chairs a financial-institutions oversight subcommittee, routinely issues press releases attacking the administration for not pursuing S&L crooks. But Annunzio was one of the top twenty-five recipients of S&L money in the Common Cause study and lined up behind the U.S. League on almost every vote.

The real trouble is that not much has really changed. Both sides are playing politics with the S&L scandal, which is how the whole thing got started in the first place. And the same system of well-heeled lawyers, accountants, and consultants who paved the regulatory way for the Don Dixons of the world are alive and well in Washington, lining their pockets at the offices of the RTC instead of at some S&L.

The RTC now is selling off piecemeal the real estate and other S&L assets that the government has inherited in its takeovers. Even its critics agree the agency faces a monumental task. Congressional auditors say that RTC red tape and mismanagement are tangling the sale of billions of dollars worth of transactions and costing taxpayers millions of additional dollars, prompting House Banking Committee Chairman Gonzalez to call the crisis "a bottomless pit."

Meanwhile, federal officials who fear that a repeat performance of the thrift crisis is evolving in the banking industry have now tightened regulation and examination of financial institutions of all kinds. The result: restricted real estate lending, an epidemic of unsold homes across the country and a credit crunch that is helping tip an already weak economy into recession.

One day all of the S&Ls that should have been shut down years ago will be closed. One day all of their assets will be sold. Perhaps the Congress or someone else will implement sorely needed reforms of the nation's deposit-insurance system. Unfortunately, the American public will probably have to pay for this mess with more than money. The system that had given the nation stability since the Great Depression is in jeopardy. Reform is needed. Perhaps only deposits of up to $20,000 should be insured. Perhaps some other scheme should be developed. But until that happens, the government will continue selling off savings and loans piecemeal and more will go broke.

The government hasn't even sold off all of Vernon Savings' assets yet. Some of Dixon's toys have been placed on the auction block. The boat and the planes have been sold, but much of the land remains in a government inventory.

So far, the results of the sales aren't too encouraging, either. At an August 1989 auction in Dallas, Dixon's *Watcher of the Plains* statue was sold. Tanner said that $125,000 of Vernon's money originally went out the door to pay for the bronze Indian guard. When it was sold recently, though, it fetched only $13,000. The remaining $112,000 is gone forever. The statue now belongs to a Texan who owns a direct-mail firm and three western-wear shops called Boot Country.

The same thing happened when the auctioneers sold some handmade covered wagons from Vernon Savings that were replicas of the kind that brought R. B. Tanner and his family to western Texas. They were sold to a developer who said he never borrowed money from S&Ls.

Dennis Cauchon, a reporter for *USA Today*, wandered through the FSLIC auction amazed at all of the S&L toys crammed in the government warehouse. Dixon's Spanish castle doors were there; so was the silver saddle he had purchased. But the item that caught Cauchon's eye was an antique mirror waiting to grace a new parlor. As rays of sunlight filtered through the warehouse windows, Cauchon could barely make out the words that someone had written with his finger in the dust on the face of the mirror:

"Don Dixon was here."

AUTHOR'S NOTES

1
Roots

PAGE 2—*At first, Tanner*—The details of Dixon's early contacts with R. B. Tanner came from an interview with Mr. and Mrs. R. B. Tanner in Denton, Texas, during November 1989. The author also talked with other members of Tanner's family. His daughter, Janet, and her husband, Frank Arnold, of Austin, Texas, were also interviewed. Various sources involved with Dixon confirmed most details used in the manuscript.

PAGE 3—*Back in Dallas*—The details on how Dixon first learned Vernon Savings might be for sale came from an interview with Woody Lemons in Vernon, Texas, during June 1989. Lemons said he had heard that a mortgage-insurance salesman who was a friend of Tanner's somehow got word to Dixon that Vernon Savings was for sale. Tanner confirmed that he had discussed the possible sale with a man who sold him mortgage insurance just before he got the phone call from Dixon.

PAGES 3–4—*Like a lot of smart people*—Interview with Gary Roth; Solana Beach, California; July 1989. Roth talked at length with the author about Dixon's business practices in California.

PAGE 5—*Tanner said there*—Interview with Mr. and Mrs. R. B. Tanner; Denton, Texas; November 1989. Some of the quotes from the interview were first reported by Douglas Frantz of the *Los Angeles Times*.

PAGE 7—*One guy in Washington*—*Washington Post*; Sunday, February 1971. Bernard Nossiter wrote an insightful and interesting story on the so-called Sharpstown Bank scandal in Texas. According to the U.S. Securities and Exchange Commission, the sitting governor, Preston Smith; Elmer Baum, the chairman of the state Democratic committee; House Speaker Gus Mutscher, Jr.; his father, Gus senior; S. Rush McGinty, an aide to the Speaker; the chairman of the House Appropriations Committee; and Tommy Shannon, the House floor leader, earned $359,150 in profits from a stock investment sponsored by the proponents of legislation to set up a Texas deposit-insurance fund. The bill was designed to circumvent a crackdown by federal regulators. Although then-governor Smith supported the bill, he later vetoed it when a controversy surfaced.

PAGE 9—*Old conflict-of-interest*—*Where Deregulation Went Wrong;* Norman Strunk & Fred Case; U.S. League of Savings Institutions, 1988; page 90.

PAGE 10—*Just weeks before*—Interview with Dale Anderson; Shreveport, Louisiana; July 1989. The author talked to Anderson on several occasions. Most of the information came from a lengthy interview in Shreveport, though. Additional details about Dixon's ties to Anderson and Herman Beebe were provided in subsequent phone calls and were confirmed by federal law enforcement officials involved in the investigation and prosecution of Herman Beebe.

PAGE 11—*It is a terrifying thing*—Anita Creamer; *Dallas Life Magazine;* May 7, 1989. Ms. Creamer wrote an excellent profile of Larry Vineyard and included direct quotes from his trial in her story.

2
The Boy in a Covered Wagon

PAGE 13—*He was six years old.*—Interview with Mr. and Mrs. R. B. Tanner; Denton, Texas; November 1989. The author talked with Tanner several times by phone, and his family made available tapes of television interviews he'd conducted.

PAGE 16—*On the other end*—Tanner said that Judge Vandergriff was the one who came up with the idea for him to get into the savings and loan business. His comment about the early days in Vernon came from one of several taped interviews between Tanner and Byron Harris, a reporter for WFAA-TV in Dallas.

PAGE 17—*bail him out.*—"A Guide to the Federal Home Loan Bank System"; FHLB Publication Corporation; Washington, D.C.; March 1987; pages 5–6.

PAGE 18—*Between 1930 and*—U.S. League of Savings Institutions; Thrift Failures—1930 to 1985.

PAGE 18—*"Depositors stood in*—Statement of Congressman Frank Karsten, Ret.; House Banking Committee Hearings; San Antonio, Texas; March 1989.

PAGE 18—*For the first time*—*Where Deregulation Went Wrong;* Norman Strunk & Fred Case; U.S. League of Savings Institutions, 1988; page

17. There were actually three laws initially passed that helped the industry enormously. One was the Federal Home Loan Bank Act of 1932. Another was Section 5 of the Home Owners' Loan Act of 1933, which created the Federal Savings and Loan System. Title IV of the National Housing Act of 1934 created the Federal Savings and Loan Insurance Corp., otherwise known as FSLIC. The Federal Housing Administration and Veterans Administration guaranteed-loan programs, passed to help Americans get mortgage loans with low down payments, also benefited the industry enormously.

PAGE 19—*The key ratio*—Although the story of the three-six-three ratio was almost folklore in the S&L industry, Rick Atkinson and David Maraniss of the *Washington Post* were the first reporters to discuss it in print, in a first-rate series on the S&L crisis that ran in June 1989.

PAGE 19—*Each month they'd*—"Federal Home Loan Bank Board Semi-Annual Report for Vernon Savings and Loan"; June 1977.

PAGE 20—*"Our lending was*—Interview with Mr. and Mrs. R. B. Tanner; Denton, Texas; November 1989. Tanner also discussed Vernon's early philosophy on a Public Broadcasting System report entitled "Money in America—The Business of Banking," which aired during 1989.

PAGE 20—*Although Tanner's deposits*—Federal Home Loan Bank Board semiannual reports for Vernon Savings and Loan; June 1977–78.

PAGE 21—*In 1972, though*—*Complete Money Market Guide*; William E. Donoghue with Thomas Tilling; Harper & Row, 1981; pages 49–50.

PAGE 22—*The process would*—Statement of George Barclay, president of the Federal Home Loan Bank of Dallas; House Banking Committee Hearings; San Antonio, Texas; March 1989; page 7. Citing government statistics, Barclay noted that money market funds between 1978 and 1980 attracted nearly one-half trillion dollars, or nearly half the savings in the U.S. Most of the growth came at the expense of savings and loans like Vernon.

PAGE 22—*"We had a lot of loans*—"Money in America—The Business of Banking"; Public Broadcasting System, 1989.

3
Faulkner Points

PAGES 24–25—*A decade of oil embargoes*—*Annual Energy Review*; Energy Information Administration; U.S. Department of Energy,

1987. Prior to 1972, oil prices had been incredibly stable. A barrel of domestic crude oil fetched $3.39 that year, a twenty-four-year high. It had not varied by more than 85 cents per barrel since 1949. On October 6, 1973, war broke out in the Middle East on Yom Kippur. America airlifted supplies to Israel during the fighting, infuriating Arabs. Nationalization of oil companies started, and Arab nations staged a boycott of oil bound for the U.S. By early 1974, crude oil was $7.67 per barrel. The Shah of Iran's fall from power and the chaos created by the rise of the Ayatollah Khomeini in Iran, a major oil-producing nation, drove the price of oil to $12.51 during 1979, $21.59 by 1980, and over $34 by 1981.

PAGE 25—*"The art world*—"Texas Financial Crisis: Reading the Signals"; M. Ray Perryman; Texas League Savings Account, May–June 1988. An economist at Baylor Univeristy in Waco, Perryman speaks and writes extensively on the Texas economy.

PAGE 26—*"Don was a natural*—Interviews with Rick Ramsey; Dallas, Texas; January 1989 and June 1989. A former executive at Raldon, Ramsey worked closely with Dixon for years and was considered his top aide for much of the time. The author interviewed Ramsey twice in person and several times on the phone.

PAGE 27—*"You've got to*—*Trammell Crow, Master Builder*; Robert Sobel; John Wiley & Sons, 1989; page 20.

PAGE 27—*A developer with a $100-million*—Interview with David Gleeson of Lincoln Properties; Dallas, Texas; fall 1989. Lincoln is a major developer in Dallas. A top executive at Lincoln, Gleeson explained that many real estate developers borrow just as extensively as Faulkner and Dixon. However, they usually invest the money in projects and add economic value that can later be converted into cash through a rental or sales program. He said the major difference between Lincoln and developers such as Dixon and Faulkner is that the projects done by the latter developers never made any economic sense. The only reason for the investments seemed to be the generation of fees and income.

PAGES 27–28—*See this building*—Interview with Preston Carter; Dallas, Texas; July 1989. Carter is quoted extensively in *Grant's Interest Rate Observer* and other publications because of his outspoken views about real estate development and financial problems in Texas. Carter says all developers are being penalized because of the sins of a few.

PAGE 28—*Building permits in*—Prepared statement of George M. Barclay, president, Federal Home Loan Bank of Dallas; House Committee on Banking, Currency, and Housing; Hearings on S&L Crisis; San Antonio, Texas; March 1989.

PAGES 28–29—*An itinerant housepainter*—"Fast Money and Fraud"; Allen Pusey; *New York Times Magazine;* April 23, 1989; page 30. A reporter for the *Dallas Morning News,* Pusey reported extensively on Empire Savings and the S&L crisis in Texas.

PAGE 29—*Hughes had hitchhiked*—Interviews with Ernie Hughes; Dallas, Texas; August 1988 and July 1989. This anecdote and many others were taken from several interviews with Hughes in person and over the phone. Eventually the government would file suit against Empire and charge Faulkner and dozens of others with fraud in connection with the collapse of the Mesquite thrift. Faulkner and his friends pleaded innocent. The charges against Faulkner would end up as a mistrial during 1989 after a lengthy trial in Lubbock. The government has vowed to retry the case and now has set a date in January 1991. Hughes, who pleaded guilty to federal charges growing out of his involvement with federally insured savings and loans, is one of the government's main witnesses in the Empire case.

PAGE 32—*As politicians like Texas*—Hughes said that Mattox attended the breakfasts regularly and was widely known to be friendly with Faulkner although Hughes did not know whether Mattox received any money at these breakfasts. Allen Pusey reported that Mattox received $200,000 in cashier's checks made out to his sister in connection with a December 1982 land flip engineered by Faulkner and his friends. Mattox would later threaten to file suit against the Federal Home Loan Bank for discriminating against Texas savings and loans.

PAGE 33—*The profits from*—"Fast Money and Fraud"; Allen Pusey; *New York Times Magazine;* April 23, 1989; page 36.

PAGE 33—*"I went down there*—Interview with Gerald Carmen, former head of the Federal Asset Disposition Association; Washington, D.C.; September 1989.

PAGE 35—*"We had an interest*—Interview with Dale Anderson, former Herman Beebe associate; Shreveport, Louisiana; July 1989.

PAGE 36—*the Texas Rent-a-Bank scheme.—The Failure of Citizens State Bank of Carrizo Springs, Texas, and Related Financial Problems;* Hearings by House Committee on Banking, Currency, and Housing; Part 1, Nov. 30–Dec. 1, 1976. The Texas Rent-a-Bank scheme is outlined in detail in this two-volume set of hearings. A confidant of politicians such as former Louisiana governor Edwin Edwards, Beebe was never accused of any wrongdoing in the hearings. But his name came up often in connection with a scheme to acquire banks by borrowing money from a bank to acquire its stock, which was used as collateral. This technique, known years later as the leveraged buyout, was considered questionable in the mid-1970s. Beebe's involvement in the acquisition and sale of several banks prompted federal bank regulators to start scrutinizing his ties to federally insured banks and savings and loans. Eventually, the federal regulators would trace Beebe to forty-one banks and savings and loans, including one bank that lent money to a firm with ties to Carlos Marcello, the reputed Mafia boss in New Orleans. But Anderson said the loans to the Marcello venture were already in the Beebe-controlled Bossier City Bank & Trust Co. in Bossier City, Louisiana, when Beebe acquired it through AMI.

PAGE 36—*It was a bright day*—"Fast Money and Fraud"; Allen Pusey; *New York Times Magazine;* April 23, 1989; page 32. This quote from Ronald Reagan had often been used by several authors and reporters. It was first reported by Allen Pusey in the *Dallas Morning News*. Pusey covered the signing ceremony for his newspaper and pioneered in the coverage of the S&L crisis in Texas and other areas of the Southwest.

4
Edwin J. Gray

PAGE 38—*"Four years later*—Interview with Ed Gray; Miami, Florida; September 1988. The author interviewed Gray on several occasions. Most of the material came from the September 1988 interview, which was extensive. Some of the background material on Mr. Gray also came from an excellent series on the S&L crisis that focused on Gray's role in the scandal, written by Rick Atkinson and David Maraniss of the *Washington Post*. The author confirmed the accuracy of any material used from the Atkinson and Maraniss series and strove to credit the two *Post* reporters for anything that they unearthed first. Atkinson and Maraniss first reported how Gray was sent to Carmel, California, to get a Bible for Reagan's swearing in.

PAGE 38—*From the outset*—"The $150-Billion Calamity—In Texas, Thrifts Went on a Binge of Growth"; David Maraniss and Rick Atkinson; *Washington Post;* June 11, 1989; page 1.

PAGE 41—*Worst of all*—*Where Deregulation Went Wrong;* Norman Strunk & Fred Case; U.S. League of Savings Institutions, 1988; pages 26–35. Strunk and Case present an excellent summary of the history of S&L capital requirements in their book.

PAGE 41—*Three years later*—Financial statements of Vernon Savings and Loan on file with the Federal Home Loan Bank Board in Washington D.C. The author used the logic presented by Strunk and Case to compute the overall capital that Dixon and Tanner would need. The official computation is far more complex. Nevertheless, the author's computation supports the general conclusion by Strunk and Case and by William Black, the former associate director at the Federal Savings and Loan Insurance Corp., that owners such as Dixon could take on billions of additional deposits with a minimum amount of fresh cash injected into an S&L. Many observers feel that the lenient capital requirements are the prime reason behind the crisis suffered by the industry.

PAGE 42—*The two men met*—Interview with Ed Gray; May 1990. Gray talked at length in this interview on his relationship with Regan. The author covered the Treasury Department as a Washington correspondent for the *Chicago Tribune* and knew personally of Regan's dislike of the S&L industry and its regulators.

PAGE 43—*But in March 1982*—Strunk & Case; op. cit.; pages 89–96. An entire book could be written on brokered deposits. Strunk and Case present a brief history in *Where Deregulation Went Wrong*. Although a publication of the U.S. League, the book is quite forthright in discussing the industry's culpability in the troubles that engulfed federally insured savings and loans.

PAGE 44—*"This was a sleepy*—"An Introspective Gray is Bloodied but Unbowed"; Jim McTague; *American Banker*; June 25, 1987. McTague, formerly with the *American Banker*'s Washington bureau and now with *USA Today*, got this great quote from Sahadi. McTague's coverage of the S&L crisis was also first rate.

PAGE 44—*Entry-level examiners*—Strunk & Case; op. cit.; pages 108–20. Strunk and Case discuss the entire problem with examiners and regulation in their book. It is clear that the number of examiners was only part of the problem. Strunk and Case document that federal regulators were not aggressive in their pursuit of fraud or dishonesty in the savings and loan industry either. They cite numerous memos from Chairman Gray in 1985 and 1986 urging examiners to get tougher and issue more cease-and-desist orders. The specific figures documenting the decline in examiners during the early years of the Reagan administration are on page 138.

PAGE 45—*By the time Pratt*—Maraniss and Atkinson; op. cit.; page 1.

PAGE 46—*He arrived a hero*—Maraniss and Atkinson; op. cit.; page 1.

5
Homecoming

PAGE 47—"*Vernon Savings is*—"Mayor to Head Vernon Savings as Plans for Expansion Mapped"; *Vernon Daily Record*; December 6, 1982; page 1.

PAGE 48—*It's an obscure place*—The author spent close to one week in Vernon, Texas, during June 1988. The description of the town comes from personal observations and research in the local library and newspaper office.

PAGE 48—*Friends said the elder*—Interview with Truman Quillan; Vernon, Texas; June 1989. Quillan is an old family friend of the Dixons and was one of W. D. Dixon's closest friends. He was also a business partner with Mrs. Dixon after her husband died. Quillan said few people knew W.D.'s real name.

PAGE 49—*W.D. figured out*—"Party Line"; W. D. Dixon; *Vernon Daily Record*; August 1947. Dixon actually called his campaign the A.R.F.N.P.S. for Anti–Red Finger Nail Polish Society.

PAGE 49—*One teacher recalled*—Interview with Mrs. Jack Eure; Vernon, Texas; June 1989.

PAGE 49—*"His Daddy would*—Interview with Diana Dixon; Laguna Beach, California; July 1989.

PAGE 49—*"He told me to*—Interview with Truman Quillan; Vernon, Texas; July 1989.

PAGE 50—*Memories differ on*—Interview with R. B. Tanner; Denton, Texas; November 1989. Tanner told the author and Byron Harris on a television report that Dixon made the after-the-fact request to buy the statue for $125,000. Some board members say they think the statute was actually acquired one year later, and some support Tanner's version of events. The actual records of the original purchase could not be traced.

PAGE 50—*Other board members*—Interview with Leon Speer; Vernon, Texas; June 1989.

PAGE 51—*Dixon soon approached Woody*—Interview with Woody Lemons; Vernon, Texas; June 1989.

PAGE 51—*He had the reputation*—Interview with Raylan Loggins; Dallas, Texas; June 1989.

PAGE 51—*But a summer job in*—Interview with Diana Dixon; Laguna Beach, California; July 1989.

PAGE 52—*Actually, Dixon funded*—"Deposition and Sworn Statement of Donald R. Dixon"; Dallas County Court, Divorce Court; Case No. 67-04360-U. May 19, 1967; Dixon testified that he borrowed money from his mother on a few occasions as an advance from his father's estate.

PAGE 53—*"He went over*—Interview with Woody Lemons, Vernon, Texas; June 1989.

PAGE 54—*"In acquiring Vernon, Don*—Testimony of Harvey McLean, *U.S. Housing Corp. v. Continental Savings Association, Continental Service Corp., Joseph S. Rice, Vernon Savings and Loan Association, and Richard A. Larsen;* U.S. Bankruptcy Court, Western District of Louisiana, Shreveport Division; Case No. 87BK-000001511; August 1987.

PAGE 54—*"I met Ron Finley*—Interview with Raylan Loggins; Dallas, Texas; June 1989.

PAGE 55—*Jack Atkinson walked in*—Letter from Jack D. Atkinson to Federal Savings and Loan Insurance Corp. officials detailing Atkinson Financial Corp. financial dealings with Vernon Savings and Loan; August 31, 1987. Atkinson's letter detailed each and every loan he made with Vernon Savings.

PAGE 56—*During a twenty-month*—"Recommendation for the Appointment of the Federal Savings and Loan Insurance Corp. as Receiver for Vernon Savings and Loan Association, Vernon, Texas"; Federal Home Loan Bank Board No. 6485.

PAGE 56—*"They ran the business*—Interview with Yvonne Robinson; Vernon, Texas; June 1989.

PAGE 56—*"Anything that was done*—"Sworn Oral Statement of Chris Barker," former employee of Vernon Savings and Loan; U.S. Bankruptcy Court, Central District of California; Case No. SA 87-02476-PE; June 1987.

PAGE 56—*The only one that we never*—"Sworn Oral Statement of Linda Shivers," former employee of Vernon Savings and Loan; U.S. Bankruptcy Court, Central District of California; Case No. SA 87-02476-PE; June 1987.

PAGE 56—*As far back as 1976*—*The Failure of the Citizens State Bank of Carrizo Springs, Texas, and Related Financial Problems;* Hearings by U.S. House Committee on Banking, Currency, and Housing; Part 1, Nov. 30–Dec. 1, 1976. Rosemary Stewart, a lawyer with the Federal Home Loan Bank Board in 1976, said Beebe's name surfaced in connection with a troubled S&L involved in the committee's investigation. Ms. Stewart would later become the director of enforcement at the Bank Board when Dixon and Beebe acquired Vernon Savings. Yet the Bank Board officials raised no question when Beebe's name surfaced, even though he had also been investigated extensively by banking regulators.

PAGE 57—*Anderson was amused*—Interview with Dale Anderson; Shreveport, Louisiana; June 1989. Anderson said he and Dixon worked closely structuring the deal and that easing the Dondi Group's debt burden was a major consideration in the reorganization.

PAGE 58—*By 1983, the board authorized*—Financial statements of Vernon Savings and Loan Association; Federal Home Loan Bank Board; 1982.

6
Gastronomique Fantastique

PAGE 59—*Interest rates were twenty percent*—Interview with Gary Roth; Solana Beach, California; June 1989.

PAGE 60—*The swap involved*—*Van Boxtel v. McLean*; U.S. District Court, San Diego, California; Case No. CV 88001325; 1988. The details of the house purchase were outlined in the court case in which Van Boxtel filed suit against Paris Savings and Loan Association and Harvey McLean. In the proposed tax-free swap, Van Boxtel never got his condos in Dallas. Eventually Beebe and Dixon would take out additional loans against the beach house. Paris Savings, which held a first lien against the house, finally foreclosed, leading Van Boxtel to file suit against Paris Savings and Loan. During the proceedings, Van Boxtel charged that Dixon and Beebe had drained his equity from the house.

PAGES 63–64—*Dixon had hired Philippe*—The details of Dixon's hiring of Philippe Junot and Philippe's background came from a sworn deposition of Philippe Junot taken in Dallas during September 1989.

PAGE 64—*We called it our Rent-a-Frenchman*—Interview with Raylan Loggins; Dallas, Texas; June 1989.

PAGE 65—*The Old World suites*—"Tour to Europe—Dallas to France; *Gastronomique Fantastique!*" This is a written account of the trip.

Government officials said the account was written by Dana Dixon. But Dixon's lawyer later confirmed that it was written by Carol Little. In any event, no one disputes that it was an accurate account of the tour. It was written in October 1983 and filed in court in connection with the Dixon bankruptcy case in U.S. District Court, Central District of California.

PAGES 67–68—*Gary Roth's phone rang*—Interview with Gary Roth; Solana Beach, California; July 1989.

PAGE 69—*Woody Lemons took care of her*—Interviews in Vernon, Texas; June 1989. The author interviewed Yvonne Robinson by phone and received Mrs. Robinson's version of the incident. A senior executive from Vernon Savings and Loan told the author of Mr. Lemons's explanation to Mrs. Robinson. Lemons later confirmed that he told Mrs. Robinson she would not be able to attend the meeting in California.

7
The Tattoo Tuna

PAGE 71—*From LBJ Freeway eastward*—"Condo Land Deals, Price Spiral Reported"; Allen Pusey and Christi Harlan; *Dallas Morning News;* Nov. 27, 1983; page 1.

PAGE 72—*Ramsey didn't know*—Interview with Rick Ramsey; Dallas, Texas; June 1989.

PAGE 72—*At a fund-raiser*—*Roundup: A Newsletter for Employees of Vernon Savings;* Spring 1984.

PAGE 73—*Each of the subsidiaries*—Interview with Rick Ramsey; Dallas, Texas; June 1989.

PAGE 74—"*We submitted our*—Testimony of Harvey McLean; *U.S. Housing Corp.* v. *Continental Savings Association, Continental Service Corp., Joseph S. Rice, Vernon Savings and Loan Association, and Richard A. Larsen;* U.S. Bankruptcy Court, Western District of Louisiana, Shreveport Division; Case No. 87BK-000001511; August 1987.

PAGE 74—*But it worked*—"Vernon, Tex., Tops ROAA at Big S&Ls"; Jeffrey Tuchman; *National Thrift News;* August 1985; page 1A; and column featuring Vernon Savings by Lynn Adkins; *Dun's Business Month;* 1985.

PAGE 75—*Dixon himself took*—Vernon Savings semiannual reports, June and December, 1984; Federal Home Loan Bank Board; and special report on Vernon Savings prepared by the thrift's staff in early 1985. Dixon told the author in a 1988 interview that he had set up Vernon Savings as a bank for developers. The data on the number of projects started also came from the special report.

PAGE 76—*The pace of the deals*—Letter from Jack D. Atkinson to Federal Savings and Loan Insurance Corp. officials detailing Atkinson Financial Corp. financial dealings with Vernon Savings and Loan; August 31, 1987.

PAGE 80—*He continued to resist*—*U.S. Housing Corp. v. Continental Savings Association* et al.; op. cit.

8
No More Mr. Nice Guy

PAGE 81—*"We've reviewed the situation*—"The $150-Billion Calamity—Turning Anger into Action on Thrifts"; Rick Atkinson and David Maraniss; *Washington Post*; June 13, 1989. Atkinson and Maraniss first reported the story about Joe Settle. Ed Gray confirmed the details in a subsequent interview, as did other Texas thrift executives and politicians.

PAGE 82—*Bowman and Durward Curlee*—"The $150-Billion Calamity—In Texas, Thrifts Went On a Binge of Growth"; David Maraniss and Rick Atkinson; *Washington Post*; June 11, 1989; page 1.

PAGE 83—*When Gray assumed the chairmanship*—Interviews with Ed Gray and L. L. Bowman; Miami, Florida, and Austin, Texas; September 1988 and June 1989. Gray said the warnings that were given him were vague and extremely superficial. But Bowman said Gray was aware of the situation.

PAGES 84–85—*"I got my first briefing*—Interview with Ed Gray; Miami, Florida; September 1988.

PAGE 85—*"I felt physically sick,"*—Frank Augustine; videotaped report to Federal Home Loan Bank Board; March 1984. Some sections of the tape were first printed by Atkinson and Maraniss in the *Washington Post*. The author had also obtained the tape.

PAGE 85—*"fiduciary pornography."*—Interview with Ed Gray; Miami, Florida; September 1988.

PAGE 86—*"All you had to do was walk up*—Interview with Ed Gray; Miami, Florida; September 1988.

PAGE 87—*Mettlen and Gray swapped insults*—"The $150-Billion Calamity—Turning Anger into Action on Thrifts"; Rick Atkinson and David Maraniss; *Washington Post;* June 13, 1989; page 1.

PAGE 87—*discrimination against the little guys.*—Letter from Roy Dickey, president, Vernon Savings and Loan; Bank Board Watch; January 27, 1984.

PAGE 88—*"This was right after we had closed Empire*—Interview with Ed Gray; Miami, Florida; September 1988.

9
The Divorce

PAGE 91—*Anderson was Beebe's right-hand man*—Interview with Dale Anderson; Shreveport, Louisana; June 1989. Anderson and several other sources said that he was intricately involved in negotiating the division of the Beebe-Dixon empire.

PAGES 91–92—*the regulators had become a nuisance*—"Recommendation for the Appointment of the Federal Savings and Loan Insurance Corp. as Receiver for Vernon Savings and Loan Association, Vernon, Texas"; Federal Home Loan Bank No. 6485.

PAGES 92–93—*Beebe's business relationships*—"Beebe's Network Casts Long Shadow in Thrift Industry"; Bill Lodge and Allen Pusey; *Dallas Morning News;* Dec. 23, 1988; page 1.

PAGE 93—*Wolfenbarger moved to Texas*—Interview with Joe Cage, U.S. Attorney; Shreveport, Louisiana; and "Appraisals for Bossier Bank & Trust Collateral"; Lender Equine Service, Inc.; U.S. District Court for Western District of Louisiana; Shreveport. Oct. 1984.

PAGE 93—*reflected the "real world"*—Interview with Dale Anderson; Shreveport, Louisiana; June 1989.

PAGE 94—*For their money, members would*—Letter from Jack D. Atkinson to Federal Savings and Loan Insurance Corp. officials detailing Atkinson Financial Corp. financial dealings with Vernon Savings and Loan; August 31, 1987. In his letter, Atkinson discussed in detail the Sugarloaf Hunt Club transaction.

PAGE 94—*"To hunt birds, you've got to have a bird dog*—Interview with Vaughn Mitchell; Dallas, Texas; September 1988. The author interviewed Mitchell on two other occasions in 1989 to further confirm details of Vernon loans.

PAGE 94—*"Don took me up to the hunting lodge*—Interview with Tom Gaubert; Dallas, Texas; October 1989.

PAGE 95—*"$1 million was transferred to Beebe's*—Interview with Dale Anderson; Shreveport, Louisiana; June 1989. Anderson confirmed the details of the Sugarloaf loan as did Woody Lemons, U.S. Attorney Joe Cage, and Jack Atkinson in interviews. Atkinson said he didn't find out about the details of the loans until the FBI told him years later. Details of the deal were also outlined in *USA* v. *Herman K. Beebe,* Factual Résumé; Criminal No. CR3-88-124-D; U.S. District Court for the Northern District of Texas, Dallas Division; April 1988; and Criminal Information filed in the same case. The author went over the details of the deal involving the Sugarloaf loan twice after the initial interview with Anderson. Dixon has never agreed that he got 25 percent of the proceeds. But U.S. Attorney Joe Cage and Lemons backed up Anderson's version of events.

PAGE 95—*To sweeten the deal, Atkinson*—Letter from Jack D. Atkinson to the Federal Savings and Loan Insurance Corp. detailing Atkinson Financial Corporation's dealings with Vernon Savings and Loan Association; August 31, 1987.

PAGES 95–96—*"I never was in any negotiations where someone put a gun*—Interview with Rick Ramsey; Dallas, Texas; June 1989.

PAGE 96—*Beebe was more authoritarian*—"Beebe's Network Cast Long Shadow in Thrift Industry"; Bill Lodge and Allen Pusey; *Dallas Morning News;* Dec. 23, 1988; page 1.

PAGE 97—*At one point, Beebe was accused*—*Van Boxtel* v. *McLean;* U.S. District Court, San Diego, California; Case No. CV 88001325, 1988. Beebe has never responded to the claim that he diverted $130,000 to his personal use, although the lien on the house suggests the money is not in escrow in the bank Beebe once controlled. The author has not interviewed Beebe, who has been interviewed only once, by a paper in Louisiana.

PAGES 98–99—*Dixon was heading for a fall*—Interview with Dale Anderson; Shreveport, Louisiana; June 1989.

PAGE 100—*"It was incredible,"*—Interview with William Hendricks, former head of the fraud section, U.S. Justice Department; Washington, D.C.; August 1989.

10
Joy Love

PAGE 101—*Bowman knew the savings and loan*—Interview with L. L. Bowman; Austin, Texas; June 1989. The author confirmed the details of the plane ride with Bowman in a subsequent phone interview in late 1989.

PAGE 102—*"What if I'm wrong*—"The $150-Billion Calamity—Hardening the S&L Battle Lines"; David Maraniss and Rick Atkinson; *Washington Post;* June 14, 1989; page 1.

PAGE 103—*The next thing everyone knew*—"Texas Most Wanted—Former Bank Examiner Is Sought in Double Shooting in Lubbock"; *Vernon Daily Record;* June 1983.

PAGE 103—*Bowman was surprised*—USA v. *Patrick G. King;* U.S. District Court for the Northern District of Texas, Dallas Division; CR-3-89-141-T; August 1989. Much of the information about the trip to California came in the sworn testimony of Patrick Malone and John Hill. In a subsequent interview, Bowman confirmed some details but didn't comment in detail on others for obvious reasons. Lemons also confirmed some details of the trips.

PAGE 103—*Those boys from Vernon*—Interview with L. L. Bowman; Austin, Texas; June 1989 and phone interviews in winter, 1989. Bowman acknowledged that Vernon officials included prostitutes on trips, but he said he didn't know at the time they were prostitutes, and he denied that he used their services. Numerous Vernon officials confirmed that Bowman didn't initially know that his dinner companion was a prostitute paid for by Vernon.

PAGE 104—*Joy was good lookin' and well built*—Interview with former high-ranking Vernon executive; Vernon, Texas, and Dallas; June-October 1989. The former executive asked that his name not be used in this book, for obvious reasons.

PAGE 104—*Dixon gripped the commissioner's hand*—Interview with L. L. Bowman; Austin, Texas; June 1989.

PAGE 104—*Back on the ground*—"Recommendation for the Appointment of the Federal Savings and Loan Insurance Corp. as Receiver for Vernon Savings and Loan Association, Vernon, Texas"; Federal Home Loan Bank Board No. 6485.

PAGE 108—*King and Woody Lemons objected*—USA v. *Patrick G. King;* U.S. District Court for the Northern District of Texas, Dallas Division; CR-3-89-141-T; August 1989. Pat Malone testified about the circumstances surrounding the employment of Joy Love under oath. Several other Vernon executives also confirmed the details. When asked about Joy Love directly by the author in an interview, Bowman confirmed that he knew prostitutes were taken on the trips to the hunting lodge in Kansas. However, he said he didn't "partake" of any sexual activities.

PAGE 110—"*I don't think you had to join*—Phone interview with Ross Ikemeir; Dallas, Texas; August 1988. The author interviewed Ikemeir for a series of stories he wrote for the *Chicago Tribune*. The series appeared in the fall of 1988 and quoted Ikemeir.

PAGE 111—*Suddenly, Don said*—*USA v. Patrick G. King*; U.S. District Court for the Northern District of Texas, Dallas Division; CR-3-89-141-T; August 1989. Testimony of Patrick Malone.

PAGE 112—*You had to hand it to Don Dixon*—Ibid. Bowman did not raise such a defense because he was not charged in the trial. King's lawyers argued that their client had to be innocent because he knew that Bowman was impotent and unable to have sexual activities. It, therefore, would have made no sense to hire a prostitute for him, according to King's lawyers. But there was also ample sworn testimony in the trial from several witnesses that Joy Love and other girls were hired by Vernon as dates for Bowman on several occasions. Bowman acknowledged that he was embarrassed by public disclosure of his medical problems. Lawyers introduced letters and documents discussing Bowman's alleged impotency in the trial, but his medical condition never became a focal point of the trial.

11
The Board

PAGE 114—"*Don got real interested in this,*"—All quotes from the board meetings were taken from tape recordings of the meetings that were made available to the author by a former Vernon executive. When the tapes raised questions about the identity of the speaker, the former Vernon executive put names together with the voices. The author listened extensively to the tapes from 1984 onward until 1986, when they were discontinued. All board member quotes not otherwise footnoted in this and subsequent chapters came from tapes of the meetings.

PAGE 114—"*I remember going before*—Interview with Gary Roth; Solana Beach, California; July 1989.

PAGES 115–16—*The board members considered*—Interview with Raylan Loggins; Dallas, Texas; June 1989.

PAGE 116—*"These people are from*—Interview with a former senior officer of Vernon Savings; Vernon, Texas; June 1989. The author refrained from using anonymous quotes wherever possible in the text. This particular individual asked not to be quoted by name in this book..

PAGE 116—*"There were all of these*—Interview with Leon Speer; Vernon, Texas; June 1989.

PAGE 120—*"So Bowman said why*—Bowman denies that he gave verbal approval of the car dealership acquisition before the fact. He said that he was informed of the acquisition after it had taken place and that he then instructed Vernon officials to remove it from Vernon S&L. However, the state took over the thrift before Vernon officials could get the car dealership off its books.

12
The Daisy Chain

PAGE 123—*"Boy, Vern, this sure is*—"The Best of Ernest P. Worrell" video; Vernon Savings and Loan Association ad; 1989.

PAGE 124—*Ernest stood around*—"Vernon Savings and Loan Features Ernest P. Worrell Series of Ads"; *Vernon Daily Record;* July 1985.

PAGE 124—*"I like the homelike atmosphere*—*Roundup*—A *Newsletter for Employees of Vernon Savings and Loan;* Spring 1985.

PAGE 124—*Dixon's thrift had reported*—"Vernon, Tex., Tops ROAA at Big S&Ls"; Jeffrey Tuchman; *National Thrift News;* August 1985. The Vernon performance was for the fiscal year that ended June 30, 1985. According to the survey by Kaplan and Smith, a nationally recognized thrift consultant based in Los Angeles, Vernon earned a return of 4.518 percent on assets of $1.031 billion. That was an improvement from the 4.228 percent return for a comparable period the year before, when Vernon ranked second in the $500-million-to-$1-billion-asset class. In 1983, Vernon Savings registered a 6.873 percent return on assets. The next highest in the rankings for fiscal 1985 was Washington Federal Savings and Loan Association, which generated a return of 2.576 percent on assets of just over $1 billion. Vernon's return was almost double the second-place thrift's. The survey attributed the superior performance to Vernon's aggressive telemarketing program in which loans were funded through its money desk.

PAGE 126—*Asset values weren't*—"Recommendation for the Appointment of the Federal Savings and Loan Insurance Corp. as Receiver for Vernon Savings and Loan Association, Vernon, Texas"; Federal Home Loan Bank Board No. 6485.

PAGE 127—*"In the trade it was*—Testimony of William K. Black before the House Committee on Banking, Finance, and Urban Affairs; U.S. House of Representatives; October 6, 1989.

PAGES 127–29—*Auditors from Arthur Young & Co.*—"Sworn Testimony of Gregory Scott McCormick in the Matter of Vernon Savings and Loan Association, Vernon, Tex."; U.S. Federal Savings and Loan Insurance Corp.; Resolution No. 86-1023. Much of the basis for the account of the Drippie transactions was taken from the McCormick deposition. Dixon later testified in a deposition about the transactions, as did John Hill, Harby Westmoreland, and several others involved. Although each party disputed certain details, the drift of the testimony was the same. The major disagreement seems to be whether Vernon Savings planned to get the loan off its books before or after everyone learned of the problems.

PAGE 130—*When bank and thrift regulators first stumbled*—Interview with William Churchill; Dallas, Texas; October 1989. Although Churchill discussed regulation of federally insured savings and loans in Texas in general with the author, he said he would talk about Vernon Savings only if the Federal Home Loan Bank Board would waive a rule that prohibited him from discussing exams of any financial institution. A spokesman for the Bank Board said it was all right to talk with the author, but the Bank Board's legal department would not issue a letter waiving its right to penalize Churchill. Therefore, he would not talk about the particulars of Vernon Savings.

PAGE 130—*Once the swat team*—"Sworn Testimony of Gregory Scott McCormick in the Matter of Vernon Savings and Loan Association, Vernon, Tex."; U.S. Federal Savings and Loan Insurance Corp.; Resolution No. 86-1023.

PAGES 131–32—*At first Dixon raised*—Testimony of Harvey McLean; *U.S. Housing Corp. v. Continental Savings Association, Continental Service Corp., Joseph S. Rice, Vernon Savings and Loan Association, and Richard A. Larsen;* U.S. Bankruptcy Court, Western District of Louisiana, Shreveport Division; Case No. 87BK-000001511; August 1987.

PAGE 132—*In case he missed Woody's hint*—Ibid.

PAGE 133—*Sandia eventually acquired*—Vernon books and records. The Drippie transactions occurred in mid-1985. According to Vernon's records, Delwin W. Morton borrowed nearly $5.7 million from Vernon Savings, secured by Sandia Savings stock, in June 1985. Charles J. Wilson also borrowed $5.8 million in June 1985, secured by his stock in Sandia Savings.

PAGE 134—*Dixon's name never really*—Sworn testimony of John Hill; *USA v. Patrick G. King;* U.S. District Court for the Northern District of Texas, Dallas Division; CR-3-89-141-T; August 1989.

13
Mr. Inside, Mr. Outside, and Mr. Inside Out

PAGES 136–37—*Prior to his death, Troop*—The background information on Glenwood S. Troop came from four sources: an anonymous interview with a lobbyist; Troop's obituary, which ran in the *Washington Post* on August 7, 1982; six *Washington Post* stories detailing the involvement of Troop with Bobby Baker that ran Oct. 26 and Oct. 30, 1963; Nov. 8, 1963; Dec. 19, 1965; and Jan. 17 and Jan. 25, 1967; and the *Congressional Record* for August 9 and 10, 1982, pages 19897–98 and 20131–32.

PAGE 137—*Late last Wednesday Glen Troop*—Statement by Sen. Donald Riegle on the passing of Glenwood S. (Glen) Troop, Jr.; *Congressional Record;* August 10, 1982; pages 20131–32.

PAGE 138—*"He knew everybody*—Interview with lobbyist who asked that his name not be used in this book. The interview was conducted in Washington, D.C. The lobbyist also provided some details about the memorial service for Troop, which he attended.

PAGE 139—*"It was a good old boy network*—Interview with Ed Gray; Miami, Florida; September 1988.

PAGE 140—*"I just wanted to turn off the spigot*—Interview with Ed Gray; Miami, Florida; September 1988.

PAGE 141—*By mid-1985, David Stockman*—"An Introspective Gray Is Bloodied but Unbowed"; Jim McTague; *American Banker;* June 25, 1987.

PAGE 141—*"Stockman was busy doing other things*—Interview with Ed Gray; Miami, Florida; September 1988.

PAGE 143—*But when they turned to O'Connell*—"Special Thrift Fund Urged"; *New York Times;* Friday, October 13, 1985. O'Connell says he was much more cooperative with Ed Gray than the former bank board chairman now suggests. However, the record is replete with instances of U.S. League opposition to Gray's proposals. In fairness to O'Connell, several sources said he struggled to forge a unified industry posture. He faced a daunting task, though. Many members of the U.S. League downplayed the problems. They didn't want to pay higher insurance premiums that would put them at a competitive disadvantage with bankers and money market funds vying for their depositors.

PAGE 143—*A California lawyer known as the patriarch*—Background on McKenna came from interviews with industry sources, newspaper stories on his career, and from the "Federal Asset Disposition Association: Report of an Inquiry into Its Operations and Performance"; *Congressional Record*; Wednesday, April 20, 1988; page H-2203. McKenna refused to talk to the author on the record.

PAGE 144—*deregulation had created a monster*—Memo to members of the Federal Savings and Loan Advisory Council, Steering and East Coast committees, from Bernard J. Carl, chairman of the East Coast Committee of the Federal Savings and Loan Advisory Council; September 23, 1985. The memo went to some of the most influential executives in the nation's S&L industry and discussed in frank terms the implications of the troubles facing federally insured savings and loans. Carl's memo documents beyond any doubt that the industry and influential members of the U.S. League knew exactly how bad the problems were and the threat that the growing insolvency of the FSLIC posed for the nation's savings and loan industry.

PAGE 145—*The situation in the deposit-insurance fund*—The S&L Insurance Mess; Edward J. Kane; Urban Institute Press; 1989; page 9.

PAGE 147—*The chartering of FADA*—"Federal Asset Disposition Association: Report of an Inquiry into Its Operations and Performance"; *Congressional Record*; April 20, 1988; page H-2203.

PAGE 147—*But the high-flying S&L owners*—Interviews with Durward Curlee and Stanley Adams; Austin, Texas; May 1988. Adams and Curlee expressed distrust of the U.S. League and William McKenna's relationship during a day-long interview in Adams's offices. The interview was originally conducted for stories that ran in the *Chicago Tribune* during 1988.

PAGES 147–48—*Within weeks of Gray's speech*—Interview with Tibby Weston; Houston, Texas; November 1989.

14
Dixons Outdo Dallas

PAGE 149—*"What a wonderful setting,"*—Phone interviews with Peggy Freeman; Rancho Santa Fe, California; April and June 1989. Ms. Freeman also talked with the local papers in San Diego about Dixon and to Douglas Frantz of the *Los Angeles Times.*

PAGE 150—*The guest list alone*—"Dixons Outdo Dallas"; Peggy Freeman; *Ranch and Coast;* Winter 1986.

PAGE 150—*"We went to the party*—Interview with Richard Rosenblatt, former publisher *Ranch and Coast;* Rancho Santa Fe, California; July 1989.

PAGE 150—*Dixon's second wife back in Dallas*—Interview with Diana Dixon; Laguna Beach, California; July 1989.

PAGE 151—*Donald R. Dixon Student Union*—Sworn testimony of Donald R. Dixon; Office of the U.S. Trustee; Central District of California; No. SA-87-02476-PE; July 9, 1987. Dixon testified about the gift of the stock in the creditors' hearing cited above and a deposition taken in June 1987.

PAGE 152—*Freeman soon found herself*—"Dixons Outdo Dallas"; Peggy Freeman; *Ranch and Coast;* Winter 1986.

PAGE 153—*Dixon and Dana moved in*—Affidavit of Gene Webb, senior field examiner, Federal Home Loan Bank of Dallas, Texas; April 1987. In his affidavit, Webb discusses Dixon's use of the Del Mar beach house extensively. According to the affidavit, practically all of the Dixons' living expenses were paid by Vernon Savings. In his depositions, Dixon does not dispute this. He says he was in California working for Vernon Savings and that the S&L should have picked up the outlays.

PAGE 153—*the house was also decorated sumptuously*—"Salute to the Sunset"; Phyllis Van Doren; *San Diego Home/Garden Magazine;* January 1986. The Van Doren story reported extensively on the Dixons' home and contained numerous pictures of the courtyard, den, bedrooms, and the deck with the ocean view.

PAGE 154—*boulders as big as Volkswagens*—Brochure on Los Torres; San Diego Polo Club Tournament Schedule, 1988/89; Plaza Properties, Rancho Santa Fe, California; June 1989; and interview with Ray Schooley.

PAGE 154—"*They never knew what they wanted*—Interview with Ray Schooley, builder of Los Torres; Rancho Santa Fe, California; July 1989. Schooley also took the author on an extended tour of the home. It was sold at a loss of about $2 million in the summer of 1989 to "a Japanese gentleman" from San Francisco, according to Schooley.

PAGE 155—*People wanted to know more about him*—Interview with Bertrand Hug, owner, Mille Fleurs Restaurant; Rancho Sante Fe, California; July 1989.

PAGE 155—*Dixon used Symbolic Motors*—Interview with Walter Van Boxtel, Rancho Santa Fe, California; July 1989.

PAGE 157—"*I was very well aware of everything*—"Break the Bank"; Byron Harris; *Texas Monthly;* January 1988. Harris also covered the S&L story aggressively and well in Dallas. His stories in *Texas Monthly* were particularly good.

15
Politics

PAGE 158—"*He spoke directly*—USA v. Patrick G. King; U.S. District Court for the Northern District of Texas, Dallas Division; CR-3-89-141-T; August 1989; Sworn testimony of Pat Malone.

PAGES 158–59—*I went to the Jewel Ball*—Interview with Ed Gray; Miami, Florida; November 1989.

PAGES 160–61—"*This guy didn't understand economics,*"—Interview with Durward Curlee; Austin, Texas; July 1989. The author interviewed Curlee on several occasions by phone and in person.

PAGE 162—*To Dixon, the most immediate problem*—Where Deregulation Went Wrong; Norman Strunk & Fred Case; U.S. League of Savings Institutions, 1988; page 113.

PAGE 162—*300 percent a year since Dixon*—"Recommendation for the Appointment of the Federal Savings and Loan Insurance Corp. as Receiver for Vernon Savings and Loan Association, Vernon, Texas"; Federal Home Loan Bank Board No. 6485.

PAGE 163—*Gipp Dupree, a Dallas loan broker*—USA v. Woody F. Lemons; U.S. District Court for the Northern District of Texas, Dallas Division; Sworn testimony of Gipp Dupree; CR-3-88-234-T; November 1989.

PAGE 163—*"You'd get some guy from Hutchinson, Kansas*—Interview with Gary Roth; Solana Beach, California; July 1989. In the interview, Roth talked about the California technique. The details of the Dallas technique came during a separate interview with a former senior executive at Vernon. Although the executive spoke with the author on the condition that his name not be used, another former Vernon executive, Rocky Crocker, confirmed details of the incidents in question.

PAGE 165—*Behind the scenes, the League*—Interviews with George Gould, a former Treasury Department official in charge of developing the Reagan administration's policy toward S&Ls and with Ed Gray. Both interviews were conducted via phone in November 1989 and early 1990. Gray insisted that the U.S. League was opposed to his policies from the start, but Gould said their opposition intensified as time passed. Both remembered well the League's instant opposition to a plan requiring the industry to pay off $15 billion worth of bonds.

PAGE 165—*Stanley Adams, a mysterious hulk*—Interview with Durward Curlee; Austin, Texas; September 1989.

PAGES 165–66—*Adams had once applied*—"The $150-Billion Calamity—Hardening the S&L Battle Lines"; David Maraniss and Rick Atkinson; *Washington Post;* June 14, 1989; page 1. Joe Selby told the author about Adams's application for the moon during a July 1989 interview. However, it was first reported publicly in the *Washington Post.* Bowman, too, confirmed the incident.

PAGE 166—*A magician performed feats of levitation*—"The Party's Over"; Byron Harris; *Texas Monthly;* June 1987. Harris first reported many details of Sunbelt in his magazine article.

PAGE 168—*Gaubert set up the East Texas First*—Interview with Tom Gaubert; Dallas, Texas; October 1989.

PAGE 168—*"He wanted a thousand-dollar*—USA v. Patrick G. King; U.S. District Court, Northern District of Texas, Dallas Division; CR-3-89-141-T; August 1989. Sworn testimony of John Hill. The donations were confirmed in records on file at the Federal Election Commission.

PAGES 168–69—*When David Farmer went to work*—USA v. Robert Hopkins, Jr., Morton E. Hopkins, and John W. Harrell; U.S. District Court for the Northern District of Texas, Dallas Division; CR-3-89-008-G; May 1989. Sworn testimony of David Farmer.

PAGE 169—*The June 1985 conversation related by Farmer came three months after*—"Chronology of the FSLIC Recapitalization Legislation"; U.S. Department of the Treasury; 1988. The Treasury chronology was introduced into Congress by George Gould at hearings on the FSLIC recapitalization bill.

PAGE 169—*The East Texas First PAC had contributed*—Court exhibits to prosecution of Hopkins et al. The check in question was made out to the East Texas First PAC for the Chapman race. But in the memo section where people usually jot down an account number or the reason for the check, Mrs. Hopkins had written Jim Wright's name. Mrs. Hopkins was questioned on why she wrote the name on the check by *Chicago Tribune* reporter Gary Marx for a story that Marx and the author prepared for the *Chicago Tribune*. Mrs. Hopkins could never really explain the notation.

PAGE 170—*Charles Keating, a well-known and politically influential*—Interview with Ed Gray; Miami, Florida; January 1990. Gray and his chief of staff, Shannon Fairbanks, say that Keating tried to lure him away from the bank board chairmanship with a job offer transmitted through a Keating lawyer and another member of the board. Gray said he sent Fairbanks to a subsequent meeting to determine who was behind the effort. She learned that Keating was the person trying to hire Gray for $250,000 a year. When the effort failed, Texas S&L executives began leaking disparaging details about Gray to the Washington press corps. Jack Anderson and Joseph Spear reported Keating's efforts to hire Gray in a column prepared for publication in November 1986.

PAGE 171—*But he felt queasy*—USA v. *Patrick G. King;* U.S. District Court for the Northern District of Texas, Dallas Division; CR-3-89-141-T; August 1989. Malone's commentary on the political contributions and their propriety came from the sworn testimony of Pat Malone in this case.

PAGE 171—*to dread Malone's visits*—USA v. *Patrick G. King;* U.S. District Court for the Northern District of Texas, Dallas Division; CR-3-89-141-T; August 1989. Sworn testimony of John Hill.

PAGE 171—*When Dickey asked about*—USA v. *Patrick G. King;* U.S. District Court for the Northern District of Texas, Dallas Division; CR-3-89-141-T; August 1989. Sworn testimony of Roy F. Dickey.

PAGE 172—*" 'Jesus, Don, you know this is adding up*—USA v. *Patrick G. King;* U.S. District Court for the Northern District of Texas, Dallas Division; CR-3-89-141-T; August 1989. Sworn testimony of John Hill.

PAGE 172—*Tom Loeffler would bring Treasury Secretary Jim Baker to Dallas*—USA v. *Patrick G. King;* U.S. District Court for the Northern District of Texas, Dallas Division; CR-3-89-141T; August 1989. Sworn testimony of Pat Malone.

16
Garden City

PAGE 173—*Joy Love was worried*—*USA* v. *Patrick G. King*; U.S. District
Court for the Northern District of Texas, Dallas Division; CR-3-89-
141-T; August 1989. Sworn testimony of Blair Davis. Davis testified
at length about his activities in the trial of King. As one of Hill's
key aides, Davis set up several of the meetings between Vernon
officials and women hired in Dallas.

PAGE 174—*Hill's contact at the saloon was Valerie*—*USA* v. *Patrick G.
King*; U.S. District Court for the Northern District of Texas, Dallas
Division; CR-3-89-141-T; August 1989. Sworn testimony of John
Hill.

PAGES 176–77—*"I first met with Ray Jeter*—"Sworn Testimony of Gregory Scott McCormick in the Matter of Vernon Savings and Loan
Association, Vernon, Tex."; U.S. Federal Savings and Loan Insurance Corp.; Resolution No. 86-1023.

PAGE 177—*But the paper game didn't work*—"Recommendation for the
Appointment of the Federal Savings and Loan Insurance Corp. as
Receiver for Vernon Savings and Loan Association, Vernon, Tex.";
Federal Home Loan Bank Board No. 6485.

PAGE 178—*Hill told me I was to pass out funds*—*USA* v. *Patrick G.
King*; U.S. District Court for the Northern District of Texas, Dallas
Division; CR-3-89-141-T; August 1989. Sworn testimony of Pat
Malone.

PAGES 180–81—*"I remember how we would come in there*—At one
point, Dixon apparently attempted to sell Vernon Savings to Charles
Bazarian, according to Rocky Crocker, Vernon's general counsel,
and according to Bank Board lawyers. Bazarian had been convicted
of mail fraud in 1980 and had several loans at Vernon. He also
leased the beach house in Solana Beach for a while and was
supposed to buy it at one point, according to Van Boxtel. By all
accounts, Bazarian was a huge man who later ran into additional
legal problems.

PAGES 181–82—*"I had one expense voucher*—*USA* v. *Patrick G. King*;
U.S. District Court for the Northern District of Texas, Dallas Division; CR-3-89-141-T; August 1989. Sworn testimony of John Hill.

PAGE 182—*He used an example that there were several bars in the
office*—*USA* v. *Patrick G. King*; U.S. District Court for the Northern
District of Texas, Dallas Division; CR-3-89-141-T; August 1989.
Sworn testimony of Ray Jeter.

17
The Alamo

PAGE 184—*R. B. Tanner caught him off guard*—Interview with R. B. Tanner; Denton, Texas; October 1989.

PAGE 185—*Tanner stopped just short*—Interview with R. B. Tanner; Denton, Texas; October 1989.

PAGE 186—*the first exam in two years*—"Recommendation for the Appointment of the Federal Savings and Loan Insurance Corp. as Receiver for Vernon Savings and Loan Association, Vernon Tex."; Federal Home Loan Bank Board No. 6485.

PAGE 186—*refused to admit Donald Hovde*—"The $150-Billion Calamity—Hardening the S&L Battle Lines"; David Maraniss and Rick Atkinson; *Washington Post;* June 14, 1989; page 1.

PAGE 188—*Vernon had lent $36.6 million*—"Recommendation for the Appointment of the Federal Savings and Loan Insurance Corp. as Receiver for Vernon Savings and Loan Association, Vernon, Tex."; Federal Home Loan Bank Board No. 6485.

PAGE 188—*The examiners concluded that some transactions*—Books and records of Vernon Savings and Loan; schedule of dividends; and "Recommendation for Appointment of the Federal Savings and Loan Insurance Corp. as Receiver for Vernon Savings and Loan Association, Vernon, Tex."; Federal Home Loan Bank Board No. 6485.

PAGES 188–89—*Included in its loan portfolio*—"Recommendation for the Appointment of the Federal Savings and Loan Insurance Corp. as Receiver for Vernon Savings and Loan Association, Vernon, Tex."; Federal Home Loan Bank Board No. 6485.

PAGE 189—*Yet the place was crawling with examiners*—Tape of board meeting, Vernon Savings and Loan Association, Vernon, Texas; Jan. 23, 1986.

PAGE 190—*He called a meeting of his twelve*—"The $150-Billion Calamity—Hardening the S&L Battle Lines"; David Maraniss and Rick Atkinson; *Washington Post;* June 14, 1989; page 1.

PAGE 191—*"He was quite alarmed*—*USA* v. *Patrick G. King;* U.S. District Court for the Northern District of Texas, Dallas Division; CR-3-89-141-T; August 1989. Sworn testimony of John Hill. Hill's testimony about the car was backed up by testimony from John Smith, who became Dondi Financial Corp.'s chief financial officer and authorized the transfer of funds to pay for the car.

PAGE 192—"*This is like the fox*—*USA* v. *Patrick G. King*; U.S. District Court for the Northern District of Texas, Dallas Division; CR-3-89-141-T; August 1989. Sworn testimony of Patrick Malone.

PAGE 193—*Woody told me in December*—Tape of board meeting, Vernon Savings and Loan Association, Vernon, Texas; April 24, 1986.

PAGES 193–94—*They decided to get Woody a plaque*—Tape of board meeting, Vernon Savings and Loan Association, Vernon, Texas; May 28, 1986.

PAGES 194–95—*It was in the summer of 1986 and it was hot as hell*—Interview with Raylan Loggins; Dallas, Texas; June 1989.

18
High Spirits

PAGE 196—"*I had seen a brochure*—"Sworn Statement of Rosswell Harbort Westmoreland III in the Matter of Vernon Savings and Loan Association, Vernon, Tex."; U.S. Federal Savings and Loan Insurance Corp.; Resolution No. 86-1023; March 1987.

PAGES 196–97—*A partnership composed of*—Interview with Woody Lemons; Vernon, Texas; June 1989; and Vernon books and records; sales brochure on the *High Spirits*.

PAGE 197—*In that forty-five year stretch*—*Where Deregulation Went Wrong*; Norman Strunk & Fred Case; U.S. League of Savings Institutions, 1988; page 13.

PAGE 198—*Gray had attempted to get*—"Federal Asset Disposition Association: Report of an Inquiry into Its Operations and Performance"; *Congressional Record*; April 20, 1988; page H-2203.

PAGE 199—*The Treasury Department backed*—Phone interview with George Gould; Washington, D.C.; January 1990.

PAGE 199—*But the U.S. League opposed*—Letter from William O'Connell to Sen. William Proxmire, chairman of Committee on Banking, Housing, and Urban Affairs, U.S. Senate; February 27, 1989.

PAGE 199—*When Gray had two officials*—"The $150-Billion Calamity—Hardening the S&L Battle Lines"; David Maraniss and Rick Atkinson; *Washington Post;* June 14, 1989; page 1.

PAGES 201–02—*Dana made sure the* High Spirits—Books and records of Vernon Savings and Loan; after-action reports, yacht *High Spirits.*

PAGE 202—*Dear Don*—"Report of the Special Outside Counsel in the Matter of Speaker James C. Wright, Jr."; Committee on Standards of Official Conduct, U.S. House of Representatives; Feb. 21, 1989; page 264.

PAGE 202—*"I was there staying on*—Interview with Tom Gaubert; Dallas, Texas; October 1989; and books and records of Vernon Savings and Loan; after-action reports, yacht *High Spirits.*

PAGE 202—*to discuss the READY*—Interview with Tibby Weston; Houston, Texas; November 1989.

PAGE 202—*Sen. Pete Wilson*—Books and records of Vernon Savings and Loan; flight logs.

PAGE 203—*Dixon spread contributions around*—Federal Election Commission reports on campaigns of various candidates and contributions to entities such as the East Texas First PAC on the Democratic Congressional Campaign Committee are replete with donations from Texas S&L executives.

PAGE 203—*The sudden abundance of charity*—Federal Election Commission reports, particularly reports for Rep. Bill Lowrey (R, Calif) for late 1985 and 1986 and East Texas First PAC, 1985.

PAGE 203—*Gipp Dupree said he*—*USA v. Woody F. Lemons;* U.S. District Court for the Northern District of Texas, Dallas Division; CR-3-88-234-T; November 1989. Sworn testimony of G. G. Gipp Dupree. A jury found Lemons guilty of federal charges in the case.

PAGE 204—*At Commodore Savings in Dallas*—*USA v. Robert E. Hopkins, Jr., Morton E. Hopkins, and John W. Harrell;* U.S. District Court for the Northern District of Texas, Dallas Division; CR-3-89-008-G; May 1989. Sworn testimony of Barbara Couch and books and records of Commodore Savings Association.

PAGE 204—*Lowery later told*—"Letter from Washington"; William Osborne; *San Diego Tribune;* January 23, 1986; Representative Lowery told Osborne that he and Kemp each netted about $50,000 on the trip.

PAGES 204–05—*the U.S. League's political*—Federal Election Commission records.

PAGE 205—*"Within striking distance of*—*USA* v. *Robert E. Hopkins, Jr., Morton E. Hopkins, and John W. Harrell;* U.S. District Court for the Northern District of Texas, Dallas Division; CR-3-89-008-G; May 1989. Sworn testimony of Barbara Couch. Ms. Couch was asked by the prosecutor to read the telegram from Jim Mattox into the record.

PAGE 205—*Keating focused on the Senate*—The donations to Sen. John McCain were widely reported and also were documented in the records of the Federal Election Commission.

PAGE 205—*He pumped $200,000 into*—"The Man Who Tried to Buy Congress"; *U.S. News and World Report;* November 27, 1989; page 18.

PAGE 206—*"Don responded by saying*—USA v. *Patrick G. King;* U.S. District Court for the Northern District of Texas, Dallas Division; CR-3-89-141-T; August 1989. Sworn testimony of John Smith.

PAGE 208—*He lost $60,000*—"Shooting the Glum Messenger—An Insider's Guide to Capital Issues"; Jim McTague; *American Banker;* March 23, 1987; page 10.

PAGE 209—*Another person whose name was put forward*—Interview with Durward Curlee; Austin, Texas; May 1988. Curlee told the author that industry officials pushed his name for the seat on the bank board. Congressional sources say that Curlee's name did arise, but that he had little chance of getting the job.

PAGE 209—*In one of his first actions*—"Bank Board's Henkel Proposed a Rule That Would Have Aided S&L Tied to Him"; John E. Yang; *Wall Street Journal;* Wednesday, December 24, 1986.

PAGE 209—*Henkel asked Reagan to withdraw*—"Federal Bank Board Member Henkel Resigns"; Reuters News Service; April 2, 1987. After numerous allegations about possible conflicts of interest because of his ties to Lincoln Savings, Henkel stepped down, saying, "I have concluded that I have not and will not be able to fully accomplish my agenda with the constant distraction of unfounded charges and the resulting investigations."

PAGE 210—*Loeffler brought Baker to*—Interview with Tibby Weston; Houston, Texas; January 1990.

19
High Noon

PAGE 211—*such as Selby had been hired*—Interview with Tibby Weston; Houston, Texas; January 1990.

PAGE 212—*Besides the salary—$165,000*—"The $150-Billion Calamity—Putting the Hammer to Lone Star Thrifts"; Rick Atkinson and David Maraniss; *Washington Post;* June 15, 1989. Atkinson and Maraniss gave the first detailed account of Selby's treatment at the bank board in their series of stories. Some of the author's material was taken from the story, but most of it came from several interviews with Selby ranging from July 1988 to January 1990.

PAGE 213—*"I was flabbergasted*—Interview with Joe Selby; Dallas, Texas; January 1990.

PAGES 213–14—*Even a cursory look*—"Recommendation for the Appointment of the Federal Savings and Loan Insurance Corp. as Receiver for Vernon Savings and Loan Association, Vernon, Tex."; Federal Home Loan Bank Board No. 6485. This lengthy document from Selby to his superiors at the bank board outlined the history of Vernon and the logic behind Selby's arguments to close it. It is also referred to as the closing memo.

PAGE 216—*"John Hill asked that the*—"In the Matter of the Investigation of Vernon Savings and Loan by the Federal Savings and Loan Insurance Corp."; Sworn statement of Nancy Horne; Vernon Savings and Loan; Vernon, Texas; April 1987.

PAGES 216–17—*Collectively, Vernon declared*—Books and records of Vernon Savings and Loan and affidavit of James S. Hinman, examiner at Federal Home Loan Bank of Dallas; April 1987.

PAGE 217—*The anointed few used*—Vernon books and records, and *Raleigh Blakely, Sr. v. Don R. Dixon, Dondi Financial Corp., and Vernon Savings and Loan Association;* Dallas County Court; No. 87-1643.

PAGE 217—*The salaries didn't include*—Vernon books and records.

PAGE 217—*"I was told that these*—Federal Savings and Loan Insurance Corp. v. Don R. Dixon et al.; U.S. District Court for the Northern District of Texas, Dallas Division; CA-3-87-1102-G; April 1987. Deposition of Brenda Bryant; Dallas, Texas; December 1987.

PAGE 219—*When Lemons, King, and the others*—"Recommendation for the Appointment of the Federal Savings and Loan Insurance Corp. as Receiver for Vernon Savings and Loan Association, Vernon, Tex."; Federal Home Loan Bank Board No. 6485; March 1987.

PAGE 219—*"Deferred compensation of*—Vernon books and records. Various memos to file, May 1986.

PAGE 219—*Big money was involved*—Vernon books and records; and deposition of Donald R. Dixon; *Don Ray Dixon and Dana Dene Dixon v. Federal Savings and Loan Insurance Corp. and Vernon Savings and Loan Assn.*; Adversary No. SA-87-0327-PE; June 1987.

PAGE 219—*Lemons and Malone got the good news*—Vernon books and records; various memos to file and canceled check dated July 10, 1986.

PAGE 220—*Bryant didn't like the idea*—*Federal Savings and Loan Insurance Corp. v. Don R. Dixon et al.*; U.S. District Court for the Northern District of Texas; CA-3-87-1102-G; April 1987; deposition of Brenda Bryant; December 1987.

PAGE 221—*Forfeiture of the fee*—Deposition of Donald R. Dixon; *Don Ray Dixon and Dana Dene Dixon v. the Federal Savings and Loan Insurance Corp. and Vernon Savings and Loan Assn.*; Adversary No. SA-87-0327-PE; June 1987.

PAGE 221—*no Joy Love in this guy's future*—"Report of the Special Outside Counsel in the Matter of Speaker James C. Wright, Jr.";
Committee on Standards of Official Conduct; U.S. House of Representatives; February 21, 1989. The report documents a smear campaign against Selby in which Speaker Wright either wittingly or unwittingly participated. The term "Fruit Loop" was not included in the report but was widely used by Texas S&L executives.

PAGES 221–22—*"I am writing because of a genuine concern*—Letter from Lawrence W. Taggart of Taggart Financial, San Diego, to Honorable Donald Regan, chief of staff, White House; August 1986. Copies of Taggart's letter were also sent to Rep. Doug Barnard, a Georgia Democrat who headed the bank board's oversight committee, and Sen. Jake Garn, the Utah Republican who was chairman of the Senate Banking Committee when Republicans controlled the Senate. The letter was later made part of the record in hearings before the House Banking Committee.

PAGE 222—*One week later Taggart*—After-action reports of Eric Estelle, captain of the yacht *High Spirits*, filed in connection with *Federal*

Savings and Loan Insurance Corp. v. *Don R. Dixon* et al.; Dallas, Texas.

PAGE 222—*Hall boldly moved into*—Interview with Raylan Loggins; Dallas, Texas; June 1989; and interview with former Vernon executive who asked that his name not be used in this book.

20
The Wright Stuff

PAGE 223—*Mack picked up the phone*—"Report of the Special Outside Counsel in the Matter of Speaker James C. Wright, Jr."; Committee of Standards of Official Conduct; U.S. House of Representatives; February 1989. The so-called Phelan report, named after special counsel Richard Phelan, who led the congressional investigation into Wright's business affairs, pieced together the Dixon story. Many of the comments in this chapter are taken from sworn testimony in the report.

PAGE 225—*"Thrift deregulation has been misused*—"Regulator Says Crooks Sink FSLIC"; William Gruber; *Chicago Tribune;* October 1986.

PAGES 225–26—*For Wright it had all started*—"Report of the Special Outside Counsel." The Phelan report has an entire section on Hall's predicament. The author also interviewed Hall in September 1988 and found some details on Wright's side of the story in *The Ambition and the Power—The Fall of Jim Wright: A True Story of Washington;* John M. Barry; Viking-Penguin, 1989.

PAGE 226—*But Hall said he couldn't even*—Interview with Craig Hall; Dallas, Texas; September 1988.

PAGE 227—*The first was to Freddy*—"Report of the Special Outside Counsel"; February 1989.

PAGE 227—*Although Hall said*—"Report on Donations to Democratic Congressional Campaign Committee, 1985–86"; Federal Election Commission.

PAGE 227—*Early the next week*—"Report of the Special Outside Counsel"; February 1989. Also, *The Ambition and the Power—The Fall of Jim Wright: A True Story of Washington;* John M. Barry; Viking-Penguin, 1989.

PAGES 227–28—*Four days later*—"Chronology of the FSLIC Recapitalization"; U.S. Department of the Treasury; 1989.

PAGE 228—*"I mean he knows Scott*—Interview with Ed Gray; Miami, Florida; September 1988.

PAGE 228—*blocked further consideration*—"Chronology of the FSLIC Recapitalization"; U.S. Department of the Treasury; 1989. Also, *Wall Street Journal;* September 1986 and February 1987.

PAGE 228—*It was a classic Washington*—"S&L Insurance Fund"; *Congressional Quarterly Almanac,* 1987; pages 633–36.

PAGE 228—*"Put yourself in our shoes*—Interview with Ed Gray; Miami, Florida; September 1988.

PAGE 229—*"They passed those bills*—Interview with Ed Gray; Miami, Florida; January 1990.

PAGE 230—*Wright suspected a*—*The Ambition and the Power*—*The Fall of Jim Wright: A True Story of Washington;* John M. Barry; Viking-Penguin, 1989.

PAGE 230—*Wright requested that*—"Federal Savings and Loan Insurance Corporation Recapitalization Act of 1987"; hearings before the Committee on Banking, Finance, and Urban Affairs; House of Representatives; March 1987; page 32.

PAGE 230—*"He insisted that Gaubert*—Interview with Ed Gray; Miami, Florida; September 1988.

PAGE 231—*Gaubert tried to get*—Interview with Tom Gaubert; Dallas, Texas; July 1988 and October 1989.

PAGE 231—*Gaubert walked into Gray's office*—Interview with Ed Gray; Miami, Florida; September 1988.

PAGE 232—*It was basically another call*—Interviews with Ed Gray, Miami, Florida, September 1988; Joe Selby, Dallas, Texas, Spring, 1989; and "Report of the Special Outside Counsel," February 1989. Although Wright has never publicly commented in detail on the thrift industry controversy that dogged him, his account of events was chronicled in John M. Barry's *The Ambition and the Power.* Wright maintains that he didn't ask Gray to fire Selby but simply questioned him about the allegations he had heard. Gray says otherwise.

PAGE 232—*Back in Forth Worth*—"Report of the Special Outside Counsel"; February 1989.

PAGE 233—*"Ed, I don't know anything*—"Report of the Special Outside Counsel"; February 1989.

PAGE 233—*"You have to remember*—Interview with Ed Gray; Miami, Florida; January 1990.

PAGE 234—*"I said, hey, be our guest*—"Report of the Special Outside Counsel"; February 1989.

PAGE 235—*Within forty-five minutes*—"Report of the Special Outside Counsel"; February 1989.

PAGE 235—*Mack from a long prison term*—"Memory and Anger: A Victim's Story, Watching as the Man Who Tried to Kill Her Rose to Power"; Margaret Thomas; *Washington Post*; May 4, 1989; page 1B.

PAGE 235—*No less an authority than*—News release; U.S. League of Savings Institutions; Washington, D.C.; March 1987.

PAGES 235–36—*Gray was livid*—Interview Ed Gray; Miami, Florida; September 1988.

PAGE 236—*"Oh, yeah," Curlee replied*—Interview with Joe Selby; Dallas, Texas; July 1988; and "The $150-Billion Calamity—Putting the Hammer to Lone Star Thrifts"; Rick Atkinson and David Maraniss; *Washington Post*; June 1989; page 1.

PAGE 236—*"Speaker Wright indicated to us*—"The $150-Billion Calamity—Gray the Re-Regulator and Wright Lock Horns"; Rick Atkinson and David Maraniss; *Washington Post*; June 1989; page 1.

PAGE 236—*Wright, who had an infamous temper*—The Ambition and the Power—The Fall of Jim Wright: A True Story of Washington; John M. Barry; Viking-Penguin, 1989.

PAGE 237—*The regulators were ready to bolster*—"Report of the Special Outside Counsel"; February 1989; and interview with William Black.

PAGE 238—*Black, a red-bearded, gutsy*—William Black discussed the meeting with the author as did George Mallick in a 1989 interview. However, the author borrowed from Barry, *The Ambition and the Power—The Fall of Jim Wright: A True Story of Washington*, because he was an impartial observer at the meeting. Barry's account seemed the most fair representation of what happened. It closely tracked the account of the meeting in the outside counsel's special report.

21
The Cops Come

PAGE 239—*"I had researched the place*—Interview with Raylan Loggins; Dallas, Texas; June 1989.

PAGE 240—*"We hired some consultants*—Interview with L. L. Bowman; Austin, Texas; June 1989.

PAGE 241—*In some cases, Hall*—Vernon books and records on file in U.S. District Court for the Northern District of Texas, Dallas Division. Comparisons of original purchase prices to subsequent appraisals suggest that Dixon paid too much for the artwork acquired. Through friends, however, Dixon maintains that Vernon should have made money selling the art. Any losses were due to inadequate marketing, according to his view as related by others.

PAGES 241–42—*"Hepworth acknowledged that Don*—Memo to Carl Asakawa from Jennifer Miller; February 1987; "Re: Phone Conversation with James Hepworth Pertaining to the Antique Containers in Dondi Design's Carlsbad Warehouse"; Vernon books and records.

PAGE 242—*Before the state had assumed control*—Interviews with Joe Selby and William Black; Dallas, Texas, and San Francisco, California; July 1988 and August 1988.

PAGES 243–44—*"We used to have a game*—Interview with Jack Atkinson; Dallas, Texas; November 1989.

PAGE 244—*Vernon reported no income*—Vernon Savings and Loan Association financial statement for December 1986. Vernon's income plunged during the first quarter of government operation. Part of the problem was probably recognition of the true losses. Vernon had been reporting paper profits as income for many months. But part of the reason was management of the institution. Vernon actually had negative operating income for the quarter. It reported no income at all from its mortgage loan portfolio, suggesting that borrowers simply quit paying on loans.

PAGE 244—*Earl looked like he was*—Interview with Raylan Loggins; Dallas, Texas; June 1989.

PAGE 245—*Of the $1.5 billion Vernon*—"Recommendation for the Appointment of the Federal Savings and Loan Insurance Corp. as Receiver for Vernon Savings and Loan Association, Vernon, Tex."; Federal Home Loan Bank Board No. 6485; and sworn statement of

Linda Shivers on file in U.S. District Court for the Northern Division of Texas, Dallas Division.

PAGE 246—*Dickey was stunned*—Sworn oral statement of Chris Barker; U.S. Bankruptcy Court, Central District of California; Case No. SA-87-02476-PE; June 1987.

PAGE 247—*The thrift was broke*—"Recommendation for the Appointment of the Federal Savings and Loan Insurance Corp. as Receiver for Vernon Savings and Loan Association, Vernon, Tex."; Federal Home Loan Bank Board No. 6485.

PAGE 247—*to sell some stock*—Interview with Rocky Crocker; Lubbock, Texas; July 1989.

PAGE 247—*The meeting on what to do*—Transcript of special meeting of the Federal Home Loan Bank Board, March 20, 1987; Federal Home Loan Bank Board; Washington, D.C.

22
The Black Hole

PAGE 253—*"Bank Board Lived Well Off S&Ls"*—"The $150-Billion Calamity—Gray the Re-Regulator and Wright Lock Horns"; Rick Atkinson and David Maraniss; *Washington Post*; June 1989; page 1.

PAGE 253—*Dingell's letter presented*—Letter to Edwin J. Gray from Rep. John Dingell, chairman of the House Committee on Energy and Commerce; U.S. House of Representatives; January 12, 1987.

PAGES 253–54—*Staffers on Dingell's*—Memo to John D. Dingell, chairman, Committee on Energy and Commerce, U.S. House of Representatives, from committee staff; "Re: Allegations of Conflict of Interest and Fraud Against the Government Involving a FSLIC-Acquired Property"; March 1987.

PAGE 254—*Then came Rep. Carroll Hubbard*—"Finding of Booz Allen & Hamilton Study of FHLBB"; hearing before the Committee on Banking, Finance, and Urban Affairs; Subcommittee on Oversight and Investigations; U.S. House of Representatives; May 14, 1987.

PAGE 254—*Hubbard told Gray*—Letter from Rep. Carroll Hubbard to Gray.

PAGE 254—*In the one month since the*—Bureau of National Affairs; *Daily Report for Executives*, February 4, 1987.

PAGE 255—*the League's O'Connell publicly*—Letter to Sen. William Proxmire, chairman, Senate Committee on Banking, Housing, and Urban Affairs; Washington, D.C.; from William O'Connell, president, U.S. League of Savings Institutions; Feb. 27, 1987.

PAGE 256—*Treasury Secretary Baker had traveled*—*The Ambition and the Power—The Fall of Jim Wright: A True Story of Washington*; John M. Barry; Viking-Penguin, 1989.

PAGES 256–57—*"Wright made a speech on the floor*—Interview with George Gould; New York, New York; January 1990.

PAGE 257—*Virtually every congressman*—Author's analysis of votes that appeared in "S&L Insurance Fund Votes"; *Congressional Quarterly Almanac*; page 29-H; votes 83–85.

PAGE 257—*"This was one of the great scams*—Interview with Ed Gray; Miami, Florida; March 1990.

PAGE 258—*"As Ed Gray, his clothes rumpled*—"The $150-Billion Calamity—Gray the Re-Regulator and Wright Lock Horns"; Rick Atkinson and David Maraniss; *Washington Post*; June 1989; page 1.

PAGE 258—*"The government didn't realize*—This particular individual agreed to talk with the author if his name was not used. Since he still works on projects with the government, the author used his quotes without his name attached sparingly.

PAGE 259—*SASA's Roger Clark took over*—In an interview during February 1990, Clark acknowledged that SASA officials and the government forced him and Vernon officials to quit some clubs and that the thrift didn't do well during his tenure. However, he said Vernon was so hopelessly shot by the time he got there that nothing could have been done. He said the clubs were simply a racquetball club and other inexpensive memberships in Dallas.

PAGE 259—*He had to bid up the interest rates*—Vernon Savings and Loan financial statements for the three months ending in September 1987; Federal Home Loan Bank Board; Washington, D.C.; and February 1990 interview with Clarke. The higher cost of money was at least partially due to a slight increase in interest rates at the time, too.

PAGE 260—*Loggins and his colleagues squared off*—Interview with Raylan Loggins; Dallas, Texas; June 1989.

PAGES 260–61—*Gary Bowser and Jim Deveney*—Bowser and Deveney eventually did a report harshly criticizing the operation of the

FADA. It appeared in the *Congressional Record* during April 1988. Among other things, it discussed inflated salaries, high costs, and other items and laid the foundation for a movement in Congress to abolish the FADA. Eventually Congress removed its authority.

PAGE 261—*By November of 1987*—Vernon books and records.

PAGE 262—*But the figures didn't tell*—"Portfolio Overview"; Federal Asset Disposition Association; Vernon Savings and Loan Association, F.S.A.; February 1988.

PAGE 262—*For Danny Wall*—"Recommendation for the Appointment of the Federal Savings and Loan Insurance Corp. as Receiver for Vernon Savings and Loan Association, Vernon, Tex."; Federal Home Loan Bank Board No. 6485; March 1987.

PAGE 266—*"I'm devastated by this*—Byron Harris; tape of series of reports that ran on WFAA-TV; Dallas, Texas; 1988.

PAGE 266—*Every morning, usually at nine* A.M.—"Money in America— the Business of Banking, A Documentary"; Public Broadcasting System.

23
Laguna Beach

PAGES 267–68—*"I'm looking for Don Dixon,"*—Interview with Donald R. Dixon, Laguna Beach, California; July 1989. The author spoke with Dixon in his California office for about one-half hour to forty-five minutes in preparation for a series that ran in the *Chicago Tribune* during September 1988. Dixon would not agree to a lengthy interview regarding the federal charges leveled against him in a lawsuit filed by the FSLIC. He said he would like to discuss his problems with a reporter, but that his lawyers would not let him talk. The quotes and comments in this chapter surfaced during a discussion in which Dixon related his general views about the S&L problems and Vernon to the author. Dixon has testified publicly in court twice in California. His deposition was also taken in July 1987. Dixon's views in *The Daisy Chain* reflect his testimony, the interview with the author, and interviews with various friends. Dixon also declined an opportunity to talk with the author at length for this book.

PAGE 268—*The first thing that went*—Affidavit of Gene Webb, examiner for Federal Home Loan Bank of Dallas; U.S. District Court for the Northern District of Texas, Dallas Division; CR-3-87-1102-G; April 1987.

PAGES 268–69—*"He told me he'd acquired*—Office of the U.S. Trustee, Central District of California; sworn testimony recorded in transcript of creditors' meeting with Don R. Dixon; Santa Ana, California; July 1987.

PAGE 269—*This West was a man*—The transaction involving the sale of the beach house was quite complex. Had the initial sale been a straight deal, Vernon Savings would have recouped some of its money. But West's company financed the purchase of the house through a note secured by a lien against his various business interests, according to lawyers involved in litigation over the transactions. In effect Vernon went from the owner of the house to a lien holder against West's business interests, which included cash that was raised from the sale of the house and invested in West's ventures.

PAGE 269—*It was an unusual sale*—Affidavit of Robert Torres, examiner for the Federal Home Loan Bank of Dallas; U.S. District Court of Northern District of Texas, Dallas Division; CA-3-87-1102-G; April 1987.

PAGE 270—*He used $100,000*—Office of the U.S. Trustee for the Central District of California; sworn testimony recorded in transcript of creditors' meeting with Don R. Dixon; Santa Ana, California; July 1987; and deposition of Don R. Dixon; U.S. Bankruptcy Court for the Central District of California; *Don Ray Dixon and Dana Dene Dixon v. Federal Savings and Loan Insurance Corp.*; Adversary SA-87-0327-PE. Under questioning and under oath, Dixon discussed his living expenses and his use of proceeds from asset sales.

PAGE 271—*His cavalier attitude*—Ibid.

PAGE 271—*"It was a family Ferrari*—Office of the U.S. Trustee for the Central District of California; sworn testimony recorded in transcript of creditors' meeting with Don R. Dixon, Santa Ana, California; July 1987. The quote about the family Ferrari was first reported by Byron Harris in a January 1988 *Texas Monthly* article.

PAGE 273—*"The bank board compounded the losses*—Interviews with officials from San Antonio Savings Association and the Federal Home Loan Bank Board in Washington. The government refuses to release the records of the transactions at Vernon when the thrift was under its control. In interviews with SASA employees and bank board officials, the author learned that the bank board placed into Vernon housing bonds and other loans stripped from sick institutions the bank board was trying to sell. Some of the institutions were purchased by people who gave huge campaign contributions to the Bush administration. The bank board contended that receivership reports on Vernon were internal documents that can be withheld from public view.

PAGE 273—*Wall was comparing Dixon*—Transcript of Federal Home Loan Bank Board meeting regarding the resolution of disputes between officials from the Federal Home Loan Bank of San Francisco and Charles Keating of Lincoln Savings and Loan of Irvine, California. The record was released during hearings held by the House Committee on Banking, Finance, and Urban Affairs, chaired by Rep. Henry Gonzalez, October 1989.

PAGE 274—*"Sure we traveled to Europe*—Interview with Don R. Dixon, Laguna Beach, California; August 1989. The author first reported this quote in a series of stories that ran in the *Chicago Tribune* during September 1988.

PAGE 274—*"You know, Mr. Hill*—Transcript of sentencing of John Hill by U.S. district court judge Barefoot Sanders; U.S. District Court, Dallas, Texas; 1989.

PAGE 275—*"I'd just like to know one thing*—Phone interview with Jack Atkinson; December 1989.

PAGES 275–76—*"Well, Mr. Lemons*—Transcript of sentencing of Woody Lemons by U.S. district court judge Robert Maloney; U.S. District Court, Dallas, Texas; Spring, 1990.

PAGE 276—*Dixon has gotten religion*—Interview with Tim Timmons, Dixon's minister.

24
The Savings and Loan Crisis

PAGE 277—*The government said Dixon*—Federal indictment of Donald R. Dixon; U.S. District Court, Dallas, Texas; June 1990; and *Dallas Morning News*, June 19–20, 1990

PAGE 279—*In fact Vernon and nineteen other Texas thrifts*—*Where Deregulation Went Wrong*; Norman Strunk & Fred Case; U.S. League of Savings Institutions, 1988; page 101; and figures compiled by U.S. League of Savings Institutions.

PAGE 280—*"The bailout to come*—Floor statement of Sen. William Proxmire; U.S. Senate; September 1988.

PAGE 281—*"Is there a book somewhere*—Statement of Donald Dixon; *Firing Line* interview with Sam Donaldson; June 1990.

PAGE 283—*Wall's job was to contain*—Danny Wall objects to the statement that his job was to put off exposure of the savings and loan problems until after the election. He says he was legitimately attempting to resolve the problem. However, there is little doubt that the policies he pursued put off exposure of the problem until after the elections, even though the Reagan-Bush administration was well aware of its severity before voters took to the polls.

PAGE 284—*Ely correctly argued*—Alexandria-based Bert Ely has consistently been more accurate with his projections than the government. Because his system seemed to present a gloomier picture of the situation, the government had criticized Ely's assessments. But time had proved Ely right. He made numerous studies of the potential loss and always came up with more accurate figures than the government.

PAGE 284—*"It is with reluctance*—Floor statement of Sen. William Proxmire; U.S. Senate; September 1988.

PAGE 286—*When Vernon Savings first went down*—"Closing of Vernon Savings Threatens Thrifts That Bought Its Loans"; Jim McTague and David LaGesse; *American Banker;* Nov. 23, 1987; page 1.

PAGES 286–87—*billionaire Robert M. Bass*—"GOP Discloses Names of Big Donors"; Charles Babcock; *Washington Post;* January 1989.

PAGE 287—*In the last five days of 1988 alone*—The lucrative nature of the tax breaks and assistance packages given to Perelman and others has been reported in numerous publications, including the *Wall Street Journal, Barron's, Grant's Interest Rate Observer,* the *New York Times,* and the *Chicago Tribune.*

PAGE 289—*"Economic conditions have*—Office of the White House, statement of the President; February 6, 1989.

PAGES 289–90—*"I suppose bad members*—Author's interview with William Seidman, chairman of the Federal Deposit Insurance Corp. and head of the RTC; June 1990.

PAGES 291–92—*"I had as much to do*—Ibid.

INDEX